The Daily

BOOK OF
MOTORING
ANSWERS

The Daily Telegraph

BOOK OF
MOTORING
ANSWERS

Honest John

ROBINSON
London

Constable & Robinson Ltd
3 The Lanchesters
162 Fulham Palace Road
London W6 9ER

www.constablerobinson.com

First published by Robinson Publishing Ltd 1997
This edition published by Robinson,
an imprint of Constable & Robinson Ltd 2000

A copy of the British Library Cataloguing in Publication Data is
available from the British Library

ISBN 1–84119–226–0

Designed and typeset by WordSpace, Lewes, East Sussex

Printed and bound in the EU

10 9 8 7 6 5 4 3 2 1

CONTENTS

INTRODUCTION

What you need to know about this book before you start reading and using it

This *Daily Telegraph* book gives you the answers to the most-asked questions about cars and motoring. How do I know this? Over the last six years I have replied to more than 30,000 letters and emails. Most sought information. But many also provided it, particularly about older cars. So, whether you're worrying about your next MOT, or you want to know a bit more about a car grand-dad owned in the 1920s, the chances are you'll find it in these pages. If you are connected, you can also visit my website at http://www.honestjohn.co.uk.

Condition of sale

You don't have to be in the motor trade to enjoy this book. You don't need to be an enthusiast. You don't even have to be remotely interested in cars. All you need to be is a car owner or driver, or simply someone looking for an answer to a car-related question – past or present. While you're looking, I hope you'll also find plenty to amuse, stimulate and maybe even annoy you enough to write to 'Honest John' at the *Daily Telegraph*.

But, a word of warning. Since all this went to press long before you laid out your money for it, and since I could not know for certain exactly what was going to happen in the future, I can't guarantee that everything in this book can be 100 per cent up to date. So, just like unwarranted cars at auction, you buy this at your own risk. Neither I, nor the *Daily Telegraph*, nor Constable & Robinson Limited, nor anyone else mentioned or involved will accept any liability whatsoever for any inaccuracies or the dating of any information in this book. Of course, unlike cars at auction, you can sneak a look inside and give it a 'read-test' at the bookshop, so you know exactly what you're getting before you make a bid to the cashier.

About the chapter headings

In editing 30,000 questions and answers down to 1,000 or so, I've had to categorise them. So what happened was that the chapter headings more or less decided themselves. This year there are new chapters, such as 'Accident Solicitors', 'De-mystified Motors', 'Out-of-Warranty Claims' and a list of cars most prone to 'Catalytic Converter Failures'.

About me

I don't have the time to do much buying and selling any more. But I still get down to the auctions around once a week. And I have my own very comprehensive computer databank of auction prices from the beginning of 1992 – so I always know exactly which way the market is going compared to the past month, the past year, and up to eight years ago.

My first contact with the motor trade was in 1959 when I started cleaning cars for Ron at Sports Motors on Orpington High Street. Ron's stock included a 1926 AC Roadster at £225; a 1930 Austin Nippy at £90; a 1932 Lagonda 2 litre two-seat special at £225; a 1938 Jaguar SS 100 at £275 (multiply by somewhere between 100 and 250 to find out just what an investment some of this older stuff has been). Ron also had comparatively modern cars, such as a pair of 1949 Riley three-seat Roadsters, MGAs, TR2s, a Buckler, a Berkeley and a gigantic Buick. Sports Motors folded in 1960, but Pete the Painter's murals remain to this day, hidden behind the dry-lined walls of the carpet shop that replaced it.

I bought my first car in 1964 and did my first deal the year after when I sold it. The car was a 1959 BMW Isetta 300, spotted rocking gently on the roof of a fabric-bodied Alvis 12/50 saloon in Shire Ted's scrapyard. 'I can drive that when I'm 16,' I thought. The car duly arrived on the end of a rope behind a 1938 Oldsmobile and, being the canny man he was, Ted gave me £2 back from my £20. Reconstruction began, and test runs were undertaken round a neighbour's garden. On my 16th birthday the bubble burst forth onto the road. A year later I sold it for £60.

Further gains (and losses) were made on a 1959 Riley 1.5 bought for £250; a 1942 Ford Jeep, bought for £20; a Thames Camper bought for £175; a modified Minivan bought for £125; a 1949 Rover P3 bought for £40; a Wolseley Hornet and plenty of other tackle, including a rear-engined Renault and a two-stroke Saab. Then, by writing the ads for a Rolls Royce dealer, I got into advertising.

Four years of this was spent conveniently close to London's Warren Street, where I shared bank, pubs and caffs with the street's car traders and did a few deals on Simcas, Minis, VW Beetles, 2CVs, Fiats and Alfas. Apart from acquiring a pair of 'D&AD' pencils, I have to admit I never really made it in adland. The recession didn't help. Then, deep in the midst of the Gulf War, I had a brainwave: I would launch a completely new type of car magazine about nothing but used cars. The aim was simply to set it going, and then flog it for £10,000 and carry on in the ad game, but instead I became indentured into the penury of freelancing features for car magazines. Since this involved reporting on car auctions, watching wasn't enough. Before long, I was back to buying cars and turning them round – retail, trade or on commission – to supplement the mag money into enough to live on.

For four months I commuted between London, Amsterdam and Nice, working on pan-European launches for the Mazda Xedos 6 and RX7. Then it was back to buying and selling, a column in *Car Week*, and an auction column in *The Daily Telegraph*'s 'Motoring' section. Life was moving along quite nicely. Then, at a contributor's Christmas party in a room above a pub in Soho, my editor, Eric Bailey had an idea.

I'd arrived at the party fresh from an auction where I'd spent £17,250 on three Vauxhalls in the space of 20 minutes, then moved them on to earn a mere £250 each. Eric thought, '£250 a car. He's far too honest for that game', and 'Honest John' was born.

In the ancient tradition of all agony columns, the first questions were made up, and they ran on the back cover of *Telegraph* 'Motoring' in the issue of 21 January 1995. The response was phenomenal: within months I was answering up to 150 genuine letters a week. By year three, the weekly mailbag sometimes hit 500. By year four, I'd even got myself onto television.

What you'll find in this book is a distillation of the best and most interesting questions and answers, mostly from the last year, but some going back to January 1995.

ACCIDENT SOLICITORS

If you have had an accident which was not your fault, you need a no-fault accident solicitor.

Here, in no particular order, is a list of solicitors specialising in 'no fault' accidents. I strongly advise anyone involved in such an accident to consult one of these solicitors before instituting an insurance claim. They will ensure that you get what you are entitled to, rather than a lesser settlement which may suit the insurers but will leave you out of pocket. The first question you must ask is whether the solicitor will handle your case on a 'no win, no fee' basis. You must then get this in writing. Do not hire a car to keep yourself mobile unless on a guaranteed 'no cost' basis.

- Claims Direct (personal injury specialists) tel: 0800 448851.

- Motor Accident Solicitors Society, Bridge House, 48–52 Baldwin Street, Bristol BS1 1QD, tel: 0117 929 2560.

- Kingsford Flower & Pain Solicitors, 7 Bank Street, Ashford, Kent TN23 1BZ, tel: 01233 665544.

- Thomas Taggart & Sons Solicitors, 27 Church Street, Ballymoney, Co. Antrim BT53 6HS, tel: 012656 62118.

- Easthams Solicitors, Continental House, 292–302 Church Street, Blackpool FY1 3QA, tel: 01253 299222.

- Brian Camp & Co. Solicitors, No. 1 Europa House, Conway Street,

Birkenhead, Merseyside L41 4FT, tel: 0151 201 8080 or freecall: 0500 122 559.

- Philip Baker & Co. Solicitors, 1st Floor, Newater House, 11 Newhall Street, Birmingham B3 2NY, tel: 0121 212 1100.

- Widdows Mason Solicitors, 2 Princess Street, Bolton BL1 1EJ, tel: 01204 528105.

- Burroughs Day Solicitors, Road Traffic Accident Unit, 14 Charlotte Street, Bristol BS1 5PT, tel: 0117 929 0333 (out of hours tel: 0117 925 0334).

- John Hodge Nichols Strickland Solicitors, 9 Queen Square, Bristol BS1 4HR, tel: 0117 9292281.

- Clarke, Willmott & Clarke Solicitors, The Waterfront, Welsh Back, Bristol BS1 4SB, tel: 0117 941 6600.

- Steele Ford Newton Solicitors, 1–3 Colne Road, Brierfield, Burnley BB9 5HW, tel: 01282 616446.

- Russell & Russell Solicitors, Belgrave Terrace, 10 Manchester Road, Bury BL9 0EB, tel: 0161 764 5424.

- Marquis Penna Solicitors, Post Office House, Elliott Street, Crook, Co. Durham DL15 8QH, tel: 01388 762466.

- Easthams Solicitors, 10th Floor, Leon House, High Street, Croydon CR9 0TE, tel: 020 8681 5464.

- McArdle, Cardwell & Mitchell Solicitors, 56 Duke Street, Darlington, Co. Durham DL3 7AN, tel: 01325 482299.

- Stephen Rimmer & Co. Solicitors, 28 Hyde Gardens, Eastbourne, East Sussex BN21 4PX, tel: 01323 644222.

- Tayntons Solicitors, Clarence Chambers, 8–12 Clarence Street,

Gloucester GL1 1DZ, tel: 01452 522047.

- Andrew M. Jackson & Co. Solicitors, PO Box 47, Essex House, Manor Street, Hull HU1 1XH, tel: 01482 325242.

- Stephensons Solicitors, 26 Union Street, Leigh WN7 1AT, tel: 01942 608942.

- Quinn Melville Solicitors, 15 Stanley Street, Liverpool L1 6AA, tel: 0151 236 3340.

- Bermans Solicitors, Pioneer Buildings, 65/67 Dale Street, Liverpool L2 2NS, tel: 0151 227 3351.

- Cotton Griffiths & Co., 880 Stockport Road, Levenshulme, Manchester M19 3BN, tel: 0161 225 5813 (not solicitors, but respected claims assessors well versed in 'diminution in value'.)

- Lopian Wagner Solicitors, 9 St. John Street, Manchester M3 4DN, tel: 0161 834 2324.

- Philip Shuker & Co. Solicitors, New Church House, 34 John Dalton Street, Manchester M2 6LE, tel: 0161 839 7900 (specialise in 'no fault' claims by motorcyclists).

- Berry & Co. Solicitors, 2nd Floor, Building 1, Wilson Park, Monsall Road, Manchester M40 8PA, tel: 0161 205 0081.

- David Harris Solicitors, Lloyd House, 18 Lloyd Street, Manchester M2 5WA, tel: 0161 834 2200.

- Colemans Solicitors, Elizabeth House, 16 St. Peter's Square, Manchester M2 3DF, tel: 0161 228 7393.

- Lyons Wilson Solicitors, Dickinson Chambers, 1 Central Street, Manchester M2 5WR, tel: 0161 834 6836.

- Sedgewick Phelan & Partners Solicitors, Argyle House, Warwick

Court, Park Road, Middleton, Manchester M24 1AE, tel: 0161 653 5299.

- Aubrey Isaacson & Co. Solicitors, 2 Scholes Lane, Prestwich, Manchester M25 1ED, tel: 0161 798 6700.

- Fennemores Solicitors, 200 Silbury Boulevard, Central Milton Keynes MK9 1LL, tel: 01908 678241.

- Poole Alcock & Co. Solicitors, Mill House, 14 Mill Street, Nantwich, Cheshire CW5 5ST, tel: 01270 625478/624560.

- Hewitt Brown-Humes & Hare Solicitors, 21 Dalton Way, Newton Aycliffe, Co. Durham DL5 4DJ, tel: 01325 316170.

- Nelsons Solicitors, Pennine House, 8 Stanford Street, Nottingham NG1 7BQ, tel: 0115 958 6262.

- Innes & Company Solicitors, 214 London Road, North End, Portsmouth PO2 9JE, tel: 01705 693052.

- Blake Lapthorn Solicitors, Harbour Court, Compass Road North Harbour, Portsmouth, Hants PO6 4ST, tel: 01705 221122.

- Whittle Robinson Solicitors, 5, 6 & 7 Cannon Street, Preston PR1 1PY, tel: 01772 254201.

- Pitmans Solicitors, 47 Castle Street, Reading, Berks RG1 7SR, tel: 0118 958 0224.

- Blackhurst Parker & Yates Solicitors, 9 Cannon Street, Preston PR1 3QD, tel: 01772 253601.

- Atkinson & Co. Solicitors, 140A Framingham Road, Brooklands, Sale, Cheshire M33 3RG, tel: 0161 976 1921.

- Windsor Bronzite Solicitors, 162 Millbrook Road East, Southampton SO15 1EB, tel: 01703 634555.

- Stathams Solicitors, Hammonds Court, 22 London Road, Southampton SO15 2AF, tel: 01703 211617.

- Brignalls Solicitors, Queensway Chambers, Queensway, Stevenage, Herts SG1 1BA, tel: 01438 359311.

- Beardsells Solicitors, Vienna House, 281 Wellington Road South, Stockport, Cheshire SK2 6ND, tel: 0161 477 2288.

- Davies & Co. Solicitors, 2a Lawton Road, Alsager, Stoke-on-Trent ST7 2BJ, tel: 01270 873132.

- Ross Aldridge Solicitors, 3 Rowcroft, Stroud, Gloucs GL5 3AZ, tel: 01453 766193.

- Smith Llewellyn Solicitors, 18 Princess Way, Swansea SA1 3LW, tel: 01792 464444.

- O'Connor & Company Solicitors, 63 Lemon Street, Truro, Cornwall TR1 2PN, tel: 01872 271919.

- Dawson Hart Solicitors, The Old Grammar School, Church Street, Uckfield, East Sussex TN22 1BH, tel: 01825 762281.

- Frasers Solicitors, 29 Old Market, Wisbech, Cambs PE13 1ND, tel: 01945 582664.

AIR CONDITIONING

Aircon specialists

" *I am retiring soon and am considering purchasing my company car, which is a three-year-old Vauxhall Omega 2.5TD Estate with 53,000 miles on the clock. Can you please advise if it is possible to retrofit air conditioning.* "

Air conditioning retrofit specialists and maintenance specialists include: Motor Climate (0121 766 5006); Alpinair, 174 Honey Pot Lane, Stanmore, Middlesex (020 8204 9633); Vehicle Air Conditioning Services: Service Centre: Unit 8, Wintersells Road, Byfleet, Weybridge, Surrey KT14 7LF; Parts: Unit A, 120 Oyster Lane, Byfleet (01932 355825); Vehvac Ltd of Fircroft Way, Edenbridge, Kent TN8 6AJ (01732 868080), Coolair UK Ltd, Kingsley Road, Lincolnfields, Lincoln LN6 2TA (01522 682288); Halfords Garages (see local Yellow Pages).

A/C expense

" *I have owned my 'N'-registered VW Passat for 18 months and in that time I have only used the air conditioning once. I tried to use it again last weekend, only to find it was not working. The VW dealer told me it needed re-charging – and re-charged me £80 for the job. Is it right that air-conditioning systems should be re-charged every two years?* "

Time for a reminder. The refrigerant in car air-conditioning systems contains a lubricant to keep the seals gas-tight. If you do not use the a/c, these seals dry out and the refrigerant leaks away. It is generally recommended that a/c should be used for 20 minutes every week to keep the seals in good shape. This is no hardship because a/c is an excellent winter de-humidifier. My a/c has been on permanently for the past four months and the only noticeable increase in fuel consumption occurs when the car is stuck in one of our Government's Integrated Traffic Jams.

Justly deserted

" I suffered problems with the air conditioning of a 'nearly new' 406 purchased from a Peugeot dealer with an extended warranty. Despite using the aircon regularly, summer and winter, it failed in September 1998. The unit and later some defective piping were changed under the terms of the warranty, then, when I really needed the a/c on holiday in Spain, it failed again. I had it repaired by a Peugeot dealer in Spain at the very reasonable cost of Ptas 55,537 (£229.67) and on my return presented the bill to the dealer for a further warranty claim. However, it now seems that the failed pipe-work was not covered under the terms of the extended warranty or by any form of goodwill from Peugeot. As a direct result, I part-exchanged the car for a Mazda 626, which comes complete with a proper three-year warranty. "

Your letter wasn't clear about the length of the extended warranty and who provided it. But, faced with strong competition from reliable cars backed by three-year warranties, Peugeot introduced one of its own in January 2000.

ALTERNATIVE TRANSPORT

Micro machines

" I have seen some tiny cars in France and Spain, which must surely represent the answer to reducing urban pollution for those who only need or want to travel short distances. Can you tell us more? "

Reliant is now importing Ligier microcars from France. They are right-hand drive, UK and Euro Type Approved, have 505 cc, two-cylinder Lombardini petrol or diesel engines and open-belt Variomatic transmission. In de-restricted UK specification, they should have a top speed of 55–65 mph and give 65–85 mpg. They should also qualify for an extremely low CO_2-based rate of VED as from next October. And, after changes in licence regulations in 1996, they can also be driven on the same motorcycle licence as a Reliant three-wheeler. Price, from £6,495. More details from Reliant Cars Ltd, Cannock Road, Chase Terrace, Burntwood, Staffs WS7 8GB, tel: 01543 459222, fax: 01543 459444. Reliant is also importing Piaggio Ape micro pick-up trucks and vans, and will probably take on the cheaper Ligier Due Microcar in the near future.

A second microcar contender is Aixam Ltd, Unit 2 & 3, Tachbrook Link, Tachbrook Park

Drive, Royal Leamington Spa, Warwick, tel: 01926 886100. Aixam has been building microcars since 1975 and offers a range of convertibles, and two- and four-seater hatchbacks with diesel engines from 276 cc to 479 cc. The UK range is all rhd and powered by the 479 cc Kubota diesel engine, which gives up to 55 mph and up to 90 mpg. Prices start at £6,530 on the road with a year's VED for the two-seater Utility, or £6,630 OTR for the four-seater Economy, rising to £8,050 for the four-seater Super. Ex-Reliant boss Jonathan Heynes is importing a range of right-hand-drive fibreglass monocoque models called Microcar Virgo. These are available with two seats, 505 cc petrol or diesel Lombardini engines giving up to 68 mph and up to 80 mpg and cost from £5,995 on the road, including a three-year warranty. Microcar UK, Park House, The Grange, Wolverton, Stratford-on-Avon CV37 0HD, tel: 01789 730094. Other microcar makers include JRD, and Erad, who will be watching the UK market to see how sales go. We shouldn't forget the lhd, 599 cc, six-speed, 87 mph, MCC Smart car, now also available as a 799 cc common rail direct-injected diesel or a convertible, from MB UK at prices from £5,995, tel MB UK on 0800 037 9966 or contact KSB MotorGroup, website: www.ksb.co.uk. (More about Smarts in 'Horses for Courses' section).

New on the scene is the American 'Sparrow' a single-seater, three-wheeler, electric microcar capable of up to 70 mph, but costing £8,750. Finally, the incredible two-seater, 50 cc, three-wheeler and 350 cc, four-wheeler Fun Tech buggies seen at the Barcelona Motor Show can now be obtained in the UK from SMC Scooters of Torquay, tel: 01803 200670 or Fun Tech UK, tel:

01803 666610, website: www.fun-tec.co.uk (prices £2,995 and £3,995).

Petrol microcar, please

" I only do very short journeys, mostly of one to five miles, and would therefore like to exchange my 1998R Rover 416Si for something more suitable. However, it must have power steering and must not be a diesel. "

'Petrol only' cuts you out of a Ligier Ambra or an Aixam, both of which are diesel. But it does put you in the market for the 65 mph petrol version of the Microcar Virgo, from £5,995 on the road (tel: 01789 730094), or the 80 mph MCC Smart Pure, also from £5,995 (see above for dealers). Neither of these has power steering for the simple reason that neither needs it. I'd also have included the Daewoo Matiz on this list, but

I was stuck behind one recently and it was still chucking out clouds of white smoke after several miles so was obviously taking its time to warm up.

Electric car conversions

" Have any of the car manufacturers cracked the electric car nut yet? Our two cars cover around 5,000 miles each, almost exclusively on three miles of country lanes to and from work. As you keep writing, a vehicle with an internal combustion engine is entirely unsuitable for this sort of use. "

Alternative Vehicles Technology (AVT) has written to say that it offers 'affordable electric cars'. Unfortunately 'affordable' is only relative because its 'lowest cost complete conversion' works out at £5,500 including batteries and charger but excluding the cost of the car to be converted – either a Mini or the old-model sump-gearbox Metro, now at least nine years old. However, kits are available for home conversions from £2,995 excluding charger and batteries. The company also offers a conversion of the later and better Rover Metro or Rover 100 and of microvans, including the Bedford Rascal, Daihatsu Hijet and Suzuki Supercarry. AVT is in the process of developing its own AVT 100E electric car, but quotes prices from £16,995 to £19,995, *plus* batteries which cost from £1,481 to £2,070, including VAT. AVT claims top speeds from 56 mph for its £16,995 plus battery PM2 model to 'over 120 mph' for its £17,996 plus battery S192 model.

The theory of electric cars is spot-on for people who use their cars for short journeys only, a job for which internal combustion engines are particularly unsuited. Unfortunately, as yet, AVT's complete vehicle prices are still too high to attract the levels of interest that the vehicles themselves should justify. AVT can be contacted at Blue Lias House, Station Road, Hatch Beauchamp, Somerset TA3 6SQ, tel: 01823 480196. 'The Electric Car Association' also operates from the same offices. Reader J.S. of Manchester reports unfavourably on Varta semi-traction batteries and warns readers to source their batteries from a British supplier instead. For more advice on electric vehicles, contact The Electric Vehicle Society on 01933 276618, website: www.evn.co.uk and the Battery Vehicle Society on 01258 455470.

ANIMALS IN CARS

Doggy wagons

Five years ago I was asked to list the most suitable estate cars for transporting dogs. The reader specified that a car for dog-lovers should have tie hooks for harnesses or dog cages, a reasonably low rear sill and, preferably no exposed seat pins which could damage a large dog's skull or ribcage. What follows is an updated list.

- Audi A4 Avant: tie hooks, no pins, 3 × 3-point belts.
- BMW E36 3-Series Touring: tie hooks, small protected pins, 2 × 3-point belts.
- Citroën Xsara: tie hooks, no pins, 2 × 3-point belts.
- Citroën Xantia: tie hooks, no pins, 3 × 3-point belts, suspension lowers which makes it easier for older and smaller dogs to jump in.
- Citroën Berlingo Multispace Forte 5-door: tie hooks, small pins, 3×3-point belts.
- Citroën Picasso: tie hooks, no pins, 3 × 3-point belts.
- Daihatsu Move: no pins, 2 × 3-point belts.
- Daihatsu Grand Move: no pins, 2 × 3-point belts.

- Fiat Marea Weekend: tie hooks, no pins, 2 × 3-point belts.
- Fiat Multipla: tie hooks, no pins, 3 × 3-point belts (the only small 6-seater MPV with room in the back for a dog).
- Ford Mondeo: tie hooks, exposed pins, 3 × 3-point belts.
- Honda CRV: tie hooks, 2 × 3-point belts.
- Land Rover Freelander five-door: tie hooks, 3 × 3-point belts.
- Mazda Premacy: no exposed pins, 2 × 3-point belts, separately removable rear seats.
- Mazda 626: tie hooks, no exposed pins, 2 × 3-point belts.
- Mercedes A Class: tie hooks, no exposed pins, 2 × 3-point belts, removable rear seats.
- Mercedes C Class: tie hooks, no exposed pins, 3 × 3-point belts.
- Mercedes E Class: tie hooks, no exposed pins, 3 × 3-point belts.
- Mitsubishi Space Star: tie hooks, no exposed pins, 3 × 3-point belts, rear sill protector, slide-forward as well as fully folding and reclining rear seats.
- Nissan new Primera SLX: tie hooks, no exposed pins, 3 × 3-point belts.
- Peugeot 306: tie hooks, semi-exposed latches, 2 × 3-point belts.
- Peugeot 406: tie hooks, no pins, 3 × 3-point belts (option of rear-facing sixth and seventh child seats).
- Renault Kangoo Combi: strong tie hooks, no pins, 2 × 3-point belts (3 × 3-point in RXE version), five doors. Very practical for dogs – and cheap at £9,750 or £10,500 for RXE.
- Renault Megane Scenic: tie hooks, no pins, 3 × 3-point belts, slide-forward as well as reclining and completely removable rear seats.

- Renault Laguna: tie hooks, no pins, 3 × 3-point belts (option of rear-facing sixth and seventh child seats).
- Seat Cordoba Vario: no exposed pins, 2 × 3-point belts, very high sill.
- Skoda Felicia: tie hooks, exposed pins, 2 × 3-point belts.
- Skoda Octavia: tie hooks, no pins, 2 × 3-point belts, high sill without optional false floor.
- Suzuki Wagon R: tie hooks, no pins, 2 × 3-point belts.
- Suzuki Baleno: tie hooks, no pins, 2 × 3-point belts.
- Toyota Corolla: tie hooks, no pins, 3 × 3-point belts.
- Toyota Avensis: tie hooks, no pins, 3 × 3-point belts.
- Toyota Yaris Verso: tie hooks, no pins, 2 × 3-point belts, low load sill (rear seats fold away).
- Toyota RAV4 five-door: tie hooks, no pins, 2 × 3-point rear belts, low rear loading sill and completely flat floor when rear seats folded.
- Vauxhall new Astra: tie hooks, no pins, 3 × 3-point belts.
- Vauxhall Zafira: tie hooks, no pins, 2 × 3-point belts, seven seats.
- Vauxhall Vectra: tie hooks, no pins, 3 × 3-point belts.
- Volkswagen Golf Mk III: no hooks, exposed pins, 2 × 3-point belts.
- Volkswagen Golf Mk IV: four strong tie hooks, no exposed pins, 2 × 3-point belts (3 × 3-point belts optional), built-in dog guard.
- Volkswagen Passat: tie hooks, exposed pins, 2 × 3-point belts (3 × 3-point belts optional, covers for exposed pins available).
- Volvo V40: tie hooks, no pins, 3 × 3-point belts.
- Volvo V70: tie hooks, no pins, 3 × 3-point belts.

BODYWORK AND APPEARANCE

Chips and scratchings

" In the past you have mentioned firms that specialise in removing minor dents, painting in stone chips, and repairing damaged windscreens. Any chance of a quick reprise? "

For minor dents of the supermarket car park variety, call Dentmaster (0800 433687), Paint Technik PDR (0800 298 5455) or Dent Devils (0402 936728), who will put you on to their nearest operator. For stone chips and upholstery repairs try Chips Away on 01562 755678. (Paint Technik also 'invisibly' repair minor paint damage.) For repairs to cracked or scratched plastic bumpers, call Plastic Technik on 01296 682105. For plastic trim and upholstery repairs call Magic Mend on 0800 901 902 or Trimline Systems on 01202 480 881. For repairs and renovation of leather upholstery call Patrick Russell Leather on 020 8878 3976. And for chipped or scratched windscreens, call Glas Weld Systems on 0800 243 274 or 01372 362362 in Surrey. On modern cars with bonded windscreens this is better than having the entire screen replaced, because removing the old one can damage the car body leading to leaks and rust. (Autoglass and Auto Windscreens and many others offer a similar service.)

Scratched screen

" *I am the lucky owner of a new Mercedes 300TD. But my luck ran out other day when I passed a pelican crossing where they had just finished coating the approaches with a new, rough 'anti-skid' gravel. Another car threw some of it on to my screen and, as it was raining, I was using my wipers. The wipers caught the grit and left a number of fine scratches on the screen. These won't wash or rub off with conventional screen-cleaning polishes, so my question is, do you know of a firm that can remove them?* "

Some Glas Weld franchises, such as Adrian in Surrey (01372 362362) have a new kit which is more effective at removing scratches than anything else so far. The national number is 0800 243 274. Another possibility is a DIY kit by Cetem (0121 786 1840) but readers have had very mixed results attempting to use this.

Cow pat repellent

" *I drive a Rover 111 Knightsbridge which has metallic purple paintwork. My problem is I live in the country in a dairy-farming area where the roads are used to bring the cows in for milking. Inevitably my car becomes splattered with cow pats which dry rapidly and are very difficult to remove even with a jetwash. Can you recommend anything to help remove them or to prevent them from sticking to the paintwork?* "

Once you have completely cleaned the car, try Autoglym Super Resin Polish followed by a couple of coats of Autoglym Extra Gloss Protection. I have 'road tested' this combination on a metallic finish for more than 12 months. The Extra Gloss Protection lasts about three months and when hand-washing the car, dried mud splatters from country roads come off easily. Small bird poop simply wipes off with a damp cloth.

Seagull strikes

" In 1998 I purchased a Daewoo car complete with a three-year warranty. This year I found a large bird dropping on the bonnet which I removed within 24 hours but which left an area of pitted paint. I was led to believe by a Daewoo rep that the bonnet would be re-sprayed under the car's three-year paintwork warranty. I have since been told that Daewoo will not pay for the re-spray because the warranty does not cover damage to the paint, only faulty materials or workmanship. Is it reasonable for Daewoo not to honour my claim, or are modern cars built to such a low standard that they are unable to endure everyday use? "

Environmentalists have persuaded governments to reduce solvent-based paints and car makers have been compelled to replace colour coats with water-based paints. These paints are not impervious to bird droppings, particularly if the tougher lacquer coat over the paint is penetrated. This is why section 8–4 of your car's handbook tells you to remove the droppings immediately. One reader recommends carrying wet wipes in the car specifically for this purpose. I find that Autoglym Extra Gloss Protection works as well at repelling droppings as can be reasonably expected, but there are other DIY and professional paint sealants.

Cover up

P.W. of Wilmslow has written to tell us that he manufactures standard-size and made-to-measure Terylene and cotton car-cover sheets in various colours from price £10. For more information please telephone 01625 527522.

Chipping away

" *I am alarmed at the amount of damage caused by stone chippings to the paintwork and windscreens of my BMW and Mazda.* "

Me too. While paint finishes are not as hard as they used to be, the main culprit is cut-backs in UK road maintenance, leading to more stones being thrown up at cars.

Top products

" *How do I look after the fabric top of my 'S'-reg. Renault Megane Cabriolet? Should I wash it? If so, what should I wash it with? Should I waterproof it or treat it in some other way?* "

Brush any loose dust and dirt from the hood, but don't apply any car-body shampoo, then hose it clean along with the rest of the car. Every six months or so it's a good idea to clean the hood properly with Renovo Pre-cleaner/ Shampoo, which comes in a spray can and costs £11.95 plus £1.95 p&p direct from the makers. Renovo also offers a Hood Reviver at £29.95 a can, an Ultra Proofer to re-waterproof a canvas hood, and a special polish to help restore transparency to scratched or opaqued plastic windows. More information on their website: www.renovointernational.com, or tel: 01444 443277, or write to Renovo International Ltd, PO Box 404, Haywards Heath, West Sussex RH17 5YN.

Door protector

" *I park next to a wall and am looking for a suitable rubber or similarly waterproof strip to fix to the wall to avoid chipping the paintwork when I open the car door. I have looked in car accessory shops, but have not seen anything suitable. What do you suggest?* "

Use a length of plastic hosepipe. Screw right through it into the wall using Rawlplugs or similar. Then use a Stanley knife to cut around the screw head on the outer surface of the pipe so it pops back out into shape. Another reader suggested using a length of boat 'defendering' available from most boat yard chandlers. If the car is parked inside a garage, yet another reader recommends fixing squares of old carpet to the garage walls against which car doors are likely to be opened.

Integrated dirt

" *I regularly integrate my transport by parking my car at a station and taking the train. However, my reward is to find its paintwork covered in a brown, rust-like deposit, which I am told is brake dust from the trains. If left untreated, this builds up into a coating, which requires abrasive polish to remove. Do you know of any non-abrasive treatment that would do the same job?* "

The dust landing on your car is iron powder, which has gradually replaced asbestos in the brake linings of cars and trains over the last 10 years or so. Readers recommend washing the car with a solution of liquidised rhubarb leaves, which contain oxalic acid. Alternatively, see if a chemist will sell you a small quantity of oxalic acid crystals and make up a weak solution of that, but do wear gloves and be careful, because oxalic acid is poisonous.

BRAKES

Dotty idea

" A knowledgeable car-racing friend of mine has suggested an alternative solution to changing brake fluid every two years or even every single year to protect ABS pumps from moisture attack. He suggests using DOT 5 silicone fluid, which is non-hygroscopic instead of the normal DOT 3 or 4. Apparently, DOT 5 will last indefinitely and is used by most sports/racing enthusiasts to give more consistent braking when the callipers are extremely hot. It's much more expensive, but would work out cheaper in the long term. "

I checked with my racing and 'track day' buddies. You're right. They do use Automec's DOT 5 silicone fluid. But it's not compatible with ordinary brake fluid so all of the old fluid needs to be completely flushed out of the entire system using high pressure equipment first. Automec, tel: 01280 822818.

Make sensor this

" I would like to use your column to warn Citroën ZX-owning readers that their brake-pad-wear sensor warning lights may not be functioning. On both our ZXs, the cable had severed and the wear on the outer pads was severe enough for the sensors to make contact with the discs. The inner pads had worn far less. "

The combined handbrake and low master-cylinder fluid-level warning light on ZXs does work quite well. But severed pad-wear sensor cables is quite common on a number of cars, especially those with power steering that make a lot of parking manoeuvres.

Parking or barking?

" I own a Mercedes Benz C250D manual, which is fitted with the same foot-operated parking brake as the automatic. In January an MB automatic rolled down an incline into a river with a child strapped into the back who drowned. The driver, who had just left the car, could not reach the parking brake to apply it and avert the tragedy. Twice my own car has rolled away from me, once when I confused the brake and bonnet release. The only way to stop the car in these circumstances is to jump in and apply either the footbrake or parking brake, a task impossible for many drivers. Mercedes Benz is fully aware of this problem, but is happy to blame the driver for not leaving the car in gear. Since they fit a lights-on warning buzzer and a buzzer to tell the driver he has driven away with the parking brake on, why can't they fit a buzzer to warn the driver he has not applied the parking brake before he leaves the car? Is there any way of getting my car modified to have a handbrake? "

MB has adopted American-style parking brakes to suit the American market where virtually every American-built car has a foot-operated parking brake because they are easier to apply fully than a handbrake. The driver of the car in which the child so tragically died was at fault either for getting out of the car with the engine running (an offence in itself), for failing to apply the parking brake properly, or for failing to leave the transmission in 'park'. This locks an automatic transmission far more effectively than leaving a manual parked in first or reverse. (See the Highway Code, rules 214 and 226.) It is true that an 'idiots beeper' would remind the sloppy and the careless, but drivers who forget simple things like applying a parking brake and leaving a car in gear on an incline should not be driving at all. You may be able to find someone who can fit your car with a handbrake to replace its parking brake. However, this will disqualify your car from any outstanding warranty, will cost a fortune and you will need to inform your insurer of the alterations.

BUYING AND SELLING

Supersites

" Where are the cheapest places to buy new cars in the UK? "

- Motorpoint, Chartwell Drive, West Meadows, Derby, tel: 01332 347357, website: www.motorpoint.co.uk
- Trade Sales of Slough, 353–357 Bath Road, Slough, Berks SL1 6JA, tel: 01753 773763, website: www.trade-sales.co.uk
- Motorhouse 2000, Wryly Brook Retail Park, Walkmill Lane, Cannock WS11 3XE, tel: 01543 462300, website: www.motorhouse2000ltd.co.uk
- www.d.c.cook.co.uk

www.ways to sell a car

" Which are the best websites on which to advertise a car I want to sell? "

- www.autotrader.co.uk (£4.95 for a fortnight)
- www.exchangeandmart.co.uk
- www.fish4cars.co.uk
- www.autohit.com
- www.autolocate.co.uk
- www.used-car-buyer.co.uk

Pros and cons

" *Your column and* Book of Motoring Answers *are valued reading, but what I believe Joe Punter also needs is a listing of popular models, giving a catalogue of pro and anti points in the fashion of your observations. For example, I was once the very satisfied owner of a Cavalier but was not aware until you told me that changing the clutch of a Vectra involves a five-fold increase in the labour cost. So, does such a list exists? If not, I reckon you are the man for the job, and put me down for a copy.* "

This list took up 274 pages in the last *Daily Telegraph* 'How to Buy and Sell Cars', has now been expanded to cover 450 models and is on my website at www.honestjohn.co.uk under 'Car by Car Breakdown'. This gives me the opportunity to update it regularly and bring you the latest information.

Going for broker

" With all the talk of buying cars over the internet, is it still worthwhile contacting a conventional car broker? "

Can be. With companies like Fiat sometimes offering 30% dealer discounts, brokers can still be a good route to a bargain. Speak to Steve Tokatlian at Quote to Quote on 020 7603 9999 (six lines) and Pat Lawless at Carfile on 01335 360763/360022 (9.15–5.45), 0410 081984 (evenings and weekends). Neither asks for a deposit.

Worth less than nothing

" Some friends who have left the country have left me with their 1984 Opel Manta to dispose of. There is too much rust in the chassis to warrant even trying to get an MOT. Nevertheless, my friends assure me that the car contains £800 worth of spares. The local Opel specialist scrap yard says it's worth £35 to them. Is there an Opel Manta Club or similar that might give me a reasonable price for the car? "

The club is the Opel Manta Owners' Club, c/o Richard Miller, 186 Norman Place Road, Coundon, Coventry CV6 2BU. Try them by all means. But on the open market a rusted-out, MOT-failure, 1984 Manta is worth no more than £35 even to a specialist scrap yard. An ordinary scrapper would charge £35 to take it away. MOT failures are now worth zilch. For the first time since the 1960s I recently saw a car sell at auction for £1. It was a 79V Princess 1700 automatic 'Wedge', frayed at the edges, but a runner. Unless the bloke in the checked shirt who bought it manages to sell it to someone from the Princess & Ambassador Club, he faces getting nothing for it from the scrapper, and that's why no one outbid him, including me.

Triumphant departure

" *I wish to sell my elderly mother's 1968 'G'-registered Triumph 1300TC, which has been in her hands since October 1977. Would this be an appropriate car for a classic car auction?* "

Yes. The front-wheel drive Triumph 1300 was the predecessor to the Triumph Toledo, the Triumph 1500, the Triumph Dolomite and the Saab 99/900. The 1300TC has a 1,296 cc, Spitfire Mk III engine (the best Spitfire engine) and is now a very rare car. (See list of classic car auction houses at the end of this section.)

What's the bidding for a genuine NG?

" *I have carefully constructed my Sierra-based pastiche NG 'Henley' to a high standard but now wish to sell it. At 70 years old, I find it a bit draughty. Ads in the owners' club magazine and relevant news-stall magazines (quoting a price of £5,500) have provoked zero response. Last Saturday's column referred to a 'market', like a car boot sale where, I believe, you can turn up and sell the car rather than its contents, but where are they?* "

I have not written about these Sunday car markets in the column, but one that ran about six years ago at Kempton Park Racecourse has been revived. You turn up, pay £20, stick a price in your windscreen and wait. (Remember to take the Sunday papers with you.) Like Marlins, NG's are well established kit cars and some of the classic car auction houses will accept them as entries. (See the list at the end of this section.)

End of the road

" *I am writing on behalf of an elderly lady friend who has just given up driving. In her garage is a 1978 'S'-reg. Ford Fiesta, which she wants to sell despite a rusty underbody which would not pass the MOT. The engine and interior are in good nick. She has driven very little over the last decade and I wondered if she could sell the car to a Ford Fiesta Club, if one exists.* **"**

There is a club: The Ford Fiesta Club of GB, c/o Mrs S. Church, 145 Chapel Lane, Farnborough, Hants GU14 9BN, tel: 01276 35422, website: http://www.fiestacentre.com. But I'm afraid that the end of leaded petrol and new environmental controls on the way cars are scrapped mean that, if the club won't take it off her hands, your friend faces having to pay a vehicle breaker £30 or more to dispose of it.

Limited income

" *I am an OAP. I have a three-and-a-half-year-old Vauxhall Corsa 1.4 litre LS hatchback, just coming up to 40,000 on the clock. Please can you advise me what is the best time financially to consider replacing it in order to get the best possible price on the secondhand market? Also, do I replace with new or newish secondhand? Bear in mind that my annual income is approximately £6,000 and the money will have to come out of fast-diminishing capital.* **"**

If your car has power steering and it suits you, why change it at all? The cold facts are that used cars are not selling well at the moment and you would be very lucky to get £4,000 for your Corsa as a private sale. I wouldn't value the car at more than £3,500 and I think that even this would be a good offer in part-exchange. A replacement 'nearly new' Corsa 1.4i Breeze with PAS should not cost you more than £6,000. If a local dealer wants more, then he should pay you more for your part-exchange and your 'cost to switch' should not be more than £2,500. But as I wrote, why waste this money when you need it for other things?

How new is 'new'?

" An advertisement in Exchange & Mart caught my eye. It read: 'Mercedes E220 W124 New Unregistered £16,995'. The car has air conditioning, electric windows, four headrests, etc. The price seems attractive, but what are the pitfalls with such a purchase? "

Production of this model ended in August 1995, so the car is at least five years old. It will have been scheduled for export to the Far East and will have either gone there and come back when the Tiger economies collapsed, or never got off the Bremerhaven dockside. As a trade import, unless it has a certificate of European National Type Approval, it is subject to SVA quotas and testing before it can be registered and the only way round this is for you to drive it in another EU country then personally import it from there as a car more than three years old, then put it through a UK MOT. It will probably have a kilometre speedometer which you will need to have re-faced with mph and kph calibrations (Reap Automotive Design, tel: 020 8863 2305). The car will suffer from all the usual problems of a vehicle left standing unused in the open for three to four years: rusty brake discs, rusty exhaust system, flat battery, possible cooling system problems, possible heater matrix problems, dodgy air conditioning, etc, etc. But at least the dealer was honest enough to describe it as a 'W124' and not try to mislead you that it was the current model E-Class.

Imprezzive money

" I have been scouting around Subaru franchises looking for an Impreza five-door. All six franchises I visited were offering cars priced at least £1,000 over dealer prices quoted in car-price guides and the more recent *cars are attracting a premium of around £1,700. This means that the cars have only depreciated by £1,800 in 20 months compared to a Mondeo's depreciation of around £9,000. How can the public rely on price guides if such disparities exist? The franchises I spoke to showed no interest in haggling and all expressed the view that they could sell at the asking prices without any trouble. A whiff of a cartel, perhaps? Could you suggest an alternative that will match the spec and quality of the Impreza at a more realistic price?* "

What you are faced with are the forces of supply and demand. Imprezas are excellent vehicles which don't break down and which are in short supply in the UK. The only way to get an Impreza more cheaply is to import it personally, which means personally owning and driving it in another country, then getting it through the SVA test once you have imported it into the UK. Speak to Park Lane on 01420 544300 or Warrender of Bolton on 01257 427700. There aren't any alternatives to the non-turbo Impreza apart from the Skoda Octavia 4x4, but a Mitsubishi Lancer Evo is a fine alternative to the Impreza Turbo.

Hong Kong klunker

" *I hope my foolishness will serve as a warning to others. Last August, against all reason and sound advice, I bought a 1983 Mercedes 500SL roadster from a Hong Kong solicitor for £10,000. It cost £2,000 to ship the car back to the UK and a further £200 to transport it to Yeovil from Southampton docks. It was only then that the true realisation of my impetuous decision dawned. The car is a rust bucket, carefully and deliberately disguised, virtually undrivable and needing thousands of pounds spending on it. Is its value no more than scrap? Should it go to auction? I enclose what purported to be a Hong Kong AA inspection report.* "

Not much wrong with the inspection report. This clearly states, 'Front right chassis, bodysills, under-floor pressing and jacking points are corroded'; 'oil sump oil seep'; 'steering hoses oil seep'; and warned that the car was not roadworthy in its present state. The car isn't scrap though. As long as you have C&E 386 to prove VAT and EU import duty have been paid, you could consign it to a classic car auction where it will make what it is worth.

Doing a Daewoo

" *Daewoo has curdled my interest with its 'all-in' prices. What is your opinion of the Matiz SE and the Lanos S? I have a 93L Micra 1.0L which I bought new, has now done 7,500 miles and is in immaculate condition.* "

The basic Matiz is a sensible, low-powered little buzz-box for pottering around in, shopping and ferrying the kids about locally. It has so little power that even on the Millbrook Alpine Route I reckon it handled more safely than the Mercedes A Class, Vauxhall Zafira and Fiat Multipla. But there is no point in paying extra for SE or SE+ spec unless you go for the more powerful 100 mph Matiz which should be arriving soon. The Lanos 1.4S is a simple, basic three-door hatch with PAS which sells for the same price as a Fiesta, but includes the 'Daewoo Deal'. If you ever intend travelling any distance, this would be a better choice than the Matiz.

Of Minor importance

" *I have a 1971 Morris Minor 1,098 cc to dispose of due to age – mine, that is, not the car's. It is in very good condition and with only a genuine 32,300 on the clock. Can you advise how best to sell it and how much I can expect to receive?* "

VED exempt, cheap to convert to unleaded, a

shape universally loved and one of the last of the line. If this car is genuinely sound underneath as well as sparkling on top, you could get as much as £3,000 for it – and a bit more if it's a half-wooded Traveller model. You could try the friendly Morris Minor Owners' Club, PO Box 1098, Derby DE23 8ZX, tel: 01332 291675, website: www.MorrisMinorOC.co.uk. You could use a photo ad in *Classic Car Weekly* (order a copy from your newsagent to obtain a form). But because viewing is a problem due to where you live, I think your best bet will be a classic car auction. The nearest is H&H, which holds sales at Pavilion Gardens, Buxton every two months, tel: 01925 730630.

How much for the old bus?

" *I had the good fortune to travel in a charming 1950s Bedford bus in Paphos, Cyprus during a recent holiday. It was in immaculate condition and I was surprised to hear that the owner/driver was thinking of selling it to retire. He asked what it would be worth in England and if anyone would be interested in buying it. I promised to try to find out by writing to you.* "

The best man to talk to is Ron Ruggins of the Bedford Owners' Club, 27 Northville Drive, Westcliffe-on-Sea, Essex SS0 0QA. Before the Afghan war, the roads there too were packed with these late 1950s Bedford 7-tonners, usually sporting the sort of decoration seen on a Manila Jeepney bus. Engines were normally 4,927 cc, six-cylinder diesels. Shipping is certainly feasible from Cyprus and rust obviously isn't a problem. On the other hand, getting permission to export the old bus and putting its mechanicals through a UK MOT might be. I have no basis from which to value it, but if any readers want to make an offer, please write to Harry Georgiades, 21 Pickwick Road, London SE21 7JN. It would be nice to see someone sponsor bringing it back for the National Motor Museum at Beaulieu as part of a post-war 'Export or Die' exhibit.

Import finance

Crown Leasing offers finance on imported cars. Rates are between 9.9%APR for over £30,000 borrowed to 12.5%APR for £10,000. The price is fixed in sterling on contract by forward-buying the foreign currency at a guaranteed rate (there is a charge for this). The deposit is 10% rather than the 20%–30% sometimes asked for by Continental dealers. The car is imported on your behalf, so the UK is its first country of registration. Residual values are fixed to match the lease-purchase balloon payment at a realistic 90% of predicted 'CAP Clean' two or three years hence. The beauty of the scheme is that, providing you eventually return the car in 'CAP Clean' condition at the agreed mileage, you know exactly what you will have to pay throughout from the moment you sign the contract. Tel: 01487 773322. Allen Fleet Services of Leicester also offer imported cars on contract hire at savings of 25% on normal rates, tel: 01455 222401.

Sera vendido

" *My wife and I have an 'H'-registered right-hand-drive Toyota Sera, properly imported and documented. The car has done about 27,000 kilometres, is in excellent condition and has been looked after by our local Toyota dealer. Its specification includes a 110 bhp, 1.5 litre engine, air conditioning, alloy wheels and power steering, but no ABS to go expensively wrong. Now we are both getting a bit ancient we find the Lamborghini-like doors a bit hard to manage and reluctantly feel that the time has come to part with our price and joy. We would be grateful for your advice about how to find it a good home.* "

I think that your best bet is www.autotrader. co.uk. I hit the site myself and found seven Seras, all 1990/91, priced from £4,700 to £7,995. £8,000 is way OTT, but if you pitch yours at a straight £6,000 (not £5,995 or you'll look like a car dealer) you may stand a chance of a nip (be prepared to take £5,000). Whenever using a photo ad, take your own photograph and go through a roll of film trying to get a good snap. This will cost you £4.99 tops, including a replacement film. Cars usually look their best side-on, preferably against the sky or a plain background.

Costa del SL

" *I plan to buy a Mercedes 300SL (89/91) to keep in Spain in the winter and in the UK in the summer. Left- or right-hand drive. Where in Europe should I look for the best price and where should I tax and insure it?* "

Buy in Germany using a magazine such as the large-format *DAZ*, which you pick up at the airport. Tax and insure the car in Spain, where the annual damage will be a lot less than in the UK, but the insurance could be a bit stiffer. You're going to have to time your trips so that Spanish tax and roadworthiness certificates do not run out while the car is in the UK.

X1/9 time

" *At last, after ten years, it looks as though I might get half my garage back, as my daughter has finally consented to my selling her X1/9 five-speed. I have just had it serviced, it passed its MOT first time and I took*

my first drive in it for 15 years. I was surprised how well it handled and how nippy it felt for a design that must be all of 25 years old. With only 53,000 miles and in excellent condition for its 18 years I wondered what it might be worth? I was told at the local garage they can fetch anything from £300 to £3,000 and that I should try the owners' club. **"**

The club is the Fiat X1/9 Owners' Club, c/o Claire Home, 37 Parklands, Uffors, Woodbridge, Suffolk IP13 6ES, tel: 01394 460883, website: www.x1-9ownersclub.org.uk. The price range you have been given is about right, and is confirmed by auction results. I suggest you ask for £2,750 in the club magazine and see what happens.

Long-range orders

" *Over the last 18 years I have bought five Mitsubishis, all from the same dealer. Recently I tried to order a new Galant 2.0iGLS in Finesse Green* *with a sunroof and air conditioning. Despite having to give two alternative colours it seems it is impossible to get the car I want. Do import restrictions limit the choice? Is there a better time to order to actually get the colour I want?* "

Favourable press reports of the amazing Galant VR4 have led to a sudden surge of interest in Galants generally. Shipments are landed roughly every month and the voyage from Japan takes three weeks. So while it cannot always be possible to obtain the precise colour and specification you want from stocks already in the UK, the Colt Car Co. can make a specific build order on your behalf and the car should not take more than 8–12 weeks to arrive from Japan.

As recommended

" *Some six months ago I wrote to you asking if you could suggest somewhere I could get a new Mazda MX5 cheaper than through a UK Mazda dealer. You suggested that I should try Park Lane in Alton, Hants (01420 544300) and recommended that I should get the 1.8 litre version rather than the 1.6. This is what I did and I now want you to know that I was satisfied with Park Lane's service and am delighted with my 1.8 MX5. Thanks very much for your help.* "

The difference between Park Lane and some of the other independent importers is that Park Lane is extremely well funded, is probably the most experienced and is very professional, tel: 01420 544300, website: www.park-lane.co.uk.

Any more Senators?

" *My wonderful 'H'-reg. Vauxhall Senator 3.0iCD has done 178,000 miles and is starting to rust in awkward places. I would like to replace it with one of the last 1994L's but am finding them to be as rare as a stiff drink in a temperance hotel. I have left my requirements with every*

Vauxhall dealer within a 25-mile semicircle around Great Yarmouth to no avail. Where can I find one? There also seems to be a severe shortage of Omega saloons in my area. "

The best two places I know of for Omegas are (franchised) Nidd Vale Motors of Harrogate (01423 500005) and (independent) DK Car Sales of Thatcham (01635 865610). DK could also be your best source of a late Senator CD. The very last Senators were held back for the police and a few may even have been registered on 'N' plates. When they came off duty, a company by the name of Portaploy used to bring them up to CD spec and re-sell them as bargain two-year-old, 110,000-mile cars (01256 322240). But as far as I know, the last were disposed of in 1999 and the two-year-old ex-police patrol cars coming through West Oxfordshire Motor Auctions (01993 774413) are now Volvo T5s, Vauxhall Omegas and BMW 325TDSs.

'Classic' coupe

" *I have been the proud owner of a Mercedes Benz 230CE coupe, fitted with £10,500 of extras, ever since it was new in 1983. It is immaculate, light blue in colour, has covered 101,000 miles and has been regularly serviced. The extras include ABS, cruise control. tinted glass, and head restraints and centre arm rests front and rear. Would you kindly give your suggestion as to the best way to sell the car?* "

A classic car auction, without a doubt, because classics are very hard to shift by advertising at the moment. The best price I have recorded this year for a 280CE was £3,229 including commission at H&H, Pavilion Gardens, Buxton in February. While the best price in recent years for a 280CE was £6,670 at Sandown Park in November 1997.

£7,999 Mazdas

" *Motorpoint of Derby is advertising Mazda 323 1.3LXIs at £7,999. The cars are apparently from Eire, so presumably they will be of a slightly different specification. Could you confirm this and possibly list the differences? Do you know of any pitfalls in purchasing a car imported from Eire? Will the vehicle registration document indicate that the car has been imported? If so, will this affect the resale value?* "

Motorpoint tells me that the only significant difference from UK spec is that the cars do not have remote locking. They do have central locking, twin airbags, power steering, etc. The cars are pre-UK registered to Motorpoint, but are not 'previously registered overseas'. Surprisingly, they even carry a thee-year warranty because Mazda's three-year warranty is pan-European. So the only warning I can give is don't overdo the celebrations over the money you're going to save. Motorpoint, tel: 01332 347357, website: www.motorpoint.co.uk.

1986 price

" *What was the 'on the road' price of a Mercedes 560SEL in December 1986?* "

The closest I have is August 1986, which was £52,750 excluding delivery and VED.

Viva the tax-free Viva

" *My mother died recently and left her mint condition, yellow, 1972 Vauxhall Viva HC X14, 1,800 cc, which has now done 76,586 miles. It qualifies as a VED-exempt 'historic vehicle'. We would like to find a caring home for it and are asking £500. Can you help? The MOT runs out on 20 September.* "

If the car is truly 'mint', you're certainly not asking too much. Try The Vauxhall Viva Owners' Club, c/o Adrian Miller, 'The Thatches', Snetterton North End, Snetterton, Norwich NR16 2LD, tel: 01953 498818.

Pre-reg value

" What is the strategy behind car dealers pre-registering vehicles? "

To turn them into secondhand cars and get rid of the damn things at whatever price the public is prepared to pay. Of every 100 mass-produced cars built, only around 5% are sold to members of the public at the full list price. Between 50% and 80% go on to fleets of some kind, and the remaining 45%–15% are either pre-registered by manufacturers or by dealers who get bonuses for every car they register by a certain date. These bonuses, plus the standard dealer discount, plus other forms of rebate are used to finance the apparent discounts at which pre-registered cars are offered to the public. One of the Competion Commission's recommendations was that pre-registering should be banned.

Full set of Vettes

" Over the years I have acquired a collection of four classic Corvettes: a '58, a '63 split-window, a '72 T-Top auto, and a '72 convertible manual. I also have a '54 Chevy step-side pick-up. Now, because I'm about to lose storage facilities on a nearby farm I have to sell most or all of them. I am told that the Corvettes could be worth more back in the USA. Is this true? Ideally I would like to sell all four vehicles as a complete collection. Where would you suggest is the best place to advertise both in Europe and the USA? "

First speak to Claremont Corvette on 01634

244444 to see if Tom Falconer will make you a sensible offer for the job lot. Otherwise, don't try to keep the vehicles together because it greatly decreases your chances of selling them. To advertise the '72s and the truck, try the UK magazine *Classic American*. I can tell you exactly what the '72 manual convertible is worth: £8,250 plus commission, because that's exactly what a good '72 manual convertible with hard-top and a/c made at BCA's Classic Car Auction at Blackbushe on 16 August 1999. The '72 T-top will be worth less, but still benefits from being VED exempt. The '58 and the '63 probably will make more money at auction in the USA where cars like this in top condition can make the equivalent of £20,000–£40,000 in megabucks. Speak to UK auction houses Christies (020 7389 2851) and Brooks (020 7228 8000) which have been particularly successful with their sales staged in the USA. Remember, though, that once you've got the cars over there, they're stuck there. If word gets around a dealer 'ring' that the cars are from England you could find yourself stitched up, particularly if the cars are in less than the perfect condition they will need to be to rise above an auction ring.

Jam sandwiches for 'T'

" I am interested in buying an ex-police Volvo but am finding it hard to locate an auction that deals in them in North Yorkshire. Do you know of any? How much can I expect to pay? And is buying one a good idea? "

The best way to buy ex-police cars is at one of the twice monthly ex-police sales held on Tuesday or Thursday evenings by West Oxfordshire Motor Auctions on the old A40 at Witney (tel: 01993 774413, email: buy@woma.demon.uk).

Throughput of ex-police vehicles is now running at 120 to 150 a week. The new bargain ex-police car is a Volvo T5 estate, many of which are automatics because this increases front-tyre life. Expect to pay £5,000 to £6,000 for a three-year-old estate with 120,000 to 150,000 miles, or around £4,000 for the much less desirable saloon (you'll get a three-year-old 100,000-mile civvy T5 saloon for around £6,250). Ex-police cars are extremely well maintained and motorway patrol cars clock up most of their mileage at 65 mph with a huge tailback behind them. But, because they almost inevitably get involved in pursuits, it is vital to inspect them very carefully for repaired accident damage. The only auction houses I know of with regular police sales in your part of the country are BCA Derby (01332 666111) and Manheim Leeds (0870 444 0407), but WOMA remains the best.

Car buyers' strike

" May I suggest a car buyers' strike? If all private UK car buyers stopped buying new cars for several months, this would force the manufacturers to reduce list prices to more sensible levels. "

This started in early September 1999 and continued right through until Summer 2000, by which time manufacturers and importers were forced to reduce prices substantially. Over the same period, sterling rose by around 15% against Eurocurrencies then fell back from early May making any purchase completed in April 2000 about the best.

Classic Saab?

" Has the old-shape Saab 900 Turbo 16 become a classic? The price

seems to have gone up by £500 since spring 1999, and I am now being asked for £3,600 for a 'perfect' 88E Turbo 16v S. I have been told that BBC2's 'Top Gear' featured older Saab 900s and recommended the 16v S as the one to get. But could the price increase merely be a passing fad? I could also buy an 87D non-S Turbo 16 for £2,355. "

Back in February 1999 on ITV2's 'Dealer's Choice' I found myself recommending a 116,000 mile 92J Saab 900 16v non-Turbo convertible priced at £8,000. My reasoning was that while Saab 900 tin-tops are weird enough to become trendy 'neo-classics', the convertibles take the game on to an altogether higher level. After all, why pay £8,000 for a restored MGB when the same money buys you a very interesting four-seater convertible with a power hood that, even without a turbo, runs rings round an MGB? Of the tin-top turbos, the only real classic is the 180 bhp Ruby – the very last old-shape 900 16v Turbo. All 16vs, apart from the APC, will run on premium unleaded, so no worries there. But for £3,600 I'd want a newer tin-top than an 88E, so if I were you I'd go for the £2,355 87D – but do make sure it's a 16v, not an 8v.

His and hers

" When we win the lottery, which must now be soon, we would like to buy examples of two cars we cherished many years ago. These were a 1959-ish Fiat 2300 and a 1960 'half wooded' Mini Countryman. We owned both outside the UK and I have never seen either here, so could it be that they were never available here? "

The twin-headlight, six-cylinder Fiat 2100 was built from 1959 to 1961, but was criticised for its coil-sprung rear end. Its successor, the more powerful, better handling 2300 was built from 1961 to 1968. Most rotted away years ago but, if you're .

prepared to take on a restoration, you may find a relatively rot-free lhd example in an olive grove in southern Italy or Spain. In the UK you stand a much better chance of securing the elegant 2300 coupe, which is far more likely to have been preserved. But first speak to the Fiat Motor Club (GB), c/o Sally Robins, 118 Brookland Road, Langport, Somerset TA10 9TH, tel: 01458 250116. The 'half wooded' 1960 Mini Countryman was one of the very first and your best bet for this is one of the Mini clubs: British Mini Club, c/o David Hollis, The Mini House, 15 Dove Ridge, Amblecote, Stourbridge, West Midlands DY8 4LE, tel: 01384 440060; National Mini Owners' Club, c/o C. Cheal, 15 Birchwood Road, Lichfield, Staffs WS14 9UN, tel: 01543 257956, email: http://www.brochure.org/moc/; Club Mini Classics, c/o P. Kershaw, 18a Douglas Road, Harpenden, Herts AL5 2EW, tel: 01582 769549.

Auction caution?

" *We recently bought a 'nearly new' Daewoo at a special sale held at British Car Auctions, Blackbushe. As with all the other cars in the sale, ours was sold with the benefit of the remainder of Daewoo Cars Ltd's three-year warranty. There was a notice to this effect in the windscreen and the warranty was also mentioned by the auctioneer. Not until later correspondence with Daewoo Cars Ltd did we discover that we only have very limited warranty cover. Servicing is excluded, as is windscreen damage and the AA cover is not as full as described in the paperwork that came with the car. While we could accept this behaviour from a backstreet trader, we find it disgraceful behaviour from Daewoo. The cars in question were sold with the balance of the warranty, not balance of warranty excluding x, y and z.* "

You got what you paid for: 9–12-month-old Daewoos with 9,000–12,000 miles are typically 42–48% cheaper in these sales than when new.

The car was sold with the balance of warranty, not any balance of the Daewoo Deal, which private buyers benefit from when they buy a new Daewoo. That's why the car was so cheap.

Minor anxiety

" We are anxious to sell our 1968 Morris Minor 1000 Traveller, which has a reconditioned body with new wood. We would consider any reasonable offer, as we are shortly to move house and will no longer have suitable garage space. "

There has always been plenty of demand for the Traveller and really first-class examples have been known to fetch as much as £5,000 at classic car auctions. However, the normal price range is £1,500 to £2,500. Try the excellent Morris Minor Owners' Club, PO Box 1098, Derby DE23 8ZX, tel: 01332 291675, website: www.MorrisMinorOC.co.uk. (The car later sold through the suggested routes.)

15,000 mile Vanden Plas

" In November 1972 my father-in-law purchased a new Vanden Plas 1300 which is, of course, VED exempt. He passed away in 1978 and the car has been owned by our family ever since. Its mileage currently stands at 14,828. Could you give us some idea of its value and how best to sell it? "

The mileage is headline material for a classic car auction catalogue. Providing the car is in first-class condition, I think it could realise between £3,000 and £4,000. That said, it's only fair and right to contact the clubs first and these are: 1100 Club (all 1100 and 1300 variants), c/o Steve King, PO Box 3326, London N1 1QD; Vanden Plas Owners' Club, c/o Nigel Stephens, The Briars, Lawson Leas, Barrowby, Grantham, Lincs.

Autumn 'Leaf'

" I have in my possession a Lea Francis 18. This car is the oldest of this model in the world and was registered 'DVG 321' back in 1949. A considerable amount of restoration work has been done on the car, which is in possible Grade B condition, and I have it insured for an agreed value of £10,000. I have tried to sell it through the club, of which I am a member, with no success. Nor have I had suitable response from advertising. How would you suggest I dispose of it? "

If all else has failed, a classic car auction. Cars which don't sell from advertising do sell at auction for the simple reason that auctions show up what the cars are really worth. Only 69 alloy-bodied 18HPs were built with four-cylinder 95 bhp 2,496 cc engines, giving them the performance of contemporary Riley RMBs and RMFs. But I'd set your sights, and your reserve price, at £6,000 rather than £10,000.

E-Type to go

" My sister-in-law was recently widowed and has been granted probate of her deceased husband's affairs. Among his possessions is an immaculate white E-Type Jaguar fixed head coupe, built in 1969, originally exported to the USA and returned to the UK in 1992, when he paid around £17,000 for it. My sister-in-law wishes to dispose of this car. How best should she go about this? "

A classic car auction is the most straightforward route in these circumstances. Upcoming sales are listed on www.mysterymotors.com.

One-two-three GT

" I have a 1968F Volvo 123GT. It's been garaged since 1980 and requires a full overhaul. Is it worth overhauling? Should I advertise it with a club? Should I simply call the scrap man? "

The 123GT is a rare model and someone, some-where, will want your car either to restore it for its own sake or for classic rallying. Contact the Volvo Enthusiasts' Club, c/o Kevin Price, 4 Goonbell, St. Agnes, Cornwall TR5 0PH, tel: 01872 553740 and the Volvo Owners' Club, c/o John Smith, 18 McCaulay Avenue, Portsmouth, Hants PO6 4NY, tel: 023 9238 1494, website: www.volvovlub.orh.uk/volvo. Please don't call the scrap man as you will probably have to pay him around £30 to take it away. (With the help of Maurice Williams of the Volvo Enthusiasts' Club, the reader eventually obtained £500 for his rare 123GT.)

Polo pointers

" *I am interested in buying a 'J'-registered VW Polo 1.0CL from a friend. She has had the car from new and it has only done 25,000 miles. Are there any problems associated with this car?* "

The timing belt turns the water pump and if the water pump fails, the belt will fail possibly lead-ing to engine damage. As a precaution, I'd have water pump, timing belt and timing-belt ten-sioner all changed as soon as you acquire the car. Sump pans can rust through, spilling oil all over your driveway. A 'J'-reg will be catalysed, but premature cat failure is not a problem area with this model and original exhaust systems last well. There should be no rust in the bodywork.

Period piece

" *Owing to the onset of arthritis my cousin has reluctantly decided to sell her 1954 Morris Oxford of which she has been the sole driver since 1955. It has only been used in recent years on the Isle of Wight and has been maintained by one garage. Recently, it has been refurbished with red leather upholstery, a respray, re-chromed bumpers, a new radiator, etc. and is now in very good condition. Can you inform me of any organisation that might be interested in finding a new owner, and also give some idea of price? The lady has great affection for the car and would like to find it a good home.* "

A 1954 Oxford could be either an 'MO', which looks like a big Morris Minor, or a 'Series II'. But I spoke to Derek Andrews who runs the Morris Cowley and Oxford Club and he actually knew your cousin's car. Derek confirmed that it has been very well maintained throughout its life and the respray was a proper job in cellulose by Prices Garage on the Isle of Wight. He tells me that the car is worth between £1,000 and £2,000 and that the best way to try and sell it would be a £26 photo ad in *Practical Classics* magazine (01733 465430). Club members tend to already have a car and anyone with a 1954 to 1959 Cowley, Oxford or Isis really should join the club to help ensure a future supply of spare parts. The address is 202 Chantry Gardens, Southwick, Trowbridge, Wilts BA14 9QX, tel: 01225 766800.

Interesting trade-in

" *I am thinking of trading up from my 1998 BMW 318iS four-door saloon. It has disc brakes on all four wheels, leather 'M' Tech steering wheel and gear knob, air conditioning, sports suspension, alloy wheels, traction control, dual airbags, BMW sports seats, BMW alarm and Tracker. It has just had its first oil service at 9,200 miles. Should I sell it or keep it?* "

Keep it. This is an interesting, run-out special which combined the old-shape 3-Series body with the 140 bhp 1.9 litre engine of late 318iS models and the all disc-braking system of a 323i. It's a desirable car which could eventually become a minor classic like the old square-rigged 318iS, but you are thinking of doing the deal too soon.

Another unwanted Allegro

" *In 1993 I purchased a 'Y'-reg. four-door Austin Allegro L from an elderly friend of my mother's who had owned the car from new. I paid well over the odds for the car because I knew its history. I had intended giving it to one of our children when they passed their test, but circumstances are changed and the Allegro now stands unused and unwanted. Bearing in mind that it would now need new tyres, battery and servicing to make it saleable, and lead-replacement additives or a new head to run it on unleaded, do you consider it has any value, or should I simply scrap it?* "

I'm still referring about one reader a fortnight to the Allegro Club International, 20 Stoneleigh Crescent, Stoneleigh, Epsom, Surrey KT19 0RP, website: www.uk-classic-cars.com/allegro.htm. Offer it to the club for nothing and if no member will take it I'm afraid you may well be faced with paying a breaker around £30 to take it away.

Type 3

" *Due to my husband having passed away I have been left with a 1972 VW Variant 1600 estate car. It is yellow, with a manual gearbox, has done 50,000 miles and is in immaculate condition. I would be very grateful if you can assist me with its value so that I can put it up for sale. I am unable to drive myself.* "

VW Type 3s like this are now very rare and *Practical Classics* magazine values them at between £500 and £3,600, depending on condition. Yours has the added advantage of being VED exempt. If I were you I would first contact the VW Type 3 & 4 Club, c/o Jim Bourne,

Brookside, Hamsey Road, Barcombe, Lewes, Sussex, tel: 01273 400463.

'Ex-Ministry'

" I am in need of a good sturdy Land Rover and I am considering an ex-MOD model. Would you say go to a dealer in the said vehicles or go to an MOD auction. If so, where are the auctions held? How do I find the details? "

British Car Auctions runs regular drive-through auctions at its Blackbushe Airport Centre on the A30 between Hartley Wintney and Blackwater and also holds auctions at MOD depots (01252 878555). The MOD and Lex Defence drive-through sales are on Fridays. The problem with ex-MOD vehicles is that they are not registered or MOT tested so, unless you have trade plates and trade insurance, you cannot legally drive them back to be tested. If you'd rather buy from a dealer who has registered and MOT tested the vehicle, the best place to look is *Exchange & Mart*.

Ageing Colt

" I write on behalf of an elderly lady who has now given up driving and is anxious to sell her car. It is a 1978 Colt Lancer 1400 automatic, which she has owned since new and which has covered 29,000 miles. As can be seen from the photograph, the car can justifiably be described as 'as new'. The owner wishes to sell to a non-local person because she does not want to see the car being driven about by someone else. It has been suggested that the car might be worth £1,500 in view of its condition. But where does one try to sell it? "

My first port of call was The Colt Car Company itself, but they already own a perfect 1974 Colt Lancer – the first to be imported to Europe.

However, they have offered to put the lady's Lancer on their franchise and club websites in the hope that a dealer or club member would be prepared to pay £1,500.

Happy Landying

" *I now have a Daihatsu Sportrak 4x4 so would like to sell my Series One Land Rover 80" hard-top. Do you have any idea what it is worth? And can you put me in touch with any Land Rover Clubs, a member of which might be interested?* "

Someone made a small fortune on a 1949 Series One Land Rover 80" last year. He bought 'PV 9208' for £6,882, including commission and VAT at a Cheffyns classic car auction on 10 April, then sold it at a Christies auction on 1 November for £18,820, including commission and VAT. Even after expenses and commission, that's a cool profit of £9,000 in seven months. Alas, your 1951–58 model Series One is probably worth between £500 and £750 if it's a runner with no serious rot. I guess from the 'Q' plate it is ex-military. But if you can find a chassis and engine number, you might be able to persuade the DVLA to issue it with an age-related registration. Land Rover 1947–51 Register, c/o Richard Lines, Ricoli, Conisholme Road, North Somercotes, Louth, Lincs LN11 7PS, tel: 01507 358314, email: 100560.560@compuserve.com, Land Rover Series One Club, c/o David Bowyer, East Foldhay, Zeal Monachorum, Crediton, Devon EX17 6DH, tel: 01363 82666 (day).

Bargain, or white elephant?

" *I have the opportunity to purchase a 70,000-mile 1992 Mercedes 400SE with full MB service history for £10,000. Can you tell me if this would be better value than a 'nearly new' family saloon such as a Vectra or Mondeo? And will it be any more expensive over a five-year period, assuming 15,000 miles a year?* "

This is the giant, slab-sided, double-glazed 'S' Class model introduced in September 1991 and at £1,450 below 'bottom book', it certainly wasn't overpriced when I received the letter. If an MB franchise was prepared to stock an 'S' Class this age, it would probably be asking more than £15,000. In five year's time, with 145,000 miles under its wheels, as long as there is no overt government legislation against big cars, the 400SE should still be worth £4,000–£5,000, which is a lot more than a 99T Vectra or Mondeo will be worth after five years and 75,000 miles. The trouble is that insurance, servicing, routine replacements and fuel will cost at least twice as much as for a Mondeo or Vectra. On top of that, if you have any serious failures, such as gearbox or engine, you probably won't be able to afford the replacements. But, of course, when you aren't worrying about these things, you and your family will feel like royalty and there is at least an evens chance you won't have any problems at all. A friend of mine runs a 130,000-mile 'E'-reg. 560SEL with complete confidence.

Net catch

" *What do you know of Autotek Imports (UK), which operates from a website: www.autotek.co.uk? On 26 May I paid them a deposit of £4,000 and was promised delivery of a Renault Scenic on 28 November. I have become increasingly concerned about the lack of paperwork and contact from Autotek. Invoice and delivery instructions are continually being promised but never arrive. I have been told by Netwatch that Autotek is being investigated by BBC's 'Watchdog'. Apparently, they know of many deposits being taken but not one vehicle ever being supplied.* "

'Watchdog' covered Autotek on 18 November and traced its operations to somewhere in Holland. I had never heard of it until I spotted a small ad in a Sunday newspaper appealing for victims of Autotek to email their problems to www.netwatchUK.co.uk. (When I visited the site there was nothing on it apart from a general appeal for emails from victims of net fraud.) There was a Rotterdam-based scam in 1998 when an outfit offered cars at low European prices from a flash, serviced office suite, then vanished with the punters' deposits before any of the cars were due to be delivered. The police were powerless to act before the first delivery date because no crime had been committed until the outfit started failing to deliver the cars. It's why I always warn buyers using import dealers to either pay their deposits by credit card or pay them into an escrow account, both of which offer protection if the deal goes wrong.

Getting them gone

" *Can you please advise me how to sell my beloved Ford XR3i convertible and how much it should be worth? It is 1989 (on a private plate at the moment), in two-tone maroon and silver with a half RS bodykit, has a power hood and windows, half-leather seats, CD player and has done 65,000 miles. Are there any clubs or organisations for this special edition model? I have tried to sell the car locally and you are my last resort.* "

Ford XR Owners' Club, PO Box 47, Loughborough, Leics LE11 1XS, or Les Gent (01509 881015). But having sold my 76,000 mile 88E Jetta 16v for £1,300 within days of putting it on the Autotrader website (which cost me just £4.95) I reckon this is one of the best as well as the cheapest ways to advertise a car. It's easy and fun to use. Just go to www.autotrader.co.uk and click on 'advertise'. Price the car right (in your case, £2,250, but take £2,000) and follow the instructions about sending a photo. Other readers will find this webside just as useful when looking for a car. To make sure the car goes to the first punter, transfer your cherished reg to a retention certificate and put it on the 'G' reg. which the DVLA will allocate. Don't answer the door to anyone who comes to see the car at night. Don't let anyone test drive it unless they're properly insured and you have one of your friends with you in the car. And insist on exchanging the V5 and keys for cash inside a bank where you can tuck it away safely there and then.

Testing my loyalty

" *I had intended changing my car for a Rover 75, and my wife was going to swap hers for a Rover 25. But we live in Hexham, Northumberland, and now that the Hexham Rover franchise has been terminated the nearest are in Newcastle-upon-Tyne (23 miles away) or Carlisle (33 miles away). So we would be daft to buy a Rover.* "

Hexham remains well covered for VW, Toyota, Citroën, Mazda, Peugeot, Ford, Vauxhall, Subaru, Daihatsu, Isuzu and even TVR. If Haltwhistle, Haydon Bridge, Allendale, Bellingham, Corbridge, Riding Mill and Stocksfield are included in its hinterland, there are easily enough potential customers to support a modern Rover franchise. The dealer Rover had in Hexham was a good one (a Vauxhall dealer has moved into its premises). It was even open at 3pm on a Saturday afternoon when I needed a part for a Rover 200 Vi, which lost its gears while I was driving it in the area.

When to swap

" Would you be kind enough to give us the benefit of your thoughts on the vexed question of when to change one's car? Manufacturers and sales-men always recommend a change, while mechanics are happy for one to stick with one's existing vehicle. I have a 1994L Granada Scorpio 2.9i 12-valve (one of the last before the 'goggle eyed' Scorpio), which has now completed 75,000 miles. Its early years were spent on motorways but, since retirement, most of its journeys are now fairly short and its fuel con-sumption is punishing. I understand that I can expect trouble from the automatic gearbox fairly soon. If I were to add £10–15k to what I could obtain for the Scorpio what would my best choice be? "

You're looking at getting maybe £3,000 in a pri-vate sale, or having to spend £1,000–£1,500 on a gearbox rebuild (King Automatics, tel: 01372 728769) in the not-too-distant future. But there's absolutely no need to spend £10,000 to £15,000 plus on replacing the car. Trade Sales of Slough or Motorpoint of Derby should be able to put you into a nine-month-old Mondeo 2.0iLX or GLX, with air conditioning and auto-matic transmission, for between £8,500 and £9,000. You won't get quite the ride quality of the Scorpio, but the Mondeo is a much better, more modern car, is roughly the same size and will return 25–35 mpg, depending on the type of use you put it to.

Low-mileage Minor

" Advancing years make it necessary for me to sell my Morris Minor 1000. It is a little unusual in having had only one owner since new on 4 November 1970 and has covered just 12,151 miles. It has been garaged in dry conditions, free from ultra-violet light, and was wax injected and properly rust-proofed when new. It is fitted with servo brakes and radial tyres. It has not been used for 25 years. How much is it worth and what would be the best method of disposal? "

Money should be spent on properly recommissioning the car with fresh oil in the engine and gearbox, fresh coolant in the radiator, fresh fuel in the tank and a fresh battery prior to getting it MOT tested and VED'd (it's a 'historic vehicle', so there is no annual tax to pay). I'd then consider two courses of action: offer it via the magazine of the Morris Minor Owners' Club, PO Box 1098, Derby DE23 8ZX, tel: 01332 291675, email: http://www.MorrisMinorOC.co.uk. Or try your local classic car auction house, which is H&H and holds its sales at Pavilion Gardens, Buxton, tel: 01925 730630, www.classic-auctions.co.uk. I would be looking for £3,500, but would not be surprised to see the car make more at auction with some suitable pre-publicity.

Registration scam?

" *I arranged a test drive of a secondhand 'T'-registered Mercedes Benz. However, when I was looking through the car's papers I found a Certificate of Conformity to EU Type Approval dated 8 October 1998. These details suggested that the car was driven in Germany prior to UK registration. When a car's age is described, is it from the date of manufacture, the date of first registration, or the date of first registration in the UK?* "

When the Tiger economies of South East Asia were booming in the mid 1990s, this fuelled huge demand for rhd prestige cars, particularly Mercedes Benz. There was even money to be made from exporting certain secondhand MBs from the UK to S.E. Asia (there is again now). But when the Tiger economies collapsed, many 1996-build rhd export orders were not cancelled until after the cars had come off the line, with the result that they sat around in compounds in Germany. A number of switched-on traders picked up on this and imported some of these rhd cars at huge discounts, but were only able to register a total of 50 of each make and model in the UK each year under SVA import quotas. Eventually the manufacturers issued the residue of cancelled rhd exports with Certificates of Conformity to EU Type Approval, allowing them to be sold in the UK. But MBUK limits its 12-month warranty on these cars to a maximum of 18 months after the car left the factory so, though new 1999/2000 build MB's now carry a three-year warranty, 1996-build cars not registered until 1999 are already well out of warranty.

Making a Motor Point

" My company car, a Citroën Xantia TD, has performed faultlessly, so we decided to replace my wife's ageing banger with a Xsara estate. You often advocate buying 'nearly new' from a car supersite and frequently mention Motorpoint of Derby. Before setting out, I checked the website (www.motorpoint.co.uk). But buying from them is not for the faint-hearted. The enormous display of cars can be bewildering with those of the same make and model not necessarily grouped together. There are no over-attentive salesmen, no test drives and no looking at the vehicle documents before purchase. However, you do get a large choice of cars, clear pricing, a straight-talking salesman and time to make a decision without being pushed. We purchased a 'nearly new' reg Xsara 1.4i X estate with 12,900 miles. When we returned to collect it a week later, the vehicle was well prepared and we discovered it came with a franchised dealer service history. The price was £6,999, plus a £42.30 'indemnity', plus £199 for an extra year's warranty. A local Citroën dealer is asking £8,495 for much the same car. "

For those of us in the South, Trade Sales of Slough offers much the same sort of new and 'nearly new' stock at similar prices with the option of an excellent 'bumper to bumper' 12-

month warranty. Both Motorpoint and Trade Sales are regular advertisers in Telegraph Motoring.

£4,125 off a Serena

" *I thought you would be interested in the deal we got on a 17-mile, pre-registered new Nissan Serena 2.0 petrol 'Excursion' model. Apparently, list price was £17,625, but we got it for £13,500 and obtained an excellent part-exchange allowance of £3,500 for our 1994 Micra SLX.* "

Purchase prices like this reflect the true state of supply and demand for the vehicle in question. For lists of similar bargains, consult the Trade Sales of Slough and Motorpoint of Derby advertisements in Telegraph Motoring. Japan now has a new Serena.

Supersite 'lemons'

" *How do car supermarkets obtain almost new cars with less than 100 miles on the clock and sell them at a discount? Could they have previously been rejected under the Sale and Supply of Goods Act, then found their way back on to the market, or is there another reason?* "

They either buy excess stock of cars pre-registered to meet bonus targets by franchised dealers, or import the cars from countries where the pre-tax prices are much lower than in the UK. Trade Sales of Slough and Motorpoint of Derby don't buy Customer Service Returns or damaged cars to resell because they are too much hassle for the very tight profit margins on which they operate.

Gas guzzler

" *An elderly neighbour has died, leaving a 1981 Daimler 4.2 Sovereign converted to run on LPG. This two-owner car was in good condition with 90,000 miles on the clock when it went into storage about 12 years ago. Can you help with advice for the family on its possible value and the best way of selling it?* **"**

Someone might want this as a project car, and may be prepared to pay £500. But for most people Devon is a long way to tow a car from on a trailer and the part iron/part alloy engine could be corroded inside. I don't recommend trying to get it started as it is because the cooling system is likely to be sludged up and this will lead the engine to overheat at the rear of the block, particularly on LPG. You could try advertising it in 'Spares Vehicles' classifieds in *Practical Classics* magazine (though free, the appearance of your ad cannot be guaranteed). Or, if you've got webbed fingers, on www.autotrader.co.uk, which costs just £4.95. Or give the clubs a call: Jaguar & Daimler Owners' Club, tel: 0121 773 1801; Jaguar Car Club, tel: 01773 741784; Jaguar Drivers' Club, tel: 01582 419332; Jaguar Enthusiasts' Club, tel: 0117 969 8186.

Back to the Landy

" *It is time to sell my 1986 Land Rover 90 County Station Wagon, which has a 2.5 litre petrol engine and has only done 56,000 miles. It is in very good condition but I do not know what value to put on it or where to advertise.* **"**

Russell, Baldwin & Bright hold the country's largest 4x4 auctions at Leominster every fortnight (01568 611166). Latest prices realised indicate that your Land Rover should be worth around £2,500 as a private sale. Try advertising in one of the numerous Land Rover magazines you will find at W.H. Smith on Guildford High Street.

Negative equity?

" Three years ago I acquired a Mercedes C250TD Elegance automatic estate on a three-year, 36,000-mile MB Personal Contract Purchase. The final payment to exercise my option to purchase the car is £18,507.83. I would like to purchase the car, but find that its true used value is more like £16,000 and I am under the impression that if the car was sold at auction it would fetch around £14,000. In the circumstances, is MB Finance being unrealistic in expecting me to pay £18,507.83? "

Slightly, but a contract is a contract and all the payments you made were based on a residual value figure of £18,507.83. Unless you are able to buy on trade terms, you are theoretically better off paying the balloon payment and keeping the car. I don't know how you got the auction figure of £14,000. I've never seen a three-year-old, 36,000-mile C250TD Elegance estate sell at auction for anything like as little.

200,000-mile Mondeo

" My 1993 Ford Mondeo LXTD is approaching 200,000 miles. I have owned it for most of its life and have a full service history. The belts have been changed every 36,000 miles and, apart from needing a replacement steering rack, there have been no major problems. It still has its original clutch and exhaust system. I now feel I should think about changing it for a newer model, possibly from one of the supersites you often mention. But would they welcome a part-exchange? Or would I do better selling the car privately? The car certainly doesn't 'owe me' anything, but I have no idea whether its high mileage makes it virtually unsaleable. "

The supersites will simply offer you what they think they will get for the car at auction (and they are very clued up about current auction values, in this case £1,000 to £1,250). So I think you would do better selling the car yourself. Try it at £1,500 in the paper and you might get a nip.

And because the car 'owes you' nothing, you don't have to wait until you've sold it before you buy your 'W'-reg or a 'nearly new' from one of the supersites. I think it's time to start a competition for Mondeo clutch life. Can anyone beat 200,000 miles?

Executor's sale

" As executor of an estate I have to dispose of a 1979 Ford Capri L hatchback, which I believe is in good condition. I have no idea how to do this. "

The best bet for an executor is a classic car auction because it neatly avoids accusations from beneficiaries that any favouritism has been shown to the purchaser.

200,000 miles down the road

" I drive a 1985 Mercedes 190E automatic, which I bought at seven years old for £7,000 and which has now done 196,000 miles. Two years ago it needed a new transmission, new valve stem oil seals and a few more things which led to a huge bill. Last year it cost me £700 to get it through the MOT, needing a new timing chain, shock absorbers, brake discs and pads as well as a service. The car is still running well and last year even got me to Austria and back. I do 12,000 miles a year and need a car for my work. My question is, should I carry on with the 190E or should I replace it? If so what would be a fair price for the car? "

The car is worth so little (around £1,000) and the gap to finance a new one is so great that you might as well keep running it until a major disaster strikes.

Voyage of Discovery

" You don't have to shop abroad to get a decent deal on a Land Rover Discovery, but you do have to shop around, as we recently discovered.

Having found a buyer for our old Discovery we checked with import specialists and found we could save up to £5,000 on a new TD5 GS7. But we would have to wait at least four months and possibly a lot longer, which was unacceptable to us. The first UK Land Rover dealer we visited wanted full list price and quoted £1,500 less than book if we traded in our old Disco. The second offered either £1,000 off list or £2,500 more for our old Disco. The third offered us £3,000 off if we settled for a 'V' rather than a 'W', but this did, of course, include the three-year UK warranty, two years' servicing and Land Rover Breakdown Assistance. We drove away happy. "

This shows that where a UK dealer is switched on, and has vehicles in stock, deals can be done. This reader's deal is preferable to waiting at least four months during which the price you expected to pay could rise substantially. But manufacturers have no excuse for deliberately delaying delivery of rhd vehicles sold by European dealers to UK nationals. This is against EU law and could eventually be punished by fines that far exceed fat UK profit margins.

Net savings nonsense

" *I feel I have been conned out of a £10 service fee by one of the widely publicised independent importers. On 5 February, I contacted P&O for a quotation for a new RHD UK spec BMW 320DSE manual in Orient Blue with climate control. I was asked to pay £10 by credit card and was promised a reply within five working days. When I received it, the reply came from 'Burbank Automotive Holdings Ltd' quoting £23,750 and requiring a £4,750 deposit. My local BMW dealer had already beaten that with a quote of £22,645, so P&O charged me £10 to quote me a premium price.* "

At the time of writing P&O Stena Lines was referring all requests to Burbank Automotive Holdings. You're not the only one getting nowhere with this much hyped service. D.C. of Bickendene could not even get through to P&O

on the widely advertised 0870 600 0613 because it was constantly engaged and the website was not yet up and running. The company has probably become a victim of its own success and in any case you can't expect it to be able to offer cars which are in short supply at a significant saving. There is a long waiting list for BMW 320DSEs, so you did well at £22,645, a figure I could not beat by visting all the other websites. The best general advice to readers looking for a cheap new car is to buy from stock either from a supersite such as Motorpoint of Derby (www.motorpoint.co.uk) or Trade Sales of Slough (www.trade-sales.co.uk) or from an overstocked UK franchised dealer, or from a franchised dealer in Eire if you can find one with any surplus stock.

Five grand in a year

" *In March 1999 I bought a 'P'-reg. Jeep Cherokee Limited 2.5TD SE for £14,995, less £2,500 P/X allowance on my old Range Rover. At the time it had 77,203 miles on the clock. It now has 93,000 miles and, though I need to sell it to reduce my fuel bill, I can't. The garage told me the best offer it had received in the trade was £8,000. But I still owe £11,500 on it. I have advertised it many times and am now down to £10,995, but would probably accept £10,000. Why has it dropped so much? And how can I shift it?* "

It dropped so much because you took it into a mileage band where few buyers are prepared to pay five figures. I think your best bet now is www.autotrader.co.uk which costs a mere £4.95 and gets great results. Or try a 4x4 auction.

Six grand in six months

" *Last year I part-exchanged my four-year-old Fiat Tipo 1.4 for a five-year-old Audi A6 2.0E Estate at £10,995, minus £3,000 for the Tipo. Now I am finding the Audi too big, but the best offers I have been able to get for it are £4,500 to £5,000. I can afford to keep it, but don't want to waste money unnecessarily. So what should I do? Grin and bear it, or take the low P/X offer to get a car with better fuel economy and lower service charges? "*

Grin and bear it. When you acquired the Audi £9,600 would have been a fair price to pay for it. At the time of writing, the same car with 56,000 miles trade booked at £5,425, but if yours has higher mileage or damage either would be good reasons for lower trade bids.

LPG Land Rover

" I own a 1993 lhd Land Rover Discovery V8i which I have had converted to run on LPG. Performance is close to running on petrol, but with the financial (if not the consumption) economy of running on diesel. The vehicle has done 87,000 miles. How do I sell it? "

The conversion is a very sensible thing to have done, but you still face an uphill struggle. I'd try ads in the specialist Land Rover magazines and on the various used car websites such as www.autotrader.co.uk.

Where's that Nippa?

" Can you possibly let me know an address for Perodua UK or a list of dealers in the London area? "

Perodua UK Ltd, Abbey Road, Park Royal, London NW10 7RY, tel: 020 8961 1255 and ask for Jutta. List prices now start at just £4,499, which can't be bad for a five-door hatchback, and the car comes with a two-year warranty. (*Autocar* did a comparison test on 24/9/97 – Haymarket Reprints: 01235 534323.)

Goddess to go

" How should my No. 1 son go about setting a price with a view to selling his 1975 Citroën Pallas, which is in generally good condition and has done about 85,000 miles? He lives in Shrewsbury. Perhaps you could you put us in touch with the trade specialists or an enthusiasts' club. "

I am assuming that this is a late DS23 Pallas, in which case it is worth between around £2,500 and around £8,000 depending on your interpretation of 'generally good condition'. The club is the friendly, helpful and very active Citroën Car Club, c/o Derek Pearson, PO Box 348, Bromley, Kent BR2 8QT, tel: 07000248258, email: http://www.ccc.uk.demon.co.uk. A DS specialist is Retromobile, Unit 74 Chelsea Bridge Business Centre, 326–340 Queenstown Road, London SW4, tel: 020 7498 7111. But you'll probably get the best price at a classic car auction. For advance notice of classic car auctions see the news page on www.mysterymotors.com. For lists of cars entered in these sales, subscribe to *The Collectors' Car Auction List*, tel: 020 8534 3883.

Two for one

" Soon we shall no longer need to be a two-car family. I drive a four-year-old Peugeot 406 LXTD 1.9 with 95,000 on the clock and full Peugeot service history. My wife drives a three-year-old 106XN with 28,000 on the clock and full history. I would like to trade in both cars together, for ease and immediacy, and buy a 'nearly new' medium hatch (206 – Focus). What would you recommend in the 206 – Focus class? "

You're asking to get your leg lifted because trading two for one is the worst way to do a deal. Obviously, the more bargain priced the replacement car, the less you're going to get for your swappers. A Focus is the best 'nearly new' car in the class for the money, but Astras are cheaper.

British built

" *Please could you list all the makes and models of cars which are built in Britain. We could all make a real difference both to employment and our trade balance if we bought Almeras instead of Meganes, etc.* "

- AC (all)
- Aston Martin (all)
- Bentley (all)
- Bristol (all)
- Daimler (all)
- Ford Fiesta (all)
- Ford Escort (all)
- HMC sports cars (all)
- Honda Logo (from September 2000)
- Honda Civic five-door and Aerodeck (all)
- Honda Accord four-door and five-door
- Honda CRV (from June 2000)
- Jaguar (all)
- Land Rover (all)
- Lotus (all)
- Marcos (all)
- Marlin sports cars (all)
- Mini (all y2k models)
- Morgan (all)
- MG (all)
- Nissan Micra (all)
- Nissan Almera (all)
- Nissan Primera (all)
- Peugeot 206 (most)
- Peugeot 306 (most)
- Reliant (three-wheelers)
- Rolls Royce (all)
- Rover (all)

- Sebring sports cars (all)
- Spectre sports cars (all)
- Toyota Corolla (some)
- Toyota Avensis (all)
- TVR (all)
- Vauxhall Astra (most)
- Vauxhall Vectra (most)
- Vauxhall Frontera (from imported kits)
- Westfield sports cars (all)

Crystal balls-up

" Recently a Government minister (can't remember who) said that they were going to 'do something' about car prices in the UK and we could expect to see a fall of 30%. My question is this: what will that do for the car trade and prices (both new and secondhand) in the interim? I have been thinking of buying a new or 'nearly new' car from an importer or car supersite. Do you think I would be better off waiting until we see what changes the Government is able to bring about? "

Government dithering and the high pound were responsible for ruining Rover and for turning what could have been 'Million Car March 2000' into a 400,000 registrations disaster. The reason the Government gave for high UK interest rates and the resultant high pound was 'to keep inflation under control'. But, of course, it didn't because instead of inflation occurring in terms of pounds, sterling itself inflated, and that accounted for the main difference between UK car prices and those in countries such as Germany. Even allowing for the relative strength of the dollar, the UK economy simply was not capable of sustaining sterling at its April 2000 rate against the Euro so, by June 2000, it had already fallen back by 15%. Continental car prices in all but subsidised markets no longer seem as cheap as they did. I can see a few mass-market cars coming down in the short-term by maybe 15% (Citroëns, Fiats, Vauxhalls, Saabs, Seats and Mitsubishis were the first). But as long as the UK demand for desirable German cars exceeds supply, the law of supply and demand will ensure that their UK prices remain high.

Classic Senator to go

" I bought an 'ex management' 1991J Vauxhall Senator CD 24v manual in 1992, have owned it ever since and it has clocked up a mere 46,000 miles. It has been serviced every year by Vauxhall dealers, with regular brake fluid and ATF changes and it is now on new tyres, not because the originals wore out but because they perished. My family has decided that the car is not earning its keep and must go, so I would appreciate your advice on my options. Since I run a classic-car insurance company, I can arrange a classic policy for the new owner at a premium from £140. "

The top specialist dealer in these cars is David Kingh of DK Car Sales, Piper's Industrial Estate, Thatcham, Newbury, Berks, tel: 01635 865610, mobile: 0831 416422, website: www.dkcarsales.co.uk.

Egg-shaped Escort

" Could you please give me some information regarding the sale of my late husband's Ford Escort saloon, cylinder capacity 1,098 cc, registration date 1/11/1970, reg. FGF 953J, condition good (it was much loved). "

This is one of the original ovular Escorts and there is a club for them: Ford Escort Mk 1 Owners' Club, c/o Larry Cross, 1 Port Lane, Colchester, Essex CO2 1JF, tel: 01206 799595. Rust-free examples are rare and if the car is in really good condition it could be worth £1,000–£1,500. Assuming the car's condition speaks for itself and there are no ready buyers in the club, try a classic car auction.

Cardata

" *A friend of mine emigrated last year leaving me to sell his Honda estate car for the best price I could get. He had placed some local advertisements with my telephone number and I started receiving calls from an organisation calling itself Cardata offering to put the car on its databank and website for £65. Eventually, I succumbed and started waiting for calls from potential buyers. After a month's silence, I tried a few local dealers and eventually sold the car for two thirds of the price my friend had been looking for. I did not contact Cardata to cancel yet still received no calls. So I would like to ask your readers if any of them have ever sold a car through Cardata.* "

Fair point. When I used Cardata to try and find cars for customers I found the service quite helpful with someone calling me up whenever they logged a car on that matched what I was looking for. But I have never sold a car through Cardata. The reason could be I was asking too much, but I would be as interested as you in the experiences of other readers (www.cardata.co.uk, or tel: 0700 222 4444).

Thirty readers then either wrote or e-mailed to tell me of similar experiences with Cardata. They placed an advertisement for their car elsewhere. They were then phoned by Cardata telesales with a promise that Cardata had a number of people looking for a similar car. They registered with Cardata at a cost of £69.99. Then they received no calls at all. If they complained, they then got one or two calls from prospective purchasers who never turned up to view the car. Only R.D. of Tarporley had any success from the service and sold his Citroën Xantia (a very hard car to shift) to a dealer at what he considered to be 'an extremely favourable price'.

Vauxhall Opels

" I see that some of the supersites are offering new Vauxhall Astras and Vectras badged as Opels at very attractive prices. Do you know if an Opel would have the same warranty as a Vauxhall? Would a Vauxhall dealer be able to service an Opel? Are there any other snags in buying these cars? "

Vauxhalls are Opels badged as Vauxhalls rather than the other way round for the simple reason that this helps to sell them in the UK. EU law decrees that all new cars sold throughout Europe are covered by a 12-month warranty. Opels aren't worth as much as trade-ins as Vauxhalls and you should check the good deals on offer at Vauxhall dealers such as Lance Owen before taking the plunge.

CRX or MR2?

" Personal satisfaction apart, do you think it is worth continuing to cherish my 1990H silver Honda CRX VTEC in the hope that my family will inherit a collector's item worth substantially more than its current value of £4,500? The car, which is spotless, has covered less than 32,000 miles, doesn't go out in the wet and never misses its annual service (including new cambelt). CRXs seem to have got left behind in the popularity stakes and I wonder if an MR2 of similar age and condition would be a better investment. Please note my car is not for sale. "

There is a lot of enthusiasm for these quick little cars, both here and in Holland. As with Mk 1 MR2s, the main problem is rust which can get so bad that good bodyshops won't even attempt repairs. I think you do have a little classic on your hands, easily the equal of a Mk 1 MR2, but, unless you've actually been offered £4,500, I'm sceptical of your valuation. You should join The Honda Enthusiasts' Drivers' Club, c/o Nigel Allen, 70

Langworth Gardens, Holbeech, Spalding, Lincs PE11 2YJ, tel: 01406 423502.

Ponton pointers

" For almost 50 years I have been the proud owner of a 1953 Mercedes 180 four-door saloon, white with red leather upholstery, which I bought when new. The mileage is only 98,564. I used to run it regularly at weekends and keep it immaculate. However, because of illness and other family problems, it has been sitting in my garage for the past eight years. I now regretfully feel I must sell it, but obviously it must first be cleaned up and recommissioned. I realise this will probably mean draining the fuel system, engine oil, gearbox oil, cooling system, brakes, etc. Could you recommend someone who would do a good job at minimal cost? Finally, could you please advise me on the best way to sell a classic car such as this, which is neither a sports car nor in the Rolls Royce league? "

This must have been one of the first 1,767 cc side-valve 'Ponton' model 180s to be imported. It's rare, but not particularly valuable which means that the cost of recommissioning it properly and obtaining an MOT might be greater than the sum you could realise. If I were you I would first contact the two Mercedes clubs: Mercedes-Benz Club Ltd, Brightstone, Over Old Road, Harbury, Glos GL19 3BJ, tel: 07071 818868; and Mercedes-Benz Owners' Association, Upper Birchetts House, Langton Road, Langton Green, Tunbridge Wells, Kent TN3 0EG, tel: 01892 860922, fax: 01892 861363, email: Join@ mercedesclub.org.uk. If you have no joy there, and you can at least wheel it out and photograph it, I'd recommend a photo ad in *Classic Car Weekly* as it is, asking £2,000, but being prepared to accept £1,000. If you can find a local mechanic (Yellow Pages) prepared to recommission and MOT it for less than £1,000 (I have no idea how much work may be required), it may be worth the gamble of entering it in a local classic car auction such as BCA Blackbushe, but you will then incur transportation costs as well as having no guarantee that you will recoup your costs. In this case the clubs should be your best bet.

Garage find

" A friend of mine has a 1956 Aston Martin Lagonda in the back of his garage where it has lurked awaiting restoration for 24 years. How could he go about selling it as it is? "

First contact the Lagonda Club, c/o Colin Bugler, Wintney House, London Road, Hartley Wintney, Hants RG27 8RN, tel: 01252 845451. If you have no joy there, try a photo ad in *The Automobile* magazine asking £500, but being prepared to accept offers.

Winging in

" A friend of mine has owned a 1955 Mercedes Benz 300SL Gullwing for some years. The car has been fully restored recently and is in pristine condition. A sale is considered. What might be a reasonable asking price and if it were yours how would you sell it? "

Racing 300SLRs are still well over a million, but standard road-going 300SL Gullwings have slipped from around £225,000 at their peak in 1990 to between £80,000 and £125,000 today, with cars realising up to £155,000 being the exception rather than the rule. Provenance and condition are everything. I'd try a classic car auction, such as the Coys sale at their excellent historic festival at Silverstone in July, tel: 020 7584 7444 for sale details.

When balloons burst

" *I have an automatic Nissan Micra 1.3SLX on a Personal Contract Purchase scheme, which ends in August. By that time it will have 24,000 miles on its clock, 50% of which will only have been short journeys. The final PCP balloon payment is £4,500. Should I make the final payment and keep it for a few more years or use my equity in the car to start a new PCP?* "

It all depends on the deal your Nissan dealer offers you. Many PCPs were sold on the unwritten promise that at the end of the term you would have enough equity left in the car to finance the deposit for a new PCP at very similar monthly payments to the existing contract. Unfortunately many of the 'guaranteed future values' on which these contracts were based have proven to be unduly optimistic, but in your case the trade value of your car should still exceed your final payment by £750 to £1,000 and the retail value by £1,500 to £2,000. If the dealer can't offer you a replacement at monthly payments within £10 of your current payments, my advice is to keep the car. Note that his offer may depend on your taking delivery of the new car in August rather than September and it having a 'W' rather than an 'X' registration, which will make it worth about £500 less than the 'X' in three years time.

Classic Car auction houses

- AMA, Aylesbury, tel: 01296 339150.

- Barons, Sandown Park, tel: 023 808 40081.

- BCA Blackbushe (A30 Surrey/Hants), tel: 01252 878555/877317.

- Brooks, various locations, tel: 020 7228 8000.

- Cheffins, Linton, Cambridgeshire, tel: 01223 358731.

- Christies, London, tel: 020 7389 2851.

- Coys, various locations, tel: 020 7584 7444.

- Greens, Millbrook Test Centre, tel: 01684 575902.

- H&H, Pavilion Gardens, Buxton, tel: 01925 730630.

- Husseys, Marsh Barton, Exeter, tel: 01392 425481.

- Lambert & Foster, Maidstone, tel: 01892 832325

- Philips, Exeter, tel: 01392 439025.

- Purely Classics, Southend, tel: 01702 461600.

- RBR Sales, Doune, Scotland, tel: 0131 449 2465.

- RTS, Godmanchester and Norwich, tel: 01603 418200.

- Stags Classic Commercials, Devon, tel: 01882 255533.

CAMPERS AND CARAVANS

Adventurous A Class

" *I own a Mercedes A160 A Class Elegance and am very interested in the ABI Adventurer caravan which has been on display throughout Europe being towed by an A160. The trouble is, my A Class is a five-speed full automatic and my query as to suitability to MBUK has so far met with a blank.* "

The ABI Adventurer is aimed at people who enjoy outdoor activities such as hill walking, surfing, windsurfing, shooting, cycling, canoeing, diving, etc. rather than at the traditional caravanner. It has a 'wet door' so that wet kit can be dumped straight into the shower compartment rather than dragged through the van. And the interior contains simple, no-nonsense accommodation for four, plus hob, fridge, etc., but a total absence of 'home from home' luxuries. Prices are £5,995 in white or £6,995 in metallic as seen at last year's London Motor Show (enquiries: 01482 678000). The bad news is, ABI has been towing it with a five-speed manual A160. You'd be all right towing with the autoclutch A160. But with the full five-speed automatic you're bound to experience torque converter slip in fifth and, without the addition of

a transmission oil cooler, you run the risk of overcooking your ATF.

Carry on camping

" *Since it was new I have owned an April 1973 'L'-registered Ford Transit 1700 V4 'Inca' camper. Its genuine mileage stands at 51,554. Due to my illness it has been garaged for the past 10 years but is now being recommissioned and MOT tested prior to sale. (It's far too good to go for scrap.) Could you suggest a suitable venue for sale, or is there a Veteran Ford Caravanette Society through which I might find a suitable buyer? Sadly, I can't foresee being able to drive the vehicle again myself.* "

If it was first registered in April 1973, there is a very good chance that the Transit on which it is based was built in 1972, in which case it is classified as an 'historic vehicle' and is VED exempt, making it more valuable. The clubs are: Classic

Camper Club, c/o Mark & Karen Smith, PO Box 3, Amlwch, Anglesey LL68 9ZE, tel: 01407 832243, email: classiccamper@cwcom.net, website: www.classiccamper.mcmail.com; Period Motorcaravan Guild, c/o M. & J. Traxton, 10 Sunnyside Cottages, Woodford, Kettering, Northants NN14 4HX, tel: 01832 734441. There is a lot of enthusiasm out there for old campers and motorcaravans and this may also generate some interest. I will forward any enquiries from readers. (In fact, this camper was later sold to a reader who paid the full asking price.)

CAR DESIGN

On reflection...

" *Last year I bought my wife a car which, whilst meeting our needs in almost every way, is dangerous to drive in sunny weather. The car is an Audi A3 SE and the reason is that the light-coloured dashboard top reflects so brightly in the windscreen that it seriously impairs the driver's ability to see the road ahead. Through the Audi dealer, Audi replied that no one else had complained of this. What's the answer?* "

This problem has come up a few times in the past. It afflicts almost any car from a Fiesta to a Passat which has a light-coloured dash-top or parcel shelf, during the periods of the year when the sun is low in the sky. Back in 1996, D.S. of Ottery St Mary supplied an answer in the form of black self-adhesive Fablon velour from a DIY shop (order code 65217). This is 450 mm wide and can be cut to shape and stuck to the reflecting areas. Though it shrinks over time, D.S. tells us it totally eliminates reflections, and can easily be removed prior to sale of the vehicle. Apparently, the glue residue can be removed with white spirit. Obviously, this will spoil the look of the interior of the car. The other answer is polarising sunglasses or clip-ons which eliminate reflections.

Column change

" No, I don't mean change the column. My question is, do you know of any current model cars which still have a column gear change? The last I can remember was a 1970s Renault 16. "

The ultra reliable Honda Shuttle has a four-speed autobox with an excellent column change. New and old model Toyota Previa automatics have column changes. New Renault Espace automatics do. The forthcoming Toyota Prius 'hybrid' petrol/electric car has a column change combined with a parking brake which works very well indeed. The Citroën Picasso, Citroën Synergie, Fiat Ulysse, Peugeot 806, Mercedes V Class and Fiat Multipla all have stubby dashboard gearlevers, a bit like the Citroën Traction, Citroën 2CV, Renault 4 and early Renault 5.

Thoroughly spoiled

" One increasingly comes across modern cars with back spoilers. For normal driving, are there any advantages, or are they merely a fashion feature? "

They serve no function below 50 mph. Above this speed, as the vehicle speed increases, they help to reduce 'lift' at the rear of the car and thereby make the car more stable. Audi did not fit a rear spoiler to the TT model, but, faced with complaints from German owners about stability problems at over 100 mph on long autobahn bends, they 'borrowed' the full-size Mercedes Benz wind tunnel. In it, they found that the curved, unspoiled back of the TT does generate lift at more than 100 mph, so a recall was prompted and the design was changed to incorporate a spoiler.

Aston outrage

" Having read Andrew English's report about the new six-litre 185 mph Aston Martin DB7, I wondered what on earth they could do next to ruin the company. They have gone bust many times with several owners and they still haven't learned the lesson. Just how many of these utterly impractical and environmentally wasteful cars can they sell? Pre-war they made the most glorious two-seater sports cars which most young men lusted after. Surely their future well being would be safer if they did this, and they have Ford's backing to make the change. I don't see, of course, that you can do much about it, but to express an opinion in print might reach the right quarter. "

The Aston Martin DB7 Vantage may not be your cup of tea, but it is Andrew English's and there are plenty of people aged 30 to 70 who will lust after a 185 mph supercar for a relatively reasonable £92,500. If it's too fast and too expensive for them, they can go for the £85,000 DB7 3.2. If that's too dear, they can pick up a Jaguar XK8 from £50,500, or the forthcoming 'S' Type roadster for around £30,000. Below these, and also from the Ford stable, are Mazda RX7s and MX5s, Ford Cougars and Pumas, and even then possibility of a £10,000 StreetKa roadster. If the Government de-restricted motorways in the early hours of the morning, cars like the DB7 Vantage could be used in the manner they are designed to be. But if practicality is the only criteria, then what is the point of any sports or performance car on our increasingly speed-restricted roads? Why pay the Government £13,777 in VAT to buy a £92,500 sports car it won't let you use? Why pay 250% tax on the fuel to run it? Why should motorists support a Government which takes £36 billion in motor tax revenue when all they get back are speeding fines and holes in the roads? Why put up with speed restrictions which make our roads so increasingly congested they create unhealthy levels of pollution from vehicles stuck in traffic jams?

'Built like a brick…'

" *I often read that a VW Golf holds its value better than, say, a Ford Focus because of its 'build quality'. Can you please define 'build quality'. For instance, is it the number of spot welds per foot, the thickness of the metal, or just simply the way the car feels?* "

The Golf Mk IV is generally reckoned to have the highest build quality in its class. This is judged by a mix of thickness of the steel, stiffness of the structure, quality of the paint, quality of the materials (particularly interior trim) and quality of assembly. Electro-galvanised steel is used in the car's construction, which is why VW is confident enough to offer a 12-year warranty against perforation by rust. Another reason why VWs hold their value so well is that VW does its best to build cars mainly to customer orders, which creates a waiting list and make the cars tantalisingly hard to get. This helps to keep them a cut above Fords and Vauxhalls, a factor which has always appealed to good, old-fashioned British snobbery. Unfortunately none of this makes a Golf any more reliable than the cars it is perceived to be superior to.

Traffic lights

" *Would it not be an idea to incorporate a series of different coloured lights into car speedometers so that, for example, an orange light illuminated when 30 mph was exceeded, a red light illuminated when 40 mph was exceeded and a blue light when 70 mph was exceeded.* "

Not a bad idea. Pre-set lights are already used

on drag racing, track racing and rally cars to tell drivers who don't have time to glance at instruments when maximum safe rpm is reached. Far better to keep our eyes on the road than to constantly refer to a rev counter or speedo.

Electric guillotine windows

" *How safe are electric windows? My old Montego has electric windows which stop when an obstruction is placed in the gap. A carrot placed between the window and frame when closing is hardly marked. However, under the same test, my Audi has electric windows which snap the carrot in two like a guillotine. Is there any record of serious injury to children's fingers?* "

A child was killed when its parents left it playing in a car, the electric windows of which could be closed when the door was open despite the ignition being off. Most electric windows now stop closing when they sense an obstruction and will not work anyway unless the ignition is switched to at least the auxiliary circuits. But leaving a child in a vehicle unattended by an adult is dangerously negligent anyway and there is a limit as to how much car manufacturers can protect owners against their own stupidity.

BMW lock-in

" May I alert you and your readers to a potentially fatal design fault of the current BMW 5-Series. I was left sitting in the passenger seat of one when the driver left the car and inadvertently pressed the locking button on his remote sender. This had the effect of locking me inside the car, with no means of getting out. The central locking button had no effect, I could not operate the horn to alert a passer by, and I was on the point of kicking out the front screen to escape when the driver fortunately returned. "

This is not a design fault, it is a design feature. When the remote sender is pressed, the doors automatically deadlock and the deadlocking mechanism is separate from the normal door-locks. If a driver leaves someone inside a 5-Series, he or she should not lock the car. Passengers can then lock themselves in using the central-locking button and can unlock the doors with the same button.

Cutting corners

" May I use your column to draw attention to a design defect of the VW Golf Mk IV? The top corners of the front doors come to a very sharp point. My wife got a severe cut in her forehead from one of these today and it looks like she might need stitches to close the wound. "

This problem is not confined to Golf Mk IVs. Another reader complained of being stabbed by the doors of his Peugeot 406. On most cars, Mondeos included, these corners are rounded off so only quite a heavy impact with them would draw blood.

Garage sale

" We have owned a new-shape Mondeo 2.0iLX for almost two years and find it excellent in every respect bar one: owing to its width and the size of its door mirrors it only just goes into the garage. After my wife got one of the mirrors tangled up with the door jamb she has refused to garage the car. We are looking for a change in the new year and want something narrower from mirror tip to mirror tip. A Focus is even wider than a Mondeo. Can you suggest something that will give us the same degree of ride, road-holding and flexibility as the Mondeo, but is narrower? "

I have exactly the same Mondeo/garage problem and think it's time to start a campaign against developers who build houses with garage entrances a miserable seven feet (213 cm) wide or less. Garage doors need to be at least eight feet (244 cm) wide and if new houses come with narrower garage doors, home buyers should boycot them. The best answer to your question is a Seat Toledo TDI 110SE or V5, which have electrically folding door mirrors. Chrysler Neons do too, and are much cheaper, but the engines are nowhere near as flexible as those of the 2.0 litre Mondeo or the two Toledos mentioned and the ride quality is not as good.

Sit up and pay attention!

" With regard to A.P. of Berkhampsted's discomfort when driving his Jaguar XJ8, may we offer a suggestion? We drive a Ford Escort van, the seats of which were plainly not designed for people. We find that the foam wedges supplied by the Essex Alexandra School (020 8220 1630) tip our

pelvises forward, enabling our backs to be more vertically aligned. The end result is we arrive at our destinations flexible and alert, rather than stiff and tense. **"**

This may be a good idea for short journeys. And indeed I have an identical wedge tipping me forward on my badly designed office chair as I write this. But a reclining position is actually much better for your back when driving a long distance. The reason is that sitting upright concentrates all your upper body weight on to the base of your spine. If you sit in a semi-reclined position, your weight is distributed more evenly, taking some of the pressure off your lower back. This advice came directly from Professor Mark Porter, head of the Ergonomics Unit at Loughborough University, and probably the most qualified ergonomist in the country. The golden rule when buying a car in which to travel long distances is to find one with a height- and reach-adjustable steering wheel; a seat which adjusts for reach, height and recline; and one in which the seat, steering wheel and pedals are all correctly aligned. Examples include: Ford Focus, some Ford Mondeos (not all have seat-height adjustment), Seat Leon, Seat Toledo, Skoda Fabia, Skoda Octavia, VW Golf Mk IV, VW Bora, VW Passat.

Safety yellow

" *I am a nurse and believe that yellow is the safest colour for a car. In December 1997 I wrote to Nissan GB asking if I could have a Micra in yellow. Nissan replied that it did not produce the Micra GLX in yellow 'at this time'. I then ordered a Micra GX in white and took delivery in August 1998. Imagine my utter shock when I saw a 'T'-reg Micra in a showroom in March 1999. I have since seen several more, so I wrote to Nissan GB asking why I had not been informed. Nissan apologised that it had not been* *able to advise me that yellow would be available on the Micra six months in advance. Should I pursue the matter?* **"**

No. Car colour availability can change every few months. 'T' registrations did not begin until March 1999, so it would have been expecting rather a lot of Nissan to have anticipated in December 1997 that yellow would be available in March 1999. I agree with you about the safety aspect, and was utterly amazed when British Telecom switched from bright yellow to dull grey several years ago. After all, if any vehicle is likely to be parked at the roadside in an unexpected place, it's a BT van.

The way they were

" *I once owned a 1938 Morris 14 which was fitted with hydraulic jacks under the car operated by a simple pump which meant I could replace the wheels with ease. But the item I now miss most is the foot-operated dip-switch fitted to the left of the clutch, an absolute boon. Will we ever see these gadgets again?* **"**

Doubtful. We don't get punctures at anything like the rate they occurred during the 1930s and the wheels of the average car only tend to be removed to replace tyres or brake parts. Finger stalks are quicker than foot-operated dip-switches, can incorporate a headlight flash mode and are less prone to moisture damage.

Automatically bad?

" *In trying to help my wife choose a new small automatic I recently test drove an 'S'-reg. Peugeot 106 auto. I was surprised to find that the front wheel arches intrude so far into the car that the very small accelerator pedal was placed alongside and virtually touching the brake pedal. All members of my family who tried this car agreed that it was* *impossible to control the car and to drive it safely. How is it that such an obvious and dangerous design fault can appear in a car that has been so highly praised?* **"**

The Peugeot 106, followed by its Citroën Saxo derivative, has been around since 1991 and right-hand-drive examples have always suffered from front wheel arch intrusion into the footwell which compels the driver to sit in an offset position. But this is not and never has been either unsafe or dangerous to drivers of normal height. I had a Saxo 1.4 three-speed auto out last year and found it fine (even the 1.4 will clock 90 in second). But if everyone in your family is all over 6ft tall, you need to look at a more upright automatic, such as a Fiat Punto, Rover 25 (my choice), Seat Arosa, VW Polo or VW Lupo. And send the family on a driving skills course to learn how to left-foot brake.

Bully bars, again

" *Is it still legal to drive a vehicle with massive 'bull bars' fitted to the front? There are large numbers of such vehicles on the roads in Berkshire. These lethal weapons are used to intimidate, maim and kill other motorists and pedestrians. There is no justification for their use on UK roads.* **"**

We have touched on this before. Off-road, they do have a purpose. Until recently there was no statistical proof that they maim and kill significant numbers of people on the road, although they obviously have the potential to do so, and I am inclined to agree with you.

Cool face, warm feet

" *At present we have a 1987 'E'-reg. Vauxhall Cavalier, which we have owned from new. Now we are thinking about switching to a smaller car,* *but cannot find one which offers cool air to the face at the same time as warm air to the feet.* **"**

A Rover 25 offers this feature. Go for the 1.4Si model and you'll get a car that's a real pleasure to drive – far better than its 200-badged predecessor.

In-car TV

" *Having witnessed evidence over many years of accidents and near-misses caused by drivers not driving with due care and attention I am amazed to see a number of high-quality cars being advertised equipped with TV monitors in the dashboard. I have also seen the units advertised separately as an accessory. I consider this to be a dangerous and unnecessary piece of equipment and would like to take the matter up with the proper authorities but am unsure who this should be. Could you advise, please?* **"**

The Vehicle Certification Agency, 1 The Eastgate Office Centre, Eastgate Road, Bristol BS5 6XX. But bear in mind that it remains illegal for a monitor to display a TV picture visible to the driver while the vehicle is moving. In a BMW 7-Series, for example, a TV picture can only be displayed when the gear-shift is placed in 'park'. All you can view on the move are information displays and, while you could argue that satellite navigation information displayed on a colour screen set low in the dashboard is distracting, it still counts as a vehicle information display and is not in itself illegal. Similarly TV and video monitors set in headrests or the backs of seats for the entertainment of rear-seat passengers are no more illegal than those in a passenger aircraft.

CAR HIRE

Hiring something special

" Next year is my father's 60th birthday. To make it special we wish to send him and my mother away for a night in a hotel and we would like them to be able to drive there in a classic car. Something like an Austin Healey or an MGA would be appropriate. So far my attempts to locate a classic car hire company have been in vain. Can you help? I also read somewhere of a classic car timeshare club. Do you have any details. "

The Classic Car Club is a sort of classic car timeshare, which costs £500 to join and £1,750 a year. This gives access to around 40 days of 50 classic cars from Fiats to Ferraris, according to the points per day required for each car (tel: 020 7713 7313, fax: 020 7713 7316). A good classic car rental company is Bespokes (tel: 020 8421 8686, fax: 020 8421 8588). Its fleet includes E-Types, older 911s, Aston Martins and Ferraris, prices from £350 a day and it also does long-term contract hire. Modena offers Lotus, Ferrari and Porsche (tel: 01676 535596). Northern Sportscar Hire has a TVR Tuscan Speed Six among others (tel: 01977 668068). Express Vehicle Rentals have Mercedes, BMW, Porsche, Lexus, Land Rover, Jeep Jaguar and Audi (tel: 020 7383 3440, website: www.express-rentacar.co.uk). Eurostyle has Ferraris, TVRs, Porsche 996s, Porsche Boxters, Mercedes and BMW (tel: 020 7624 1313, website: www.eurostyle.uk.com). Miles & Miles Prestige Car Rental offers new BMWs, Jaguars and Mercedes (tel: 020 7591 0555). Carriages Vehicle Agency offers a wide variety of classic vehicles from a 1920s Dennis bus, through 1930s Rolls Royces, to a 70s VW Beetle cabriolet (tel: 01737 353926). Ray Tomkinson offers a range of classic taxis from 1930s Austin Landaulettes to late 70s Checker Cabs (tel: 01204 533447). Hanwells of London W7 has a late model Rolls Royce and Bentley rental fleet (tel: 020 8567 9729, website: www.hanwells.com). Budget Rent a Car (now owned by Team Rental) aims to offer anything from a Harley Davidson motorcycle to a Jaguar XK8 convertible (see Yellow Pages). Euro Style in London offers TVRs, Boxters, SLKs, Range Rover 4.6HSEs and even a Bentley Azure (tel: 020 7624 1313). Tangerine offers every kind of track day and off-road driving experience you can think of (tel: 0800 975 7299, website: www.tamgerineuk.com). Warning: if hiring a car for road use and paying a substantial deposit, inspect the car with a fine-tooth comb before taking delivery so you cannot be charged for damage you did not do.

Nice surprise

" *I pre-booked a hire car in Italy on Air Miles through Avis in the UK. When I went to pick up the car I was told that the insurance I had paid for at the time of booking was insufficient. I then paid £50 more for additional insurance. I queried this with Avis in the UK on my return, was told I had been ill advised in Italy and that my £50 would be refunded.* "

It's by no means the first time Avis has given refunds when its foreign subsidiaries have overcharged.

Hire before you buy

" *I am considering buying an Audi A3. But before I take the plunge I'd like to hire one for a fortnight to make sure it's what I really want. Do you know where I can do this? My local Audi dealer does not hire them and passed on the message from Audi that no car rental company has A3s.* "

Europcar had some (Northampton office, tel: 01604 785178, central reservations, tel: 0345 222525). The company rents cars by group and won't officially guarantee you will get an A3, but you should be able to come to an arrangement. Other companies offering more 'interesting' hire cars (but no A3s at the moment) are Budget's London Bridge branch (020 7702 1777) and The Civilised Car Hire Company (020 7735 9911). Audi has now revised its A3 line-up to include such delicacies as a TDI PD 130 bhp with a six-speed gearbox to differentiate the A3 from the much cheaper Seat Leon.

Photocards again

" *Just a reminder, that if any of your readers are expecting to hire a car in Europe on the strength of their photocard licence, they may find they need the paper counterpart as well so that endorsements can be checked.* "

Thank you. This is a real pain, but very valuable advice.

CATALYTIC CONVERTER FAILURES

The CAT Report

After more than 400 reader responses, this is a summary of what's been going wrong with advanced emissions systems.

I first ran a reader survey into how car 'advanced emission systems' were holding up when testing of them was introduced in August 1995. It turned out there were so many technical glitches in the testing equipment and software that the test itself had to be suspended from February to September 1996. Since then, the failure rate (or at least the reader complaint rate) seemed to have settled down. Now, seven years after catalytic converters were made obligatory, the failure rate has started to rise again, as I had expected.

Advanced emission system failures needn't be confined to catalytic converters to prove expensive. Other parts of the system, such as Lambda (oxygen)-exhaust-gas sensors, air-flow sensors, air-temperature sensors, crankshaft-revolution sensors and electronic control units have been failing too, sometimes creating a knock-on series of failures. Some makes and models have proved very expensive. What follows is a make-by-make summary of readers' experiences.

Alfa Romeo: Very low rate of failure. Only one recorded in 1999, but emissions problems with a 1994L 155 resulted in two massive bills of £775 and a jaw-dropping £2,494.

Audi: High rate of failure. Seven recorded 1995–98, 28 recorded in 1999. Cats for V6 petrol-engined cars are expensive at £700 apiece, and these cars have two. Very high failure rate of oxidising cats on A4 TDIs built between March 1995 and August 1998 explained by failure of welds holding the cat matrixes in place. Most of these £400 cats were replaced under warranty and cats fitted from August 1998 should not give any trouble. Cats on Audi 80TDIs were never a big problem area and I know of one which did more than 200,000 miles.

BMW: Low rate of failure. None in early survey. Six across the range in 1999 survey, but four of the cars were V8s. Cats on a 19,000 mile, 840 Sport cost a total of £2,058.96 to replace.

Chrysler: Low rate of failure. None in early survey. Three in 1999 survey. Two of the three were replaced under Chrysler's three-year warranty. One wasn't because the car was an import.

Citroën: Average to high rate of failure. Nine in early survey, eight in 1999 survey. Most of the early failures were Lambda readings outside the MOT parameters. Variety of causes included dirty sensors, poor ECU connections, faulty ECUs. Most late problems Lambda sensors or cat failures.

Fiat: Average to high rate of failure. Three in early survey, nine in late survey. Early failures were all cat failures. Late failures mostly Lambda sensors at cost of between £120 and £170. But a cat for an Uno is quite dear at over £400.

Ford Fiesta: Comparatively high rate of failure on pushrod engined cars, especially 1.1i, despite high number of registrations. Five in early survey, ten in late survey. Fortunately, these cats are cheap at £200.

Ford Escort and Orion: High rate of failure, even in context of high number of registrations. Twelve in early survey, 11 in late survey. Most required new cats at cost of £200 to £300 inclusive. In some cases, Ford paid part of the cost out of goodwill.

Ford Mondeo: Average rate of failure in context of high registrations. Six in early survey, four of which were 24vs, seven in late survey, one of which was a 24v.

Ford Granada/Scorpio/Galaxy: Comparatively high rate of failure for relatively small number of this model on the road. Four in early survey, seven in late survey. Low replacement cost in case of 2.0 litre cars, but five of the failures were on 2.9 litre 24v models, which have multiple cats and which also seem to be prone to multiple HEGO (oxygen)-sensor failures.

Honda: Low rate of failure. One in early survey, two in late survey. One

Civic cat cost a high £509. Other two were Lambda sensors at £250–£270.

Hyundai: Low rate of failure. Just two in late survey. Both cats, comparatively expensive at £460.

Jaguar: Low rate of failure even accounting for low number of registrations. The only failure noted was a Lambda sensor in a 94M 4.0 litre Daimler XJ40.

Land Rover: Low rate of failure. Just one Discovery 2.0MPi and one Range Rover 4.0SE for which cost of replacement cats was a high £1,155.

Mazda: Low rate of failure. Just one 323 1.6F. Replacement from exhaust centre cost £470.

Mercedes Benz C180/C200/C220: High rate of failure. None in early survey, but nine in late survey, most at around 50,000 miles. Part or full refunds in three cases, but others had to pay £767–£869.

Mercedes Benz E and S Class: Low rate of failure. Two (one cat, one Lambda sensor) in late survey. New cat for S Class fitted FOC.

Morgan: Low rate of failure. One 1996 Plus Four fitted with Rover T16 engine.

Nissan: Low to average rate of failure. Four in early survey, four in late survey. Across the range from Micra to Primera. Even mix of Lambda sensor, cats and inconsistent testing equipment.

Peugeot: High rate of failure across the range. Fourteen in early survey, 14 in late survey. Most problematic seem to be 306 1.8XTs (six in total). High incidence of ECU and sensor failures. Three 406 cats failed at or soon after first MOT.

Proton: Low rate of failure. Just one MPi model at 72,000 miles in late survey. Replacement cost £350.

Renault: Average to high rate of failure across the range. Eight in early survey, 15 in late survey. Most were straightforward cat failures. Replacement costs reasonable at £250–£350.

Rover Mini and Metro: Very high early rate of failure, but just two in late survey. Of the 19 failures in the early survey, some were caused by confusion over test procedures. It is possible that new MOT test software may have solved this.

Rover 200/400/600/800: Average rate of failure taking account of high number of registrations. Six in early survey, nine in late survey. Early problems due to test procedure confusion. Late problems mostly straightforward cat failures. Replacement costs reasonable at around £300.

Toyota Carina E and Avensis: Comparatively high rate of failure of oxygen sensors. One in early survey, six in late survey. This essential part of Toyota's 'lean burn' system is expensive at £340, but Toyota has now extended its warranty on it to four years.

Toyota (general): Very low failure rate. One in late survey. Cat and Lambda sensor of RAV 4 failed. Replaced with secondhand cat from breakers and new Lambda sensor costing £269.67.

Vauxhall: Average failure rate taking account of high number of registrations. Ten in early survey, twelve in later survey. Nine of early failures were cats. Five of late failures were Lambda sensors. No real pattern to failures. Highest cost £348.50. One Cavalier cat lasted at least 244,784 miles.

VW (general): Comparatively high failure rate. Two in early survey, 18 in late survey. Mostly Lambda sensors, but figures included seven cats. Some £700 bills.

VW Passat: Very high failure rate of oxidising cats of late model Passat TDI (see Audi). One in early survey, 19 in late survey. Most replaced under warranty and problem now said to be cured (see Audi for explanation).

Volvo: Average failure rate. Five in early survey, seven in late survey. Some met with part-refunds under Volvo 'Lifetime Care'. Others meant bills of £500 to £840.

D.H. of Batley's 1991 Volvo 960 3.0 24v has covered 243,741 miles on the same engine, gearbox, catalytic converter and 'all the other bits'. But the record so far for catalytic-converter life has to go to J.M. of Chesterfield whose 92K Cavalier 2.0GLSi recently passed its MOT on the original cat at 244,784 miles.

So what's the verdict? Some companies, notably Ford, seem to have cleaned up their act and late model Mondeos in particular seem to be very little trouble. Others, such as Peugeot, Renault and, to a lesser extent, Citroën clearly still experience a complicated mixture of problems, some of which can have financially devastating knock-on effects. The high number of failures on four-cylinder C Class Mercedes at around 50,000 miles should have been met with more goodwill than proved to be the case.

Power Steering Services (020 8853 3343) is now offering cut-price cats and it's also worth checking with your local Kwik-Fit or other fast-fit exhaust centre, particularly if an OE cat is as expensive as the Mercedes item and you're thinking of selling the car. But make sure the replacement cat is Type Approved, as shown by an 'E' mark, or it could fail the MOT as from October 1999. Cats of cars first registered before 1 August 1992 can still be legally removed.

In the USA, the emission control system of cars, including ECUs, Lambda sensors and catalytic converters are required by law to be guaranteed for the first 50,000 miles.

Cat behaviour patterns

" *Later this year I will probably make the switch from a non-catalysed car to a catalysed one. I only drive 3,000 miles a year: 2,000 miles on journeys of 30 miles or more; 850 miles on journeys of 7–10 miles; and 150 miles of 1–2 mile journeys. Are the cats of some vehicles more tolerant of short journeys than others? Would it be helpful to run the engine on fast idle for a couple of minutes before or after a short journey? For an average car and driver, how much would the cat's life be reduced by my sort of use? And when the cat fails, does it do so suddenly, or are there any warning signs? I am surprised that no manufacturer has produced an electrically self-heating cat to get the matrix up to operating temperature before the engine is started.* "

Generally, the closer a cat is to the exhaust manifold of the car, the faster it will reach operating temperature. (Sometimes it's actually in the exhaust manifold.) Years ago, Tickford was experimenting with cats which incorporated an electrical heating element and I actually rode in a Mondeo fitted with one, but the most practical solution has been to locate the cat as close as possible to the engine heat source. No, you should never fast-idle a catalysed car. Best simply to drive it, but an electric engine pre-heater such as the Kenlowe Hotstart will help reduce engine and exhaust system condensation on start-up during the winter (01628 823202). Low-mileage use will give the cat a harder life, but it's impossible to quantify how much, as this will depend on a lot of other factors. When a cat fails, the ceramic matrix breaks up and gradually blocks the car's exhaust system. The effect is a gradual loss of power, culminating in the engine being unable to breathe out at all, at which point it stops running. Generally, the smaller the car's engine, the less problems you should have from short-run syndrome, which is why the new breed of non-catalysed, 500 cc, diesel-powered microcars should be particularly suitable for low mileage motorists. (See 'Alternative Transport'.)

It's a cat's life

" *I have just been quoted £1,215 to replace the two catalytic converters of my 119,000-mile BMW 740i bought in September 1994. (It was one of the first of the current shape 7-Series.) I was also a victim of premature bore wear for which BMW blamed inferior UK petrol. Could there be any connection between the two? If not, is five years and 119,000 miles the expected life of a cat and is the estimate reasonable?* "

It is remotely possible that a small amount of oil, burned as a result of the bore wear problem, hot-spotted the cat matrixes with red hot particles of carbon. But five years and 119,000 miles is an average to good life for a pair of catalytic converters. Some last longer; some don't last as long. Ford cats are the cheapest, but if you own anything else it's always worth getting competitive quotes from specialist exhaust centres for after-market cats which are likely to be needed in increasing numbers as the cat crisis widens.

Cats for big cats

" Further to the Cat Report, your post-August 1992 Jaguar-owning readers might be interested in a source of cheap, high-quality catalytic converters for their cars. It is Fuel Parts UK, tel: 01527 835555, website: www.fuel-parts.co.uk. Their cats are warranted for five years or 50,000 miles, whichever comes first, and the main cat for an XJS is £127.63, Lambda sensor £99, fuel pumps from £80.46 to £92.44. "

Many thanks. These prices could soon make the difference between keeping an older catalysed Jaguar on the road and being forced to scrap it.

Toyota comes clean

After the comparatively high number of expensive Lambda sensor failures on Toyota Carina E models, exposed in the Cat Report, Toyota has extended its manufacturer warranty on this part to five years or 100,000 miles whichever comes first. In Toyota's words, 'This is part of a warranty programme designed to reduce the cost of ownership of certain items when the original comprehensive manufacturer's warranty of three years or 60,000 miles expires.' Highly commendable. And many thanks to C.J. of Burntwood (no connection with the factory) for bringing it to our attention.

Cat out of the bag

" What would happen if I removed the catalyser from the exhaust system of my 'M'-reg. Rover Montego Estate 2.0LXi and replaced it with a simple length of pipe? "

You might get away with it because the Montego is not listed for advanced emission-system testing as part of the MOT (it was one of the exemptions and is not included in the 5th edition of the Emissions Standards book). Check first to make absolutely sure that it is not in the test equipment software. Leave the Lambda sensor in place in the exhaust system (if it's in the cat you will need to relocate it). You may find that reducing the exhaust back pressure leads the engine to run leaner, which can be solved either by re-programming the ECU or by adding back pressure by replacing the cat with a silencer box.

CHERISHED REGISTRATIONS

Austin 7 GT

" *I am only the second owner of my 1931 Austin 7 'Box' saloon and have had it for 37 years. This year I decided to put it up for sale, but sadly most of the response has been from people after the registration, 'GT 6193', which seems to be worth £3,000. Should I separate it and the registration? What value would you put on the car alone?* "

The car looks really nice in its period wheel covers (this reader sent a photograph), but without a proper look I can't tell its true condition. What I can say is I haven't seen one in the condition yours appears to be sell for less than £3,000 over the last five years, with a best price for a real 'Condition 1' car of £5,929, including auction commission. So, if you've been offered £3,000 for the registration alone, take it. (Your car will then be allocated a new age-related registration which will never be transferable.) Then either advertise it in one of the Austin 7 club magazines, or try a classic car auction. Three club addresses are as follows: Austin 7 Owners' Club (London), c/o Yvonne King (memb sec), PO Box 77, Esher, Surrey KT10 8WZ, tel: 01372 466134, email: king yvonne@hotmail.com; The Pre-War Austin Seven Club Ltd, c/o Steve Jones,

1 The Fold, Doncaster Road, Whiteley, nr Goole, East Yorks DN14 0JF, tel: 01977 662828; Midlands Austin 7 Club, c/o John Roberts, 18 Oaktree Lane, Cookhill, Alcester, Warwks B49 5LH, tel: 01789 765349 (before 9pm).

Disgusted of Tenterden

" *It's typical of wheeler dealers like you to advise the owner of the 1931 Austin 7 to separate it and its registration to raise the maximum amount of money. Don't you have any regard at all for this important piece of our automotive heritage?* "

Normally I would support your point of view and had R.M. of Hornchurch been as rich as you seem to be, then my answer would have been different. But he obviously had to sell his pride and joy in order to raise much-needed cash and he had already been offered £3,000 for the registration alone. If you are so concerned about the car and registration being separated, then make him an offer of £6,000 for the car with its registration and I'll forward this to him.

E 9

" *I have a Vauxhall Astra 1300, driven out of the Hammersmith garage brand new on 16 November 1983 and with myself as the only owner. It has just passed its MOT at a little over 79,000 miles and is kept in first-class condition by my local garage, Hampstead Motor Services. Do you have any idea of its value? The number plate is 'E 9' which has been in our family in Staffordshire since cars were invented.* "

On the open market a car like this is now worth virtually nothing: £200 tops, unless you are lucky enough to find an eccentric individual who must have an immaculate 1983 Astra 1300 at any price and is prepared to pay maybe £500. The 1904 registration, on the other hand, is worth a five figure sum. So, whatever you do, don't allow the car to be sold for buttons with the registration still on it. Transfer the registration to another vehicle or to a retention certificate before you advertise the car. This will cost you either £80, or £80 plus £25. You need form V778/1 – which comes with instructions – from your local vehicle registration office. Most post offices offer free lists of vehicle registration offices.

Goodbye, Dolly

" *I have decided to part with my car which is a 1979 Triumph Dolomite 1500 Highline in yellow with 47,000 miles and which I have owned since new. The body is rusting, but otherwise there is nothing wrong with it. It was suggested that maybe we could sell the number plate: 'RKB 97T'. How much do you think we could get for the car and the number plate, separately or together? And how do I go about selling them? The car has not been taxed or insured since last year because it was not being used.* "

You can't sell a registration separately unless the car has been taxed within the last six months, even if it qualifies for a free of charge 'historic vehicle' tax disc. If the car has not been taxed for some time, it will need to be MOT tested and insured before it can be taxed. From your description it doesn't sound like classic car auction fodder and is probably worth no more than £200 without MOT or tax. I don't think you'd get enough for the registration separately to justify the cost of putting the car through the MOT, insuring it and taxing it.

411 NMJ

" *This registration was assigned to my 1958 Dodge Sierra station wagon in June 1964. I then returned to Texas in June 1966, re-registered the car in Texas using the old green log book, and lost the log book. In 1967 I retired from active duty with the USAF and in 1969 my wife and I returned to England and have lived in Abbotsley ever since. For sentimental reasons I would now like to try to get my old registration back and transfer it from car to car as and when I need to. How can I go about this?* "

First, find out if the registration is available for transfer by calling the DVLA Hotline on 020 8200 6565. If it is, you will be given a price and will be required to pay an additional transfer fee of £80 to transfer the registration to an MOT tested and VED'd vehicle. If the registration is not available for transfer, check if it has been issued by writing to Customer Enquiries (Vehicles), DVLA, Long View Road, Swansea SA6 7JL or by faxing 01792 783657. You will get a simple 'yes' or 'no' answer. If 'yes', the Data Protection Act prevents the DVLA from telling you who to, so you will either need to employ a cherished-number dealer to try and find it for you, or advertise for it. If the registration turns out to be attached to a vehicle which is not VED'd or MOT tested and cannot economically be made to pass an MOT, it may be possible to buy the wreck and have it officially disposed of, in which case the registration mark will revert to the DVLA and should become available for re-issue at a negotiable price. If a reader happens to have '411 NMJ' on an MOT tested and VED'd vehicle and wishes to sell the registration to you, I will put you in touch. To complete the transfer you will then need to obtain form V778/1, which comes with full instructions, from the DVLA or from your local vehicle registration office.

How old is 'OT'?

" I recently bought a registration to take the age off my car. The letters are 'OT' and it has been suggested to me that this is, in fact, a very old registration. Do you know how old? And is there a 'trainspotters' book for registrations? "

'OT' was issued in Hampshire from January 1926 to November 1928. 'OT' Hampshire registration records (not *all* registration records) are held by The Hampshire Record Office, Sussex Street, Winchester SO23 8TH, tel: 01962 846154 and by a charity, The Kithead Trust at De Sallis Drive, Hampton Lovett, Droitwich Spa, Worcs WR9 0QE, tel: 01905 776681. Contributions are welcomed in exchange for a search. The DVLA does not necessarily have pre-computerisation registration records unless old registrations have been revived, but having a mark assigned to you does entitle you to know whatever history of it the DVLA holds. A book on the subject is *How to Trace the History of Your Car* by Philip Riden, ISBN 1-898937-25-7, priced £5.95. Another book, *Car Numbers 2000* was published on 20 December 1999, priced £40 including p&p, from Noel Woodall, Blenheim Street, Ribbey Hall, Wreay Green, Lancs PY4 2PA, tel: 01772 672870. You might also be able to find a secondhand or remaindered 1994 copy of Noel Woodall's *Where's it from? When was it issued?* (ISBN 0-9502537-7-4).

Losing a number

" Something has happened to me which I feel is very unjust. It appears that even though I paid the DVLA £250 for the cherished registration 'L10 EOD' I have now lost it. I think the situation is deplorable. I know of no other circumstances under which, after the purchaser pays for an item in

full, the vendor has the right to take it back. All I did was forget to renew my entitlement to hold the registration on retention after the first 12-month period elapsed. **"**

The terms and conditions for holding a cherished registration on a Certificate of Entitlement (retention certificate) are clearly set out on the certificate. No private individual 'owns' a registration. He or she merely leases it from the DVLA on the DVLA's terms, which require that the registration is either put on a vehicle or, if kept on a retention certificate, a fee of £25 a year is paid. In your case, the assignment fee of £80 was pre-paid as part of the original £250, so you could have transferred the registration to a vehicle first registered in August 1993 or later at no further charge.

Dodgy registrations

" *Through no fault of my own I am about to lose a cherished registration for which I paid £1,600 plus £80 transfer fee four years ago. It transpires that the plate was transferred from a scrapped pre-1972 car for which a fake MOT was obtained by the vendor. He then 'taxed' the car free of charge as a 'historic vehicle', establishing a history of taxation before offering the registration for transfer (the DVLA does not ask to see the car the registration is coming from if it has a history of being taxed). Now the cherished number dealer is under investigation by Humberside police and because my registration was illegally obtained in the first place it looks like I'm going to lose it. How can this be when I am the innocent victim of the DVLA's incompetence?* **"**

It shouldn't be. As long as the registration is not cloned, you should be allowed to keep it, or should be refunded your £1,680 by the DVLA for its part in transferring to you the 'illegal' registration. This kind of non-serious fraud should be stamped out once MOT testing stations go on-line and the entire system is tightened up. But other readers should be aware that a registration offered for transfer may not be legal and, as yet, neither the DVLA nor anyone else offers any means of checking its legality.

No room for Reg

" *I bought a new 'W'-registered car in March and specifically requested 'EU' plates. When I went to pick it up, the salesman told me that the garage could not fit 'EU' plates because they would be illegal. If this is true, why do I see hundreds of cars 'illegally' driving around with EU plates?* "

When a registration has seven digits and some of them are wide, such as 'W', there is no room on a standard plate for both the EU GB symbol and seven correctly sized, correctly spaced digits. With a six- or five-digit registration or one with narrow digits there is no problem.

CLASSIC CAR CLUBS*

Microcar rally

" *Further to your article about new microcars on 12 June, there will be a 25th National Micro Car Club rally at Toddington and Winchcombe stations on the Gloucestershire Warwickshire steam railway on 4/5 September. More details on 01242 621405.* "

> Club details are: Register of Unusual Microcars, c/o Jean Hammond, School House Farm, Hawkenbury, Staplehurst, Kent, tel: 01580 891377; Micro Maniacs, c/o Roger Bentley, 3 Pine Tree Lane, Hillam, Leeds LS25 5HY.

World's biggest bay window

" *On 11 September 1999 you helped us publicise our attempt to achieve the world's biggest bay window at the 1999 Vanfest. The weather was awful, but we did get the 514 VW vans we needed to park up in the shape of a second-generation rear-engined VW 'Type 2' Transporter. Many thanks for your help.* "

> And many thanks for the photo. It's a great way

---

* There is an up-to-date list of classic car clubs permanently on display at www.mysterymotors.com.

to show the huge size of the hobby of preserving and enjoying older vehicles. Politicians, please take note. Anyone seeking information about the next vanfest should call 01902 674760 or 01235 863664.

Split-window Beetle

" My daughter is now coming up to her 17th birthday and wants a split-rear-window VW Beetle as she feels these are the most beetle-like. Could you say which is the best model Beetle to buy irrespective of price, and also name a source. "

Assuming you can find one, I wouldn't recommend that your daughter tried to learn to drive in one of these, as rear vision is very strictly limited. After Major Ivan Hirst put the post-war VW Beetle into production (Type 60 KdF saloon on Type 82 Kubelwagen floorpan), split-rear-window models were built from 1946 until 1952. These were designated 'Type 51' and 'Type 53', which had a sunroof. Engines were 25 bhp 1,131 cc flat-fours, increased to 1,295 cc and 48 bhp for the 1951 Okrasa modified 'export' version as owned by Keith Seume. If you can find one, that's the split-rear-window model to go for. On 16 July, auctioneers Sothebys sold a black 1947 split-window Beetle in fairly poor condition for £8,510 at their sale at Brooklands Museum. You will discover a lot more about VW Beetles by buying *The Beetle*, a superb large-format book by Keith Seume (ISBN 1-85833-438-1) and by joining the Historic Volkswagen Club, c/o Rod Sleigh, 28 Lognor Road, Brooklands, Telford, Shropshire TF1 3NY, tel: 01952 242167. Sadly, Major Hirst passed away in early 2000.

Sera club

" *Regarding the Toyota Sera, uninitiated owners might like to know that I have established a register for these cars. Through Omnicron Engineering of Norwich (01508 570351) I have imported spare parts that Toyota (GB) Ltd is unable or unwilling to supply and I also have full workshop manuals and parts books for these cars, so it's well worth owners joining the register.* "

I have added this to my clubs list at www.mysterymotors.com, which now contains more than 400 car clubs. Readers wishing to join the Sera Club should contact Andrew Cliffe, 10 Glendinning Road, Norwich NR1 1YS, tel: 0498 651441, fax: 01508 570795, email: andrew@omnicron.uk.com, website: www.omnicron.uk.com/sera.html.

A Princess for £1

" *I have owned an Austin Princess 1800HL saloon in bronze metallic since new in September 1976. It has now covered 64,500 miles, is in fair condition and I would like to sell it. Should I try a classic car auction, an advertisement or is there a classic car club for this model?* "

Sadly, a Princess just happens to be the cheapest car I have ever seen sell at auction since the 1960s. It was a 79V 1.7 automatic with 150,000 miles unwarranted and, at BCA Blackbushe on 30 April 1999, it went to a chap in a checked shirt for £1. He probably had the good sense to offer it straight to the club which grew out of the defunct Wedge Owners' Club (Princess & Ambassador Owners' Club, c/o Peter Maycroft, 26 Castlehall, Glascote, Tamworth, Staffs B77 2EJ). Yours will probably be a much better car, but it will still require a £200 cylinder-head conversion to run satisfactorily on unleaded petrol and is unlikely to be worth more than £400. For proper BMC 'A' and 'B' Series unleaded conversions contact Ron Hopkinson, tel: 01332 756056. (Note: any further junk mail about so-called petrol 'catalysts' will be binned without acknowledgement.)

Collectable Maestro?

" *I bought one of the last Maestro Vanden Plas cars in March 1989 and it is still in excellent condition after almost 74,000 miles. Do you think it will become a collector's item? And is there a Maestro Owners' Club?* "

This is the model launched with a talking dashboard from which the synthesised voice of actress Nicolette McKenzie reminded Chris Goffey and a colleague to check their oil pressure after they rolled the car on a test drive. Thankfully, by the time yours was built, the talking dashboard had been dropped and the cars were fitted with proper 'S' series engines rather than the awful 'R' series which gave Maestros a reputation for unreliability. It's collectable enough for two clubs: Vanden Plas Owners' Club, c/o Nigel Stephens, The Briars, Lawson Leas, Barrowby, Grantham, Lincs; and Austin Maestro Owners' Club, 2 Compass Close, Littlehampton, West Sussex BN17 6SA, tel: 01428 641032, website: www.maestro.org.uk, email: jpsellars@maestro.org.uk.

Small Chevy society

" *My wife has owned a 1980 Vauxhall Chevette L hatchback from new and it is still immaculate with just 30,000 miles under its wheels. Is there a Chevette club or some other organisation she should join?* "

Yes. The latest address in the definitive *Practical*

Classics magazine clubs list is Vauxhall 'Cavette' Club (Mk 1 Cavaliers and Chevettes), c/o Peter Norrish, 67 Riley Lane, Bradshaw, Halifax HX2 9QE, tel: 01952 274608.

Smart club

" *A few friends and I are in the process of setting up a members' club for Smart Car owners in the UK. This should be helpful for any Smart owners as we can answer queries about the cars and discuss general matters referring to them. We also hope to negotiate discounts for accessories and spares, or import them ourselves.* "

Either email Robert Eatwell at rob@ robmanns.fsnet.co.uk or hit the website at http://clubs.yahoo.com/clubs/smartclubuk. His postal address is 9 Honeysuckle Court, 43 Grove Road, Sutton, Surrey SM1 2AW.

Latin-American Talbot

" *I have owned a 'Y'-reg. Talbot Samba cabriolet ever since it was ten months old and it now has 78,000 miles on the clock. It is very pretty and original. Can you tell me if there is an owners' club and what value would you put on the car?* "

The club is the 79–86 Talbot Owners' Register, c/o David Chapman, 18 Cavendish Gardens, Redhill, Surrey RH1 4AQ, tel: 01737 765331. The value is a bit of a stab in the dark, but it is spring and your car does have a soft top so I'd reckon on £1,250 to £1,500. Mechanical parts aren't a problem because they are all basically Peugeot and early 205s inherited some of them.

Harbour lights

" *I have a 1976 Morris Marina 1.3 Coupe which is running well and next year will be exempt from road tax but has a few rust patches here and there. Would a vintage car collector be interested?* "

Your car will not be VED exempt. The date for exemption is fixed at 31 December 1972 and applies to vehicles built (but not necessarily registered) before that date. Even though the car has no value, a member of one of the following clubs may be interested: Morris Marina Owners' Club and Ital Register, 39 Portley Road, Dawley, Telford, Shropshire TF4 3JW, tel: 01952 504900, email: ajmmarina@aol.com (450 members); Marina & Ital Drivers' Club, c/o John Lawson, 12 Nithsdale Road, Liverpool LS15 5AX (35 members); Morris Marina Enthusiasts' Club, 45 Oak Drive, Acton Vale, Acton, London W3 7LD, email: alan@mmec.freeserve.co.uk, website: www.mmec.freeserve.co.uk/mmec.htm (35 members). Club data from the directory in *Practical Classics* magazine which is updated every month.

CLASSICS AND NOSTALGIA

First car in England?

" *While rummaging through some old photographs, my wife turned up a picture of her great uncle, on the back of which is inscribed, 'Charlie SANTLER – builder of the 1st car in England'. He lived in Malvern, Worcestershire and, at the time of the picture, taken around 1920, he was more than 60 years old. So, assuming he was about 30 when he built the car, he must have done so between 1880 and 1890. It would be most interesting to know if any of your readers can shed more light on this.* "

The Santler car, registered 'AB 171' actually survives in full running order in Monmouth and takes part in the annual Emancipation Run from London to Brighton, but first a bit of history: Jean-Joseph Etienne Lenoir drove the world's first internal combustion engined car from Paris to Joinville-le-Pont in 1863. But in the UK, restrictive legislation held back the birth of the motor industry. The Red Flag Act of 1865 decreed words to the effect that at least three persons shall be employed to drive or conduct such a locomotive – one to precede it on foot carrying a red flag constantly displayed – and that any person with a horse and carriage could stop it simply by raising their hand.

The Act also imposed a speed limit of four

mph in the country and two mph in towns, while the Highways and Locomotive (Amendment) Act of 1878 laid down the first emissions regulations by requiring that a mechanical vehicle 'should consume its own smoke'. These petty restrictions left the field open for Panhard et Levassor, Gottlieb Daimler and Karl Benz to build the first practical cars elsewhere. Charles Santler worked with Benz on the very early three-wheeler cars. But he fell out with the great man, possibly over his ideas for creating a steerable four-wheeler car, returned to Malvern Link and, in 1889, with the aid of his brother Walter, began to build 'the first four-wheeler car in Britain'. The similar Benz 'Velo' was not launched until 1894. Santler's 'Malvernia' was first powered by a steam engine, which was replaced by a gas engine in 1892 and finally a petrol engine in 1894. It was laid up in a blacksmith's yard from the late 1890s until around 1907 and then appears to have been parked near a cricket pavilion where it deteriorated quite badly.

Another scratch-built car was by Frederick Bremer of Walthamstow between 1892 and 1894 (this car survives, reg. 'NJ 733'), followed by Herbert Austin who built the first Wolseley tricar in 1895 (this also survives at the Heritage Centre, Gaydon) and Frederick Lanchester who built his first, totally original, car in 1895. One book credits Edward Butler as building the first truly British motor car at the Merryweather Fire Engine Works in Greenwich in 1888. Apart from these five, my sources tell me that cars built in the UK before 1900 were close imitations of Panhards (Coventry Daimlers and MMCs) or Benz Velos (Marshalls from Manchester, Stars from Wolverhampton and

Arnolds from Paddock Wood in Kent). Santler went on to build light front-engined cars in 1906 and 1913, then diversified into manufacturing a motor plough in the 1920s.

Another motoring pioneer

" *A friend, now living in Majorca, has supplied information about his father who was a motoring pioneer. His name was Albert Farnell and the specification of the tri-car he built in 1897 was as follows: Independent 'sliding pillar' front suspension, 1.25 hp air-cooled motor, tubular chassis, belt drive via three step cone pulleys (an early 'CVT'). He later fitted a 'Starley' rear axle, his own patent four-speed, non-crash gearbox and worm and sector steering by wheel rather than lever. His address was 75 Manningham Lane, Bradford. Albert Farnell also raced Daimlers in the Isle of Man from 1902 to 1912 and took part in speed trials on the sands at Scarborough and Morecambe.* "

This is one for the motoring historians because it's not in Georgano's *Complete Encyclopaedia of Motorcars 1885–1968*, Culshaw & Horrobin's *Complete Catalogue of British Cars 1895–1975* or Hugo Wilson's *Encyclopaedia of the Motorcycle*. The reason for this may be that Albert Farnell only ever built one vehicle, which was quite common among early motoring pioneers.

100,000 miles in three years

" *In exactly three years between 1926 and 1929, my father, Sydney Taylor, managed to clock up 98,243 trouble-free miles in his 1926 AC Acedes, chassis no. 30618, reg. 'TD 7546'. AC used his letter in a testimonial advertisement in The Motor magazine on 17 September 1929. My father previously owned a Maxwell, then a Morris, about both of which he had much criticism, but he was full of praise for the AC. He sold it several years before I was born and, curiously, never owned a car again. Is there any possibility that his car might still be extant?* "

It's worth writing to Tony Morpeth of the AC Owners' Club, The Clovers, Mursley MK17 0RT. The overhead-cam, six-cylinder, 1,991 cc engine remained current from 1921 until the early 1950s when it was often supplanted first by BMW-based Bristol Sixes, then the 2,553 cc, overhead-valve Six from the Ford Zephyr. In 1926, an AC Six registered 'PE 7799' was the first British entry to win the Monte Carlo Rally, while a stripped-down AC 16/66 set the world 24-hour speed record of 82.58 mph at Montlhery. I cut my motor-trade teeth polishing a 1926 AC Six at Sports Motors on Orpington High Street in 1959.

Scrap yard special

" *Please could you give me some information regarding a car I bought from a scrap yard in Munster, Germany a couple of years after the end of WW2. It was called an Adler. But I have never seen or heard of one since.* "

Adler began making bicycles in the late 1800s, followed by cars in 1900. This car is a four-cylinder, 1,943 cc, side-valve, rear-wheel-drive Adler Favorit of 1929–33. In 1932 Adler showed a new, advanced front-wheel-drive model at the Frankfurt Motor Show named the 'Trumpf' which formed the basis of a number of special-bodied, speed-record-breaking cars. Production of private cars ended in 1939 and the company is now best known for its typewriters.

Definitely one of Syd's

" *I seem to remember a relative owning an Allard Monte Carlo. Could you tell me anything about it? The registration began 'DG'.* "

Only 11 Allard P2 Monte Carlos were built between 1952 and 1955. Engines were usually 3,622 cc Ford or 4,375 cc Mercury side-valve V-8s, but Lincoln, Cadillac and Chrysler OHV V-8s were also fitted. Sydney Allard himself won the 1952 Monte Carlo Rally in a P1, which was an earlier incarnation of the 'tin-top'. 'DG' is a Gloucester registration mark and records of first and subsequent owners in Gloucester from 1929–74 are held at County Record Office, Clarence Row, Alvin Street, Gloucester GL1 3DW, tel: 01452 425295 (expect to be asked for a modest search fee). The Allard Drivers' Club may also have records of the car c/o Michelle Wilson, 10 Brooklyn Court, Woking, Surrey GU22 7TQ, tel: 01483 773428. Philip Riden's Book, *How To Trace the History of Your Car* has now been updated, price £5.95, ISBN 1-898937-25-7.

Missed history motors

" *You have featured my 1934 Aston Martin Le Mans 'DS 1873' several times and I am still piecing together the missing parts of its past. I have now worked out that it may have been sold to Gentleman Motors of Wishaw near Motherwell and spent its war years in Scotland. That would fit with its ownership from 1946–65 by Frank Sugden of Carlisle. I have been surprised to find myself starting to receive information by email. Do you think there is scope to set up a Missing Motors and Missing History website?* "

Have already done so on www.mysterymotors.com, but it can't survive without sponsorship. 'DS 1873' is on there with several pictures. The owner can be emailed at richardwhite@supanet.com.

Sphinxed

" *I have a car mascot in the shape of a sphinx sitting on my mantelpiece. Can you tell me where it originated?* "

Armstrong Siddeley. Siddeley Deasys of 1912–19 and Armstrong Siddeleys of 1919–32 sported an upright Sphinx. Armstrong Siddeleys of 1932–34 had a recumbent Sphinx on the radiator cap, remodelled in 1934. Later models had a Sphinx head bonnet ornament; a Sphinx head with jet engines was used on the 346 model (1953–58); then a smoother recumbent Sphinx on the Star Sapphire (1958–60). A book, *Automotive Mascots* by David Kay and Lynda Springate (Veloce publications, ISBN 1-901295-42-7) reveals much more about mascots generally.

Yet another Siddeley

" *My father bought a yellow Armstrong Siddeley 14HP Light Six, registered 'CGH 815' brand new for £260 in 1936. Stupidly, we let her go for a song in 1953 (but then everyone did). I remember her self-jacking system, the whine of her pre-selector gearbox and her beautiful set of spanners, which I still have. I would give a lot to buy her back.* "

Talk to the Armstrong Siddeley Owners' Club Ltd, c/o Peter Sheppard, 57 Berberry Close, Bourneville, Birmingham B30 1TB, tel: 0121 459 0742. 'GH' London registration records have been destroyed, so you won't get any joy there. These cars had a very low 5.33 rear-axle ratio to help the 45 bhp, 1,666 cc, overhead-valve small Six pull around 25 cwt of bodywork, but they gave a refined ride.

Who knows what Kate got up to?

" *'Kate' is our March 1934 Austin 7 box saloon – one of the last before the Ruby came along. Her registration is 'VN 5960'. She was registered to the Hall family in Corby and Peterborough in the 1950s. But does anyone know anything of her past in the 1930s and 1940s. We would be glad of any photos or memories.* "

'VM' registration records have been destroyed, so this sort of appeal is the reader's only chance of uncovering what happened to Kate in her early and teenage years. Would anyone who knows anything please contact Barry Davis on 0121 711 1452.

Reunited

" *In November 1997 I wrote to you regarding the whereabouts of my late grandfather's Bentley (originally 'MB 4483', later 'XMF 547' and now 'GX 3993'). Between you, your readers and the Bentley Drivers' Club, the car was traced to its current owner, a Mr Clive Jones. I got in touch with Mr Jones and with his kind permission I visited him to see the car, which he has now owned for 41 years. He took my girlfriend and me for a drive in it and this was a great experience. I had a number of photos of the car from the 1950s showing it with different bodywork, and I made copies for Mr Jones's album. I'd like to thank you, your readers and the Bentley Drivers' Club who made this possible, and also Mr Clive Jones who spent a couple of hours talking about the car and taking us for our drive.* "

That's nice. Glad we could be of help.

First of the 'Blower' Bentleys

" *Following the death of his grandfather, my son inherited a painting of a vintage Bentley, registration 'YU 3250'. Is there any way the car can be identified? It would appear that it might have been raced as it sports a Union Jack and a racing roundel.* "

'YU 3250' was and still is the first ever 'Blower' Bentley built from the standard 10ft 10in. wheelbase, 4.5 litre model raced in the 1928 Brooklands Six Hour race and featured in *The Autocar* on 5 July 1929. It was not ready for Le Mans that year, but was entered with two other Birkin/Paget 'Blower' cars in 1930. Sadly, 'YU 3250' was a non-starter, but a 6.5 litre Bentley 'MT 3664', driven by Glen Kidston and Woolf Barnato won and another 6.5 litre 'GF 8507' driven by F.C. Clement and R. Watney was second. 'YU 3250' retired from the 1930 Brooklands Double Twelve but covered 65 laps in the Irish Grand Prix in 1930 (a handicap race) and came 11th in the 1930 Tourist Trophy. It was briefly reregistered 'JH 3115', then returned to 'YU 3250'. In 1978 it was still owned by Ann Shoosmith.

The name is Bond

" *I am trying to locate and buy a very rare car, namely a Bond Mini Car. My next-door neighbour in the mid-1950s owned one. From memory, it had a very long bonnet and a motorcycle engine at the front, which turned with the front wheel enabling the car to turn in its own length. Is there an owners' club for this model?* "

The owners' club is run by Stan Cormack, 42 Beaufort Avenue, Hodge Hill, Birmingham B34 6AE, tel: 0121 784 4626, website: www.uk-classic-cars.com/bond.htm. The man to sell you one is the larger-than-life Alan Hitchcock of Alan's Unusual Automobiles of 56 Lechlade Road, Faringdon Oxon SN7 8AQ, tel: 01367 240125 (visits by appointment only).

A.E. Merrill, where are you?

" *I'm in the process of restoring my JAP-engined, 1928 Brough Superior SS80. It is unusual in that the machine record card shows it was set up as an off-road or trials outfit for a Mr A.E. Merrill, who collected it from the works on 20 March 1928. I have no record of it ever having been registered. Could you possibly place an appeal to your readers for any information about A.E. Merrill and what he used the motorcycle for?* "

Said and done. Would readers with any information about Mr Merrill's motorcycling activities please phone Dave Clark on 01727 764637.

COY little number

" *'COY 266' is a red 1937 Series IV BSA Scout originally purchased from Godfreys of Croydon in March 1937. As the DVLA has no records prior to computerisation and I have no log book, I do not know anything about it until the car was purchased in 1984 and partially restored. However, I understand that the previous owner lived in Croydon and it was his widow who sold it after he had laid it up for 30 years. Would anyone, maybe a former Godfreys employee, remember seeing it and know the names of its owners from 1937 to 1984.* "

No COY joy from pre-computerised Croydon registration records because they have been destroyed. So would any reader with any information, please write direct to Mrs S. Mills, 18 Outram Road, Croydon CR0 6XE.

Christmas time again

I received a lively response to John Christmas of Wells-next-the-Sea's appeal for information about his family's coachbuilding and garage business which traded under the Christmas name (26 June). D.B. of Honiton wrote that many years ago her father was in the motor business in North London and once told her that the Christmas garage actually took horses in part-exchange for horseless carriages. B.M. of Harlow identifies the garage shown as having been on the High Road at Bushey Heath, and tells us that it later became Fuggles, which was famous for dealing in Bristol cars. S.M. confirms this, but states that in the 1950s Fuggles was next door to The Alpine Restaurant, so must have taken over these Christmas premises at a later date. B.T. of Watford recalls the garage in the same location in the 1950s when it had petrol pumps with long arms to bring the pipes over the footpath to the road, but thinks this must have been the second Christmas premises. J.J. of Norwich clears up the mystery by referring to the *Book of Watford* which shows a garage with the caption, 'A. Christmas & Co. Ltd – garage at rear of Clock House, 54 High Street – were previously at mid Lower High Street at 141/143 and were established in 1822 as coachmakers'. Apparently, Miss

Elsie Christmas, who was related to the owners, ran a dance studio in Watford and later married Mr T. Rigby Taylor, Mayor of Watford from 1937 to 1938. Motor Historian, David Culshaw, found an entry for A. Christmas & Co. Ltd in the 1923 *Michelin Guide*. The address was Junction of High Street and Water Lane, Watford and they were listed as agents for Vulcan, Albert and Wolseley. A.H. of Boxmoor, Hemel Hempstead, found Thomas Christmas listed as a carriage builder of 13 Marlowes, Hemel Hempstead and even sent a copy of a contemporary o/s map showing the location of the works for me to forward to J.C.. *The Gazette*, 39 Marlowes, Hemel Hempstead, HP1 1LH has a heritage section which may be able to provide further information. J.M. of Hemel Hempstead confirms that there had been a Christmas garage in Marlowes, Hemel Hempstead and that the Methodist chapel which stood to its right is still there. At the time he knew it, ownership had passed to George Chatten, so it would seem that Christmas had three, not two, premises over the years, first in Marlowes, then in mid Lower High Street, and finally at 54 High Street. J.M. also provided some interesting history of the Christmas coachbuilding business during the First World War. Apparently, in 1916 Thomas Christmas asked that he should keep Alfred Cook, a painter, because he had already released seven painters to the forces. C.H. of Hemel Hempstead's 1890 *Kelly's Directory* lists a Mrs Christmas at 24 Marlowes which was the house next door to Thomas Christmas Carriage Builder of (confusingly) 13 Marlowes. He thinks that the coachbuilders was taken over by James Chatten who owned it from 1917 to 1927. C.H. knew the premises as 'The County Garage', owned by Mr H. Keat from 1937 to 1945 and tells us that it and the house next door were demolished for town-centre redevelopment in the early 1960s. Finally C. Collins of Crown Motors, 45/46 High Road, Bushey Heath wrote to tell us he bought the A. Christmas Watford garage in 1960 and would like to get in touch with John Christmas to discover more.

Cord concession

" Do any of your readers know anyone connected with R.S.M. (Automobiles) Ltd who imported Auburn, Cord and Duesenberg cars to the UK until 1937, then Nash cars until the company's demise. I am particularly interested in import figures for Cords from 1936 to 1937 and any sales records if they exist. R.S.M. was located at 26 Bruton Street, Mayfair, London W1 in 1936, then in Grosvenor Square in 1937 when the name changed to Clifford Taylor (Automobiles). The company ceased trading in 1942. "

This is a genuine enquiry from a Cord owner and I will be equally interested in the information.

Pre-war Fiats and a rather special Bugatti

" In the late 1930s my father, F. Macario, was the enthusiastic sales manager of Hanover Motors Ltd, London West End distributors for Fiat cars. The 500 'Topolino' convertible coupe was priced at £125 and the 1,089 cc, 508C Millecento pillarless saloon was £198. These cars were shipped to the UK as bare shells and were upholstered and painted in the UK. My father offered a modified version fitted with an Arnott Concentric supercharger by Carburettors Ltd of Grange Road, Willesden Green, N10 and this version was tested to 80 mph and 0–50 in 12.6 seconds by The Light Car magazine in November 1938. Since the model was also fitted with independent front suspension, it had handling to match the performance. Another unusual car was the smart rhd spider, based on a 500 Topolino. Can you tell me anything more about this? After the war, my father worked for Car Mart Ltd of Euston Road and a very smart Bugatti four-

door saloon passed through his hands (reg. 'FUW 180'). He was forced to sell this after being caught doing 80 mph down Albany Street. Can you tell me anything about the Bugatti and whether or not it survived? "

There is a very unusual car in the showroom photo: a 1939/40 model Fiat 500 four-seater built for the UK market only (sitting behind a pair of Fiat 1500s with faired-in headlights). Abarth, Cisitalia, Ferrari, Giannini, Moretti, Siata and Stanguellini all built sports cars using Fiat components, as did Pininfarina, Vignale and other Italian coachbuilders. Does any reader know more about the pretty little 500-based spider? Your father's Bugatti is a Type 57C model with a standard Bugatti-commissioned coach-built body, but I don't know who by. It even has Fiat-like door handles. You might be able to identify it from a book, *Bugatti Type 57 – the last French Bugatti* by Barry Price, on special offer at £27.50 from Bookstop, tel: 01932 868518. The Bugatti Owners; Club Ltd, c/o Sue Ward, Prescott Hill, Gotherington, Cheltenham, Glos GL52 4RD should be able to tell you if 'FUW 180' is still among us.

On Topo what?

" *The Fiat Register has been trying to solve a mystery for years and it occurred to me that one of your readers might know the answer. The Fiat 500 Convertible Four was a unique version of this car built for the 1939 model year and for the British market only. The questions we have are: Who built it? Where was it built? Was it built on Topolino convertible coupe chassis, or (more likely) that of the Topolino van? Why was it only available in Britain and only for one year?* "

Back in August I received a fascinating letter from J.M. of Milton Keynes whose father ran the Fiat showroom in Hanover Square from 1938 to

1939 (see above). One of the prints sent by J.M. clearly showed a 500 Convertible Four at the back of the showroom. Other unusual Fiats at the time included an Arnott supercharged Millecento and a tiny sports roadster based on the 500. J.M. told us in his letter that Millecentos were shipped from Italy as bare shells and were upholstered and painted in the UK, so perhaps the same coachworks built the 500 Convertible Four. I have put L.H. in touch with J.M., but would any other readers with information please write to Les Humphreys, The Fiat Register, 58 Messingham Lane, Scawby DN20 9ND.

T.H., a former treasurer of the Fiat Register then threw more light on the subject. The late Michael Sedgwick had written that the cars were imported in primer and finally painted by 'local firms'. The four-seater was only possible after the 1938 introduction of a longer chassis with half-elliptic rear springs intended for the van version. It also had a lower rear axle ratio. A 1992 Italian book, *Fiat 500 Topolino* (edited by Giorgio Nada) confirms that the four-seaters were built in Turin and finished and upholstered in the UK.

The Filey Fiat?

" *I'm conducting some research for the Filey Museum. It seems that in the early 1900s an Italian gentleman, reputed to be a Count, was conducting speed trials on the beach here in a FIAT car which had no less than 12 cylinders. Drive was transmitted by a pair of big flapping chains, one of which broke and decapitated the unfortunate Count. His family took his body back to Italy, but the car is rumoured to have been buried in the sands. What we would like, if possible, are details of this incident, including names, dates and, best of all, a photo if any exist in an archive somewhere.* "

There may be two strings to this. Fiat did indeed field some huge engines, including the 18.2 litre Mephistopheles which definitely reached these shores in 1908, and the S.76 which had a four-cylinder, 28.3 litre airship engine and was timed at 132.37 mph at Ostend in 1913. The other string is that J. Parry Thomas was killed at Pendine Sands in Wales when a drive chain broke while he was attempting a record run in the Leyland Higham Special, nicknamed 'Babs'. There was a myth that the drive chain decapitated him. 'Babs' was buried in the sands, but has been exhumed and restored to full running order by Owen Wynn Williams. Your best source of further material and possible archive pictures is the library at The National Motor Museum, Beaulieu, tel: 01590 612345.

Whose Ford?

" *I found a photo during a clearout of family snaps. I thought you might like to retain it in case anyone enquires after 'BCD 174'.* "

This is a stripped-down, 1933/34 Ford, Model 40 V8 and the photo sent in by my correspondent looks like it was taken at the Brighton Speed Trials in the late 1930s ('CD' is a Brighton registration). It is probably quite a famous car, and may even have been one of the Ford V8 specials with 60-gallon fuel tanks built for the 2,000 km, 1934 Deutsche Trial. Roger Davey, County Archivist at East Sussex County Council Records Office, very kindly supplied me with the information that it was originally registered to Moodys (Motors) Ltd, automobile engineers of 115 Western Road, Hove, on 16 October 1934, then to Mr G.S. Mathias of 9 Langdale Road, Hove on 31 October 1934. The Kithead Trust was able to tell me it later went to Hampshire, but that is all they know.

30s MPV

" Paul Hudson's review of the Renault Kangoo Combi on 11 September last year was headed: 'The van that thinks it's a family estate'. I have to tell you it wasn't the first. Way back in 1938, Kevill Davies and Freddy March designed the 'Brakenvan' based on a Ford 10 Prefect. It converts from a van to a six-seater in under 30 seconds and better access to the rear can be achieved simply by sliding the side windows into the roof. It isn't the fastest thing on four wheels, but even after 62 years is still proving extremely useful. "

Freddy March was responsible for a lot of good car design in the 1930s. But the concept of this one is very close to that of the Ford Model A 'Woody' of 1928, ten years earlier. 1930s to 50s 'Woody' estate cars are now in great demand to tow racing cars to Goodwood revival meetings organised by none other than the present Lord March. Very soon you will be able to buy a brand new MPV that looks like a customised 1949 Ford Prefect E493A saloon (the one with its headlights in the front wings). The new version is both super trendy and very practical. It's the Chrysler PT Cruiser.

Grandma's forgotten bequest

" My grandmother, Mrs M.S. Smith of The Homestead, Moreton Road, Upton, Wirral, Cheshire, had a 1936 Frazer Nash BMW. The colours were red and beige, and at one time a German mechanic was employed to look after it. The car was promised to me when I could drive but in 1957, when I was 16, my grandmother gave it to her gardener/handyman, a Mr Moore. I would now like to trace it. If I find it can you tell me its approximate value? I cannot remember the registration, and it cannot be read from the original print. "

This is a BMW 315 of which 9,765 were built between 1934 and 1937 and which was sold in the UK with rhd as a Frazer Nash BMW Type 34. It had an overhead-valve, 1,490 cc, six-cylinder engine, four-speed gearbox, transverse-leaf independent front suspension and, with a top speed of 70 mph, was very well thought of. BMW 327s and 328s from the 1930s make a lot of money, but this should not mislead you into overvaluing the car, presuming it still exists. I'd say around £10,000 in good condition, rather than the £25,000 to £40,000 a 327, 328 or even the sports version of the 315 might make. The club is BMW Car Club Historic Section, secretary Mark Garfitt, tel: 01633 871704. Dennis Jenkinson's Frazer Nash Archives are kept going by Laurence Harwicke at Coxin House, tel: 01491 411491.

Dumfries and...?

" In 1931 when I was 17 my Grandma bought me a two-seater car with a dickey seat. It was a nice Galloway, made in Dumfries, Scotland. Would it be possible to let me have an address or note in your column? "

These cars were built by Galloway Motors Ltd of Heathall, Dumfries. They were very sturdy, but little known outside Scotland. There is a photo of a 1924 Galloway two-seater with dickey on page 394 of Culshaw & Horrobin's *Complete Catalogue of British Cars 1895–1975* (ISBN 1-874105-93-6). The 10/20 model has a side-valve engine of 1,528 cc to around 1927, after which it became the 12/20 with an overhead-valve engine of 1,669 cc. The Myreton Motor Museum at Aberlady, East Lothian has a 1927 Galloway saloon (tel: 01875 870288). And there is a 1924 10/20 two-seater with dickey at the Museum of Transport, Kelvin Hall, Glasgow (tel: 0141 287 2720).

Welsh wheels

" If possible, kindly let me know if there has been a sports car manufacturer based in Wales since 1950? "

Very much so. In 1959 Giles Smith and Bernard Friese combined their Christian names and set up Gilbern Sports Cars of Llantwit, Pontypridd to build GRP-bodied, four-seater GTs with BMC running gear. Engine options included the 1,098 cc, ohc Coventry Climax or BMC 'A' or 'B' series engines, standardising on the 1,798 cc twin-carb 'B' series from 1962. In 1966 a larger model called the Genie was also offered with 2,495 cc or 2,994 cc iron-block Ford V6 engines. In 1969 this grew into the attractive Invader with Bertone-like lines which was also available as a 'GTE' type estate. Before the 1970s fuel crisis bit 600 Invaders were built. The company went bankrupt in 1975 and a rescue bid finally failed in 1976.

Ginetta letter

" I would be very grateful for any history of my Ginetta G2 which your readers can provide me with. It has a distinctive Cheshire registration, '329 EMA', and though I have been able to trace the original owner as well as owners from the 1960s, there is still a significant gap over what may have been its competition heyday in the 1960s. My name is Trevor Pyman, I am the registrar of the Ginetta Owners' Club, and I can be contacted on 01621 855879. "

Dare UK Ltd, who still build Ginetta G4s and G12s for the Japanese market, also confirmed that our 24 July 'Special' was not a Ginetta G2. Dare now makes the exciting 145 mph, supercharged Ford powered Dare DZ Gullwing Coupe, seen at the 1998 Motor Show and can be contacted on 01206 382987.

Mystery racer

" Could you, or any of your readers identify this 1920s single-seater racing car? Could it be a Guyot? "

Fifteen readers attempted to identify the mystery racing car from the reader's photo, shown in my column on 18 March. Answers ranged from an American Miller (because it looks front-wheel-drive) to an Amilcar C6 'Course' (an 1,800 cc, 83 bhp, six-cylinder racer of 1926). However, the most convincing identification came from R.M. of Hook who has a copy of the same photograph, plus another showing the car in action, driven by Albert Guyot. He tells us it was built by Albert Guyot in 1925 using a Rolland Pilain chassis and a 2.0 litre, sleeve-valve engine (possibly Schmid) which developed 125 bhp. Three further cars were built with 1.5 litre engines for the Indianapolis 500 in 1926, but on these the exhaust emerged from the left-hand side and the steering drop-arm was mounted on the scuttle. None met with much success.

Mystery father

" My father, James Thomas Skinner, was motoring correspondent for the Financial Times in the 1930s. He took part in a Hillman promotional trip in June 1934, as shown in the photograph. He wrote for The Autocar, The Motor and The Morning Advertiser. He also took part in the Monte Carlo Rally several times in the 1930s. But his extensive library was destroyed by a bomb in 1940, and I am trying to establish his career between 1910 and 1932. I know he was associated with the Starmer Group of newspapers in the 1920s and also The Westminster Gazette, and would be grateful for any further information your readers may be able to supply. "

The car in my correspondent's photo looks like a 1933 Hillman Wizard 75 straight-six side valve. The factory cars had 'KV' registrations.

But the timing is unusual because by 1934 production of Rootes big cars had been rationalised and the smaller Humber-engined Hillman Wizard 65 had been replaced by the Humber 16/60. If any readers remember James Thomas Skinner, please contact Raymond Skinner directly on 01793 731340.

Early E-Types

Two readers have followed up on the restoration of the original 150 mph, road-test E-Type Jaguar '9600 HP'. J.E., who owns the white 32,000 mile Series II he recently recommissioned from hibernation in his garage asks if 'HP' was the personal registration of H.N. (Tim) Priaulx, managing director of *The Autocar* in 1961. J.E. got a job with the magazine at that time, at the princely salary of £7 10s 0d a week, and remembers Tim Priaulx driving him down Victoria Street at 70 mph in the E-Type to help him catch his train. J.B. of Rochdale is also restoring an early E-Type, this one a cream roadster built in April 1962, chassis no. 850502, originally supplied to Lad & Co.. It was imported from Pakistan in 1989 and since only one E-Type was exported to Pakistan in 1962, he wonders if his is the same car.

The car in his life

" *I am compiling an illustrated account of my father's life. A photograph taken in the mid-1920s shows him in his car. Could you identify it?* "

The distinctive shoulders of the radiator clearly identify it as a French Leon Bollee. Leon Bollee started making tricars in his father's factory and these were among the fastest cars of the 1890s, winning the first London to Brighton Emancipation Run. But by 1903 Bollee had moved on to large four-wheeled cars designed for the American market with 4.6 litre and 8.0 litre, four-cylinder engines and, by 1907, an enormous 11.9 litre Six. Electric lighting, as fitted to your father's car, was introduced in 1913 and 'LL' is a London registration issued from March to July 1914, which pins down the date of first registration to Spring 1914, but 'LL' records have been destroyed.

Straight and true in Booleroo

" *During a recent visit to Australia I spotted a 1924 Maxwell tourer on show as part of an interesting collection of old tractors and traction engines at Booleroo Centre, South Australia. The engine number is C497033. Can you tell me anything further about the car?* "

Maxwell was an American company which grew out of Maxwell-Briscoe. Once Jonathan Maxwell began to specialise in simple four-cylinder cars and trucks in 1912 he was very successful and output grew to 100,000 in 1917. But he was taken over by Chrysler in 1923 and because the Chrysler Six outsold the Maxwell Four, production of the Maxwell was discontinued in 1925. Chrysler later developed a low-cost Chrysler Four which became the Plymouth marque in 1928. Note the dodgy combination of no front brakes and no 'roo' bars.

The Clarabelle con

" *I bought 'Clarabelle' from a destitute friend of my 23-year-old brother for £40 in 1961 and, after several fun-filled drives to local pubs, hostelries and the like while on leave, returned to work in Bangkok. Foolishly, I expected to find her still in residence on my return two years later. But it was not to be. He had re-sold her to another of his 'friends' for 'an unknown sum', which he had long since swallowed. My feelings need no explanation or clarification. I'd give my eye teeth still to own 'UC 4029' and have often speculated whether or not she is still alive. I'd love to know – and to see her restored to the sort of condition I'd planned.* **"**

Looks like a 13.9HP 1926–30 Flatnose Oxford to me. You won't get any joy from 'UC' London registration records because they have been destroyed. But you might have some success making enquiries with the Morris Register, c/o Donald Moore, White Cottage, Jasmine Lane, Lower Claverham, Bristol BS19 4PY, tel: 01934 832340; and the Morris Cowley & Oxford Club, c/o Derek Andrews, 202 Chantry Gardens, Southwick, Trowbridge, Wilts BA14 9QX, tel: 01225 766800. Because the car had survived from the 1920s to the 1960s, there is a good chance that someone has preserved it.

M–O spells MO

" *An elderly friend of mine cannot drive any more and has sold his car. But in his garage he also has a 1950 Morris Traveller in good condition as far as I can see. It is the type with the split windscreen. May I ask if you can tell him where and how he can sell it and give him some idea of its value?* **"**

It can't be a Morris Minor Traveller because there was no such thing until October 1953. It can't be a Morris Oxford MO Traveller either, because these did not arrive until 1952. (You can tell the MO from the Minor because besides being bigger it has a column- rather than a floor-gearshift and a much bigger, chromed grille.) Try an ad in *Practical Classics* magazine, which values Morris Minor Series II Travellers at £450 to £3,100 according to condition and MO Travellers at £500 to £2,850.

Commercial conundrum

" *In 1949 in Gloucester I passed my driving test in a 1926 Morris Commercial One Ton lorry. It had wood-spoked wheels, rear-wheel brakes only, cork clutch, three forward gears with a gate change, magneto ignition, no self-starter, gravity fuel tank, door on passenger side only and a maximum speed of just 25 mph. It would go anywhere in top gear and was used both on road and farm. I drove it for nearly two years on two trips from Dymock to Gloucester each week to collect pig swill from hotels and restaurants and in that time it never broke down. I would love to know if the lorry survived and, if so, where it is now.* "

Can any reader help? These trucks had the 1,802 cc, 13.9 HP, side-valve engine from the 'Oxford'. In 1926 alone 7,561 were registered, and some have survived, as British Car Auctions sold a 1924 van version in 1995 and Sothebys sold a 1926 tipper in 1996. The Historic Commercial Vehicle Society has already helped as much as it could. Its address is Iden Grange, Cranbrook Road, Staplehurst, Kent TN12 0ET, fax: 01580 893227.

Figaro, figaro, figaro!

" *I saw a smart-looking little car the other day and don't recall having seen a similar one before. It was a rhd 'J'-reg. Nissan Figaro. Could you please tell me something about it?* "

This is a bit of a celebrity motor in the UK as Vanessa Feltz, Betty Boo and Mrs Jonathan Ross have all owned Figaros. They were the last and best of a series of retro-styled cars built at Nissan's Pike factory which began with the 1.0 litre, Mk 1 Micra-based Be-1, progressed through the 1.5 litre, Sunny-based, S-Cargo van and 1.0 litre, Micra-based, Pao utility car and ended with the turbo-charged, air-conditioned, automatic, 1.0 litre, Micra-based Figaro. The Figaro was built in 1991, was limited to 20,000 units and prospective buyers were chosen by lottery. Colours are grey and cream or pastel green and cream – similar to the colours of the 1950s Goggomobiles which inspired the Figaro. The full-length sun roof and rear window fold away. Prices reflect 'want factor' and scarcity, but have gone off from the £15–£18k of a few years ago to £8k–£12k now. One was entered in the H&H 'Classic' sale at Pavilion Gardens, Buxton on 16 February 2000 and fetched £8,205 including premium.

Cutting a dash

" *I have a 'Merry Olds' Oldsmobile which was imported from the USA in 1959. It appears to be a 1905 car, but is fitted with a 1950s Kohler engine. Could you help me on values: 1905 if original and 1950s if a replica. It runs well and is taxed and MOT tested for road use.* "

If it was a genuine, original 1901–04 'Curved Dash' Oldsmoblie, then it would be worth £13,000–£14,000. But I don't think it is, and have a dim memory of replicas being made. If it is a replica, then I wouldn't reckon on more than £2,000–£3,000. The best source of advice about its pedigree is the Veteran Car Club of Great Britain, c/o Margaret Golding, Jassamine Court, 15 High Street, Ashwell, Herts SG7 5NL, tel: 01462 742818, fax: 01462 742997.

Risen from the ashes

" *This happy, group picture was taken by my recently demobbed father in 1919 or 1920 outside the family home in St. Leonards-on-Sea. We think that the car was a Phoenix. Looking at the rear it would appear to have no back seats or even a dicky. You may be able to throw some light on this.* "

You're right. It is a Phoenix 8/10 HP, built from 1909 to 1913. This had a transversely mounted, side-valve, vertical, two-cylinder engine of 1,272 cc with primary drive by chain to a three-speed gearbox and another chain driving the rear wheels. The model was superseded by the 11.9 HP which had a conventional in-line engine and gearbox, but a Renault-like coalscuttle bonnet and radiator in the scuttle. The original Phoenix factory was in North London, but manufacturing moved to Letchworth, Herts in 1911. There is a photo of the 8/10 HP on page 237 of *The Complete Catalogue of British Cars 1895–1975* by Culshaw & Horrobin, now in reprint (ISBN 1-874105-93-6). The back is exactly as you thought.

Poles apart

" *Following the death of my father-in-law I acquired his FSO Polski Fiat 125P. It is box-shaped and looks very similar to a Lada. I have never seen another of its kind, so wondered if you could tell me anything about it and, more importantly, where I can get spares.* "

The original Russian-assembled Lada 1200 was the 1960s Fiat 124, adapted for Russian conditions, and built on the original Fiat 124 production line exported to Russia. At the same time, Fiat moved its production line for the 125 model to Poland. The 125 was a 124 with a longer bonnet and boot, originally fitted with useful 1,608 cc, twin cam engine. But the FSO 125 P had engines and gearboxes from the Fiat 1300/1500 which pre-dated the 124. It later turned into the FSO Polonez, and later still into the FSO Caro, which was still around in the 1990s. Amazingly, there is an FSO Owners' Club (including Polski Fiat register), c/o Simon

McDonald-Elliott, Cottage Workshops, The Graig, Water-Trough Lane, Llanwenarth Citra, Abergavenny NP7 7EN, tel: 01873 810517. This should be able to help you with spare parts and advice. Fiat has now gone full circle and continues to produce both the Panda and the Seicento at its Polish factory.

Babs's steering wheel

" I unearthed and restored the Higham Special, 'Babs' ,which took the world land speed record of 171.09 mph on Pendine Sands in 1926. Parry Thomas was killed the following year while he was trying to break Malcolm Campbell's new record of 174.88 mph and the remains of the car were buried for 42 years. When I commenced restoration of 'Babs', I loaned the original, damaged and heavily corroded steering wheel to The Steering Wheel Club in London in 1977. The club has now vanished, and so has my steering wheel. Do any of your readers know what happened to it? "

This could well have been stolen and illegally sold on. Would anyone with any information as to its whereabouts please telephone Owen Wynn Owen on 01690 720216.

Mays days

" I was pleased to see the Raymond Mays get a mention in the list of English V8s on 29 April. He used the 1936–38m side-valve, 2,868 cc Standard V8 in the five Raymond Mays cars built in 1939. Two still exist. I own the prototype, 'FLN 386' while a Carlton coupe 'FLN 388' was recently sold to a collector in the USA. If any readers have any information about the Raymond Mays cars I would be delighted to hear from them. "

Alan Mowlem's address is Water Farm, Sogursey, Bridgwater, Somerset TA5 1PS.

Rusting in pieces

" I need to dispose of the remains of a 1938 Riley, which is still registered in the name of my father who died a few years ago. If wondered if, at most, it might be restorable or if, at least, it would yield some parts to an enthusiast. Or should I send it to the scrap yard? "

I think this is an example of the rare Riley Victor (not to be confused with the unique Victor Riley) and should be preserved if at all possible. In any case, the breaker might charge up to £50 to take it off your hands, so your best financial option is to give the car to an enthusiast on condition he takes it all away. The two clubs to contact are: Riley Motor Club Ltd, c/o J.S. Hall, Treelands, 127 Penn Road, Wolverhampton WV3 0DU, tel: 01902 773197; and Riley Register, c/o Jim Clarke, 56 Cheltenham Road, Bishop's Cleve, Cheltenham, Glos GL52 4LY, tel: 01242 673598, website: www.uk-classic-cars.com/rileyregister.htm.

Any other reader with a rusting and unwanted relic should contact the appropriate club of which there is a directory in every issue of *Practical Classics* magazine.

Imp and reg reunited

" *In 'Mystery Motors' on 20 March and pages 197–198 of last year's Book of Motoring Answers you kindly featured my request for information about the early life of a 1935 Riley Imp, chassis no. 6027678, which has unique, smooth-edged wings. I was then sent a photo of several UK number plates, screwed to a wall in Texas, and one, 'BRA 763', turned out to have originally been allocated to a Riley Imp in 1934. A little later, I had a call from a reader who believed that the car had been owned by Neville Duke in 1945. So I wrote to Squadron Leader Duke and received a very nice letter back with a couple of photographs confirming that the registration had, indeed, been 'BRA 763'. I then traced the original county council records and found that the chassis number and registration matched. After a bit of a struggle, the original registration has been reallocated to the Riley by the DVLA and it is now very much as it was in 1935, so thank you to all concerned.* "

Excellent news. Thanks to everyone.

The Ghost of Donald Dale

Peter Baines of The Rolls Royce Enthusiasts' Club has supplied details of the origins of the Rolls Royce Silver Ghost 'SD 6295' pictured on page C11 on 1 May. Its chassis number was 61 JG. It was delivered in chassis form to the Clyde Automobile Co. Ltd, 96–102 Renfrew Street, Glasgow on 14 September 1921, fitted with 'springs for a Landaulette body weighing approximately 9.75 cwt, seating 7'. The first owner was J. Arthur Findlay of Beith, near Glasgow. According to Rodney Dale, his father bought the car in 1952 and sold it to a film company in

1953. They modified it to make it look like a Hispano Suiza for the film *Beat the Devil*, which was set on the European Mediterranean coast and in North Africa. The RREC does not know what became of the car.

How Rover 8s were made

" *I was fascinated by the extract from Rodney Dale's Halcyon Days published on 1 May, in particular the piece about the Rover 8. I can supply a little bit of history about this car. After the First World War, Rover took on the munitions factory at Tyseley (formerly a steam locomotive works). Through most of the 1920s Rover 8s spilled out of there, but not as complete cars. The factory was not big enough to build the bodies as well, so one of each pair was fitted with a temporary body and towed the other bare chassis 15 miles to West Orchard Works, Coventry where the bodies were fitted. Buyers might get a partly run-in car or one that had not been run at all, but they never knew which it would be!* "

Readers tell me that there are around 30 survivors of the original 17,700 built and have sent pictures of their own cars. R.R. of Wigston has a brown 1923 two seater, a photo of which he asked me to send to G.S. of Margaretting. He tells us that the main problem with early cars was that the cylinder heads were held on by metal straps and it was not until late 1921 that the heads were fixed in place by five studs. Meanwhile, J.C. of Duffield wrote of how he performed a nostalgic reunion between Mrs Nina Salter of Shrewsbury and his Rover 8, similar to a car in which she was driven all over Middlesex in the early 1920s by her mother. British Aerospace was criticised for applying the Rover name to small cars such as the Metro and Mini, so when the 'Rover' Mini is revived by BMW next year, people should remember that the first Rover 8 appeared in 1904 and the later type of

1919–24 was Britain's most popular small car before the Austin 7.

French, but British

" I owned a magnificent British Salmson 12/55, four-seat tourer (reg. 'YJ 3744') from 1960 to 1962 and it was rare even then. French Salmsons were, of course, famous for their racing successes in the 1920s. My Raynes Park, Wimbledon-built car was a coach-built tourer, not a racer, with a 1,471 cc, twin-cam, hemi-headed engine that was so well balanced it would idle at 200 rpm. (The bores were guaranteed for 40,000 miles.) My car drew attention wherever it went, but the downside of ownership was an unreliable Dynastart and self-wrapping Bendix cable brakes, which called for extreme caution in the wet. I believe that only 27 examples survived when I owned my car. I sold it for £110 and have discovered that it was last registered in 1971. There used to be an owners' club, but I have lost track of it. "

The latest address I have for the British Salmson Owners Club is c/o D. Cannings, 61 Holyrood Gardens, Edgware, Middlesex HA8 5LS. Salmsons continued to be built in France until 1957, but the British factory closed on the outbreak of war in 1939. The car was important enough for Dinky Toys to make a model of it in the 1930s.

Salmson and Djerba

" Some years ago while on holiday on the island of Djerba in southern Tunisia I saw a car parked under a tree looking as if this had been its home for some time. Its badge bore the name 'Salmson', it was right-hand-drive and the number plate appeared to be local. "

It's a French Salmson 14HP, imported to the UK by British Salmson with rhd as the S4–61 and tested by *The Autocar* on 17 February 1939. The body was a four-door, pillarless saloon, the engine a four-cylinder, twin overhead-cam unit of 1,730 cc and gearbox a four-speeder. It was advanced for its day, with transverse-leaf independent front suspension, cantilever rear suspension and servo brakes. *The Autocar* got a 'best' top speed of 73 mph from it.

Air Mail Motor

" *Can you tell me anything about a 'streamlined' car registered 'BLB 444' and in the livery of Royal Air Mail Services, circa 1935.* "

The car is a 1934–36 Singer 11 HP 'Airstream' modified from the A pillar back with special streamlined bodywork. Dinky Toys did a model of this in the 1930s (No. 34a Royal Mail Air Service Car), now worth £300 plus, and even did an Air Mail Pillar Box (No. 12c). Both were painted blue.

My old smoker

" *The Kaye Don Singer shown on 26 June reminded me of a six-cylinder Singer, 'AYY 191', I once owned. It was 1957 and I was working for Vauxhall Motors in Luton when I answered a box number advertisement in Motor Sport. The ad ran: 'Dear old lady requires a good home. 1.5 litre Singer. Offers.' Being impecunious at the time, I offered £30 unseen. The owner turned out to be a bank manager who wrote back to say that if I saw the car I would increase my offer appreciably. I wrote back, stating that my offer still stood, heard nothing for four weeks, then received a letter that, in the absence of any other offers, mine was accepted. All for a car I had not even seen. The car turned out to be a 1934 Singer 1.5 litre Grand Touring model. It had an overhead cam, in-line six with twin Solex carbs, four-speed crash box, 14-inch Lockheed hydraulic brakes, a bonnet that disappeared over the horizon and an exhaust pipe you could almost crawl up. Inside were leather seats with inflatable cushions, a lovely sprung, four-spoke steering wheel and no less than three cigarette lighters. And in the boot were two boxes containing more than £30 worth of spares. What a buy.* "

This was quite a highly regarded car, with a four-main bearing, 1,493 cc engine and 70 mph capability. The three fag lighters make me wonder if it might have been an Alfred Dunhill special. The people to tell you more (and whether or not it survived) are: Martin Wray, Singer Owners' Club, 11 Ermine Rise, Great Casterton, Stamford, Lincs PE9 4EJ, tel: 01780 762740; Peter Hart, 27 Rivershill, Watton-at-Stone, Hertfordshire SG14 3SD, tel: 01920 830419; or Anne Page, Association of Singer Car Owners, 39 Oakfield, Rickmansworth, Herts WD3 2LR, tel: 01923 778575, email: http://www.uk-classic-cars.com/singer.htm. A similar car, bored out to 1,600 cc and rebuilt into the 'Cannizone Special' sold at British Car Auctions, Blackbushe on 20 February 1995 for £11,763, including commission. Unfortunately it was uncatalogued, so I have no further details.

S - SAIR - HEID - NODDIN?

" My father, who is now aged 88, had his first ever car ride in this splendid old vehicle. He and his brother referred to it as 'S - SAIR - HEID – NODDIN', which I think may be a child's misinterpretation of its real but unfamiliar name. When photographed, I think that the car was parked in Great Western Road, Aberdeen and, in view of the wheels, perhaps a ride in it did give the young passengers a 'sore head nodding'. Cold you please let me know the car's real make? "

It's a Sizaire Naudin of either just before or just after WW1.

SS100 hunt

" I am trying to trace the history of my SS100, registration 'GLB 300'. So far I have got back to 1950 when the car was owned by Capt. George Rollison in Cheshire. I know that the car was sold new in 1941 by Henly of London and that at that time it was black. I would be interested to hear *from anyone who may have owned, worked on or remembers the car during the period 1941–50. It may be of interest to other SS aficionados that for years I have been compiling a register of SS100s and so far can account for 266 of the original 309 produced, but my research has left me a little puzzled on some details of the following registrations. If anyone can help me with information about these, or knows if they still exist, I would be very interested to hear from them. I would also like to hear from anyone who owned an SS100 between 1940 and 1970 and has the details. I may be able to advise them what happened to their cars.* "

- BPH 800: M. Day, London, early 1950s
- CWT 192: M. Newton, London, late 1950s
- SS 4690: R. Paul, Burton Wood, Lancs, early 1950s
- FAU 620: Hampshire, mid 1950s
- EN 7800: Camberley, Surrey, 1958
- FYH 956: Liverpool, 1955
- DDU 822: Malden, Essex, 1960
- FGX 312: Liverpool, 1960
- CYU 483: B. Mason, early 1950s
- DAF 257: Cornwall, late 1940s
- JV 5950: London, mid 1950s
- GS 8040: London, mid 1950s
- FLO 348: London, early 1950s
- GND 171: Kent, early 1960s
- DXT 800: Kent, early 1960s
- CYR 339: Eastbourne, late 1940s
- KDG 620: H.A. Mecrow
- AFR 866: Dora Sheldon, Blackpool, 1940s
- DSD 100: Bolsover, Derby, 1960s
- BWX 1: Yorkshire, 1940s
- HMX 1: London, 1950s
- CPL 943 (SS90): Portsmouth, 1950s
- XG 4673: Wales, 1957
- CDA 431: A.R. Twentyman, Wolverhampton, early 1950s

Would readers with any information, please telephone Graham Bull on 01252 614163, or fax him on 01252 629298.

Tell me about my Talbot

" *Could any of your readers fill the gaps in the history of my 1925 Talbot 10/23 Tourer, reg. 'XX 5363'. All I know is that it was delivered to Warwick Wright Ltd in 1925, although a plate on the instrument panel states, 'Supplied by Wallace Turner & Co. Ltd, 94 Baker Street, London W1'. The earliest owner in the old green log book is a Percy Gilbert of Cobham, Surrey, who had the car in 1939.* "

London 'XX' registration records have been destroyed. Would readers with any information please contact R. Heald on 01547 540477.

14/45

" *In 1939 my father and a couple of his pals went on a tour of the West Country from Gillingham in Kent. They did this in a four-year-old, 14-horsepower Talbot drop-head coupe. I am keen to find out more about this type of car and wonder if you could shed any light on its history.* "

The history of Talbot/Darracq and Sunbeam, and their eventual emasculation by the Rootes brothers is a long and complicated one. But a 14/45 (known as the '65' from 1932) is a genuine Talbot, built from 1926 to 1935. The car had an exceptionally smooth, 1,666 cc, six-cylinder, overhead-valve engine designed by Georges Roesch developing 46 bhp and giving the car a top speed of 65 mph with an average fuel consumption of 27 mpg. A total of 11,851 were built. There is a picture of a 1928 14/40 tourer on page 310 of Culshaw & Horrobin's *Complete Catalogue of British Cars 1895–1965* (ISBN 1-874105-93-6). You could order a copy of *Georges Roesch and the Invincible Talbot*, priced £49.95 from Mill House Books on 01205 270377. They also offer a slimmer volume, *Pre-War Talbot*, for £9.95.

Pretty special

" *Back in 1958 my brother and I had a small business producing GRP mouldings, including the 'Townend 581' body for Ford 8/10 chassis. Although, as the designer, I say it myself, I think the body was very good looking for its day. Other models were planned, but the advent of the Mini killed off the special building movement. Is there any chance that 'SNU 208' or any other Townend 581s could have survived?* "

I agree, it is a very pretty shape. Your best hope is to contact Richard Disbrow of the Historic Specials Register, 16 The Close, Blandford Forum, Dorset DT11 7HA, tel: 01258 454879. But have any readers stumbled across a Townend 581? And does anyone know what happened to 'SNU 208'?

Rally Triumphs

" *Donald Healey did not drive a Triumph Dolomite Straight Eight in the 1935 Monte Carlo Rally. The car destroyed on a level crossing was an Invicta. The Straight Eight Dolomite was not developed until 1937/38 and was a two-seater open car fitted with a Wilson self-change gearbox. I drove it many times prior to 1939, but it was never put into production. As co-driver to Healey, I drove a 1,500 cc Triumph Vitesse in the 1937 Harrogate to Hastings RAC rally, passing through Norwich, Gloucester, Penzance and Andover. We drove day and night in those days and we won the 1,500 cc class.* "

We stand corrected. But Sedgwick & Gillies *A to Z of Cars of the 1930s* gives the production years of the Straight Eight Dolomite as 1934–35 and states that three prototypes were built with four-speed Wilson pre-selector boxes. This is why I did not alter D.H.'s account of the level-crossing incident.

Waterfall grille

" *I drove 'DDU 872', a 1.5 litre Triumph Dolomite roadster in the Blackpool RAC Rally of 1938. In 1997 I attended the RAC dinner in Cheltenham as a veteran rally driver and watched the start of the 1997 event the following morning. I am now 92 years old, am still driving my 120,000 mile VW Scirocco regularly and hope to continue doing so for many years to come.* "

As long as you remain fit in mind and body and undergo regular eye tests, age should not be an obstacle to driving. John O'Doherty of Hayes owns a similar car to your 1.5 litre Dolomite roadster. His is a 1939 model, reg. 'FYX 243' in metallic red and has a perfect hand-made replica waterfall grille which took hundreds of hours to cast, braze together and plate. There is a model-specific club: Pre-1940 Triumph Owners' Club, c/o Jon Quinney, 2 Duncroft Close, Reigate, Surrey RH2 9DE, tel: 01737 247218.

Pre-war trio

" *The photograph on the home page of www.mysterymotors.com shows my father's Vauxhall lined up with a Crossley (left) and a Dennis (centre). Can you tell me the registration date of the Vauxhall? The Crossley had acetylene lighting. When did acetylene give way to the electric lighting of the other cars?* "

'BY' was a London registration from December 1903 to 1922, but these London registration records have been destroyed. I think the car is a Vauxhall B11 30 HP, introduced in 1911 with a six-cylinder engine cast in two blocks of three after the 27 HP monobloc six of the previous year proved prone to cracking. Vauxhall offered optional electric lighting from 1910, but other makers caught on gradually and it was not until after the First World War that it became almost universal. Eric Dymock has written a nice history of Vauxhall, entitled *The Vauxhall File* and covering all models since 1903 (ISBN 0-9534142-1-3).

Which Wolseley?

" *Would it be possible to trace the history of a Wolseley? The registration is 'OB 8117' and the photo was taken in the early 1920s. The car bears an AA badge on its radiator cap and an RAC badge in front of the screen. How much would a car like this have cost?* "

I think it's a 4,961 cc, Wolseley 24/30 HP, six-cylinder Torpedo of 1914 or 1915. Not 1913 because 1913s had a more rounded, old-fashioned scuttle. Taking the information from Charles Neville's book *Wolseley Cars in Canada 1900–1920*, these cost $5,000 and I think about £650 in the UK. Records of 'OB' Birmingham registrations have been destroyed, but you may be able to find out more from The Wolseley Register c/o Mike Schilling, 46 Manse Wood Road, Glasgow G43 1TN.

P.M. of Thatcham later identified the car as a 1914 16/20 Special Sporting model which is differentiated from the 24/30 by having cut-away rear doors to clear the rear mudguards.

I got a real buzz out of this

" *Back in November 1997 I sought your advice in tracing 'GY 3279', the 1932 Wolseley Hornet Special Swallow model which I owned from 1939 to 1946 and, of course, never found much time to use. Roger Banks and the Wolseley Hornet Special Club were a huge help, telling me that the car had been restored by Aubrey Kirkham of Shropshire in 1991. I eventually traced it to the Roman Garage near Grantham in Lincolnshire where I visited the car with a large contingent of my family and found it to be in as fine condition as it was in 1939. The car has now been sold to another private owner.* "

Many thanks for letting me know the outcome. Anyone with a Wolseley Hornet Special would be extremely foolish not to join the Wolseley Hornet Special Club, c/o Chris Hyde, Kylemor, Crown Gardens, Fleet, Hants GU13 9PD, tel: 01252 622411. This is a very active club which organises events and rallies all over Europe.

Yak yakkety yak

" *My friend Colin has bought a 21-year-old Yak Yeoman. Everyone thinks it's a kit car. We think it was manufactured in Gorton, Manchester and may be related to the 'Africar'. It has a 1300 cc Ford engine and high- and low-range gears with a Sure Drive locking differential. Do you know any more about it? Apparently there was once a small fleet used for deliveries in Rumney, Cardiff. Is there an owners' club? Are any more left?* "

Got nothing on it apart from a brief mention in Chris Rees's *British Specialist Cars* (Windrow & Greene). He tells us it was the final product of Grantura Cars which lasted from 1968 to 1973, kicked off with a TVR-like Ford V6 coupe called the Gem and followed up with 'the Mini-based Moke-style Yak (production 150)'. Colin's Ford engine, reduction gearbox, limited slip diff and what appears to be a winch give the lie to this, but that's all I can tell you. The Africar project was much later, in the 1980s, and ended badly. Your best bet for further information is one of the kit-car magazines, even though this Yak looks to have been professionally built.

The Stanbury TT

" *Please could you include my car in 'Mystery Motors'? It is a one-off*

Triumph-Herald-based special, reg. 'BYA 234B', and I was informed by the previous owner that it was built by a chap in Yeovil as a replica of 'a 1930's Stanbury TT'. I can find no record of this maker and would like to complete the car to make it as close to the original concept as possible. Could anyone with any knowledge of the Stanbury TT, or the original builder of the car, please contact me? "

The usual sources list a 'Stanbury' 12 HP model as having been built and tested in 1903, but that is all that is known about it, and your car is obviously not a replica of this. Perhaps someone built a Standard sports special in the 1930s and called it the 'Stanbury'. Or the chap from Yeovil who built your car was called 'Stan Bury'. Would readers with any information please contact Michael Clissold direct on 01794 884454.

Mystery racing career

" *My father was a modest man and was particularly economical with stories of his escapades as a racing driver for fear of being thought a 'show-off'. He actively drove Lotus and Jaguar cars, mainly for privateer teams, and may have even raced for Aston Martin, for whom he was a test driver. His name was John Sutcliffe and he ceased racing when he married my mother. Can any of your readers help me piece together his racing career?* "

Would readers with any information please write to Dr Peter Sutcliffe at 37 Aquila Way, Langtoft, Peterborough PE6 9NN, or email him at peter.sutcliffe1@virgin.net

COOLING SYSTEM

Blowing his top

" *I have a top-of-the-range VW Golf VR6 and I am now faced with a bill of £7,000 for replacing its entire engine. The car is a 1993 model with 65,000 miles on the clock, mostly driven carefully in town. Last year I had to spend £2,000 replacing the distributor, the cooling system, all fuel pipes in the engine and the clutch. This year, while driving on a French autoroute, the cooling system warning light came on. I continued driving for 4–5 miles searching for somewhere to stop. The car could not then be restarted and had to be recovered by transporter. Once it was repatriated I commissioned an AA report which revealed that the piston crown of no. 5 cylinder had been completely burned away and there was evidence of massive overheating. VW has considered my case, but rejected any claim. What happened to VW reliability? I am an extremely dissatisfied customer.* "

Driving a powerful car in London year after year is one of the worst things you can do to it, so a clutch life of 55,000 miles or so is not unreasonable. The VAG VR6 is one of the most 'bullet-proof' performance engines ever built and there is no doubt in my mind that the problem which caused the engine failure was set in motion by last year's cooling system failure – itself probably the result of overheating in traffic. The VR6 is a narrow-angle 'V' with all cylinders sharing the same cylinder head. This is a big area to keep sealed and the cooling system failure of 1998 will have weakened the cylinder head gasket adjacent to no. 5 cylinder. At the high temperatures generated by your French autoroute trip, the gasket will have given way, allowing coolant into the combustion chamber. What then happens, according to Keith Rhoods of Wheelbase, who races a Vento VR6, is that the steam creates an extremely weak mixture in that combustion chamber leading to massive overheating and the melting of the piston crown. By not stopping as soon as the warning light came on, you destroyed your own engine. However, you don't need to pay £7,000 to have it replaced. Call Keith or Colin at Wheelbase on 01932 252515 and they will quote you a much lower price.

Hot and bothered

" I own a 1983 Jaguar Daimler 4.2 Sovereign, which is still in beautiful condition and goes like a bomb. However, ever since I purchased it some four or five years ago I have needed to top up the radiator cooling system quite regularly. I use a 3:1 antifreeze mixture and there is certainly no leak. The oil colour is perfect and certainly as good as most cars, and there is no sign of the water having found its way into the sump. Can you offer any guidance? "

Nottingham Jaguar specialist David Marks (01159 405370) gave me the reason for this several years ago. The iron and alloy Jaguar engine is a corrosion battery which requires a thorough flush of its cooling system every two years, followed by replacement of its coolant with a Trigard MPG solution, the corrosion inhibitors of which last longer than those in an MEG solution. Unless this is done, corrosion sludge collects in the waterways at the rear of the block, blocking them and causing localised overheating. This in turn creates steam, leading to air-

locks which blow out some of the coolant. It does not register on the temperature gauge because the temperature sensor is at the front of the block. If left unattended, this can result either in the burning out of no. 6 and no. 5 piston crowns, or head gasket failure. The answer is to knock out the rear-block core plug and thoroughly flush out the sludge. This is important because combustion temperatures are higher when running on unleaded petrol than leaded, so the engine must be properly cooled around each combustion chamber.

All steamed up

" *My wife has owned a Citroën ZX 1.9D Avantage since new in 1992. This has generally been a very reliable and useful car with the exception of the heating system. The matrix has now been replaced no less than five times. My son has had two Peugeot 405 TD estate cars and on these he has had the matrixes replaced twice. Is there a problem with PSA heater matrixes?* **"**

It's not a materials problem as has been the case with Renault Lagunas. It's due to the cooling system becoming excessively pressurised because of airlocks. All iron-block engines with alloy heads are corrosion batteries, and corrosion inhibitors in the coolant usually become ineffective after about three years. The area around the cylinder head and the cylinder head gasket then start to be eaten away and the sludge this creates can cause partial blockages in the system leading to air locks. The other difficulty with PSA's XUD engine is replacing the coolant, because if this is not done very carefully with due attention paid to ridding the system of any air, it will pressurise and find its weakest point. A few years ago, VW recalled most of its model range going back ten years, firstly to fit pressure-relief valves in the system and secondly to replace the heater matrixes free of charge if these had become sufficiently weakened to spring a leak. The reason was that if a heater matrix burst when the outside temperature was sub-zero, the car would instantly steam up leaving the driver with no visibility. Not what you want at high speed on the autobahn.

Heads together

" *Your advice to 'hot and bothered' regarding his 1983 Daimler 4.2 was extremely helpful. Fitting a temperature sensor at the rear of the block to warn of localised overheating is virtually impossible, so preventative measures of regular flushing and use of a high-boiling-point coolant such as 'For-Life' or Trigard MPG is the only way. But instead of scrapping a cylinder head with badly corroded waterways, we can weld and* *re-machine to the original size, thereby saving a rapidly disappearing commodity.* "

This came from Engine Machine Services (UK) Ltd of Worksop, tel: 01909 482649, website: www.engine-machining-services.co.uk, which is also so honest it recommends oil changes at least twice as frequently as manufacturers include in service schedules.

Losing your cool

" *I read 'Hot and Bothered' with interest. I have the same problem with my 1986 BMW 318i. Again there is no evidence of a water leak except for a spot below the lowest point in the exhaust system which is more likely to be condensation. Engine performance is good, but petrol consumption is only about 35 mpg on a long trip. The radiator was re-cored three years ago, but had to be replaced this week due to the top tank developing a split. Yet the coolant loss persists.* "

In 1998 170,000 E30 BMW 3-Series were recalled because the radiator cap pressure valve may seize up and over-pressurise the cooling system, leading to fracturing of the heater matrix and steaming up inside the car. So visit a BMW franchise and make sure your car has been fitted with a modified radiator cap. Next, get rid of any airlocks inside the system by running the engine from cold with the cap off and gently squeezing all the rubber pipes as they heat up and soften. If that doesn't solve it, then you have a constriction in the system somewhere caused by corrosion. This is most likely to be in the water-heated part of the inlet manifold, so pull the pipes off and have a look in there.

DE-MYSTIFIED MOTORS

1 What is a warranty?

Most secondhand cars sold by dealers come
with a warranty which is either part of the deal
or optional at extra cost. Unless this warranty
is the balance of the original manufacturer's or
importer's 12-month, 24-month or 36-month
warranty, it is not what most of us understand
as a guarantee. Instead, it is mechanical breakdown insurance (MBI), underwritten and ad-
ministered by an insurance company. The cover
provided by MBIs varies hugely, from 'bumper
to bumper' including some wearing items (as is
the case with Warranty Holdings warranties negotiated by Trade Sales of Slough) down to
'major components only' up to £100 per claim.
A vital term of the warranty contract is that you
must get any replacements or repairs approved
by the warranty insurer beforehand, or your
claim may be turned down. Before paying for
an MBI warranty, ask to see a sample warranty
booklet or document and read it thoroughly so
you fully understand exactly what is covered
and on exactly what terms. Warranties are sold
on commission, so the last thing you want to do
is buy a £300 warranty of which £250 is com-

mission and only £50 actually pays for the mechanical breakdown insurance itself.

2 What is a Personal Contract Purchase?

Personal Contract Purchases (PCPs) were an idea dreamed up in the USA and imported to the UK as a means of extracting full list prices for new cars from private punters. This is how they work: the punter pays a deposit (which may be in the form of a part-exchange) and contracts to pay the difference between list price and what the car will be worth in two or three years' time, plus interest, in easy monthly instalments. This 'future value' is put on the car up front and when the contract comes to an end the punter has three choices: pay the 'future value' as a lump sum and keep the car, use any difference between the 'future value' and the car's true trade value to part-finance the deposit on another PCP, or walk away with nothing. The trouble is that PCPs were launched at a time when used-car values were high, and since then values have collapsed. So, unless the dealer puts a falsely high value on the car at the end of its contract, most Personal Contract Purchasers are left with no equity to finance the deposit on their next PCP. If the dealer does put a falsely high value on the returned car, he has to finance it by over-pricing the replacement car. You can't win.

3 'Classic' conundrums

L.J. of Huddersfield asks what is meant by the terms 'classic car', 'historic vehicle' and 'VED exempt', all of which appeared in the column on 25 September. Defining what is and is not a 'classic car' is guaranteed to start a protracted argument. So I will say it is any car which a significant number of people regard as 'classic' either because of its age or its aesthetics or both. The Schlump brothers who amassed a vast collection of Bugattis would hardly regard a 1963 Ford Consul Classic as 'classic'. But the man who lovingly polishes his immaculate Consul Classic every Sunday would, and there's even a club for them (Ford Classic and Capri Owners Club, c/o Ray Brandon, 1 Verney Close, Covingham, Swindon, Wilts SN3 5EF). 'Historic vehicle' has now come to have a technical meaning in the eyes of the DVLA (Driver and Vehicle Licensing Authority). It is any vehicle built (not necessarily first registered) *before* 1 January 1973. These vehicles are 'VED exempt' which means that the owners are exempted from paying vehicle excise duty, but must still display a zero-duty-paid tax disc on the windscreen. To get this they have to show a current MOT and insurance certificate.

4 'Screamers' and 'Dreamers'

Some car trade argot is based on Cockney rhyming slang, such as 'Nelsons', 'Billies', 'sausaged', etc. Other terms are just a bit of fun, made up on the spot, including 'crocodiled', 'bidet', 'camel' etc. 'Nelsons' is derived from 1930s crooner Nelson Eddy whose surname just happens to rhyme with 'readies'. A 'Billy Bunter' is a punter. 'Sausaged' comes from 'sausage and mash' which, of course, rhymes with 'crash'. 'Crocodiled' is a highly technical term used to describe car upholstery which has been eaten by a pet dog. A 'bidet' is exactly what you'd think: a rear wash/wipe. While a 'camel' is, of course, a car with an odd and undesirable specification. Getting a bit more personal, a 'screamer' is not a high-revving engine. It is a revved-up customer with a penchant for complaining. 'Dreamers' are punters who don't have the money or the credit rating. 'Tyre kickers' are 'experts' who don't know the first thing about cars but have heard somewhere that it's the done thing to kick the car's tyres. A 'score' is £20, a 'pony' is £25, a 'nifty' is £50, a 'ton' is £100, a 'monkey' is £500 and a 'gripper' is £1,000. 'Spinning for it' is the means auction ringers use to divide up the spoils after a sale. This causes serious 'grief' to the auctioneers, who then have to re-invoice the cars to different account customers than the ones who made the successful bids.

5 Fuel consumption

We buy our fuel in litres, so why do we persist in using 'miles per gallon' as a basis for comparing economy? The answer is that most of us simply would not understand or relate to the Continental method of measuring fuel consumption. When excited engineers refer to 'the three-litre car' they're not talking about the swept capacity of its engine. Instead, they mean that the car will require just three litres of fuel to travel 100 kilometres. 'Litres per 100 km' is how fuel consumption is measured throughout Europe. But it's not too hard for us to start measuring this way as well. For a start, your till receipt shows how many litres you have bought, not how many gallons. Mark your mileage on the receipt after you have filled your tank to the brim. Then brim it again next time you fill up and mark the mileage on that receipt. Subtract the first mileage from the second mileage and multiply the answer by 0.0161. Then divide the litres you have used by the answer and you get your fuel consumption in terms of litres per 100 kilometres. For example, I recently travelled 391 miles on 32.94 litres of DERV in a Seat Toledo TDI 110. Multiply 391 by 0.0161 and you get 6.295. Divide 32.94 by 6.295 and you get 5.23 litres per 100 km. For simplicity's sake, 8 litres per 100 kms = 35.31 mpg; 5 litres per 100 km = 56.5 mpg; and 3 litres per 100 km = 94.16 mpg. To convert mpg to litres per 100 km, a booklet from Citroën tells us to divide 282.5 by the mpg achieved, and to convert litres per 100 km to mpg divide 282.5 by the litres used.

6 'Multivalve' engines

These days, you can buy a four-cylinder engine with eight, 12, 16 or 20 valves. Many readers have asked why the added complexity? And what effect do 'multivalves' have on an engine's performance? Obviously, the bigger the throats that can be opened by the valves, the better the engine will inhale air and fuel, and exhale burned gases. There is a limit to how big two circular valve heads can be in a combustion chamber, so the best way to increase the total size of the valve throats is to increase the number of valves serving each cylinder. Morris Minor engines have two. Audi A3 1.8s have five. Unless an engine with more than three valves per cylinder also has variable valve timing or variable intake ducting, the engine will tend to develop its power and torque quite high in the rev range. This is particularly true of most six-cylinder engines below 2.5 litres and most four-cylinder engines below 2.0 litres, and makes them less than ideal when combined with torque-converter automatic transmissions which can 'bog down' at low revs. Four-cylinder, 20-valve engines are also unlikely to meet future emissions limits without the aid of a turbocharger to help them burn their air/fuel mixtures more completely and emit fewer unburned hydrocarbons. This is why the VAG group has reverted from non-turbo, 20-valve 1.8 litre engines to 8-valve, 2.0 litre engines in the Golf IV and Skoda Octavia.

7 'Understeer' and 'Oversteer'

Readers have offered at least a dozen different definitions of these two characteristics. Leaving wit at the roadside, the simplest definition is 'what the car does in relation to what you ask it to do with the steering wheel'. If the car turns less than you ask it to, it 'under-steers', if it turns more, it 'over-steers'. Depending on how fast it is asked to take a corner, every car will do one or the other at some point, and might even switch from one to the other. The faster it can take corners without doing either, the more 'neutral' the handling is deemed to be. Skilled drivers usually hate understeer and prefer a car to handle neutrally, then gradually oversteer at the limits of adhesion. One of the best cars in this respect is the Porsche 968 Club Sport, but because oversteer can be dangerous in the hands of unskilled drivers, manufacturers have collectively taken the decision to design it out of the handling of most cars. Legendary Swedish rally driver Eric Carlsson told me that the Vauxhall Vectra-based Saab 9-5 is designed to understeer consistently (like the Vectra) and demonstrated how hard it is to provoke any sort of oversteer from this car. A 'Legends' racing car, on the other hand, with its locked and offset solid back axle, oversteers luridly at the earliest opportunity and takes a lot of getting used to.

8 Understanding car auctions 1: The fake 'sale'

When punters first start attending auctions regularly and see the same car seemingly sold week after week, they begin to wonder what is going on. It's really very simple. On the one side, you have vendors who may be car manufacturers, fleet owners, finance companies, dealers, traders or, rarely, private individuals. They are represented by the auctioneer. On the other side you have buyers who may be dealers, traders or members of the public. The vendor sets a 're-serve' price for the car, which is the minimum he says he is prepared to accept. Trade buyers buying for stock know what they can sell the cars for, so naturally try to bid as low as possible in order to maximise their profit. When times are hard, like now, they may want to pay a lot less than the vendors want for their cars. And this is why, at some sales, cars will be 'knocked down' (apparently, but not actually sold) in order to stimulate some action. Auctioneers can be extremely cunning at this. I have seen cars about to be 'knocked down' to a light fitting, then out-bid at the last second by a waste-paper bin. Don't believe everything you see. Keep an eye on the screens at BCA auctions to see which provisional bids really have been accepted. And you'll gradually start to get the feel of the place. (To be continued…)

9 Understanding car auctions 2: 'Trotting'

Last week I mentioned auctioneers taking bids

from light fittings and waste-paper bins in order to give the impression that cars were selling when they weren't. They may also do this against genuine bids when cars have not reached anywhere near their reserve price. This means that, though you think you are bidding against a fellow bidder, what you are really engaged in is a psychological battle of wits with the auctioneer. He will 'run you' or 'trot up' your bids to precisely the point where you will stop bidding. One auctioneer I know is so good at this, I sometimes wonder if he has telepathic powers. Other unscrupulous auctioneers may overdo it, take a high bid 'off the wall', then, finding you do not respond, ask the fictitious 'high bidder' if he really made a bid or was waving to a friend. As the 'under bidder' it is then up to you to decide whether to let your bid stick or not. If you want the car, fine. But if you smell a rat, don't be bullied. Everyone knows what was really going on and the auctioneer probably won't press you if you want to back out.

10 What is a 'grey' import?

With unofficial car imports now soaring towards the 100,000-a-year mark, the word 'grey' is being used to denigrate more imports than it should. If you go to Europe and buy a 'UK spec' rhd, European Type Approved car from an EU franchised dealer, it is not a grey import. It is a 'parallel' import. There is little or no difference between your car and one of the same make and model imported by the official importer. A grey import, on the other hand, is a car built for a non-EU market which will does not conform to EU Type Approved regulations. The vast majority of these are 'Jap Scrap': cars which were headed for Japanese breakers yards but which have been more lucratively exported to poorer countries such as the UK. All such cars less than three years old (and, from March, all such cars less than 10 years old) are subject to a Single Vehicle Approval inspection, which they must pass before they can be registered. But large numbers of 'Jap Scrap' over three years old have been 'personally imported' by dealers, MOT tested and sold on to unsuspecting members of the public. These cars may have been modified to run properly on lower grade UK petrol, but very few will have been rust-proofed to UK market standards which is why it is quite common to see grey imports as young as five years old already in an advanced state of decay. The AA Experian car data checks now cover whether the car you are about to buy is registered as a grey import with the DVLA, tel: 0800 234999 (have your credit card handy).

11 What is a 'chameleon?'

This is a car of many colours, or, more likely, many shades of the same colour. Some colours, especially solid, non-metallic reds such as VAG's old Tornado red, are notoriously difficult to match because they start oxidising as soon as the car is parked in bright sunlight. I had a racing red Alfa once which I bought cheaply because it had been vandalised. The damage was patch-painted. Then someone reversed into the front of the car while it was parked, necessitating another 'hot job' (quick part-respray). It looked all right in the daylight, but under sodium streetlights it resembled a patchwork quilt. The trick with damage is to repaint the whole of the surrounding area up to a natural break. For example, if you scrape the bottom of a door and there is a rubbing strip along the side of the car, have the whole of the side under the rubbing strip repainted. A minor mis-match will then be much harder to spot than if you only had the one half-door re-painted. If you smash a door above the waistline, you may need to have the whole side of the car repainted (front wing, both doors, and rear panel from the roof to the back bumper). A pro will spot this straight away (and check by peeling back the rubber trim strips). But it will make paint mis-matches harder for the average private punter to spot. If you are a damage-prone driver, the best colour to match is and always has been solid dark blue, known in the trade as 'doom blue' because it's one of the hardest colours to sell.

12 What is a 'froster'?

Thanks to the RAC Foundation we have a new vocabulary for the various easy means by which cars or their contents can be stolen. 'Jacking' is the term for hijacking an unlocked car by force at traffic lights, either kidnapping the driver in the process or leaving him or her at the road-side. The same thieves also target handbags and mobile phones left on nearside passenger seats, so always keep your doors locked in town. 'Frosting' is stealing a car while the owner has left it idling to de-frost outside his or her house (leaving a car idling from cold also damages the car and causes severe local pollution). 'Sneaking' is the term for stealing the ignition keys of a car from the owner's house. Far too many people simply leave them hanging on a hook by the door. 'Hooking' is using a stiff piece of wire through the letter box to hook car keys off a hook or a table. 'Gifting' is stealing gifts from cars. Far too many people use their cars as car-park warehouses for the first and second batches of shopping while they go out to buy the next batch. If anything of value is left visible in the car, it's an open invitation to be stolen.

13 What is 'bowler hatting'?

In the good old days when a trader sold a car to another trader, if it turned out to be a dud there was an understanding that he would take it back. Less-scrupulous traders, stuck with a bad car, developed the technique of 'bowler hatting'. They would visit a dealer well off their patch who didn't know them, pretend to be the last owner listed in the log book and either plead poverty and sell the car to the dealer, or swap it for something different of the same value. One lad, nicknamed 'Spider' because he lived by the quotation, 'Oh what a tangled web we weave when first we practise to deceive', came unstuck when a BMW 5-Series he'd bowler-hatted turned out to have a cracked cylinder head and burned-out autobox. The receiving dealer figured out who he really was and sent a professional leg-breaker by the name of 'Frankie the Criminal' after him. Fortunately Spider's garage was right out in the sticks, and when he came up behind a car with a pair of shoulders completely filling the back window, he realised that returning to base wasn't an option. As to be expected, Spider's business methods and severe aversion to paying tax paved the way towards his current status as a land-owning multi-millionaire.

14 What is 'car cloning'?

Very simply, it's running more than one car on the same registration. Photocopies of V5 registration documents are made while cars are 'in the trade'. I won't go into the various ways in which duplicate or 'change of keeper' V5s can then be obtained from the DVLA, but, once they are, a near-identical car is stolen to order, its VIN and registration numbers are changed to match the car it has been cloned from and it is then re-sold with a genuine V5. A pre-purchase check with the data registers rarely helps unless a detail mistake has been made. Alternatively, a trader importing cars less than ten years old not UK Type-Approved may clone successive cars to one with a pukka SVA and V5. But by far the most common form of cloning is the simple 'registration swap' to avoid prosecution for speeding and traffic-light offences caught on camera. All the dodgy owner has to do is spot a car of the same model, colour and year as his own, write down its registration, and have a set of its plates made up to fit on his car. Obviously, there is an element of risk attached. He can't park anywhere patrolled by parking wardens who may spot the discrepancy between plates and tax disc. And he can't afford to get stopped by a police patrol car. But if, say, he already has nine points on his licence and needs it to earn his living, he might consider the risk worth taking. So next time you receive a Fixed Penalty Notice for a speeding offence you definitely did not commit, you'll know why.

15 What is 'lean burn'?

Lean burn is a generic term for engines which are capable of running on a considerably higher proportion of air to fuel than the stoichiometric level of 14.7:1, known as Lambda 1. Honda V-Tech E engines; Toyota Carina E and Avensis 1.6 litre and 1.8 litre engines; and Mitsubishi's 1.8 litre and 2.4 litre GDI's are all capable of running with air to fuel ratios of up to 40:1. The obvious benefits are reduced fuel consumption and reduced emissions through more complete burning of the fuel. Unfortunately, in Europe, lean-burn engines have been legislated against in favour of catalytic converters, the testing of which requires all engines to be capable of running at very close to Lambda 1 in a specified rev band between 2,000 and 3,200 rpm and this has compromised the effectiveness of lean burn. Driving a lean-burn engine requires a different technique from normal economy driving: comparatively high revs with small throttle openings rather than low revs with early upchanges. The reason why so many Carina Es tend to need very expensive Lambda-sensor replacements early in their lives could be the failure of their owners to drive them as instructed by Toyota and instead adopting time-honoured economy driving techniques which are harmful to the extra-sensitive Lambda sensor.

16 What is a 'chip shop'?

'Chipping' is the generic term for re-programming a car engine's electronic management system for increased performance, different performance characteristics, better fuel economy, or to run on a lower grade of fuel. This can be done internally, by dismantling the engine ECU and either replacing or re-programming the chips inside, or externally, by altering the signals from the ECU to the fuel-injection system and ignition igniter. Both petrol and turbo-diesel engines can be 'chipped'. Prices start at £100, but are more usually in the £300–£400 bracket. Practitioners of the art include BBR or Brackley (petrol and diesel Starchips), tel: 01280 700800, website: www.bbr.gti.demon.co.uk; Superchips of Buckingham (petrol and diesel), tel: 01280 816781, website: www.superchips.co.uk; Milford Microsystems of Kidlington (system developments), tel: 01865 331552; AMD, Oxon, tel: 01865 331226; Tim Styles Racing, Somerset, tel: 01278 453036; Siegerland (UK), tel: 0191 4286226, website: www.tuningbox.com; Prima Racing, tel 0115 949 1903; Van Aaken Developments of Crowthorne, tel: 01344 777553, website: www.vanaaken.com; Jetex of Stratford-upon-Avon, tel: 01789 298989, website: www.jetexlimited.

freeserve.co.uk; Webcon of Sunbury (Diesel Torqmaster), tel: 01932 788630, website: www.webcon.co.uk; Darley Specialist Services (Diesel Powerchip), tel 01332 553143. Please note that if you alter the specification of your car in any way you must inform your insurer or your insurance could be void.

17 How do I rate an engine oil?

Readers keep asking and, thanks to Adrian at the Castrol Technical Department, this should provide all the answers. Eighty per cent of an oil is the base oil, which may be mineral, synthetic or a mixture called 'semi-synthetic' (the other 20% is additives). Undesirable compounds cannot be completely refined out of mineral oil, so the purest base oil is fully synthetic. The Society of Automobile Engineers (SAE) ratings of 0W/40, 20W/50, etc. refer to the oil's viscosity (or resistance to flow) at −20°C compared with its viscosity at 100°C. A low cold viscosity oil (0W) has its viscosity at high temperature increased by viscosity-improving additives, which is how 0W/40 or 5W/40 is achieved. Matters have been complicated by new ratings systems devised by the American Petroleum Institute (API) and the Association de Constructeurs Europeans d'Automobiles (ACEA). These are arrived at by testing the oils in engines. For oils for petrol engines, the API rating of SG corresponds with the ACEA A1, SH with A2 and SJ with A3. For oils for diesel engines the API CD corresponds with ACEA B1, CE with B2 and CF with B3. The telephone number of the Castrol technical help desk is 01793 452222 (oils for modern cars) or 01954 231668 (oils for older cars).

18 How do I read my tyres?

Modern tyres are covered in hieroglyphics. Where the main ones read something like '195/60 R 15 87V', 195 is tyre width in millimetres; /60 is the ratio of height to width expressed as a percentage (the lower the figure, the less cushion in the tyre and the harder the car's ride will be); R 15 signifies that the tyre is radial ply and for a 15-inch wheel rim; 87 is the carrying load index; and V is the speed rating. A speed rating of R is up to a maximum of 105 mph, S up to 113 mph, T up to 118 mph, U up to 124 mph, H up to 130 mph, V up to 150 mph, W up to 169 mph, Y up to 175 mph, ZR 150 mph plus with no upper limit. (Some of these ratings are now obsolete and no longer appear on new tyres.) Obviously we don't all drive at these speeds, but if a car comes with V-rated tyres, the tyres should be replaced with Vs to give the overall level of performance the car needs. Though these are the main symbols, a tyre may be sold anywhere in the world from Swindon to San Francisco, and markings applicable to other markets also appear. In the USA, for example, tyres are tested for tread wear so a wear rating may be included. Many thanks to Brian at Micheldever Tyres for his help with this.

19 When is a 'write-off' not written off?

The answer is, when it's a Category C or Category D insurance 'write-off'. An insurance assessor will 'write a car off' when it is stolen and not recovered or when the cost of repairing any damage to it exceeds 60% of the car's trade value. The insured owner is then paid the car's private sale value, while the car is registered on the national Vehicle Condition Alert Register (VCAR) and becomes the property of the insurer. If the assessor has deemed it a Category A write-off, that's the end of it and the remains of the car must be crushed. If it's deemed a Category B, it cannot be put back on the road, but it can be used as a donor car to yield spare parts for other vehicles. Category C means damaged, but repairable, so the car can be sold with a V5 for repair. Depending on the car's value, a professional repairer may then have his repair checked by an alignment specialist such as Autolign (01604 859424) or Popplewells (01992 561571) and a 'pass' will be entered on the VCAR. Category D means that damage is confined to windows, locks and possibly a few bent panels, but the car remains roadworthy. This is often the state in which stolen cars are recovered after the insurer has paid out. These cars are the easiest to fix. HPI Equifax (01722 422422) and AA Experian (0800 234999) each offer history checks on vehicles which include their VCAR status (have a credit card handy when you phone).

20 What is the difference between diesels?

These days you can buy a diesel car with at least nine different types of injection system. The first is indirect injection (IDI) where diesel fuel is pumped to the injectors by a distribution pump, then fed through to the combustion chamber via a pre-combustion antechamber. IDI engines can be made more efficient by compressing the air fed into the combustion chamber with a turbocharger. A turbocharged diesel engine can be made still more efficient by cooling the turbocharged air with an intercooler.

This explains badges such as D, TD and TDI on the backs of cars. But badging has been complicated by the advent of direct injected diesel engines, first built for cars by Perkins, where the fuel is fed directly into the combustion chamber. Direct injected diesels may also be turbocharged and charge-cooled, and may be badged SD, DI, DT, DTI or TDI. VW/Audi has taken direct injection a big step further by introducing 'pumpe duse' injector pumps where each individual injector contains a pump to increase the pressure at which fuel is pumped into the combustion chamber, enabling the dosage to be more finely controlled. The other method of achieving this at slightly lower pressure is 'Common Rail Direct Injection', the route favoured by Mercedes Benz, Fiat and PSA. Instead of distributing the fuel charge to each injector, the pump feeds a 'common rail' of fuel from which each injector is fed at high pressure and the dosage fed into each combustion chamber is finely controlled. The air supply to common rail direct injected engines is invariably turbocharged, and for more efficient, more powerful versions it is turbocharged and intercooled. CD tends to mean common rail direct injected. CDI usually means intercooled as well.

21 What is the difference between an automatic gearbox and a CVT?

A lot of readers are still confused about the difference between conventional automatic transmissions and continuously variable transmissions. I'll try to explain. Instead of a clutch, a conventional automatic box uses a 'fluid flywheel'. In very simplified terms, oil is thrown by one turbine wheel on to another, creating a flexible drive which becomes more positive as engine speed increases. This allows sequential gear changes up or down two, three, four or five ratios according to road speed, the extent to which the accelerator is pressed, an electronic programme or a manual override. The advantage is reliability. The disadvantages are a fixed set of ratios, a sometimes sluggish response and overheating when the car is heavily laden or towing. Instead of a torque converter, most current-generation transaxle CVTs use a pair of multi-plate clutches or an electromagnetic clutch to take up drive from standstill much more positively than a conventional autobox. Instead of having fixed gear ratios, a steel belt runs between two pulleys which expand and contract in diameter, theoretically giving continuously variable ratios between the lowest and highest. However, the latest CVTs have six or seven lockable ratios, so upshifts and downshifts can be manually controlled if the driver desires. Confusing matters further, for the latest 'Hypertronic CVT M6' transmission fitted to some Primeras, Nissan has adopted a torque converter instead of an electromagnetic clutch. The new 'Torotrak' CVT does away with belts, feeding drive directly from an input cone to an output cone.

22 What do the flags mean at a motor race?

The F1 season is under way again and, while wives and children groan, blokes up and down the country will be glued to their goggle-boxes every Sunday afternoon. You might find the procession a bit more interesting if you know what the marshals' flag signals mean. A blue flag held out in front of a driver means he must let a faster car overtake. A waved blue flag means he must do it now. A yellow flag held out means there is a hazard ahead and drivers must not overtake. A waved yellow flag means the hazard is imminent and drivers must be prepared to stop. A black flag held out with a driver's number means he has committed an infringement and must pull into his pit either to suffer a stop/go penalty or to be disqualified. A red flag means that the race has been stopped. We all know what a chequered flag means, but there are several other flags which may be used. A yellow and red flag signifies oil on the track ahead (when waved, immediately ahead). A white flag signifies a much slower car is ahead (when waved, immediately ahead). A black and white flag is used to warn a driver of unsporting driving. A green flag indicates the end of a danger area previously signified by a yellow flag. Red flags waved by people in the crowd mean they're Ferrari fans.

23 What makes a cheap tyre expensive?

The answer to this one came from Justin Edgington of Michelin, after I raised the matter of the safety of cheap replacement tyres fitted to some fleet cars on 26 February. He explained that the main reason why budget tyres wear comparatively quickly is insufficient support of the tread by the steel bracing. On a high-quality radial ply tyre, the bracing extends into the shoulders but requires an expensive flexible compound or cracking will occur there. To prevent cracking on a hard-compound budget tyre, the bracing stops short of the shoulder and the result is abnormal wear on the tyre shoulders. (The reason for this is often mis-diagnosed as under-inflation.) Another effect is poor water dispersal via the 'sipes' (small channels cut in the edges of the tread pattern) which either close up or get worn away. The most dangerous road surfaces are when rainwater has dried and left behind a film of oil and road grime on the surface. If the tyre sipes cannot cut through it, these are the conditions where the tyres can 'viscoplane', which is actually far more dangerous than 'aquaplaning' on a cushion of water.

24 What is a 'small child' in the eyes of the law?

R.B. of Stratford-upon-Avon asked if I could clarify the law concerning small children riding in the front seats of cars. Sections 15(2) and 15(4) of The Road Traffic Act 1988 states that it is an offence for any person without reasonable excuse to drive a motor vehicle on a road unless any children under 14 in the front or rear seats of the vehicle are wearing seat-belts which conform to the regulations. A child under one year old can travel in the front in a carry-cot restrained by straps. Children under three years old can travel in the front seats if they are wearing approved child restraints. A 'small child', defined as aged between three and 12, and less than 1.5 metres tall (4ft 11in), can travel in the front or rear using an adult belt if no approved child restraint is available. If there are no belts in the back and the front passenger seat is unoccupied, the 'small child' must travel belted in the front. There are further exceptions for disabled children and children holding medical certificates. There are more exceptions for motor vehicles first registered before 1 January

1965 if the vehicle has no rear seats or if no seats apart from the driver's are fitted with seat-belts appropriate for a child. And, of course, there are yet more exceptions for buses, vans, trucks, etc. Rear belts must be fitted to all cars first registered on or after 1 April 1987. Many thanks to *Hughes' Guide to Road Traffic Law for the Enforcement Officer*, copies of which can be obtained from Motorvation Consultants on 01908 639233 in file form or on CD Rom.

25 What is fuel tax?

Fuel tax is the fixed amount of tax you pay per litre of fuel before the cost of the fuel itself is added and VAT is imposed on both the fuel tax and the petrol. The new rates are: ultra-low-sulphur unleaded ('city' petrol) 47.82p per litre; premium unleaded 48.82p per litre; superunleaded and LRP 50.89p per litre; and unleaded low-sulphur diesel 48.82p per litre. If you pay a pump price of 79.9p a litre for premium unleaded, 19.18p pays for the petrol, 48.82p is the fuel tax and 11.9p is the VAT, so 76% of the cost of the petrol is tax and the actual tax rate on the petrol works out at 316.58%. The SMMT has now provided CO_2-based VED tax bands for new cars as from 1 March 2001. Up to 150 g/km CO_2 the owner will pay £90 for a gas-fuelled car, £100 for a petrol-fuelled car or £110 for a diesel. Up to 165 g/km the rates will be £110 for gas, £120 for petrol and £130 for diesel. Up to 185 g/km the rates will be £130 for gas, £140 for petrol and £150 for diesel; and over 185 g/km (anything from a Nissan Primera 1.6 at 186 g/km to an Aston Martin V8 Vantage at 511 g/km) the rates will be £150 for gas, £155 for petrol and £160 for diesel. So the owner of a low

CO_2 'Y'-prefix car, such as a VW Polo 1.4 TDI which puts out 119 g/km, will only benefit financially by 29% compared to the owner of a 'Y'-prefix Aston Martin V8 Vantage, despite the fact that the Aston puts out 329% more CO_2 than the Polo. The chancellor has, however, brought all older cars under 1,200 cc into the same £105-a-year tax band.

26 What are regional registrations?

From 1 September 2001, vehicle registrations will begin with one letter denoting the region, followed by one letter denoting the vehicle registration office (each VRO will have 5 to 25 letters, depending on how many of them in the region). This will be followed by two numbers giving the period of registration. And this will be followed by three random letters. So 'AA 01 ABC' will mean that the car was registered in the Anglia region at the Norwich VRO between 1 September 2001 and 28 February 2002 and is the only 'AA 01' registered car with the random letters 'ABC'. Because of the twice-yearly registration change, the year figures get a bit complicated. 02 will mean 1 March 2002 to 31 August 2002; 52 will mean 1 September 2002 to 28 February 2003; 03 will mean 1 March 2003 to 31 August 2003; 53 will mean 1 September 2003 to 29 February 2004; and so on. The regional letters will be A: Anglia; B: Birmingham; C: Cymru; D: Deeside to Shrewsbury; E: Essex; F: Forest and Fens; G; Garden of England; H: Hampshire and Dorset; K: Luton; L: London; M: Manchester; N: North; O: Oxford; P: Preston; R: Reading; S: Scotland; V: Severn Valley; W: West Country; Y: Yorkshire.

27 What are residuals?

The phrase 'residual value' appears quite a lot these days and salesmen dealing in prestige cars often stress the importance of a 'high residual value'. Unfortunately, 'residuals' quoted as percentages of car list prices can be a misleading basis on which to buy. Let's say the 'list price' of the car is £20,000, but metallic paint, a stereo upgrade and a few other knick-knacks add a further £2,500, against which you get a discount of £1,000. The car has cost you £21,500. But if you are quoted a high residual value of 50% in three years' time, it will be based on the list price of £20,000 and the assumption that the average prestige car is fitted with a bundle of extras. So, when you come to avail yourself of that residual value, you will get £10,000 and will have therefore lost £11,500. If, on the other hand, you buy a heavily discounted mass-market car listed at £15,000, but actually sold to you for £11,000, which has a three-year residual of 30% of list, the figures pan out very differently. The car may only be worth £4,500 but, instead of losing £11,500 on it, you will have lost a mere £6,500 and will have had the benefit of the interest on an extra £10,500 which you did not spend in the first place.

28 What is a 'Top Car' auction?

Most auction houses hold themed sales. For example, Russell, Baldwin & Bright of Leominster hold some of the country's biggest auctions of 4x4 vehicles, twice a month (tel: 01568 611166); and West Oxfordshire Motor Auctions hold twice monthly sales of retired police cars (tel: 01993 774413). But the first and best known

theme sales are BCA's 'Top Car' auctions. These are held on alternate Mondays at its Blackbushe auction centre (tel: 01252 878555) and once a month at Brighouse (01484 401555), Edinburgh (0131 333 2151), Measham (01530 270322) and Nottingham (0115 987 3311). The sales are divided into two sections: 'Elite' for the newer, lower mileage cars and 'Prestige' for those with higher mileages or more than four years old. The great advantage is that a large number of classy cars are conveniently offered in one auction hall on the same day. The obvious disadvantage to bidders is that this attracts large numbers of specialist dealers and private buyers competing for the same cars, so prices tend to be slightly higher than at general fleet auctions where a mixture of cars are offered.

29 What is 'SPECS'?

This is a sinister new system being used to curtail the movement of people around the country by creating such severe traffic congestion on motorways that many travel plans will be abandoned. Motorways are our safest roads by a long way and were previously speed camera enforcement free zones. But Home Office Type Approval has now been given to a new generation of 'SVDD' (Speed Violation Detection Deterrent) equipment to be installed on motorway bridges which will be invisible to drivers until their photos are taken by digital flash cameras. The new system is known as 'SPECS' (Speed Police Enforcement Camera System) and works by pairs of digital cameras with time and average speed computers automatically calculating the speeds of vehicles passing between them, then taking digital colour images of vehicles going faster than a pre-set speed and recording them together with speeds, times, dates and locations on large-capacity CDs inside boxes attached to the camera units. Fines are being increased to £60 to pay for the new equipment but, as drivers slow down, creating and getting stuck in more traffic jams, returns from the fines will diminish so speed limits and tolerance limits will have to be reduced in order to keep the systems profitable, putting yet more people dependent on the motor industry and free travel out of work. Many thanks to the Association of British Drivers for the information on SVDD and SPECS. (The ABD fulfils the function for which the AA was originally established but long since abandoned.) To join, visit www.abd.org.uk or telephone 07000 781 544.

30 What is a three-litre car?

In mainland Europe the standard for vehicle fuel consumption is obviously not 'miles per gallon'. But it's not 'kilometres per litre' either. Instead, fuel consumption is measured in terms of 'litres per 100 kilometres'. Taking reader G.B. of Oakhampton's formula, it is relatively easy to translate 'mpg' into 'l/100 km' by dividing the figure 282.5 by the mpg achieved. Thus 30 miles per gallon translates to 9.4 litres per 100 kilometres; 40 mpg translates to 7.06 l/100 km and 94 mpg translates to 3.0 l/100 km. This is the target figure set by VAG engineers for a new generation of super-economical diesel cars such as the VW Lupo 1.2TDI. It's actually quite easy for us to start thinking in terms of litres per 100 km rather than mpg, and obviously a lot more relevant than some halfway house figure such as 'miles per litre'. All we have to do is make sure we brim our tanks on every fill up and note the odometer mileage on our till receipts. Subtract the previous mileage from mileage on the latest receipt; either divide by 5 and multiply by 8 or, more accurately, multiply by 1.60934; divide the result by 100; then divide that into the litres shown on our till receipts. Thus, on a recent series of 'brim to brims' travelling through France, Belgium and Holland, my 836 miles translated to 1,345 kilometres which, on 97.39 litres of Shell Premium Unleaded, worked out at 7.24 litres per 100 kilometres, or 38.95 miles per gallon.

31 What is car benefit tax?

This is the tax drivers of company cars pay for the benefit of their private use of the car. The system for calculating this tax will change from 6 April 2002 and there will no longer be any discount for a high business mileage. Instead, drivers will be taxed on 15% of the car's list price, with the tax base increasing by 1% for each 5 g/km CO_2 the car emits over and above 165 g/km. For tax year 2003–2004, the base CO_2 will be 155 g/km and for tax year 2004–2005 the base CO_2 will be 145 g/km. So, effectively, the tax base for a £15,000 car emitting 185 g/km will rise from 19% (or £2,850) in 2002–2003 to 23% (or £3,450) in 2004–2005. Because they emit less CO_2, diesels will be hit with a 3% surcharge, and no driver will be taxed on a base of more than 35% of the car's list price. So, as with VED, there is no benefit to be had from driving a company car with an ultra low CO_2 rating, which is extraordinarily hypocritical for a tax which is supposed to be CO_2-based. Instead it has merely become an over-complicated banding exercise but with the environmental benefit of abolishing discounts for high business miles. List prices and CO_2 tables and can be found in *What Car?* and *Diesel Car* magazines, but drivers will need to subtract registration tax and VED to arrive at the taxable list price.

32 What is GEODESY?

Everyone has heard of radar and laser speed-trap detectors. But GEODESY is an entirely different dash-top system which relies on Global Positioning System technology to alert a driver that he or she is approaching the location of a known electronically mapped speed trap. If a user spots a speed trap which the GEODESY has not alerted them to, a press of a button will store its location in the unit's memory. The user then plugs the GEODESY into a self-dialling land-line interface to both upload latest speed-trap location data into the GEODESY and download the locations of any new data into the data bank (every confirmed new location earns the user £50). Of course, GEODESY cannot identify which speed traps are active but, assuming the traps have been set up in known accident black spots, it will encourage users to take extra care when approaching them and thus makes a valuable contribution to road safety. Obviously, if the speed trap is simply there to earn revenue, then the GEODESY helps to prevent it from doing so. For more information, contact Morpheous Limited, tel: 0870 2401701, website: www.morpheous.co.uk, email: info@morpheous.co.uk, product test on www.speed-trap.co.uk, product description on www.speed-trap.co.uk/geodesy.doc.

33 What is a roadster?

This is guaranteed to promote argument. In the old days, the word 'roadster' usually described an open two seater with cutaway doors, side-screens and a rudimentary canvas top, which the driver had to assemble. More luxurious open two seaters with folding hoods and wind-up windows were called 'drop-head coupes'. Possibly the best examples of the difference were Jaguar's XK series Roadsters and DHCs. The Roadsters were two seaters with no space behind the seats, rudimentary frame-and-canvas tops and, until the arrival of the XK150 Roadster, side-screens rather than wind-up windows. XK DHCs, on the other hand, all had folding hoods, vestigial rear seats (or space for them) and wind-up windows. By this definition,

Triumph TR2s, TR3s and TR3As were all roadsters even though there was a bit of space behind the seats. But TR4s had wind-up windows
and later versions had folding hoods, so they
became true DHCs. All MGA roadsters were
true roadsters but, like TR4s, MGBs soon
switched from frame-and-canvas tops to proper folding hoods. So how do we define a roadster these days? The Lotus Elise has a canvas top
supported by side members which have to be
removed and stored in special compartments.
The Audi TT Roadster has an electrically folding hood with a glass rear window and electric
side windows. The same goes for the Honda
S2000, which has a plastic, rather than glass,
rear window. Same for the Toyota MR2 and
Mazda MX5, which have glass rear windows but
no electric assistance to the hood mechanism.
While the hood of the MGF folds by hand and
has a plastic rear window. Today these are all
considered roadsters, but I have to draw the line
at the Mercedes SLK which, as everyone knows,
has a fiendishly clever electrically folding hard
top. Even though the new SLK 320 six-speed
goes like stink, it's definitely a drop-head coupe.

34 What is a 'vis-à-vis'?

I threw the cat among the pigeons by attempting to define the difference between a roadster
and a drop-head coupe. Now we'll move onto
some more straightforward coachwork de-
scriptors. 'Dos-à-dos' and 'vis-à-vis' are exactly what you would expect. In a turn of the
century 'dos-à-dos', two rows of passengers sat
back to back, while in a 'vis-à-vis' they sat face
to face, which was hardly conducive to safe driving. A 'brougham' and a 'sedanca de ville' are

large chauffeur-driven cars in the style of an early taxi, where the driver sits out in the elements while the passengers are carried in a snug, closed compartment. A 'sedanca' is a two-door coupe on which the rear seats are covered by a fixed roof, but the front pair are either open or covered by a removable top. A 'landaulette', on the other hand, usually has a roofed driver's compartment and roofed centre section with a folding top over the rearmost pair of seats. A 'limousine' is a stretched closed car with a glass window between passengers and driver and, usually, seating for four or more in the passenger compartment. 'Saloons' and 'sedans' are closed cars with two rows of seats and a 'B' pillar between the front and rear doors. (Without 'B' pillars they're described as 'hardtops'.) 'Estate cars', 'shooting brakes' and 'station wagons' are saloons with folding rear seats where the roof continues horizontally over the load area, which can be accessed by a door at the back. Cruder versions of estate cars are sometimes described as 'utilities', except in Australia where a 'ute' is a car-based truck.

35 What is a 'tourer'?

I gave you a break from soft-tops for a week, but now I'm going to try and define the difference between a 1930s-to-1950s 'tourer' and a full-blown convertible. To me, when applied to a car, the word 'tourer' conjures up a picture of a low-slung four-seater open car with two or four doors, but the front pair cut away to give infinite elbow room. The top will usually have a fully folding frame mechanism, but the only glass will be in the front and possibly rear windows. Canvas and transparent plastic side screens are the order of the day. An 'all weather tourer', a 'convertible' or a 'cabrio', on the other hand, is an altogether heavier and drier conveyance, with wind-down glass front and rear side windows. BMW Bauer cabrios had solid, removable roof panels between their roll bars and the top screen rail, and a folding hood behind. These should be not confused with a 'targa', which has an integral roll-over bar, usually supporting two solid pieces of roof between it and the top rail of the windscreen, but a fixed roof and rear screen behind.

DISABLED DRIVERS

Small auto

" I am a disabled driver and three years ago asked your advice about a family-sized car. Now I am looking for a much smaller car, which nevertheless offers high levels of comfort, easy access and power steering. "

The next letter I opened came from M.F. of Torquay who is delighted with both her Seat Arosa 1.0 and the service she gets from her local Seat dealer. So that's what I'd go for if I was you. Make sure you opt for the 'SE' model and get height-adjustable seats as well as a height-adjustable steering wheel. I personally prefer the 1.7SDI diesel, but if you are used to an automatic, the Arosa 1.4 auto is ideal and if there are no Seat dealers in your area, go for the upgraded VW Lupo equivalents.

Zafira diesel automatic

" As a tall and bulky disabled driver I am disappointed to find that the new Vauxhall Zafira is not going to be available as a diesel automatic. As I need a diesel automatic for economy, I'm finding it increasingly difficult, and uncomfortable, to drive my Peugeot 405 manual. I need a small MPV with power steering and air-conditioning for less than £15,000. "

Demand for the excellent Zafira is high throughout Europe, which limits both the allocation and the model range available in the UK. The DI engine and autobox work extremely well together in the Astra, but they probably wouldn't in the Zafira which is 600lbs heavier, even before two extra people get into the back seats. And, of course, you'd be looking at a lot more than £15,000 to buy one if it did exist. Renault offers a diesel automatic Scenic, but it's much harder to buy diesels at big disounts than petrol-engined Scenics. If you can find a late secondhand Mitsubishi Space runner with auto and a/c, that might suit you very well because the tall fourth gear ratio gives excellent economy of around 36 mpg even with the a/c on. A late used Toyota Picnic automatic with auto and a/c might also do the job. If you can put up with another car rather than an MPV, either a late used Astra DI auto estate with a/c or a late used VW Passat TDI S auto with a/c will probably give you the best combination of automatic gearbox, comfort and economy.

Excellent for the handicapped

" On 3 July you recommended the Seal Arosa 1.4SE automatic to a disabled reader. I am surprised you did not also mention the Hyundai Atoz automatic. As well as qualifying for reduced rate VED, mine has an ideal seat height for easy access, power steering, good visibility, plenty of headroom and room behind the rear seats for my wheelchair. It even has the luxury (some may call it a necessity) of air-conditioning. "

Point taken for smaller readers. But the Arosa SE has much wider opening doors and suits a greater variety of statures than the Atoz. Probably a better bet now is the Hyundai Amica automatic, which, from June 2000, has been fitted with a four-speed rather than three-speed autobox. Any Amica bought before March 2001 will continue to benefit from lower rate VED.

More pedal pushers

On 31 July, in reply to a reader concerned about sitting too close to her driver's airbag, I mentioned pedal extenders by Eze Drive Limited of 169 London Road, Leicester, LE2 1EG, tel: 07970 571407, email: EzeDrive@aol.com. Another supplier, providing a range of adjustable, removable and permanent pedal extenders is Roland Kerr Ltd, PO Box 8896, London SW15 3ZA, tel: 020 8546 8125, fax: 020 8546 7145.

Orange Badge abuse

" On applying for renewal of my Orange Badge (now the Euro Blue Badge), originally granted seven years ago, I was told that I no longer qualified. Apparently Badges are now only issued to those 'unable to walk more than 50 metres without stopping, without severe discomfort or without help from another person'. Has this new rule been applied nationwide? "

Yes. Widespread abuse of the Orange (now Blue) Badge scheme by able-bodied drivers had filled too many Badge spaces and left seriously disabled people unable to park sufficiently close to their destinations or in a slot wide enough to get out of their cars and into their wheelchairs. While there may now be a need for an intermediate semi-disabled badge of another colour, any fully able-bodied driver carrying fully able-bodied passengers who parks in an Blue Badge slot simply for convenience should have their car clamped and the release fee paid into a charity for the disabled.

In and out

" As my wife has arthritic knees and ankles we would like to buy a car which satisfies Test No. 5 in Bryan McIlwraith's article on 7 August. (Kerb height: place your right foot on the ground, as if getting out; try to ensure that your lower left leg is vertical. Your right thigh should be sloping down towards your knee.) We think the Renault Scenic may be suitable. Do you know of any other, the smaller the better? *"*

Any new shape Fiat Punto five-door model. These all have upright bodies, power steering, height-adjustable steering wheels, height-adjustable driver's seats and, by virtue of front doors which open right up to the foot pedals, are the easiest cars to get in and out of that I know. The driving position was designed by The Ergonomics Group under Professor Mark Porter at Loughborough University. The Colt Space Star is also very good in this respect. The Scenic, 'A' Class, Zafira and the Far Eastern 'minibox' cars are harder to get in and out of because of the longer step down. But, apart from the disadvantage of a large driver's door, the VW Lupo and the Seat Arosa SE are close to the Punto in ease of ingress and egress and comfortable driving position.

Small with easy access

" My husband suffers from Parkinson's disease and is becoming increasingly disabled. Could you recommend a car which will accommodate a folded wheelchair and is reasonably high to make access easier into the front seats. We do not want a large vehicle, but are there any makers of smaller 'people carriers'? *"*

I was impressed by the Toyota Yaris Verso, which is a mini-MPV-version of the highly acclaimed Yaris, last year's European 'Car of the

Year'. Readers think highly of the new Suzuki Wagon R+ and Vauxhall Agila. Don't forget the Fiat Punto which, since Fiat dealers have been on a 30% margin, has been selling for less than £6,000 brand new. Going up a size, it's worth taking a look at the Renault Kangoo Combi and the Citroën Berlingo Multispace because you won't even need to fold the wheelchair to get it into the back of one of these.

A car for stiff knees

" *I am becoming troubled by an arthritic and stiff left knee, so am considering buying an automatic car. Could you please advise on the pros and cons and reliability of fully automatic, CVT and semi-automatic gearboxes? Would taller vehicles such as 4x4s, small people carriers, a Mercedes A Class or a Toyota Yaris be likely to be better for me than a conventional automatic?* "

CVTs (continuously variable transmissions) are brilliant in theory, but have a relatively poor record for reliability. Using just your right leg you will have less control over a fully automatic car than over a semi-automatic because the semi-automatic is much easier to knock out of gear if you ever get confused between the brake and accelerator. You can get a semi-automatic Yaris or A Class. A tall car is good, but a long step down to the ground isn't. The Yaris and Yaris Verso are extremely easy for those with stiff limbs to step in and out of, as are the Fiat Punto, Suzuki Wagon R+ and Vauxhall Agila.

Moulded seats

" *I have a back condition which makes it impossible to sit upright when driving without the seat half reclined and bulked up with cushions to give my spine flexibility. This means that the head restraint is in the wrong place to prevent whiplash in an accident. Is there a company which makes custom moulded injection foam seats which would fit my spine and enable me to sit more comfortably and safely?* **"**

Otto Bock Orthopaedic of Leeds (0113 388 3100) makes various types of moulded seats and 'Technogel' cushions. Your local consultant is Andy Wadie on 0797 062 8975. He will visit you at home in order to make the necessary measurements, achieved by lying in a sort of 'bed of nails' which send signals to create a precise computer model of the shape of your back.

Driven with dignity

" *My wife has suffered several strokes and is confined to a wheelchair. She is in a nursing home and I would very much like to take her out for short trips, but this would mean pushing the wheelchair into a vehicle and anchoring it there. Are there any suitable vehicles for purchase? Who could I contact? How much do they cost?* **"**

When the Citroën Berlingo Multispace was launched I suggested to Rod Brotherwood that it would make an excellent vehicle for one of his conversions. The philosophy behind them is that a disabled person in a wheelchair should be transported with as much dignity as possible, preferably between two other members of the family, with everyone sitting at the same height. His first conversions were to the VW Sharan, and a built-in ramp allows the wheelchair to be pushed or driven into its place between the two rear seats. The same conversion is now available on the Citroën Berlingo Multispace, but at much lower cost, from £15,000 (automatic gearbox optional). Though this seems a lot, these vehicles hold their value well and a significant proportion can usually be recouped when the vehicle is sold. You may even find a used version on offer. Speak to Rod Brotherwood, Brotherwood Automobility Ltd, Pillar Box Lane, Beer Hackett, Sherbourne, Dorset DT9 6QP, tel: 01935 872603. Another company building and selling similar vehicles is Gowrings Mobility of 3 Arnhem Road, Newbury, Berks RG14 5BU, tel: 01635 529000, which offers conversions of the Citroën Despatch Combi from £16,705, Fiat Fiorinos from £12,140 and a wide range of secondhand vehicles. It's also worth considering the Fiat Multipla because it may be possible to remove two of the three front seats so your wife can sit beside you in the front. Don't ignore the Renault Kangoo Combi which is very good value from £9,500. And don't forget the small, but versatile, Toyota Yaris Verso which has a low rear sill and just about enough room to park a wheelchair in the back.

Fingerlight

" As a disabled driver leasing a car on the Motability scheme I face penalties each time the three-year lease comes up for renewal. My cars have to be modified with ultra-light power steering but, when they go back, I have to restore them to standard specification, which costs a fortune. I get no credit for extra-cost extras specified, such as a passenger airbag, and no credit for much lower than average mileage. Yet I am hit by further penalties for small holes in the floor left by the removal of a wheelchair hoist. "

Though a registered charity, the Motability scheme involves buying and selling cars, and residual values are affected by cars being of non-standard specification. If Motability were to allow for cars to be returned in a non-standard spec at the end of the lease, it would have to increase the lease payments to account for this. But there is an answer to the power-steering problem. Every new-generation Fiat Punto comes with two levels of assistance to its electric power steering as standard, switched by a button on the dash marked 'City'. With the 'City' button pressed its PAS is one of the lightest I have ever felt.

In-car facilities

" My wife uses a wheelchair and we make regular journeys between the UK and Spain. Finding a suitable loo at the right moment can be a nightmare. What we want is an upmarket vehicle with easy entry, level access from a swivel passenger seat to a WC in the rear and plenty of luggage space. Any bright ideas? "

Yes. A VW Sharan, a Renault Espace or a Chrysler Voyager. The latter pair come in two lengths: normal or 'grand', all are available with diesel engines, or V6s with manual or automatic transmissions. Swivel passenger seats are fitted to some models (but don't swivel very easily, so try them first). The Sharan and Espace are available with accessory pods which fit in place of the individual rear seats and in some markets include a portable toilet. Because the Peseta is hovering at around 275 to £1 as I write, lhd 'on the road' prices in Spain are currently 30% to 40% lower than rhd in the UK. But if you can't get precisely what you want in Spain, buy the base vehicle there and have the modifications carried out by a UK specialist such as Brotherwood Automobility Ltd, Pillar Box Lane, Beer Hackett, Sherbourne, Dorset DT9 6QP, tel: 01935 872603, or Gowrings Mobility of 3 Arnhem Road, Newbury, Berks RG14 5BU, tel: 01635 529000. I'd go for the new Sharan TDI 115

PD six-speed because the fuel cost will work out at less than half that of the VR6 and the Sharan is the nicest of the three to drive, with the least wind noise. Don't forget the similar Seat Alhambra TDI 110 five-speed if the price is substantially lower than that of the Sharan.

DISPUTES WITH GARAGES

Inspection rejection

" *In April I bought a Renault 19 diesel from a dealer who advertises his stock as 'No Risk Car Purchase' and 'RAC Inspected and Warranted'. Item 13 on the inspector's report stated, 'rh front brake calliper seized'. The dealer told me this had been freed. Four days later, after a journey of 13 miles, I noticed smoke coming from the rh front wheel and a strong smell of burning. I then checked the RAC warranty, only to find that brakes were specifically excluded. I also phoned the RAC to discover that its inspectors do not re-inspect vehicles to ensure that listed faults have been put right. The dealer did not argue over the repair, and explained that when new discs and pads had been fitted not enough clearance had been allowed. Then, since I was dubious about the quality of the service the car had been sold with, I put it in to an independent service depot for another one. The report revealed leaking rear-brake cylinders, ridged rear drums and faulty wheel bearings. These on a car which had passed its MOT and been RAC inspected within the previous month. So I then approached the local Trading Standards Office who added my experience of the dealer to its database and gave me some useful general advice, but could not act against the dealer on my evidence alone. I then spoke to the dealer again and he told me that since he had the car inspected by a neutral organisation and repaired by another neutral business, he had fulfilled all his obligations. I have returned to my view that car dealers should be treated with suspicion and the RAC with contempt.* "

The dealer was legally obliged to sort out the original brake problem anyway, which he did, and he seems to have been straight enough to have fitted new discs and pads prior to offering the car for sale. As for the leaking rear-brake cylinders, ridged drums and faulty wheel bearings, it's not the first time I have heard of service-centre chains 'finding' these faults during an otherwise routine service. Don't take the word of a service outfit which stands to profit by remedial work for the faults it finds. The only answer to all this seems to be that if you buy an 'RAC inspected' car, you should immediately have it inspected by the AA, and vice versa if you buy an 'AA inspected' car.

Service stitch-ups

Two readers have complained of unexpectedly huge service bills. T.H. of New Barnet was asked to pay £503.77 by the garage which sold her an 'N'-reg. Astra when it was new but has since lost the Vauxhall franchise. The extra costs were for replacing the front brake pads, deglazing the rear brakes, changing the brake fluid and for a new headlamp and replacing the oxygen sensor to enable it to pass its MOT test. The trouble is, even with a low-mileage car, brakes usually do need this sort of attention at four years old, and a broken headlamp and excessive emissions are both MOT failure points. So what looks like a horribly high bill is unavoidable unless you do the work yourself. This is what M.C. of Derby suggests, using a Haynes manual and parts supplied by his company, Parts Direct (01332 290833). He gives the example of a Mr Naylor of Chesterfield who asked for the brakes of his 'G'-reg. Citroën BX to be checked and renewed if necessary. For this, he was charged £675.80, including £213.65 for parts and £414.14 for labour. The labour charge was explained by a rate of £49.35 an hour, and three men working for nearly three hours each. But M.C. contends that Mr Naylor could have done the job himself for a total cost of £110.50 using parts from Parts Direct. Parts Direct's website is at www.partsdirectderby.co.uk.

Low-mileage damage

" *In August 1998 I paid a London Mercedes Benz dealer £23,000 for a 22,000-mile 1988E Mercedes Benz 560SEC. When I checked the levels after 70 miles I found I needed a quarter of a litre of oil and a litre and a half of coolant. I also discovered that the windscreen-wash reservoir was contaminated and the washers would not work. Then, 5,000 miles later, I found that the front offside tyre was badly worn on the inside due to misalignment, the brakes needed replacing, the brake fluid had not been changed for years, the sparkplugs were ancient, the distributor cap was cracked, the HT leads were faulty, the CO level was too high, the fuel gauge was under-reading, the oil pressure gauge was inaccurate and the air-conditioning was not working. This leads me to believe that the car was not checked over at all prior to sale and I have had to pay a local garage £1,186.05 to put everything right.* "

You were out of your mind to pay £15,000 more than this car was really worth on the strength of its low mileage. (A pal of mine paid £4,800 in September 1998 for a perfect 100,000-mile 88E 560SEL.) Most of the problems you have encountered are the direct result of the car sitting unused. But, though your comments about the dealer are unprintable, I have some sympathy with you. When a dealer sells a car for £15,000 more than its true value on the strength of its low mileage, he should, at the very least, have ensured that it was properly recommissioned and properly serviced prior to sale, and if the dealer did not, he should have coughed up your £1,186.05 out of the profit of at least £10,000 he made out of you on the car.

Mystery origin

" *I paid a well known garage £21,000 for an 'R'-registered Toyota MR2 T-Bar. I found its condition on delivery unacceptable. A back light was cracked, the brakes pulled dangerously to the right, the electric aerial was broken, I was given no review of the controls and I was not supplied with a driver's handbook. When I eventually received the handbook, I found that the radio was different, and possibly inferior, to the one for which instructions were given. I wrote, expressing my discontent, to the dealer principal on 25 April and again on 10 May, but have so far not even received a telephone call in response. What is my next step?* "

You did not tell me when you purchased the car, and this will determine what action you could take under The Sale and Supply of Goods Act, 1994. But from your descriptions (no handbook, wrong radio), I strongly suspect that you have unwittingly purchased a grey import. Check the Vehicle Identification Number with Toyota (GB) Ltd (01737 785002). If it is a grey import and you weren't told, then there is a clear case of deception and Toyota itself will probably help you take action against the dealer. Alternatively, pay for ABS Vehicle Services, (0345 419926) to give it a full inspection and report, then act on that, involving the Trading Standards Office which covers the dealership where you bought it if necessary.

Noddy car porkies

" *On 16 April I purchased a secondhand, 9,750-mile Micra for my daughter from a Nissan dealer, which was apparently half-owned by Nissan (GB) Ltd. I was told that the car was either ex-management, ex-staff or had been out on loan and that the registration document was with Nissan. I was also told that the car was registered in January 1998. Hours before I picked it up, this was corrected to December 1997. The registration document did not arrive until 21 June when, to my horror, I discov-*

ered that the previous registered keeper was Avis. I phoned Nissan GB who firstly told me that the supplying garage was part of Avis and secondly told me that Nissan GB had loaned the car to Avis as a trial. The people at Avis itself were exceptionally helpful and told me they had purchased the car in December 1997 on a 'sale and buyback scheme', and it had gone back to Nissan in April 1998 with a mileage of 9,250. This implied it had been in storage or on forecourts for a year before I bought it. When I remonstrated with the garage I was offered a choice of another secondhand Nissan, a new car, if I paid the difference, or three years' 'free' servicing. I would either like my money back in full so I can purchase a car from a more honest garage, or a reasonable amount in compensation – say £750 to £1,000. Do you think I am being fair? Do ex-rental cars have a lower value and are they harder to sell? I would not have bought an ex-rental car had I known. "

I have bought loads of 'nearly new', ex-rental cars in my time. There is nothing wrong with them at all, as long as you know what you're buying. In fact my current 'smoker' is a well specced, air-conditioned, ex-Thrifty Mondeo. You did not mention what you paid for the car. To my mind, a fair retail price for an ex-rental, 10,000-mile 97R Micra 1.0L three-door in April 1999 would have been £5,250 tops, to include balance of manufacturer's three-year warranty. If you paid more, and can prove you had your leg lifted over the description, see if the dealer will agree to settle via the Small Claims Court. (Not worth the expense of a County Court case.) If the dealer won't play, pull in the Trading Standards Office which covers his area. As I have written before, the only safe assumption to make about any six-to-nine-month-old 'nearly new' car is that it is ex-rental. Holding back ex-rentals in compounds after they come off the fleets can increase their age to as much as 18 months. Your car's year sitting on an airfield somewhere will mean premature rusting of the brake discs and exhaust system, a duff battery (probably already replaced), and possible corrosion in the braking and cooling systems.

Dirty dealings

" *The automatic gearbox of my much-loved 12-year-old Suzuki Swift 1.3GL lost 'drive' in 'D'. Using '2' I drove to the nearest garage. They said they would look for a replacement gearbox, warning me that it might cost as much as the car was worth, and I limped the car home. After a couple of days they rang to say they could not find a replacement box and suggested that they would 'get rid of the car for me', which I took to mean they would sell it. When I next phoned to ask what was happening, the garage men told me my car 'had to go for scrap' and there was no money for me. A few days later, my daughter saw my car, looking like new, freshly taxed, parked by a block of flats, with a label in the back window stating 're-paired and serviced by' the very garage which had told me it was scrap. Neither the police, nor Trading Standards, nor Citizens Advice Bureau nor two solicitors want to get involved. Their only advice was to personally confront the garage.* "

Send the garage a bill, with words to the effect 'to one Suzuki Swift 1.3 automatic, reg (whatever it is), price £750, date of sale (whatever it was)'. If the garage doesn't pay up, take your case to the Small Claims Court. What the garage may do is contest that it provided services up to the value of the car and seized the car under its right of lieu. But I very much doubt that the judge presiding over a Small Claims Court hearing would see matters that way, particularly when he learned that the car was alive and well and living by a block of flats in the next town. API (0500 830530) could probably have supplied a secondhand replacement gearbox imported from Japan. King Automatics of Epsom (01372 728769) could probably have repaired the existing gearbox.

Non-stop Citroën

" *I have a 95N Citroën Xantia TDSX, which I purchased from a well known Citroën dealer in March 1997, and which has covered 46,000 miles. Since then, I have spent over £500 on repairs, receiving only £100 back from the warranty insurer. Then, on 28 August, as I was driving on the M60, the engine began increasing revs by itself. Black smoke was pouring from the exhaust as the car moved faster and faster. I changed into neutral, stopped on the hard shoulder and switched off, but the engine continued to run at well past its governed maximum revs. Eventually, it stopped, and the car was recovered to an independent garage at a cost of £58. A major piston/injector fault was diagnosed and I then paid a further £40 to have the car taken to the dealer I purchased it from. I was later told that the dealer could do nothing for me because the car had not been serviced by Citroën agencies. In fact, I had serviced the car every six months, with an oil change every three months. After a heated discussion, I was told I must remove my car from the dealer's premises asap and I am now faced with the cost of over £1,100 to replace the engine with a secondhand one. I feel I have been treated extremely badly by the dealer and request your assistance in getting some satisfaction from him.* "

The most likely explanation for what happened (a 99:1 certainty) is that at its last oil change the engine was over-filled with oil. The sump oil then became drawn through the engine's breather system until the engine began running on it. This explains why the revs rose even though your foot was off the accelerator and why the engine continued to run at maximum revs even after switching off had operated the solenoid on the fuel pump to prevent further fuel oil from the tank being sucked into the engine. The phenomenon was quite well known on older diesel truck engines after the 'kill' knob had been pulled (remember the case of the runaway truck on the M1 in 1998). So I'm afraid yours is an example of over-enthusiastic home maintenance causing total engine failure

– something neither the Citroën dealer nor Citroën itself can be held accountable for.

Story full of holes

" *On 24 February this year my August 1993 Senator was inspected by a Vauxhall engineer, Mr King, who approved the replacement of the two rear doors due to rust perforation under the Vauxhall six-year body warranty. The Vauxhall dealer told me it would take two or three weeks to obtain new rear doors. Nothing happened, so I began chasing up and it was not until 30 June that the car was booked in for the work. I was then told that the wrong doors had been ordered. The next development was that the dealer lost its franchise in August. I was promised the paperwork showing approval of the work, but it did not arrive. Now Vauxhall HQ tells me that because the car is out of warranty the approval no longer stands. Any suggestions?* "

Vauxhall offers an entirely different sequence of events. The company states that B.K. bought the car secondhand on 6 January 1998 in full knowledge of the rust on the rear doors, the cause of which was outside the Vauxhall warranty, and B.K. paid a price which took account of this. B.K. then commenced his campaign to get two new doors, free of charge under the Vauxhall warranty. On 23 January 1998 (not 1999), purely as a goodwill gesture, Vauxhall offered B.K. 50% of the cost of the new doors. Correspondence went to and fro and the last time Vauxhall wrote to B.K. making its offer of 50% was 22 October 1998.

Fair deal, or foul?

" *In May 1999 I bought a brand new Ford Fiesta 1.4 16v Ghia from a Ford franchise at a discounted price. There were mechanical problems from day one, which the dealership tried to resolve without success. Finally, last week, Ford agreed to exchange the car under its*

'Commitment' scheme but, by that time, I had lost faith in Fiestas and wanted a Focus. Ford now says that if I wish to upgrade to a Focus, I will have to pay the full list price for the Focus, minus the discounted price I paid for the Fiesta. Surely the deal should be discounted price against discounted price, or list price against list price. "

> Not at all. If you were being offered a 'new' 1999 model year 'V'-reg. Fiesta 1.4 Ghia as a direct swap for your 'T'-reg. Fiesta, Ford was playing fair. If you want something different, you can't expect Ford to discount an alternative car which is not an outgoing model.

85k in seven months?

" I suspect I may have bought a car which has been 'clocked'. It is a Scorpio Ultima TD, first registered on 17 October 1996, which I purchased in November 1998 with 16,000 miles on the clock. Since then the failure of the water pump, four wheel bearings, gearbox and catalytic converter have led me to believe it may have covered a much higher mileage. The AA Equifax service checked DVLA records, which showed mileages on disposal of 82,000 on 3 October 1997 and 167,000 on 9 May 1998. I enclose relevant documents for your perusal and ask if you think I have a case to bring against the Ford franchise which sold me the car. "

> The V5 records show that the car did 85,000 miles in 213 days, which is 400 miles a day, and unlikely unless the car was a taxi. You now need to obtain a full list of past owners from the DVLA and contact the two who disposed of the car on 3 October 1997 and 9 May 1998 to find out if they really did enter 82,000 miles and 167,000 miles on their V5 disposal slips. If they did, the dealer who sold you the car is guilty of a criminal offence for not showing 'due diligence' in checking the mileage of the car before sale. But I think an extra zero has somehow crept into the mileages registered on the data-

base. The car seems to have gone through the Ford Direct refurbishment centre at Tilbury at 8,234 miles before being serviced at Polar Motor Co., York at 8,402 miles on 2 October 1997, then 14,678 miles on 16 January 1998. This would be consistent with mileages on disposal of 8,200 on 3 October 1997 and 16,700 on 9 May 1999.

Mis-built Mondeo

" *My 1996, 2.5 Mondeo failed its first MOT in November because its offside headlamp was for a left-hand-drive car. I contacted the 'Ford Direct' dealer from whom I bought it only to be told they could not help because the car was out of warranty, but gave me the phone number of the Ford Customer Assistance Centre. The lady I spoke to consulted a colleague, then came back to tell me that Ford could not assist because the car was out of warranty. Have I a case for reimbursement of the £102 cost of the headlight?* "

I'd say yes because what you describe is a classic mis-build. Rhd and lhd cars are built on the same production line, but where the line is predominantly lhd a worker may accidentally fit a lhd part to a rhd car, or may have no rhd parts to hand, and fit a lhd part so the line is not held up. Manufacturers will tell you that the process is computerised and robotised. In fact, the fitting of smaller parts and trim is invariably done by hand using parts in bins beside the line. Once you explain to the Ford Customer Assistance Centre that your car is a mis-build and you had no way of knowing until the first MOT, I am sure your money will be promptly reimbursed.

Nuts

" *Normally I check my car very regularly and service it every 5,000 miles. But a protracted house move delayed this and it was not until eight and a half months, 9,500 miles and after a tyre change that I discovered one of the wheel bolts to be cross-threaded and not fully home. It sheared when I tried to remove it and a new wheel hub had to be fitted by a Renault dealer, the cost of which was £280.43. Clearly the fault lay with the tyre fitter. I took the matter up with the tyre specialists but they have denied any liability. I would appreciate your comments.* **"**

I believe you. But your problem is that due to the passage of time you cannot prove your accusation against the tyre fitter. You might find a judge in a Small Claims Court who is prepared to believe you, but I think this involves taking too much of a chance to justify the costs involved and you would be better off forgetting the matter.

Same job – £534 difference

" *I thought you would be interested in two different job sheets to correct the same problems with the ABS light and a trim bracket on a VW Polo 1.6GL. One VW franchise charged £74.03 to analyse what was wrong, then estimated £507.11 to repair it. The other charged £47.00 (including VAT) to analyse and sort both problems. Needless to say, I won't be going back to the first VW dealer.* **"**

This is shocking. Tellingly, both VW dealers used their VAG 1552 diagnostic interrogator (a paperback-sized computer) to find out what was wrong. But any piece of kit is only as good or as honest as the bloke using it. I had been getting an uncomfortable number of complaints about VW dealers. Most are good (Station Garage, Hexham, Northumberland, for example). But too many were downright greedy. I followed up by forwarding the letters direct to the MD of Volkswagen Group, VAG UK. All were thoroughly investigated and complaints about VW dealers slowed to a trickle.

Free gifts on the bill

" *I have just had my wife's 1997 Corolla serviced and MOTd at a Toyota dealer. It underwent the three-year 'B' (27,000 mile) service at a cost of £223.34, plus £32.11 for the MOT, plus £10.26 for new wiper blades, which it needed to pass. When we got the car home we found a bottle of screen-wash additive in the glovebox and thought, 'nice touch' until we spotted that it had been charged for on the bill at a cost of £2.35. Do hidden extras like this get up the noses of other readers?* "

Yes, but the screenwasher has to be working for the car to pass its MOT, which is why screen-wash additive is routinely included in the bill. Your reservoir must have been full when you submitted the car and I agree that, unless you had signed for a 'menu service' that automatically included screenwash, charging for the bottle in the glove compartment was completely unjustified.

Long time in Transit

" *I ordered a 17-seat, diesel LWB Ford Transit minibus from a Ford truck dealer last April. I was quoted a three-month delivery date, but because the old Transit 17 seater was one of the safest on the market I was prepared to accept this delay. The date was not met and in December I was told there would be a further delay due to a shortage of seats. The vehicle eventually arrived at the dealers at the end of January 2000, which was a quiet period for us, so I opted not to register it until 1 March on a 'W'. Then, when I went to collect it, I found a fault in the paintwork between the body panels. I maintain that this should have been spotted by quality control at the manufacturers, or by truck-dealer personnel during the pre-delivery inspection. The dealer said the minibus would have to go back to his bodyshop. Three days later I was told that Ford would not approve and pay for the repair. The dealer refuses to accept any responsibility stating that our contract was with Ford, despite the fact that his dealership took our order, deposit cheque and final payment.* "

If this is true and if all cheques were made out to the dealer, then the dealer is lying through his teeth. Under the Sale and Supply of Goods Act 1994, responsibility for any goods being of 'satisfactory' quality rests squarely with the supplier, not the manufacturer. In your case, it is possible that a court would rule that you have not 'accepted' the vehicle until it was put right (see my interpretation of the Sale and Supply of Goods Act 1994 under 'Legal Matters and Consumer Rights'). Though there was a considerable passage of time between the vehicle arriving at the dealer and the dealer's final refusal to take responsibility for the repair, you may still be within your rights to hand it back and demand your money back in full.

Something for nothing

" I bought a new Renault Megane in May 1999 and included in the deal
was, to quote, 'two years' free servicing' for which I was supplied with two
vouchers. These stated 'exected (sic) mileage 12,000' and 'exected mileage
24,000'. But when I tried to redeem the first, I was told that the 9,000 miles
I had driven the car was not enough to qualify for the 'free service'.
Apparently my mileage had to be within 10% of the mileage stated.
Naturally enough I made a fuss and the dealer ended up servicing my car
free of charge, but receiving no reimbursement from Renault. Apparently,
because the service was advertised as free, Renault has no contractual
obligation to honour it. "

I think this must be a simple matter of misinterpretation of the rules. Normally 10% would
be the limit above 12,000 miles at which the service remains free, with no lower-mileage limit.
In contract law there is no contract without con-
sideration, so someone offering something for
nothing is under no contractual obligation to
provide it. But if the so-called 'free service' is a
condition of a larger contract for which payment is received, then I don't see how calling it
'free' qualifies as a get-out clause. I've sent your
file on to Fenton Bresler who might use it for a
future article on 'free offers'.

Ford fiasco

" A week after passing her driving test, my daughter bought a 56,000-
mile, 'L'-registered Ford Fiesta 1.1i from a garage in Sutton Coldfield. She
paid £2,410. A couple of days later it went back to the garage because it
would not start. The garage owner told her there was nothing wrong. The
car remained difficult to start, kept flooding and used a lot of fuel, so she
took it to an independent garage in March. She was given a printed report
stating that the injection system was over-fuelling, that this had caused
severe engine wear and that the oil-pressure warning light, which should
have warned her of this, had been disconnected. Though the selling

garage offered to pay half the cost of a partial engine rebuild and £100 to-wards sorting out the fuelling, the cost has now escalated because the re-pair garage tells her that on further investigation the engine is not repairable. My daughter is on a limited income, finds it hard enough to pay the £200 a month she owes on the car and is distraught with worry. What can we do? ”

Back in December 1999, £2,410 was a normal retail price for a 94L Fiesta 1.1i base model with 55,000 miles. If the dealer bought it at auction at the normal trade price, his gross profit won't have been more than around £600 on the deal (he'll have a receipt for what he paid). Nevertheless, the car clearly was not of 'satis-factory' quality under the terms of the Sale and Supply of Goods Act 1994 and, because your daughter did not buy it at a cut price, she has every right to expect it to have been of 'satis-factory' quality. I would guess that the dealer is already offering all of his net profit on the sale and, unless it can be proven that he discon-nected the oil warning light or he has a history of shady deals, I doubt that Trading Standards would be prepared to pursue him any further. If he bought the car at auction, the oil pipe was very probably disconnected before he bought it. What I think you should do now is re-nego-tiate on the basis of fitting a secondhand engine from a crashed Fiesta 1.1i. This should not work out significantly more expensive than the ini-tial quotation for the engine rebuild.

DRIVING ABROAD

Pre-Spain service

" I own an 'L'-reg. Mondeo TD, which has 96,000 miles on the clock. I service it myself, changing filters, fluids and belts at the correct intervals. This summer I intend to drive to and explore northern Spain, so obviously want to prepare the car and carry essential spares in order to avoid any major problems. Can you recommend any publications which will help me prepare the car, and do you have any advice as to the spares I should carry? Soon after I return, the car will need timing-belt and alternator-belt replacements. Should I also replace the timing-belt tensioner? "

Consult the Haynes manual pages 0.7 to 1.26, paying particular attention to the cooling system. Replace the belts and tensioner before you go rather than after. Take with you a spare rhd clutch cable because you can only get lhd cables off the shelf in Spain. (Note: later Mondeos, 'N'-reg. on, have hydraulic clutches.) You will do everyone else a favour if you fit a large pair of mudflaps to the rear of the car to help prevent flying stones. It's a good idea to take an emergency windscreen. In Spain you need an insurance bail bond, you *must* carry a spare set of bulbs and, if you are a spectacle wearer, a spare pair of spectacles. While driving through France, you are not allowed to wear sunglasses or tinted spectacles when driving at night. You should also carry *two* warning triangles, a first-aid kit and fire extinguisher (compulsory in some, but not all EU countries.) Take at least £100 in both Pesetas and Francs to pay off 'on the spot' speeding fines. Take a set of Torx screwdrivers in your toolkit. One final tip, make sure the windscreen-washer pipe curls gently next to the bonnet hinge because they have a nasty habit of kinking, cutting off the water supply to the nozzles and blowing off the pipe at the pump where it's a bugger to get at.

Focusing to the right

" Having hired a Ford Focus on several occasions I am very impressed with the car and am considering buying one. However, I travel to the Continent frequently and therefore the dipped headlights of my car need to be deflected to the right on dip. There is no marking on the polycarbonate lenses of the Focus lights to show me where to apply beam deflectors. Is there a cheap, convenient and effective method of deflecting the beams for Continental driving? "

When the Channel 4 'Driven' programme took a Focus estate to France they applied black beam deflectors to the centres of the lenses. When I ferried a Focus Zetec to Holland several months earlier, like you, I was unsure where to place the deflectors. So I simply used the electric load compensator to point the beams downwards. Not one oncoming driver flashed me. If you're going to be running solo most of the time, the tall-geared Focus 1.6 Zetec S will prove to be the most efficient. But if you will be carrying four or five passengers plus luggage, you will be grateful for the extra grunt of a 1.8 or 2.0 litre Zetec E. Be sure to specify the £500 climate pack which includes a/c.

Confuserisation

" *Being about to motor abroad on holiday, I turned to pages 24 and 25 of the latest, somewhat improved AA members' handbook and dialled the insurance number to request proposal forms for car and personal insurances while in Europe. I was then passed from one telephone number to another for what seemed like an age, eventually spoke to someone who seemed to know what I wanted, and requested the proposal forms. They never arrived, so I had to arrange my travel insurance through my bank. Why is it that computers are supposed to make everything happen at the speed of light, but it takes the poor old customer twice as long pressing buttons and listening to synthesised messages?* "

The AA handbook shows a general insurance number (0800 444 777) on page 25 and a separate number for Five Star Europe (0800 444 500) on page 24 under 'Motoring in Europe'. I tried this myself. First I had to press < * > then < 1 >, then I had to listen to a disembodied voice which gave me three choices, of which I picked < 1 > and got straight through to Carol Davis who promised to send me the Five Star proposal forms. (You don't need forms. You can simply book Five Star over the phone.) As a test, I then asked if I could be transferred to 0990 500 600 for travel documents, and was. To order the *AA Guide to Motoring in Europe*, which includes an application for an International Driving Permit, I had to give my membership number and my credit card number because the documents now cost £2.95. After ordering the form and information on a Friday they arrived the following Tuesday.

Dippy advice

" *I have received conflicting advice as to how to cut and where to put the beam deflectors on the headlights of my Peugeot 306 GTi-6. How can I be sure who is right?* "

Find somewhere at night where you can park your car facing a wall and about 20–30 feet from it. Switch on dipped beam and see where it falls. Then use strips of black insulation tape to mask your headlights in such a way that the dipped beams fall lower and would not shine directly into the eyes of a driver approaching on the left-hand side of the road. Also experiment with the car's electric beam-height adjuster. With many cars, simply turning this to its lowest setting is enough to dip the beams well below the eyeline of approaching drivers on the left-hand side of the road, making bits of sticky tape redundant. Of course, either way, your forward vision on dipped beam will be seriously impaired.

From dip to dipstick

" *Your readers have previously warned about the French service station nail-in-the-tyre scam. Another is the dry dipstick routine. Ever-so-helpful attendant dips the oil and presents the driver with a half-dipped dipstick showing the merest hint of oil on the bottom. An oil change is then recommended, which I refused. But I then made the mistake of allowing said attendant to top the oil up from a two-litre container for which he charged me Ffr 215 (about £23). When I got back to Blighty I had to have the excess oil in the sump drained off.* "

After this appeared, only three other readers complained of the same scam. But there have been warnings of a nasty form of highway robbery in Spain. While your car is stopped at a service area someone sticks a nail into one of your tyres. You recommence your journey and are forced to pull on to the hard shoulder to change tyres. A car full of 'friendly' Spaniards then stops to help you change the tyre. While this is being done, one of the other Spaniards steals all the valuables left in your car. You notice the theft as soon as you get back inside, then find that another tyre has been punctured so you can't give chase and are also left with a flat tyre and no spare.

Another rip-off

" *To add to the nail-in-the-tyre number and the un-dipped dipstick dodge at French service stations, may I add my own experience in Italy? There, the obliging attendant pointed out that my wiper blade was torn and offered a new one. I suspected a scam when I noticed the large quantity of wiper blade packages spilling out of a waste bin.* "

Thank you for the tip. Only three readers experienced the lubrication leg-lifter, so I'm not sure that this is as widespread as was originally assumed.

Towcar tragedy

" *During a recent caravanning holiday in Portugal, our 1984 Granada Ghia X automatic broke down. Our Green Flag emergency cover paid for it to be taken to the brand new Ford dealer at Beja, and our caravan was placed in the local campsite. However the Ford workshop foreman was clearly scared stiff of our car and refused even to touch it, despite my offer to pay for four hours' labour whatever the outcome. As a result, we were told that if we wished to continue to be assisted by Green Flag we had no alternative other than to abandon our old friend there and then, and agree to be flown home. Green Flag then paid for me to hire a towcar and return to Portugal to collect the caravan. I have lost a car, which was irreplaceable, and have written to Ford to complain about their dealer's service. But could Green Flag also be at fault for not taking the car to a competent garage?* "

It depends on the terms of your Green Flag policy document, which does not seem to have covered repatriation of your 15-year-old car in the event of a breakdown. There is a limit to what these policies can cover for an affordable premium. The foreman of the brand new Ford dealership had probably never even seen an old fuel-injected, 2.8-litre V6 coupled to a three-speed, in-line autobox, carried no spare parts and had no means of getting any in Portugal. He and Green Flag must have taken the pragmatic view that it simply was not worth even attempting a repair, especially if the problem was transmission failure. Had the car been returned to the UK, any competent automatic transmission specialist would know the old Ford three-speeder very well, and parts could have been obtained to fix it, if not through Ford, through one of the Granada Clubs. But that would have required repatriation of the car as well as the caravan to be covered.

Going South

" I will be driving my ageing 108,000-mile Volvo 440GLE to the South of France at the end of August. It gets a full service and semi synthetic oil change every year and had new timing belts at 40,000 miles and 80,000 miles, plus a throttle cable at 82,000 miles. What precautions should I take prior to the journey and what spare parts should I take with me? "

Years ago, without any preparation, a neighbour bundled his girlfriend and her two kids into his rusting boat-tail Alfa 1750 Duetto Spider and drove to Spain and back with no trouble at all. But he was a gambler (a croupier, actually) and you might not be so lucky. Problems are most likely to arise in the cooling system, so have it flushed and reverse-flushed, have a new thermostat fitted, replace any perished or seeping hoses and consider replacing both the water pump and the thermo switch to the electric fan. If the brake fluid has not been changed in the past three years, change that. Replace any perished tyres. And I would give the oil and filter a mid-year change. Carry with you a spare rhd clutch cable (because there can be a long delay on parts specific to rhd cars in France). Buy a spare bulb kit, a warning triangle, a first-aid kit, a fire extinguisher, dipped-beam converters and a GB sticker. Also remember to take with you the car's V5 registration document as well as your driving licence and paper counterpart and your insurance certificate. The AA does a useful guide, *Driving in Europe*, tel: 0117 930 8242. Vauxhall dealers are offering a travel pack of warning triangle, first-aid kit and spare-bulb kit for £31.

You have been warned

" *A couple of seasonal warnings, if I may. When using your own car to travel to the airport, make sure you take with you your driving licence, counterpart (if a photo licence), insurance certificate and MOT. If you don't, and get stopped by the police, you won't be able to show your documents at a police station within the required seven days. When using your own car for a holiday in France, make sure you take all its documents, including the V5 registration document and make sure your beam converters are permanent. Also display a full-sized GB plate, because last year French police were gleefully fining Brits who had nothing on the backs of their cars apart from the new Europlates.* "

I'm not sure I agree about the beam deflectors. The 'crime' is dazzling oncoming motorists, and the most effective way to prevent this is to use the headlamp-beam height adjuster to point your dipped beams further down. This can't be done on Citroën Xantias though, because their suspension keeps them level, so beam-height adjusters aren't fitted.

DRIVING CONDITIONS

A flash in the pan

" I find it very difficult to accept that most Gatso cameras can possibly aid road safety. The A40 into London is one of our busiest roads. Three Gatso cameras on this road are situated where the speed limit abruptly changes: from 70 to 50, and from 50 to 40. The result is three lanes of traffic braking hard to lose 20 miles an hour of speed past the cameras, then allowing their speed to creep up, only to brake again for the next camera. There are also Gatso cameras on the 70-mph limit stretches of this road. Imagine driving out of London in the usual nose-to-tail traffic, someone moving out to overtake and everyone being temporarily blinded by the two flashes of the camera. This is potentially lethal. "

I have actually seen police accident 'appeal for witness' boards propped up against Gatsos on the A40, so it may well be that they are causing more accidents than they are supposed to prevent. If a driver were to be involved in a serious accident as a direct result of being dazzled by the flashes of a Gatso camera, this may provide the scenario for a test case. To lay blame successfully on the dazzle from the camera flashes, there would have to be no other contributory factors. The driver would have to have been complying with the Highway Code to the letter, and would also need to prove he or she had excellent eyesight. But since it is an offence under Regulation 27 of the Road Vehicle Lighting Regulations 1989 to use 'any other lamp... so as to cause undue dazzle or discomfort to other persons', it may be possible to contend that the police officer who drove to the camera site and set the camera had committed an offence which caused the accident, and was therefore liable.

Flash crash

" *I agree that allowing a very bright Gatso flash to dazzle an oncoming driver at night creates a traffic hazard. I nearly had an accident on the single carriageway near Chessington when the Gatso there flashed and dazzled me so badly I had to stop to recover my night vision. It was very dangerous and unnerving, and could have been disastrous if there had been a car in front of me. I accept the necessity of speed cameras, but I hate the pettiness of the way so many are sited where the speed limit is ambiguous (or inadequately signed). The A3 is a classic mess of confusingly variable speed limits, with cameras deliberately positioned behind road signs, seemingly to entrap rather than modulate traffic. Why can't the police have a more consistent policy of fitting speed-limit reminder signs whenever a new camera is installed – and stop the nonsense of hiding the cameras. The fact that they don't, suggests that the Gatso's main function is to make money rather than prevent accidents.* "

I quote from the thinking behind Australia's 'Operation Victoria', which has been adopted in Lancashire. An internal police report dismissed the idea of placing speed cameras at accident blackspots stating, 'insufficient numbers of motorists would be booked, making the camera of little *fund-raising* benefit'. The other anomaly is that while the police are responsible for installing speed cameras, they are not responsible for putting up speed-limit signs and reminder signs. Any reader who wants to become active in opposing heavy-handed polic-

ing designed only to increase revenue from
fines would do well to join The Association of
British Drivers, PO Box 19608, London SE19
2ZW, tel: 07000 781544. But always remember,
the less motorists pay in tax and fines, the more
the Government will need to raise from other
forms of taxation.

Cat's-eyed

" *On the night of 4 March I was driving along the B1190 road near
Lincoln when I heard a bang. I got out to find that the offside front wheel
and tyre of my car had been destroyed by a Cat's-eye which had become
dislodged from its hole in the centre of the road. I am in possession of
both the damaged wheel and the Cat's-eye which damaged it. I also took
photos of the scene. I wrote to the council and received a promising letter
by return, which said they were 'considering' the situation. I then received a further letter stating that since the road had been inspected and
found to be all right within six months of the incident, under the
Highways Act they did not accept any liability, and so would not be making me any offer. The cost of a new wheel and tyre, and suspension re-
alignment amounted to £400.* "

Go to your local County Court and ask for the papers to take a Small Claims Court action against
the council. In Irish law if the accident was the result of the council's negligence in carrying out
road works it would be judged as mis-feasance
and the council would be liable. If the accident
was the result of the council's failure to carry out
works, it would be judged as non-feasance and
the council would not be liable. But in UK law
there is no such distinction between mis-feasance
and non-feasance. Anyone wanting to take action
against a council for mis-feasance (for example,
the incorrect and dangerous installation of traffic calming measures which damaged their car)
would have to prove that the measure contra-

vened Government guidelines. First you need to obtain an index to the various Traffic Advisory Leaflets which give these specifications which is 4/99 'Traffic Calming Bibliography', available free from Traffic Advisory Unit, Zone 3/23, Great Minster House, 76 Marsham Street, London SW1P 4DR, tel: 020 7676 2478. Readers might also want to obtain Leaflet 2/93 'The Highways (Traffic Calming) Regulations 1993' from Network Customer Services (Operational Strategy), tel: 020 7921 4531.

Deadly weapons

" Regarding your suggestion that 'considerate Volvo drivers' should use their headlamp load compensators to 'turn down their daytime running lights', I think you're on to a loser. In my experience and that of my motorcycling friends, there is little chance of encountering 'a considerate Volvo driver'. I do not mean to mock the poor unfortunates who are visually impaired, but it does seem that a large proportion of Volvo drivers are completely oblivious to the existence of motorcyclists – even those riding in bright clothing and with their headlights on, as recommended by the Highway Code. "

I'm afraid I live in a part of Surrey where many Volvos and even most Jeep Grand Cherokees are driven very considerately. But no harm in reminding motorists to 'Think Bike' and avoid entanglements with the Ogris and Malcolms of this world.

Bicycle manners

" I am not an 'eco warrier'. I cycle four miles from my home in Islington to work in the City and back again each day for the simple reasons that it is free and takes 20 minutes, whereas a car, bus or underground would take at least twice as long. But every day I am struck by the appalling road manners of my fellow cyclists and amazed that more are not killed by their

own stupidity. Not all car drivers are perfect, of course. But cyclists who ride through red lights or use the pavement have no grounds for complaint if they are knocked over. I have been cycling in London for 30 years (and driving for 20) without a problem, but I do follow the Highway Code. **"**

Only a cyclist could have made this point without arousing accusations of being 'anti cyclist'.

Life's too short

" *Further to the letter concerning 'eco-worriers' on their bicycles, I would like to add that the pro-bike, anti-car lobby is robbing me of the most precious commodity of all, which is time. They should also remember that a commuter is someone trying to get to and from work, to earn money, to pay taxes, which end up being used to subsidise cycle lanes.* **"**

In Barcelona, they recently cut week-day tolls by 40% on an autopista to a dormitory town from which many workers commute into the city. But instead of cutting them at weekends, they actually raised them by a few Pesetas, reasoning, as you do, that people *have* to go to work. They don't *have* to use the autopistas for leisure journeys.

White van Samaritan

" *On Saturday we ran out of petrol in our MGTD in the middle of nowhere. Since we are covered by breakdown insurance I could have called them out using my mobile phone, but was reluctant to do so over such a trivial matter. Then a young man driving a white Transit van stopped. On hearing of my problem, he drove back home some six miles to Winsford, collected a fuel can, drove to a filling station and, half an hour later, delivered 11 litres of four-star to us together with a filling station receipt. He didn't ask for, nor expect, any reward. In a world of road rage he restored our faith in human nature.* **"**

Just goes to show you can't judge a person by the colour of his van.

Speeding

" I read in one of my local newspapers that motorists are saying that they will continue to travel in excess of speed limits unless the police crack down on all of the culprits. Would it not be an idea for any 'minor' motoring convictions to be noted at the time of occurrence and then be brought to the attention of the motorists when they either come to renew their road tax or sell the vehicle to someone else? The use of fixed cameras such as speed traps and junction watchers would also increase the probability of catching these culprits. "

Business motorists naturally need to get from A to B as fast as they possibly can, so take a calculated risk by driving as fast as they think they can safely get away with. If, in so doing, the vast majority of them break the limits set by law, then the law is at fault and some of these limits need looking at with a view to raising them. If the risk of getting caught speeding increases, more motorists will comply with speed limits even if they are set at unreasonably low levels and even if this forces them to spend more time on the road. More people driving slowly will put more cars on the road for longer and have the tangential effect of slowing traffic down even further. Besides the high levels of pollution this will create, traffic jams will increase, appointments will be missed and the UK economy will slow down appreciably. It might be an idea to de-criminalise out-of-town speeding by making all trunk-road and motorway speeding offences within 30 mph of the limit subject to no more than a progressive series of fines – say £20 for 10 mph over, £40 for 20 mph over and £60 for 30 mph over. The fines would then serve their principal purpose of raising extra taxation revenue without affecting the ability of drivers to earn their livings in a fast-paced society.

Traffic-harming measures

" Have you ever conducted a public debate on the effects of various traffic-calming measures on the vehicles they are supposed to calm? "

Yes. We covered the unnecessarily high and viciously dangerous chicane kerbs on Copse Hill, Wimbledon in some detail in 1999. There is no doubt that tight, high-kerbed chicanes and pinch-points cause damage to vehicle suspensions, tyres and bodywork; road humps cause suspension, exhaust system and underbody damage; and mini-roundabouts promote severe tyre wear. Not only that, braking and gear-changing for slow-speed road humps and chicanes create additional, unnecessary pollution. I'm not against 20-mph limited residential zones as long as these are not imposed on main routes. You only have to visit Germany or Holland to see how traffic-calming restrictions can be applied wisely and well without impeding traffic flow and creating pollution from extra traffic jams which, in the UK, have increased by 26% since 1997.

Gatso alley

" Back in February 1996 I was prosecuted for exceeding a variable speed limit on the M25. It was alleged that at the hour of 23.15 I drove under a gantry displaying a 50 mph limit at 67 mph. I took the case to court, pleading that the 50 mph speed limit was not displayed when I drove under the gantry, but this was ignored and I was fined £80 with £60 costs and four penalty points. I will never come to accept this gross injustice. The road was completely clear at the time. There was no traffic jam ahead. So imposing the 50 mph limit was completely unjustified anyway. The fact that the equipment used to display the limit failed only adds to my agony. "

There were some teething troubles with the M25 variable limits. I can't tell you whether the sensors which are supposed to control the variable limits failed, whether the gantry was being tested, or whether the limit display actually did fail. But the police should have been able to present video-camera evidence that the limit signs were in fact lit when their systems told them they were lit. If no visual evidence is presented that the gantry was displaying a limit lower than 70 mph, then this should be a defence for other cases and should be properly tested in a higher court.

Eco-warrior strikes

" I was stuck in a congested London street, then we all moved forward. From somewhere to the rear of my car I heard the squeal of a cyclist's tyres as he frantically braked. A few minutes' later he shot past me, inflicting a deep scratch along the side of my vehicle, before disappearing with two fingers in the air. My dealer quoted £565 for the repair and respray, but I managed to get the job done satisfactorily by a small operator for £270. The point is, what can be done about these two-wheeled hooligans? "

Nothing. You pay a fortune in taxes to take your car on the road. He pays zilch. He does not even have to be insured. The answer is to try not to bring your car into London. This may mean travelling in filthy, overcrowded, inconvenient and infuriatingly unreliable public transport. But soon the only three ways to avoid a grim rail journey will be to work from home, to get a bicycle of your own or to become a Labour Cabinet Minister.

Choked off

" I note with concern that Mr Prescott is considering allowing local authorities to reduce speed limits in certain built-up areas from 30 mph to

20 mph. Has the man no conception of the increased pollution this will cause? I do not know of one family car that will travel in any gear higher than second at 20 mph. Yet quite a few will manage 30 mph in top. Thus, to travel the same distance, a car engine will have to run at more rpm at 20 than at 30, thus putting out proportionately more exhaust gases. The official line is that more people are killed or seriously injured at 30 mph then 20 mph. In Central London, the average speed is approximately 11 mph, yet Central London has the highest number of road casualties. **"**

I have no problem with residential areas or high-pedestrian areas which are not through-routes being restricted to 20 mph at times when there are likely to be a lot of people about. My problem is that most of the time there won't be, so a 20 mph limit will impede traffic flow unnecessarily. This is the fundamental problem with speed limits. Most of the time it is entirely safe to travel at far higher speeds than the limit, but some of the time even the limit is too high. Where do the police spring speed traps? At the points and the times within a limit where drivers feel it is safe to drive at a higher speed. Life should not be about imposing more and more restrictions, then heavy-handedly enforcing them. It should be about using common sense. Only a homicidal maniac would drive past a school at 30 mph when hordes of kids are spilling across the street. But when the school is shut and the area is deserted, higher speeds can be justified in the interests of efficiency. I don't get your point about engine revs and gear speeds. Cars pollute the most at low revs before they are warmed up properly, which is what happens in traffic jams. Eliminate traffic jams by encouraging traffic flow and you will soon see pollution levels fall.

A nation of criminals

" *My wife and I have each been driving for more than 20 years and until recently had never been convicted of any motoring offences. Recently, we both received fixed penalty notices for speeding. My wife's arrived much to her surprise because she was completely unaware she had been clocked. The notice contained no evidence of the offence, merely a very poor description of the location, a speed marginally over the limit, a date, and a time. In my case, I was caught by a hand-held, laser speed detector, about the size of a Sony Walkman. I was pulled over and was shown a digital readout of the speed I had supposedly been doing. The police officers were using two of these devices at the time and I was not given any evidence that it was my car that had, in fact, been clocked. Where do we stand on this? Should we fight our cases in court and risk a greater fine and a greater number of penalty points on our licences?* "

The more ordinary, normally law-abiding citizens who are fined and criminalised for speeding for the first time in their lives, the more of an issue this is likely to become. It used to be possible to be convicted for speeding on the evidence of one police officer corroborated by another. Now, the evidence is supplied either by the speed detection device corroborated by the officer using it, or by the speed detection device corroborated by two photographs taken in a fixed time, which show the distance the car travelled in that time and from which its speed can be calculated. If you are convicted on the evidence of an unmanned speed camera, you can insist on seeing these two photographs, but that means taking your case to court where you inevitably face a more severe penalty than the fixed one. There is some doubt as to whether digital images can be used as corroborating evidence because they can easily be 'enhanced' or altered. This needs to be tested in the courts. P.B. of Rotherham has also written of being fined after a 30 mph limit was suddenly extended into a previously de-restricted area and a speed trap set up to catch unwitting 'offenders'.

The perfect high street

" You say you have 'no problem with 20 mph restrictions where there are likely to be a lot of people'. We have one of these on Berkhamsted High Street. Admittedly, it lasts for 24 hours, but, combined with car parking both sides of the street and the relatively new A41 by-pass, it has had the effect of rejuvenating our town centre. This is pedestrian-friendly, full of attractive, prospering shops and, with shoppers visiting from miles around, is now more bustling and busier than ever. "

That's the way to do it. Welcome cars, let them park briefly in the street, but keep their speeds pedestrian-friendly and give through-traffic an excellent high-speed by-pass. If only the planners at Oxford and Reading thought like this instead of making their centres car-free and hence shopper-free zones.

Hey, that's us!

" *In past years the description 'motorist' referred to a minority of the population who were wealthy or fortunate enough to have a car. Today, when most households have access to at least one car, would it not be in order to drop the term entirely? It is being used by the anti-car press, the anti-car BBC and the Government whenever new legislation or taxation is announced as if it is almost a third sex and only applies to the rich few, when in reality it hits practically all of us. The inference is: 'don't worry, we are only hitting those who can afford it'. Perhaps the title 'car user' would make everyone aware that the increased cost was going to hit them and not some rich and unknown 'motorist'.* "

Some recent Government statistics may be helpful here. At the end of 1998 the number of people holding a full driving licence in the UK rose to 31 million; the number of cars taxed for road use reached 23 million; and the total number of vehicles taxed for road use rose to 27,500,000. Lord MacDonald has stated that he regards the 'Rail Users Association' as his 'eyes and ears'. Perhaps he would regard a 'Car Users Association' similarly. I once proposed that the 'Association of British Drivers' changed its name to the 'Road Users Association'. But this was rejected because it would have included potential 'enemies', such as cyclists and equestrians, who don't pay for their use of the roads. Our next obstacles will be persuading my editor to change the name of this publication to 'The Car User's Telegraph' and getting Mike Rutherford to re-name 'The Motorists' Association'.

Speed and schools

" *I note the frequent correspondence and articles on the subject of safety vs speed. The present answer seems to be to reduce speed limits regardless of circumstances and conditions. Outside a school when children are about, a speed limit of 15 mph would be a sensible thing. But outside the same school at midnight a speed of 60 mph may well be perfectly safe. Why do we not adopt the system widely used in the USA? A few hundred yards on the approach to a school are notices with flashing lights, which say, 'when lights are flashing speed limit is 15 mph'. The lights are programmed by the school to operate at appropriate times of the day and can also be manually switched on for special occasions. From my observations, the limits are generally very closely observed, police enforcement is rigorous and understood to be in the best interests of society, so enhancing their standing with the public. Another rule, universally applied, is 'no overtaking of school buses when the lights on them are flashing'. We need a generally more rational approach to the subject of speed vs safety.* "

I agree. The Spanish have one of the best systems in the world for slowing traffic down when entering a high-pedestrian area. Sensors detect when traffic is exceeding the speed limit and light up red 'stop' signals over the road. As soon as the traffic slows down to the limit, the sensors pick this up and change the lights to green. We don't adopt this extremely sensible and well respected system because it doesn't generate any revenue from fines.

M6 madness

" *Please ask Paul Ripley to drive south from Lancaster to Birmingham on the M6 motorway. Totally unnecessary 50 mph limits are posted at half-mile intervals. How would he handle the frustration of obeying the law while everyone else belts past at 80 mph?* "

Like everyone else, I expect. I found myself on this stretch a couple of months ago. At first, the traffic was meekly obeying the 50 mph limits and, of course, the result was enormous knock-back jams with traffic stationary for miles going into each 50 limit. Then, as the traffic got further south, every single driver on the motorway began to totally ignore the 50-limit signs. The nearside lane travelled through at 60 mph; the centre lane travelled at 70 mph; and the outer lane moved at 80–90 mph. So what thick-headed jobsworth ever put these signs there in the first place? Whoever it is should be forced to compensate every driver held up by his rampant stupidity out of his pension fund. Then perhaps he'd feel the pain his actions have caused to people who have to earn their living out in the real world.

Turning motorways into bridle paths

" Mike Rutherford made an excellent point about motorways losing their motorway status and being turned into 'Gatso alleys' to entrap anyone attempting to drive at the motorway limit. But there is another, even more serious hazard. The loss of motorway status means that these roads can now be used by traffic prohibited from motorways, including learner drivers and pedestrians. "

My copy of the Highway Code includes the following additional hazards, all of which may use the new 'non-motorways': horses, motorcycles under 50 cc, cyclists, agricultural vehicles and most invalid carriages. Mike Rutherford can be written to directly at The Motorists' Association, PO Box 325, Longfield DA3 7JU.

Observations

" I drive 25,000 miles a year, mostly commuting from Maidstone to London, and offer two observations from this experience. A lot of cars less *than three years old are driving around with two failed brake lights. Since cars are not first tested until they are three years old, I think that all new cars should be fitted with brake-lamp-failure warning lights. On the M20 at rush hour I also regularly spot a police Volvo travelling on the nearside lane at a mere 50 mph. The results of this are severe tail-backs, dangerous heavy braking and the possibility of knock-on accidents in the traffic up to two miles behind. Why can't they drive at 70 mph like everyone else?* **"**

Two very good points. The police officers may be under orders to conserve fuel or to 'slow down' the traffic flow. Time is not money to them like it is to everyone who has to earn a living in the commercial world. That said, do you really need to commute into London by car? Or are your 'Integrated Transport' station-parking charges and rail fares so ridiculously high that using the car remains the best option?

Towing the line

" *I represent a club for individuals working for roadside assistance organisations. Increasingly, we are finding that when the police come across a stranded motorist, the officers insist on calling out a recovery truck contracted to the police for which a statutory charge of £105 is imposed. Our members then get the flak, despite the fact that they are often the self-same recovery drivers who would have been called out free of charge under the stranded motorists' roadside assistance insurance.* **"**

This issue first came up a few years ago when, apparently, the grounds for preventing the motorist using his or her own recovery organisation was that it could not get to them for more than half an hour. It is part of the job of the police to get the stranded vehicle removed as soon as possible for safety reasons. But if any readers feel they have been unjustly charged for a police tow-away, please write, giving location, date and the police force concerned.

Towaway tactics

" I was most interested to read the letter about the police dropping stranded motorists into the jaws of recovery sharks. It is blatantly obvious that 'back-handers' are taking place and so many of us are suffering this experience it is high time something was done about this police corruption. I am frequently told that I must be naive to travel on a motorway without a mobile phone, and that I must never use the motorway phone under any circumstances. What a country we live in! I was transported 12 and a half miles back up the motorway, in the opposite direction of my destination, to a remote, decrepit and filthy depot, where I was told to pay £125 cash on the nail or my car would be impounded. A most intimidating situation. Not a way to treat two elderly people shaken up in a nasty accident in the fast lane. After submitting to this blackmail, the RAC Relay arrived ten minutes after my call and got me home with an efficiency which really cheered my heart. Their depot was nearer to the accident than the recovery sharks' and they told me they hadn't been busy and had several recovery vehicles available. No doubt if one were to complain the police would get their revenge by trumping up some charge over the accident. I used to hold the police in very high regard but not any more. It is little wonder that they get no help from the public in solving serious crimes. "

Steady on there. These are serious accusations against the police. If there is any bribery involved I will eat one of my hats. But this has become a national problem. On the one hand the police will block a road for hours while they measure up an accident, even, in some cases, preventing fire engines and ambulances getting too close for fear of destroying 'scene of crime evidence'. On the other hand, the police say they have a duty to clear the road quickly by using priority-contracted recovery outfits which charge the victims a fortune. If a car is damaged in an accident it is possible to reclaim the recovery charges on an insurance policy. According to an independent insurer, this is already adding £20 to premiums for motorcycle insurance and even more to policies for cars.

M.S. of Manchester and P.S. of Boncath had similar experiences where the police called in a cash-payment contractor, which charged up to £170 without even giving them a chance to contact the roadside assistance organisations of which they were members. Most amazing of all was D.W. of Cambridge's account of what happened after her Mini Metro was stolen from the station car park at Haslemere in August 1998: 'A member of the public reported to the local police that the car was being driven 'in a suspicious manner' in a very exclusive area. The next day the car was found parked next to a house which had been burgled, and the police ordered that it be towed to a local garage where it was to be examined by their scene of crime officer. I then phoned the garage and was asked to provide full details of my car insurance, which I did. The garage told me it needed my insurance details so it could bill my insurance company for its services in transporting my car from the burgled house and storing it so the SOCO could check it out. I could easily have collected the car from where it was dumped and the only reason it had needed to be moved was for the police investigation. Not only that, the bill increased for several days' storage because the SOCO could not get to it straight away and I had to pay the bill in cash before the garage would release the car. (The bill was less than the damage would have been to my no claims bonus if my insurer had paid.) I have absolutely no proof whatsoever that the police received any backhanders from the garage for this.'

Not for turning

" *Many motorists feel that 'no turning' notices placed at the end of driveways are yet another example of 'Little England' mean-mindedness and make three-point turns in them anyway. What they don't realise is that using their power-assisted steering to turn their front wheels lock to lock wears away the tarmac creating holes which cost around £100 a year for repairs. A slight spin from rear wheels reversed into a driveway causes similar damage. We can't gate our driveway turn-ins to prevent turning because it would negate the point of a driveway turn-in, forcing us to stop on the road while opening the gate. Please could you bring this to the notice of your readers and request them to drive on until they reach a designated turning place.* **"**

Fair enough.

'See-through' cars

" *Would you agree that people who plaster dark tinting over their front and rear screens are causing difficulties for the rest of us? On a busy road, being able to look through the rear and front screens of the car in front can help to see hazards ahead.* **"**

You are right. It is useful to be able to 'see through' the vehicle in front, which, of course, is impossible if it happens to be a truck, van, large MPV or big 4x4, in which case you should increase the cushion of space between you and it, or move to a different lane. Drivers of high vehicles enjoy a huge advantage over car drivers in being able to see over the tops of the cars in front, which is why they are able to spot hazards far sooner, as long as their own view is not blocked by an even higher vehicle in front.

Law enforcers who don't know the law

" *I was interested to read Mike Rutherford's comments about a Basingstoke police officer who clocked over 7,000 speeding motorists. I was a victim, and was perfectly prepared to accept the 'fixed penalty' alternative to a court appearance. But I was not allowed to because I had a German licence. Not only that, Hants police refused to even accept that* *my German licence was a valid document and also prosecuted me for driving without a licence. I countered that this action was in direct contravention of Section 99A (1) of the Road Traffic Act 1988 as amended by EC Directive 91/439, which fully harmonised the use of any EU licence in any EU country. I eventually secured compensation after threatening to sue the Chief Constable of Hampshire for malicious prosecution and the public expense of my case was considerable. I have now reluctantly changed my perfectly valid German licence for a UK one to avoid any repetition of this saga.* **"**

There is absolutely no excuse for ignorance of road traffic law by any road traffic officer. Motorvation Consultants Ltd publishes a paperback-sized loose-leaf file entitled *Hughes Guide to Traffic Law* which is updated on subscription every six months, and is now also available on CD Rom at £17. Every traffic officer should have a copy, at least of the file, and it's not a bad idea for every driver to subscribe as well. For more information, telephone 01306 713543 or visit the website: www.motorvation.co.uk.

Unposted limits

" *Don't you think it would be a good idea if the post for every speed camera warning sign also bore a repeater sign of the limit for that particular stretch of road? I made this suggestion to the Chief Constable of the West Midlands, and also wrote to the Department of Environment, Transport and the Regions. All I received in return was a reply from some minion stating that it was the responsibility of the local authority properly to mark the speed limits within its boundaries.* **"**

This is about as obvious as the need to fit a car with brakes and a steering wheel. But the minion is right. I think that the Roads Minister, Lord Witty, will be more responsive and might persuade his department to issue guidelines to local authorities which include your suggestion.

How refreshing

" *My local paper has revealed that South Yorkshire Police has come up with a novel way of encouraging road safety. It is to pre-publicise the sites of its mobile speed-check cameras on its website: www.southyorks.police.uk. In the words of Superintendent Stuart Chapman, 'If we don't catch anyone then we will have succeeded. We are not out to fine people. Our aim is to cut down on speeding.' He added, 'There have been calls to paint the fixed cameras a bright colour to make them stand out. But that's a matter which local councils will have to decide.' However, police attitudes are very different in Manchester where mobile speed traps are concealed inside unmarked white vans, which constantly change position.* "

Anyone who needs to pass through South Yorkshire on the A1, M1, M18, etc. had better check this website before they set out. Or keep their speed under 75 mph if they have the time to do so. Of course, speeding never killed anyone. Crashing is what kills people.

Not out to get you, yet

" *What are those strange-looking blue objects appearing at the sides of carriageways and on motorway bridges? They remind me of up-dated Gatso speed cameras, but appear to face the wrong way.* "

They are usually part of the Trafficmaster traffic-jam early-warning system. They can take pictures of passing cars, which are transmitted to control centres, but apparently only register the centre digits of the registration. Vodafone shops sell a useful little AA gizmo for £30 which sticks on to your car windscreen and picks up the Trafficmaster signals warning of traffic jams ahead or on the roads either side of your direction of travel. It's £30 well spent. Unfortunately the similar-looking SPECs speed-trap equipment is painted the same Trafficmaster blue.

Speedtraps on the web

" As well as the South Yorks Police website there is a less official, website directory of speed camera locations at www.ukgatsos.com. I am not sure it is approved of, but publication of the site should help every driver be more responsible. "

It's a good site, particularly in alerting drivers to fixed speed cameras hidden by trees, shubbery and direction signs as well as the favourite spots for laser traps, which by no means correspond with accident black spots or 'red zones' as they are called in Surrey. But some temporary, roadworks speed traps, which disappeared long ago have not been deleted from the lists. Another really excellent site is www.speed-trap.co.uk. Run by Chris Longhurst, this site tests radar detectors, has links to the official police websites, sends (free) subscribers e-newsmails, and alerted us to GEODESY. (www.abd.org is yet another.)

Holier than thou

" I replaced my old Peugeot 505 with a 406, and although in most respects it is a fine car I find the ride very hard over bad road surfaces. Please advise what other make of car would give a smoother ride. "

Over the past two years the quality of town and suburban road surfaces has deteriorated so markedly that even well suspended cars, such as the 406, will jar over the many ruts and potholes. So the answer is a large 4x4 with balloon-type tyres which, unfortunately, will do further damage to the road surface, particularly when manoeuvring. It would seem that moneys for road maintenance have been cunningly diverted into 'traffic-calming measures' such as humps and chicanes. Since motorists pay around £36 billion a year into Treasury coffers in the form of VED, fuel tax and VAT, they deserve a lot better than the worst roads in Europe.

Nitty gritty

" Last winter I had a serious accident after my car skidded on ice on an ungritted road. The car was written off and, more seriously, I was unable to work for nine months. Can I hold the council liable for what happened to me? "

It depends on the circumstances, and where the accident happened. On 15 June 2000 in a case against East Sussex County Council taken to appeal in the House of Lords, five law lords ruled that there is no statutory duty on English or Welsh councils to salt or grit roads. The council's duty to 'maintain the highway' is confined to keeping roads in good repair. Lower courts had previously held that the 1980 Highways Act imposed a wider duty on councils, including gritting. In his judgement, Lord Hoffman stated that it seemed to him that Parliament might take the view that there should be a duty to keep roads free of ice and snow, but with a defence against compensation claims except where they had acted unreasonably. In this case, after a forecast of freezing conditions, East Sussex County Council had sent out gritting trucks at 5.30am with the order that gritting should be completed by 7.30am, but they had not reached the place where the accident occurred at 7.10am. In Scotland the 1984 Roads Act does specifically provide that road authorities 'take such steps that are reasonable to prevent snow and ice endangering the safe passage of pedestrians and vehicles over public roads'.

DRIVING COURSES*

NOTE: 'Pass Plus' is a course of six post-test lessons aimed to familiarise a new driver with aspects such as night and motorway driving not covered in the driving test. Courses are available with BSM and other approved driving instructors and the cost is usually offset by a discount offered by most insurers on the new driver's first year's cover.

- Driving Development, 61 Holly Bank, Ackworth, Yorks WF7 7PE, tel: 01977 612094.

- Aintree Racing School, tel: 01928 712877, website: www.aintree-racing-drivers-school.co.uk.

- Ecole de Pilotage Winfield, c/o Winfield Motorsport, PO Box 839, Ascot, Berks SL6 7SB, tel/fax 01344 876169. (Advanced Racing Driving Techniques, including 'trail-braking'. Possibly the best racing driving school in the world. Techniques taught in Formula Renault cars at the Paul Ricard Circuit, South of France. First two days: £700; next two days £660.)

- Aviemore Off-Road Centre, tel: 01479 831 329.

- Defensive Driving Consultants, Litton House, 52/56 Buckingham Street, Aylesbury, Bucks HP20 2LL, tel: 01296 398783.

---

* Driving courses/skid training/circuit courses listed in alphabetical order of office address.

- AA Driving School Head Office, Basingstoke, tel: 01256 20123 (press office).

- Benniworth Springs Off Roading, Lincolnshire, tel: 01507 313 682.

- Road Safety Services Ltd, 162 Eversley Road, Bexley Heath, Kent DA7 6SW, tel: 01322 337523.

- RoSPA , Edgbaston Park, 353 Bristol Road, Birmingham B5 7ST, tel: 0121 248 2000. (Defensive Driving Courses. RoSPA 'Advanced Drivers' are re-tested every three years.)

- Lancs County Council Road Safety Office, tel: 01772 264472. Lancs Road Safety Centre Office runs £10 Skid Control Courses at its Road Safety Training Centre, Ewood, Blackburn, tel 01722 254868.

- Bill Gwynne Rally School, Turweston Aerodrome, Westbury, Brackley, Northants NN13 5YD, tel: 01280 705570, fax: 01280 701691, website: billgwynne@email.msn.com.

- Brands Hatch: 'Earlydrive' and all circuit courses, tel: 01474 872367. (Circuit itself, tel: 01474 872331.) Basic track course in BMW 318i and single-seater £85 (highly recommended for learning braking and gear-changing disciplines); skid-control courses £59.

- On Track Trackdays (previously Club 89). An excellent club providing on-track instruction, rides with British Touring Car Championship drivers and the chance to drive your own car on racing circuits throughout the UK. Tel: 01953 888 989, website: www.brands-hatch.co.uk.

- Builth Wells: Advanced Driving School, Land Rover Tower, Royal Welsh Showground, Builth Wells LD2 3SY, tel: 01902 551555, website: www.advanced-driving.org. Skid Car Courses £59–£95; one-day Advance Car Course £179–£249; two-day ACC £329–£449; three-day ACC £495–£649; one-day Explorer Experience (4x4) £199–£249; two-day Explorer Experience £349–£449.

- Defensive Driver Training Ltd, Business & Technology Centre, Pound Road, Old Bury, W. Midlands B68 8NA. tel: 0121 552 8844.

- Motor Safari, Milestone Inn, Milestone Trail Park, Ruthin Road, Bwlchgwyn, Wrexham LL11 5UT, Wales, tel: 01978 754533. Half-day off-road courses from £89.

- Cadwell Park, Lincolnshire. All circuit courses tel: 0990 125 250. (Circuit itself, tel: 01507 343248.)

- System Advanced Driver Training, 62/66 Lowther Street, Carlisle, Cumbria CA3 8DP, tel: 01228 515914.

- Forest Experience Rally School: Tony and Christina Higgins, Carno, Montgomeryshire, Wales SY17 5LU, tel: 01686 420201.

- Castle Coombe Racing School, Chippenham, Wilts SN14 7EX, tel: 01249 782417, website: www.castlecombecircuit.co.uk. Skid pan courses from £49.50.

- Peak Performance Management, The Stables, Walton Lodge, Chesterfield, Derbyshire S42 7LG, tel: 01246 568953.

- Institute of Advanced Motorists, IAM House, 259/365 Chiswick High Road, London W4 4HS, tel: 020 8994 4403.

- Jim Russell School at Rockingham Raceway, Corby, Bedfordshire, tel: 01858 5655580, website: www.rockingham.co.uk.

- 'Drive and Survive' skid control courses, Crowthorne, Berks, tel: 01344 751117, website: www.driveandsurvive.co.uk.

- Croft Racing School, Croft Circuit, nr Darlington, North Yorkshire, tel: 01325 722031. Courses in single-seaters from £85.

- Donington Rark Racing School, Derbyshire, tel: 01332 850417, website: www.donington.co.uk.

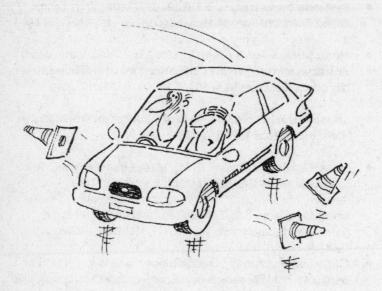

- Jim Russell Racing School, Donington Circuit, Donington Park, nr Derby, tel: 01332 811430 (re-locating to Rockingham Raceway, Corby, Northants late 2000). Also Jonathan Tait Skid Control, Donington Circuit, Donington Park, Derby, tel: 01332 811430.

- Road Sense Ltd, Royal Highland Centre, Ingliston, Edinburgh EH28 8NB, tel: 0131 333 3000.

- Driving Services, Portside House, Lower Mersey Street, Ellesmere Port, Cheshire L65 2AL, tel: 0151 355 2873.

- Driving Management Ltd, Midlands Skid Pan, Fradley nr Lichfield, Staffs, tel: 01264 771074.

- Goodwood Racing School, Goodwood Motor Circuit, Goodwood, Chichester PO18 0PH, tel: 01243 778118. (Single-seaters, also rides in Ferrari F40 3 laps £50.) Goodwood Skid Control courses, tel: 01903 691810.

- Harrow Driving, Cycling and Road Safety Centre, Christchurch Avenue, Harrow, Middx HA3 5BD, tel: 020 8424 1993. (Eight-session driving course for 16 year olds: three theory, five in-car; £80.)

- Highlands Park, Hampshire: Tank Driving Courses in Chieftain Tank, Alvis Stalwart 6x6, APC 432, tel: 01264 850702.

- Drive & Survive UK Ltd, The Maltings, Bridge Street, Hitchin, Herts SG3 2DE, tel: 01462 441844.

- Under Seventeens Car Club, 59 Coleridge Close, Hitchin, Herts, SG4 0QX, tel: 01462 457813. (Sponsored by BP Oil.) Membership Secretary: Eileen Simpkin, 51 Deerhurst Chase, Bicknacre, Chelmsford, Essex CM3 4XG.

- The Cardrome, Upper Rainham Road, Hornchurch, Essex, tel: 01708 471340. Off-road 'real road' system where youngsters of under driving age can learn to drive safely and in safety, from £9.

- Autodriva Driving Instructor Training Courses by Margaret Stacey in preparation for the ADI Parts 1, 2 and 3. Margaret Stacey, The Mount, 53 Heanor Road, Ilkeston, Derbyshire DE7 8DY, freephone 0500 55 57 57.

- AA Training Services, AA College, Widmerpool Hall, Keyworth, Notts NG12 5QB, tel: 0121 5017389.

- Phil Price Rally School (RAC MSA approved), Coed Harbour, Llangunllo, Knighton, Powys LD7 1TD, tel: 01547 550300, website: www.kc3.co.uk/rally.

- Knockhill Circuit and Racing School, Fife, tel: 01383 723 337, website: www.knockhill.co.uk.

- Road Skills, Hill Rise, Canada Crescent, Rawdon, Leeds LS19 6LT, tel: 0113 250 1756.

- Paul Ripley Driving Courses, Paul Ripley Promosport, PO Box 2,

Horsforth, Leeds LS18 5UE, tel: 0113 258 5194.

- Driving Management Ltd Skid Control Course, Lichfield, tel: 01264 771074. (Also at Thruxton Circuit.)

- British School of Motoring Head Office, London, tel: 020 8540 8262 (press officer Leslie Miles). BSM 'Masterdrive' two-hour course at £49 to check and brush up observation

- Lakeland Off-Roading Centre, West Lothian, tel: 01506 858543.

- Everyman Driving Centre, Mallory Park Circuit, Leicester LE9 7QE, tel: 01455 841670. (Drive anything from a go-kart to a tank or a helicopter.)

- Formula 1 Driving after ARDS instruction at Mallory Park, from £599; Ferrari Driving after MSA instruction at circuit on Presswold Hall airfield, Leicester, from £175; Rally Schools at Presswold Hall and Enstone (Oxon). Tangerine, Millennium Business Centre, 3 Hudson Road, London NW2 6DW, tel: 020 8208 3333.

- City of Manchester Road Safety Unit, tel: 0161 234 4480.

- DriveTech, 32 Beechingstoke, Marlow, Bucks, SL7 1JH, tel: 01628 473537.

- Fusion Centre, Millbrook Proving Ground, Bedfordshire, tel: 01525 404918.

- Drive Alive UK. Rowan House, 26/28 Queen's Road, Hethersett, Norwich NR9 3DP, tel: 01603 259989.

- Snetterton Racing School, Norwich. All circuit courses tel: 0990 125 250. Circuit itself: 01953 887 303.

- James Pritchard Associates, 3 Bolts Close, Old Marston, Oxford OX3 0PP, tel: 01865 241854.

- London Rally School (Oxford area), tel: 01869 278199. Half days £95; full days £180.

- Drive It All Rally Driving Courses, The Rally and Off Road Driving Centre, Church Enstone, Oxfordshire OX7 4NP, tel: 01608 678339, website: www.driveitall.co.uk.

- Highland Off-Road, Perthshire, tel: 01350 728 700, website: www.highlandoffroad.fsnet.co.uk.

- PGL Adventure Holidays, Alto Court, Penyard Lane, Ross-on-Wye, Herefordshire HR9 5NR, tel 01989 764211. Offers 'Grand Prix' children's holidays in which they learn to handle go-karts, trial bikes and ATV Quads at Borreatton Hall, Shropshire and Myerscough College, Lancs from £259; 'Motocross' children's holidays on trials bikes and Quads at Beam House, Devon, Dalguise, Perthshire and Tan Troed in the Brecon Beacons, from £249;Driver Awareness Courses of six half-day sessions of theoretical and practical instruction in dual-control cars at Court Farm, Herefordshire; The Bluecoat School, West Sussex; Moreton Hall, Shropshire and Myerscough in Lancashire, from £289.

- Rothiemurcas Off-Road Centre, Invernesshire, tel: 01479 81858.

- Aintree Racing Driver's School, 1 Fairoak Court, Whitehouse, Runcorn, Cheshire WA7 3DX, tel: 01928 712877. ARDS approved. Prices: £95–£155. Courses at the Three Sister's Circuit, Wigan.

- Chris Birbeck International Rally School, Manx Lodge, Low Farm, Brottom, Saltburn, Cleveland, tel: 01287 677512. Half day: £99; full day: £160; weekend course: £300.

- Rally Drive International Rally School, Kings Street, Sancton, Yorkshire YO4 3QP, tel: 01430 827430.

- Santa Pod drag strip, tel: 01234 782 828.

- Scottish Forest Rally School, tel: 01467 267311. Courses from £99.

- Silverstone Driving Centre, nr Towcester, Northants NN12 8TN, tel: 01327 320412, website: www.silverstone-circuit.co.uk. Silverstone Rally School, tel: 01327 857413, website: www.silverstonerally.co.uk.

- Land Rover Experience, Solihull, West Midlands, tel: 0121 7004 619.

- Driver Education Centre, Canute Road, Southampton SO14 3FJ, tel: 023 8033 3058.

- All-Terrain Services Off-Road School, Swansea, tel: 01792 862 669.

- Oulton Park Racing School, Tarporley, Cheshire. All circuit courses including Earlydrive, tel: 01829 760381; circuit itself, tel: 01829 760301.

- SAGA Group Car Confidence Courses, Centrex Centre, Telford, Shropshire, tel: 0800 300 500. Basic seven-night residential course: £399; advanced course £499. Reduced price rail or coach travel to and from Telford can be arranged.

- Driving Dynamics, 19 Town Street, Thaxted, Essex CM6 2LD, tel: 01371 830496.

- Driving Management Ltd, Thruxton Circuit, nr Andover, Hants SP11 8PW, tel: 01264 771074. Skid control courses.

- Ian Taylor Motor Racing School, Thruxton Circuit, nr Andover, Hants SP11 8PW, tel: 01264 773511, website: www.iantaylor.co.uk.

- AGS Formula 1 driving, Circuit du Luc, Hyeres/Toulon, Var, France. Agents in the UK: Wildside Adrenalin Sports, tel: 020 8366 1766. Cost: at least £1,000.

- Tunbridge Wells 4x4 Driving School, 23 Pennine Walk, Tunbridge Wells, Kent TN2 3NW, tel: 01892 514389. Courses £69 and £99.

- Advanced Tuition and Skid Training, Hanger 1, Hurricane Way, North Weald, Essex CM16 6AA, tel: 01992 522287.

- High Performance Course (John Lyon), HPC Ltd, 21 Church Street, Wellesbourne, Warks CV35 9LS, tel: 01789 841229. Prices from £125.

- Brooklands Auto Project, c/o Paul Jobson, Elmbridge Area Youth Office, Public Library Building, Church Street, Weybridge, Surrey KT13 8DE, tel: 01932 840986. (Pre-driver training for 15–16 year olds over four Sunday mornings at Brooklands, price £20.)

- North Yorks Off-Road Centre, Whitby, tel: 01947 880 371, website: www.mywebpage.net/off-road.

- BSM Qualified Driver Training, 81/87 Hartfield Road, Wimbledon, London SW19 3TJ, tel: 020 8545 1350.

- Corporate Driver Training Ltd, Elnup House, 6 Sherington Avenue, Wigan, Lancs WN6 8AT, tel: 01257 422331.

- Professional Driving Instructors Group, High Wycombe, tel: 01494 813064. Day course for 16 year olds on Bovingdon aerodrome.

- T.I. Rally School, The Airfield, Seaton Ross, York YO4 4NF, tel: 01759 318820. Half-day courses from £95, full-day from £129.25, inc. VAT.

Local driving schools and instructors recommended by readers

- Birmingham: Graham Birchall, tel: 0121 456 4244.
- Kenilworth: Brian Snook, tel: 01926 852206.

- Wembley, London: Neil Wallace, tel: 020 8902 9498.
- Hampshire: Adrian Dobson (disabled-driving instructor), tel: 01264 736262.

Advanced motorcycle road riding

- BMF Rider Training, tel: 01825 712896.
- Cooper Bile Training, tel: 01633 374782.
- Institute of Advanced Motorists, tel: 020 8994 4403.
- Highway Rider Training, tel: 0121 742 2936.
- Newcastle Rider Training, tel: 0191 276 1972.
- Open Road Advanced, tel: 01375 382124.
- Roadcraft, tel: 01489 896041.
- Shire Training Services, tel: 01480 464689.
- Road Runner, tel: 0114 278 9943.

Motorcycle track days

- Circuit Breakers, tel: 020 8330 3351 and 09733 61858.
- Honda Britain Performance Riding School, tel: 01455 251800.
- Kawasaki Riders Club, tel: 01652 680060.
- No Limits, tel: 01952 606777.
- Redline, tel: 01244 680000.
- Ron Haslam Racing Academy, tel: 01332 883323.
- Speed Freak and James Witham, tel: 0161 487 2222.
- Track Attack, tel: 01332 810048.
- Track Time Promotions, tel: 01384 278387.
- Yamaha Race Schools, tel: 01507 343555.

DRIVING TIPS AND LAWS

Rule of thumb

" *In the mad, mad world of the motor car, '60 mph and approaching a blind corner' (the caption to the Alfa 154 Selaspeed advertisement) is nothing special. It happens all the time, yet there's a chronic ignorance of the fact that on a left-hand corner the speed merchant will drift across into the face of oncoming traffic; and on a right-hand corner he will be launched out of his lane, smashing into the customary tree. An everyday story of motoring folk.* "

More like an everyday story of morons driving early-model Vectras too quickly into blind bends. The Alfa 156 Selaspeed's thumb buttons enable you to brake and change down at the same time without taking your hands from the wheel – whether you drive two-footed or not. This puts you into the right gear to accelerate at the right moment, ensuring that you don't 'drift across into the face of oncoming traffic'. Of course, anyone following Paul Ripley's rules would not actually enter a blind corner at 60 mph because there might be a horse, cyclist or pedestrian in the unseen road ahead. What he would do is brake down to a speed he could stop from, using the Selaspeed's thumb selectors to drop the box into the right gear to accelerate out of the corner as soon as he could clearly see the road ahead was free of any hazards.

No steering, no brakes

" *I have read of a number of accidents where drivers claimed that the vehicle's steering had 'locked' or that its brakes had 'failed' when all that had really happened was that power assistance had been lost. Please could you issue a warning to drivers, particularly smaller people driving large 4x4s, that they might be relying too heavily on power assistance to the steering and brakes. It would be a good idea for them to find a safe place with a gentle incline, where they can get an idea of how the vehicle feels when this power assistance is lost. It won't then come as such a surprise and they will stand a better chance of remaining in control if such a failure occurs.* "

This is a very sensible suggestion. Both the power-steering pump and either the brake vacuum servo on petrol-engined cars or the brake vacuum pump on diesels rely on the engine running. If the engine fails for any reason (exhaust blockage from catalytic converter failure or snapped timing belt or chain), power assistance to the steering will be lost immediately and power assistance to the brakes will be lost gradually. Switch the engine off, turn the key to unlock the steering, then gradually release the parking brake on a gentle slope and you will get a feel of unassisted steering and brakes.

Belt and braces automatic

" *I now have a car with an automatic gearbox. I am a little confused with the use of the 'N' and 'P' positions of the selector lever when parking. Why use the 'P' position? Isn't placing the lever in 'N' and applying the handbrake satisfactory?* "

No. Using 'P' holds the car more effectively than the parking brake. See rule 226 of the Highway

Code. If you are new to driving an automatic I strongly advise you to find a large empty space and see if you can train yourself to drive the car 'two-footed' (left foot for the brake, right foot for the accelerator). This will help you to avoid 'unintentional acceleration syndrome' accidents while manoeuvring. If you can't easily adapt to 'two-footed' driving, stick to one foot but be aware that there will be times where the engine-management system gives the engine enough revs for the car to move of its own accord. Don't let this take you by surprise.

Where are we all going?

" You have frequently mentioned the dazzle caused by drivers whose cars have high-level brake lights, holding them on the brakes in traffic. Another serious problem is the failure of drivers to use their traffic indicators properly. This is particularly dangerous on roundabouts and when overtaking. "

Unnecessarily giving way to roundabout traffic which exits before it reaches you, holds drivers up and causes congestion. The most courteous and sensible thing to do is to signal right when rounding a roundabout, then signal left as soon as you have passed the last exit before the one you want to take. You then tell every other driver exactly what you propose to do and help keep traffic moving.

Another lead from Jersey

" Further to your item on 24 July stating that bull bars had been banned in Jersey, well ahead of the rest of Europe, I thought you should know of another of our unilaterally imposed laws. As from 18 March 1998 it has been made a specific offence for vehicle drivers to use hand-held mobile phones on the move. "

Jersey is a small island just nine miles by five, with narrow lanes and a high percentage of holiday hire cars. So, in the circumstances, this law makes sense and should be followed by a similar local law banning smoking, eating and drinking by vehicle drivers on the move. Smoking is potentially far more dangerous than using a hand-held mobile phone because smoke or ash can blind a driver, and the burning tip of a cigarette may fall off on to the driver's clothing. Drivers in the UK who frequently need to switch from car to car can buy an excellent 'hands free' device from Vodafone shops for £40. This comprises a combined cigar-lighter, power-plug and speaker, a length of cable and a mike at the end which plugs into the phone. Though I don't make calls on the move, I do use one of these gizmos to answer them and find it far less distracting than changing channels on the radio. But I won't be trying this in Jersey.

Slowness kills

" *As the performance of modern motor cars has increased dramatically over the last 30 years, why do the majority of British drivers insist on joining a motorway or dual carriageway from a slip road at between 25–35 mph. I was always taught to accelerate along the slip road, then blend in at the same speed as the vehicles already in the nearside line.* "

What you do is exactly what the Highway Code tells you to do. The fact is, any HGVs in the nearside lane are going to be travelling at between 50 mph and their governed maximum speed of 60 mph. Any drivers trying to join a motorway at 25–35 mph put themselves and everyone else in considerable danger. But, of course, a good driver, especially when following other vehicles down a slip road, will always anticipate such stupidity and make the necessary allowances.

Speedy response

" *Perhaps you can answer this conundrum. On 1 October the Daily Telegraph carried a report of a man being clocked driving a Porsche Boxter at 149 mph on the M20. He was banned for eight months and fined £3,000. On 2 October the Telegraph carried an advertisement for a BMW 530 diesel which proudly proclaimed it was capable of 140 mph. How can this be?* "

A Porsche Boxter is safer at 150 mph than a 15-year-old Ford Fiesta is at 70 mph. The problem is not that modern cars are capable of more than twice the motorway speed limit. It's that the UK motorway speed limit is ridiculously low. A significant number of cars using the motorway system have to travel at 10–25 mph more than the speed limit to clear road space for other cars, in order to prevent gridlock and the UK economy grinding to a halt. A speed of 149 mph can be safe in the right conditions and even the police test their cars to maximum speed on motorways because cars can safely reach higher speeds on them than on any closed race or test track.

Wanted: 'J633 CUU'

" *Someone is driving around in the London area in a grey Mercedes Benz 190E, sporting the registration 'J633 CUU', and accumulating parking tickets. The trouble is, I am the registered keeper of a grey MB 190E, reg. 'J633 CUU', which never goes near the London area, and each time I get a ticket I have to go through the rigmarole of proving it wasn't me. If any of your readers see a grey 190E, reg. 'J633 CUU' parked in the London area, please would they inform the police so that this impostor, or at least his car, can be arrested.* "

What G.C. describes is known as 'cloning'. With the proliferation of enforcement of excessively low speed limits by camera, cloning is bound to increase. Law enforcement by camera requires our co-operation in order to work. But if normally law-abiding citizens start to find their livelihoods at risk as a result of heavy-handed policing, they are likely to resort to subtle changes of registration plates in order to try and frustrate camera enforcement.

Manning 'U'-turns

" I wrote to Metropolitan Police Assistant Commissioner, Paul Manning, on the subject of 'zero tolerance' enforcement of the 30 mph urban speed limit and received a courteous reply. In it, A/C Manning states: 'The current regulations, under an EEC Directive, require that speedometers are accurate to within 7–13% but never under-estimate. This latter point together with the fact that it is not our intention to prosecute at small margins over the limit removes the likelihood of minor infringements being penalised.' "

Good. And a triumph for common sense.

Driving in a 'public place'

" The car parks in several of our local shopping centres are divided into 'one-way streets' with signs and road markings generally imposing the least convenient route. As a result, many drivers take short cuts the wrong way, often at high speed, clearly believing such markings have no legal force. Yet the Highway Code states that the Road Traffic Act applies to 'any highway and any other road to which the public has access'. Can you confirm that this dangerous practice is illegal and they are liable to prosecution? "

Yes, but in practice they are unlikely to be prosecuted unless they hit another vehicle or, worse still, a pedestrian. While the fault really lies with the idiot who devised the car-park traffic system, anyone who drives at speed in a car park full of shoppers and their children is being extremely irresponsible.

Red rage

" Please settle a dispute for me. I drive an automatic car. If I am stuck in a long traffic jam, for example at a level crossing, or if I am stationary for more than a couple of minutes, I shift the selector into 'N' and apply the parking brake. One of my 'expert' friends says this is the right thing to do. Another says, when the engine is running, always keep it in gear. Please put us out of our misery, and tell us who is correct. "

Your first expert friend. Though moving the selector lever from 'D' to 'N' will result in a tiny amount of wear to the mechanism, you should always shift to 'N' and put the parking brake on in traffic to prevent your brake lights blinding the driver behind. If you don't, you are committing an offence under Regulation 27 of the Road Vehicle Lighting Regulations 1989. I should add that the best defence by the driver behind against an infra-red suntan is to pull down his or her sunvisor and blot out the high-level brake light. Don't flash your headlights or take any other action that might enrage the driver in front.

Identity cards

" Due to a change of address I recently applied for a replacement driving licence. Instead of the licence, I received a letter from the DVLA informing me that I must now apply for a photocard driving licence. I personally do not want a credit-card sized licence, particularly as it advertises the UK's membership of the EU. Were you aware that the law had recently changed? "

Yes, and I have reminded readers of this before. However, a significant change has taken place in the documentation we are obliged to supply with our photocard licence applications. When I obtained mine (long before they became compulsory) I was only required to submit a verified photocopy of my passport or my birth certificate. When my mother received the forms just before Christmas 1999, this requirement had changed, and we must now submit our actual passport or birth certificate and marriage certificate with the application. Since processing can take up to six weeks I suggested that DVLA allow applicants to submit their documents at Vehicle Registration Offices rather than trust them to the post. Instead, the DVLA went one better and now allows applicants to submit their documents for checking at the 208 main post offices which also process passport applications. Both services cost an extra £3.50, but are well worth this for convenience, efficiency and peace of mind.

Illogical

" Why is it that when an American citizen arrives in the UK, he or she can pick up a hire car straight away and drive it on an American licence for up to a year. But if the American remains in the UK for more than 12 months, becoming thoroughly acquainted with the UK traffic system and obviously a far better UK driver, to continue driving in the UK he or she must then pass a UK driving test? "

The rules have all been explained to P.B. by a particularly patient civil servant at DETR. The freedom to drive in another country for up to a year is a travel concession conferred by the 1949 Geneva Convention on Road Traffic. Drivers from all EU or other designated countries who become UK residents can exchange their licences for UK photocard licences, but in the USA the driving test varies so much from state to state that some states do not even recognise driving licenses issued in other states. An expat skydiving instructor I met in a bar last Christmas told me that passing the driving test in Florida was such a doddle he could not imagine anyone ever failing it. As an aside, visitors to Indonesia should be warned that before they can legally hire a car on islands such as Bali, they must obtain a local driving licence by passing the local written and practical test.

Dip the clutch

" *The recent icy conditions resulted in a spate of cars spun off the road, often with nasty results. Now that front-wheel drive is virtually universal, I feel that drivers should be warned of its predisposition to front-wheel skids. A driver's automatic reaction is usually to ease off the throttle, but this usually has disastrous results. Stamping on the clutch seems the only hope.* "

This is very sensible advice and is the first thing a skid-control instructor teaches you. By dipping the clutch you disconnect the drive wheels from any torque reaction caused by lifting off, and this makes it much easier to regain control of the car. It's also the reason why Saab fitted freewheels to all its cars up to and including the last 96.

When to sit on the brakes

" *I disagree with the advice you gave to automatic drivers on 15 January about blinding the driver behind with their high-level brake lights. Back in 1962 in a pea soup fog on the A580 I came up behind two cars stopped side by side at traffic lights. One had its brake lights on. The other did not, and was almost invisible in comparison.* **"**

There is a clear distinction between illegally blinding the driver behind in a traffic jam by lazily sitting with one's foot on the footbrake, and warning drivers some distance behind that they are approaching an unexpected stoppage. Paul Ripley's advice in these circumstances is to stop at least several car lengths behind the stoppage, keep your foot on the brake to display all your brake lights, keep your eyes on your mirror, and be prepared to move forward into the cushion of space you have created in front of you if a car coming up behind can't stop. Depending on the circumstances and the potential speed of traffic approaching from behind, use hazard warning lights as well as, but not instead of, your brake lights and give yourself a bigger cushion of space. This has saved me a crumpled car boot and possible whiplash injuries several times over the past few years.

Road works Gatsos

" *A speed camera recorded my car travelling at 76 mph on the A1(M) in South Yorkshire in February 1999. There was a temporary 50 mph speed limit on this stretch of road due to road works. I pleaded guilty, so did not attend the court hearing. To my great surprise I was fined £150 with £30 costs. Worse still I was 'awarded' six penalty points on a licence which had been clean for the past 20 years. Is it too late to contest this?* **"**

Your problem is that the 26-mph speed differential disqualified you from the option of a 'fixed penalty' and meant that the case automatically went to court. Whatever speeds I may drive at on clear, open roads with good visibility, I am cautious at genuine motorway roadworks subject to a 50 mph limit. They are a

favourite spot for speed cameras and, wherever motorway traffic is forced to run both ways on the same carriageway, they are also very dangerous. Yes, it's too late to contest the magistrate's decision.

Asleep in charge

"A hypothetical question. I emerge late at night from a remote pub and suspect that I am over the limit. I propose to sleep in my car. What steps must I take to prevent myself being charged with 'drunk in charge'? (Forget the obvious caveat about the morning-after risk.)"

Hughes Guide to Traffic Law states, 'A person shall be deemed *not* to have been in charge of a mechanically propelled vehicle if he proves that at the material time, the circumstances were such that there was no likelihood of his driving it so long as he remained unfit through drink or drugs.' Also, if your car is in a pub car park which is gated and the gate is locked, this ceases to be a 'public place' for the purposes of the Road Traffic Act. *Hughes Guide* can be obtained by phoning 01908 639233, price £17.00; six-monthly updates £5, or website: www.motorvation.co.uk.

Obstructive attitude

" *Just because the motorway speed limit is 70 mph, it doesn't mean you have to drive at this speed. Within reason, you can legally drive as slowly as you like providing you are not causing a hazard. In case you are thinking I am an 80-year-old woman driver, I'm actually a 23-year-old Lotus Esprit driver who regularly drives at 50 mph on the motorway. Also I've discovered a solution to the 'boy racers' who enjoy sitting two inches from my rear bumper. I simply slow down even more. Just to prove that a Lotus can drive a lot slower than a Ford Escort (or whatever it is) as well as a lot quicker!! They never dare try to overtake and eventually you'll find they just drop back and give up!* "

L.H. describes himself in his address details as 'Boy Racer Killer'. I'll leave readers to form their own conclusions.

Over here

" *My wife is American and is a 30-year holder of a full American Driver's Permit. I have tried to have her included on my UK motor insurance policy, to allow her to drive in the UK, but my insurers (Privilege) say that they will only allow her to drive in this country for a maximum period of one month, and that premiums must be pre-paid at the rate of £10 a week. My policy is due for renewal this month and I would like to know whether you are aware of any insurance companies which would permit her to drive, or should I shop around?* "

You are trying to have something complicated incorporated into a direct policy, the rating structure of which does not allow for it. Speak to a good broker such as ABM on 020 8681 8986 or Rauch & Stallard on 01702 348261. But remember, if your wife is now resident in the UK she must obtain a UK licence within a year of her arrival in the UK for the simple reason that the address on her American Driver's Permit is no longer her address.

Speedo failure

" The speedometer of my car failed when I was emerging from a service station on a journey from Sunderland to Manchester. I called at a few garages but was unable to find a mechanic, so phoned Green Flag. I was told that driving the car was legal and that I should make my own way to a garage. This I did and found a very helpful Rover dealer who installed a new speedo cable for just £18 plus VAT on the spot. But was the advice correct? "

Yes. You can continue if the speedometer fails during the journey you are undertaking. Even afterwards you can carry on driving as long as steps have been taken to effect a repair 'with all reasonable expedition'. This came from *Hughes Guide to Traffic Law*, a file book which costs a reasonable £15, plus £9 a year for six-monthly updates (01908 639233). Every driver should have a copy.

EPHEMERA

Bookworms

Though this information was in the last three books, readers continue to ask how they might dispose of old motoring literature. The answer is to try the following, all of whom take stalls at various events and 'autojumbles' throughout the year. (Remember, most have day jobs so it's better to call them in the evenings.) Kenneth Ball Autobooks Ltd, tel: 01273 845000; Eoin Young, tel: 01483 283311 (summer only), Anton Spencer, tel: 020 8337 7452; Peter Davidson, tel: 01295 810853; Graham White, tel: 01243 771961; Alan and David Burden, tel: 01923 246668; Les Wilson, tel: 01270 812410; David Ellnot, tel: 01524 762271; Andrew Currie, tel: 01276 477201; and Alan Riley, tel: 01327 351203. Don't expect magazines from later than the 1960s to be worth much, though. The dealers who attend 'automobilia' events are not very interested in them because of the sheer weight they would have to carry around. Some shops which deal in collectible motoring literature are Chaters Motoring Booksellers of 8 South Street, Isleworth, tel: 020 8568 9750; The Vintage Motorshop in Batley, tel: 01924 470733; Collectors Carbooks in Woburn, tel: 01525 290088; Connoisseur Carbooks in Brentford, tel: 020 8560 3404; Simon Lewis Transport

Bookshop in Lydney, tel: 01594 843151; John Knowles in Great Ellingham, Norfolk, tel: 01953 452257, Pooks Motor Bookshop in Rothley, tel: 0116 237 6222 and Ray Roberts' 'Wheels, Wings and Water' of Whiston, tel: 01785 712232, but don't expect them to come and collect. To advertise, try *Practical Classics* and *The Automobile* magazines, both of which have a Motoring Literature classified section.

Kosher brochures

" *I have a few original items of sales promotion for American cars of the 1930s. They are well illustrated, and stamped with the name of the showrooms they originated from. I also have a couple of manuals for British cars of the same period. Are these likely to be of any interest to collectors?* "

The friendly and very helpful chaps at Chaters Motoring Bookshop of Isleworth (020 8568 9750) put me straight on to two brochure dealers: Andrew Currie (01276 477201) and Pooks Motor Bookshop in Rothley (0116 237 6222). Obviously the value of these items will depend on both their scarcity and the demand for them.

Diesel road test data

" *I recently purchased a late registered 98R Citroën ZX 1.9SXTD. It is the first diesel car I have driven so I am at a loss regarding what sort of performance, mpg, etc. to expect from it. How do I find this out?* "

From *Diesel Car* magazine back-number road tests. The May 1997 issue (no. 104) carried a report of a road test of the three-door ZX SXTD. This is available from Future Publishing Ltd, Freepost (BS4900), Somerton, Somerset TA11 6BR, tel: 01458 271149, fax: 01225 822523, price £3.50 (best ordered by credit card).

H.J. gets booked

I've both bought and been sent five books recently all of which are worthy of a mention. The most fun is Nick Baldwin's *Classic Tractors of the World* (ISBN 0-896858-394-5) which is worth £19.95 for Andrew Morland's wonderful photographs of some of the weirdest vehicles I've ever seen. Next, Andrew Jenkinson's *British Trailer Caravans 1919–1959* (ISBN 1-874105-96-0) which contains fascinating old photographs showing the Great British Public out and about in their mobile households from the early days, price £14.99. Its companion volume *British Trailer Caravans From 1960* (ISBN 1-901295-53-2) is more for the dyed-in-the-woolly-hat caravanner than the rest of us. Burke and Price have managed to publish their *Guide to Motor Museums of the British Isles* (ISBN 1-901295-39-7), which contains locations, descriptions and abbreviated exhibits lists for over 150 museums and collections, which can be cross-referenced via the index. Good value at £9.99. But most impressive of the lot is Dave Thornton's *Grey Guide to Japanese Imports* (ISBN 1-901295-70-2). This £9.99 book provides a huge amount of bang-up-to-date detail you simply won't find anywhere else, and is a must for anyone even considering a grey-market Japanese import.

Midnight oil for motor engineers

" Will you please advise me of any individual or organisation which may be interested in acquiring the full set of Motor Engineering magazines published in 32 weekly parts during the 1930s. "

Britain's top dealer in pre-war motoring magazines, motor show guides, catalogues, annuals, books, programmes and catalogues is Kenneth Ball of Autobooks Ltd, 2 South Street, Ditchling, East Sussex BN6 8UQ, tel: 01273 845000, email: autobooks@autobooks.co.uk.

Skip find

" I found a brass foot pump in a skip and cleaned it up. From the photo, can you tell me how old it might be, and whether it is of any interest to enthusiasts or a museum? "

As far as I know, Kismet foot pumps were a popular accessory from the 1930s to the 1950s. This is the ideal sort of thing to tote along to an autojumble in the summer, and offer to a stallholder. Or try The Complete Automobilist, 35 Main Street, Baston, nr Peterborough, tel: 01778 560 312. Dealer asking prices tend to be in the £25–£40 bracket.

Seal of success

I appealed for a supplier of leather cup washer piston seals for the otherwise everlasting Kismet foot pumps which date back to the 1920s. Previously, most owners have had to make do with making their own washers, but a reader from St Albans put me on to Peter Donnelly of Donnelly UK Ltd, 70 Soho Road, Birmingham B21 9SR, tel: 0121 554 4212; fax: 0121 554 0007. Donnellys not only supply washers for Kismet pumps, but all manner of leather and rubber components for vintage and post-vintage cars. Pneumatic Components (0114 248 2712) also do pump seals, as do Pump and Farm Supplies of Helston, Cornwall (01326 565454).

FUEL AND EMISSIONS

The four-star question

" I have an older car designed to run on four-star leaded petrol. What should I be using now? "

First off, let's establish that 'Ron' = 'Research octane number'.

If your car is post-1990 it should be capable of running on unleaded petrol of the correct octane without any additives. Nearly all 1980s Japanese cars or 1980s cars with Japanese engines are designed to run on unleaded. Many cars with aluminium cylinder heads have been fitted with hard exhaust valve seat inserts made of chrome steel rather than cast iron.

The oil companies have agreed that all UK LRP will contain potassium instead of lead, now dosed at 10–12 mg per litre, which may still not be enough to protect the exhaust valve seats properly. If your car has a compression ratio of 9:1 or higher, you may find it both cheaper and safer to run your car on premium unleaded (always the same brand) octane boosted with exactly the correct quantity of either Castrol Valvemaster *Plus* (phosphorus-based, from Halfords) or Millers VSP Plus or Carplan *Nitrox*

4-Lead (both manganese-based – the favoured additive in Canada).

If your car has a compression ratio of less than 9:1, you can use 95Ron unleaded (preferably Shell) dosed with a wider choice of additives which includes: standard Valvemaster (phosphorus-based), Millers VSP Plus (manganese-based), Superblend Zero Lead 2000 (potassium-based), Nitrox *Four-Star* (potassium-based), Redline (sodium-based) or Wynns (sodium-based).

Note that sodium can damage turbochargers. *Never* mix petrol containing one LRP additive with petrol containing another and never over-dose it. Never mix manganese-based Nitrox 4-Lead with potassium-based Nitrox Four-Star.

If your engine has hard exhaust valve seats but is unhappy on 95Ron or even 97Ron petrol you can boost the octane from 95 to 97+ and from 97 to 98+ by using Millers Octane+. This costs around £3 for enough to boost 40–50 litres of petrol.

Castrol (Valvemaster), tel: 01793 452222; Superblend, tel: 0116 291 1700; Red Line, tel: 01732 866885; Millers, tel: 0800 281 053; Carplan Nitrox, tel: 0161 764 5981.

All the additives mentioned have been extensively lab tested and approved by the FBHVC at the Motor Industry Research Association.

Four-star filling stations

" Where can I still find four-star leaded petrol? "

You will find a full list at www.bayfordthrust. co.uk.

Running on gas

" Where can I get my car converted to run on LPG? "

UK LPG (Liquefied Petroleum Gas) is wellhead gas, rather than refined from crude oil and current estimates are that there is enough under the North Sea to last 40–60 years. There are now 221 LPG filling stations in the UK, there should be 400 by the end of the year, and by the end of year 2000 there should be 800. The latest LPG filling station information is available on two websites: www.lpga.co.uk and www.autogas.lpg.com.

There is now a standard conversion of the Perkins 180 diesel engine for buses and trucks, enabling them to run on LPG at the increased consumption rate of 25–50%, but using a fuel which is less than half the price of diesel. Conversion cost of cars and vans typically runs at £800–£1,200, and approved conversions to cars less than one year old qualify for a 75% Powershift grant. New Citroën Xantias, Ford Mondeos, Vauxhall Vectras and Volvos with LPG conversions all qualify. The LP Gas Association (tel: 01425 461612, website: www.lpga.co.uk) can recommend LPGA accredited converters whose conversions on new cars qualify for the 75% Powershift grant. Without the benefit of the grant, conversions for older vehicles cost between £850 and £2,000. Tanks are available to fit the car's spare wheel well.

LPG conversion specialists include: Autogas 2000 of Thirsk, tel: 01845 523213; Gentrac Systems Ltd of Chandlers Ford, tel: 0203 8025 4744; Key Autogas of Leicester, tel: 0116 2608813; Marine Ecopower Ltd of Lymington, tel: 01590 688444; Millennium Autogas of Basingstoke, tel: 07771 993459; and LPG Auto

Power UK of Bradford, tel: 01274 729425.

The Natural Gas Vehicle Association, tel: 020 7388 7598, can supply a list of CNG (Compressed Natural Gas) 'Gas Stations'. The phone number for British Gas for vehicles is 01784 646030. The Autogas Installers and Retailers Association (01663 732030) clams to supply 'the only completely accurate and up-to-date list of outlets'.

TDI MOTs

" *I have just had terrible trouble getting my old shape Passat TDI through its first MOT. I followed all your recommendations: fuel-injector cleaner, new air filter, taking the car for a hard run to blow all the cobwebs out beforehand, yet it still needed another hard run to pass. The tester said I'd done all he'd have done to get it through, but is there a better way of tackling this problem?* "

Yes. In the case of VAG TDIs you need to find a VW, Audi, Seat or Skoda franchise or an independent specialist with a VAG 1551 or VAG 1552 electronic interrogator, as used by Colin Marshall at Wheelbase (01932 252515). This plugs into a point in the car and checks out the car's systems including the fuel system. It's quite common for TDIs to over-fuel, and the fuelling can be re-set with the interrogator. You need to do the other things as well to pass the MOT, but resetting the fuelling is the proper long-term answer.

Low-sulphur lowdown

" *I own a Discovery TDI. I have read several letters in Land Rover magazines from owners complaining of poorer performance, heavier fuel consumption and diesel-pump failure from using low-sulphur diesel. I now avoid these environmentally friendlier fuels and my Disco certainly seems to drive better. What is your opinion?* "

Greenergy's 'City Diesel' sold in the UK has always contained the lubricity enhancer Paradyn 631. Shell 'Pura' also contains a lubricity additive, while Elf assures me that its ultra-low-sulphur diesel is tested for lubricity at the refinery. Ivor Carroll, editor of *Diesel Car* magazine, tells me he has had no reports of pumps failing on current generation ULS diesel, but if performance seems down the answer is probably that the pump needs recalibrating to suit the lower-density fuel. Once this is done, ULS diesel certainly reduces emissions of the larger unburned hydrocarbon particulates which gave diesel its undeserved reputation. The fact is, if a diesel engine pulls a vehicle 50% further than a petrol engine on a given amount of fuel, it must burn its fuel more efficiently and emit less unburned hydrocarbons. You may not be able to see petrol-engine emissions, but that doesn't mean they're not more plentiful and more harmful.

Emission missive

" *I took my 'M'-reg. Rover 214Si for an MOT at 9 in the morning. When I went to collect it at 10am I was told there was a problem with the exhaust emissions and that a rear tyre was worn below the legal limit. I agreed to purchase a new tyre, then took the car to a local Rover dealer for the emissions problem to be solved. At 12 noon, the Rover dealer phoned to tell me that the emissions were within the pre-set MOT limits but its tests would cost me £25. I took the car back to the MOT station at 4.30pm where it was re-tested and where it still failed on emissions. To cross-check its own equipment, the MOT station took my car to another MOT station where, once the gas analysers and the car engine were up to test temperature, it passed. After a heated argument with the proprietor of the original MOT station, he agreed to fund the cost of the replacement tyre in lieu of the £25 I had to pay for testing at the Rover garage. Do you consider this to be sufficient compensation for my time between 10am–6pm wasted due to faulty testing equipment?* "

Yes. The MOT advanced emissions test is at best a compromise test, and testing equipment can go out of calibration. At least in your case you found a very efficient and obliging Rover dealer who checked out your car at short notice, and the proprietor of the MOT testing station was honest enough to cross-check his equipment against that of another test centre.

Will it run on unleaded?

" Can you tell me what to do to adapt my car to run on unleaded petrol? It is a 'V'-registered MGB GT. "

It might run on Lead Replacement Petrol, or on Superunleaded plus an additive. But the best thing to do is to purchase a fully reconditioned head with new hardened valve seats, new valves, new guides and new springs from a specialist such as Ron Hopkinson, 850 London Road, Derby DE24 8WA, tel: 01332 756056, then run the car on superunleaded. An exchange lead-free head for a 'B' Series engine is £195 plus VAT. The DETR has printed a brief leaflet on the subject which refers anyone worried about unleaded compatibility to the *Unleaded Petrol Information Manual*, 3rd Edition (ISBN 0-85666-544-4), published by Autodata and available from Autodata Limited, Priors Way, Maidenhead, Berks SL6 2HP, fax: 01628 770385, email: sales@autodata.ltd.uk.

Tax-free pollution

" Incensed at paying more than 250% tax on petrol while the airlines get away with no tax at all on aviation fuel, I wrote to the DETR. I received a reply which stated, 'In the UK emissions of carbon dioxide from road transport are the fastest growing contributor to climate change – the

greatest global environmental threat facing the international community and road traffic is also adding substantially to the local air pollution that is damaging our health and hastens the death of thousands each year.' It goes on to state that 'Aircraft engines are believed to contribute about 2–3% to the global total of man-made pollution' and that aviation fuel cannot be taxed by international agreement. It does not state how much of 'man-made pollution' is attributable to motor vehicles. "

'Global Change Biology' 1-1 by David S. Schimel (copyright Blackwell Science Ltd 1995) contains a chart showing that only 3.5% of all CO_2 emissions come from fossil fuels and cement production. The sea and vegetation absorb more CO_2 than they emit. Changing land use emits more than it absorbs. But none of the CO_2 emitted by the burning of fossil fuels is re-absorbed by its source. However, only about 13% of the CO_2 emitted by the burning of fossil fuels comes from cars, so cars are responsible for 0.455% of total CO_2 emissions, which could easily be countered by the simple expedient of stopping deforestation and growing more trees. Last year, the British travelled 619 billion kilometres by car and taxi, 43 billion by bus and coach, 41 billion by rail, 4 billion by motorcycle, 4 billion by bicycle, and only 1 billion by aircraft. If aircraft are responsible for 2–3% of 'man-made pollution', by my reckoning, that makes aircraft vastly greater polluters per passenger kilometre travelled than cars. But motor fuel is taxable by national governments, whereas aviation fuel is not. I think it would be far more honest for our Government to state that it *needs* the £30 billion plus it nets from motorists (8–10% of total tax revenue) rather than to argue it is taxing motorists to help the environment. Lower trunk-road speed limits and increased speed-limit enforcement has slowed traffic down by

6% and directly lead to increased congestion which causes the greatest amount of pollution from road traffic.

Which petrol?

" *I have a 1986 'C'-reg. Volvo 340GLE with the B172K 1,721 cc Renault engine. Apparently it can't be modified to take account of the withdrawal of leaded petrol at the end of the year. I am told that my options are to use 98Ron Superunleaded, 97Ron/98Ron Lead Replacement Petrol, or 95Ron Premium unleaded with one of the four approved additives. What is the correct information?* "

According to *Glass's Guide* 'Green Guide', your car will run on either 97Ron Superunleaded or 97Ron LRP. Volvo made this clear to you in its letter to you of 9 June. Your car might run satisfactorily on 95Ron Premium Unleaded combined with Millers VSP Plus Lead Substitute Additive because that contains an octane enhancer bringing 95Ron Premium up to around 97Ron. But the problem with your engine is octane rating alone, not valve seat recession. Later model 1,721 cc 340s from late 1987 to 1990 can run on either 98Ron Superunleaded or 95Ron Premium Unleaded without modification.

High octane Audi

" *In August 1998 I asked you if my Audi 90, fitted with a 'PS' series engine, could be run on unleaded petrol. Using VAG's 1988 booklet Unleaded Petrol (part No. 000 VAG 312), you replied that it should only be run on 98Ron Superunleaded or unleaded four-star based on 98Ron Superunleaded. At the time (14 months ago) you thought that the LRP to be introduced for year 2000 would be based on 98Ron Superunleaded. My question is, now that LRP will be 97Ron rather than 98Ron, will the timing need adjusting? (The setting for 98Ron is 18 degrees TDC plus or minus one degree.) I was also told that the 'PS' code engine could be run on 95Ron Premium Unleaded if the timing was retarded to 12 degrees TDC plus or minus two degrees, which is contrary to the instructions in the VAG booklet. Or should I use a fuel line 'catalyst'. "*

Malcolm McKay has established that, in conjunction with the October reduction in fuel duty, the octane rating of Superunleaded will be reduced from 98Ron to 97Ron to make it cheaper to refine and hence cheaper at the pumps. Though the British Standard for leaded four-star was 97Ron, most of it in the UK and all of it in Europe was 98Ron, so the tuning of many 1980s European cars was optimised for 98Ron. I tried running a VAG GTi engine on 97Ron Shell 'low lead' four-star and found that it pinked. Even retarding by two degrees did not completely solve the problem. Try this with your Audi 90 timing and, if you still get a bit of pinking, either switch to a different brand that might be of slightly higher octane or add an octane booster to the petrol. I don't recommend retarding to 12 degrees TDC and running on 95Ron Premium Unleaded because the engine was not designed to give its best performance on this petrol and you may find that acceleration, fuel consumption and eventually emissions are adversely affected. The Federation of British Historic Vehicle Clubs does not yet recommend any form of petrol tank or fuel line 'catalyst', so if you believe the claims and testimonials for these devices, that is entirely up to you.

Unleaded low-down

Texaco has produced by far the best guide to which 80s cars will run on unleaded petrol and which need Lead Replacement Petrol. The very clear listings show if cheaper Premium Unleaded can be used with or without a timing adjustment, if Superunleaded can be used with no adjustment and if LRP is necessary. The guide, using technical data from Autodata Ltd, is entitled 'Don't throw your car away' and is free from Texaco service stations. Texaco also runs a helpline on 020 7719 3737, has a separate helpline for AA Members on 0990 500 600, and an email address: ukcustser@texaco.com.

Off with their heads!

" *You have recommended Ron Hopkinsons (01332 756056) several times for their unleaded cylinder-head conversions for BMC 'A' and 'B' series engines and for the 1500 cc; four-cylinder Triumph. However, we are Europe's largest classic engine re-manufacturer and supplier to most classic clubs of cylinder heads modified for use with unleaded petrol. We specialise in engines for post-war British sports cars and would be only too willing to offer informed advice to classic car enthusiasts and collectors.* "

This is from Susan Williams of Engine Machining Services (UK) Ltd, Kirkham Works, Central Avenue, Worksop, Notts S80 1EN, tel: 01909 482649, website: www.engine-machining-services.co.uk. EMS is a member of the Federation of Engine Remanufacturers and is British Motor Heritage approved.

Declining diesels

" *I've been driving Golf diesels since 1981. My first was a Jetta LD which, over 130,000 miles, returned 54 mpg. My second was a Mk II GTD, which returned 48 mpg. But my third, an 'atmo' Mk III LD has only managed 42 mpg over 3,022 miles in the last six months. Am I right in being disappointed?* "

One reason for the decline is that over the years

Golfs have been putting on weight. Your first Jetta ~~weighed 850 kg, your Golf Mk II weighed~~ 940 kg, and your current Mk III LD weighs 1,115 kg. Another is you've gone down from 80 bhp in your Mk II GTD to 64 bhp in your Mk III LD. (A 90 bhp Mk III TDI is not only much quicker, it is also much more economical.) But the main reason is that you're doing less miles and this almost inevitably means a greater proportion of short runs from cold starts during which the injection system has to over-fuel.

Duff DERV?

" *I wonder if the problem with R.C. of Rossendale's Audi TDI V6 (16 October) is the stuff he's putting in his tank. I run a low-mileage Landcruiser VX 4.2 Turbodiesel, which had considerable performance until about six months ago when I noticed that the mid-range pick-up had deteriorated. Talking to a technical contact in an oil company I was told that the green diesel now available is of lower calorific value with all engines using it producing between 10–15% less power and 2–3% increased fuel consumption.* "

I don't think so. I had a Seat Toledo TDI 110 out on test and not only did it perform very impressively, it did so at the rate of 52.5 mpg, which is better than I have ever seen before from any other VAG TDI 110. I put this down to the fact that I ran it entirely on Shell Pura diesel which is claimed to offer better performance and economy as well as low sulphur levels. It could be that your Landcruiser needs looking at by a diesel specialist. Some careful re-mapping may be needed to get it running properly on the new diesel. But if that doesn't work, use a detergent additive which incorporates a Cetane improver such as Millers DieselPower Plus, which has been reformulated specially for use with low sulphur diesel (tel: 0800 281 053 for stockists).

Lousy LRP?

" *My first experience of LRP may serve as a warning to others. I had always used leaded four-star in my immaculate 71,000-mile Audi 80SC. Then, on 11 October, I purchased a tankful of Esso four-star under the impression that I was buying leaded petrol. My car misbehaved on this tankful, leading me to wonder if I had inadvertently filled it with something else. I had. The four-star tank now contained LRP. My engine now rocks on its mountings at idle: something it never did before. And, with the engine under load while ascending gradients on the M40, I have noticed hesitation and loss of power. Theoretically, my car can run on Superunleaded so I am going to try that next. But I wonder if the potassium in Esso LRP interfered with chemical deposits already in my engine causing the valves to stick.* "

Could be. But Esso LRP should contain adequate detergent to prevent this. Also please note that to coincide with the tax reduction on Superunleaded as from 1 October, most refiners have also reduced its octane rating from 98Ron to 97Ron. Anyone used to running an older car with no 'knock sensor' on 98Ron Super may need to have the timing retarded by one or two degrees or may need to use an octane booster.

Unleaded Aston

" *I own a 1973 Aston Martin V8, which covers a mere 2,000 miles a year, and I would appreciate your advice on running it on unleaded petrol. Astons have offered a factory conversion at about £4,500 plus VAT. But as the beast is only valued at, say, £20,000, is it worth it, or can I safely run it with additives? Alternatively, the Broquet Catalyst has been recommended. Any assistance would be appreciated.* "

The sure way is to go for the AM head conversion. Despite thousands of testimonials, the Broquet Catalyst has not passed the FBHVC tests at the Motor Industry Research

Association (no tin-based 'catalyst' has). You could ask its suppliers to contract that, should your AM V8 suffer valve-seat recession after running on Premium Unleaded and the required number of Broquet catalysts, they will pay for a full engine rebuild by Aston Martin. If no such reassurance is forthcoming, then you could try one of the lead-replacement and octane-boosting additives which passed the FBHVC tests at MIRA (see 'The four-star question' at the beginning of this chapter).

Stuck up Mondeo

"I have had a most unfortunate experience with my September 1994 Ford Mondeo 1.8iLX which had covered 27,034 miles at the time. I took it to a Ford dealer with what I considered to be a minor fault, but was then told to sit down and take a deep breath because it was going to be a big job. Afterwards I was told that the valves had been sticking and the cylinder head had been removed to free them off. I cover about 3,000 miles a year, mainly short journeys. I enclose a copy of the bill and think there may have been a design fault."

A life of short runs from cold often wrecks an engine within 30,000 miles. But if the engine has 16 valves and is run on petrol without adequate detergent content the valves could start sticking earlier. Ford and GM Vauxhall were not to know that their engines would suffer such abuse but, when the problem started to arise, came up with solutions and fitted them as 'in service modifications' free of charge. Your engine escaped this because the problem did not occur until so much later in its life that a free modification would not have been appropriate. But the real culprit is lousy petrol. Switch to Texaco or Shell, which have good detergent packages and, with your modified engine, you should have no further problems from sticking valves. Also take the car for a reasonable run of at least 20 traffic-free miles at least once a week, or get rid of it and buy a microcar which would be more suited to your type of use.

Old Vauxhalls never die

" *I have an immaculate, rust-free Vauxhall Viva HB 1600 De-Luxe two-door saloon, which I think is a 'classic' whatever the Schlump brothers may have thought of it. My problem is what do I run it on? I'm not a 'potterer' and see 5,500 rpm quite often, so LRP will probably wreck my exhaust valve seats. I'd rather find a permanent solution than have to measure additives whenever I fill up.* "

I have great news for you. The Vauxhall Heritage Service is aimed at preserving 'classic' Vauxhalls such as yours and is offering an unleaded cylinder-head conversion service. Heads of Vivas, Magnums, Chevettes and Ventoras can all be modified by Lynwood Engineering who fit hardened valve seats and valve guides. More information from Peter Blinlow on 01582 426056.

Beetle juice

" *I run a VW Beetle 1300, first registered 7 October 1970 which has an AB code engine. The car has been in our family since 1980 and as far as I know its 87,555 miles have all been run on four-star leaded petrol. Now I don't know what to do. Should I use LRP in place of leaded petrol? Should I mix LRP one tank to four with unleaded? Or should I use an additive? Or, since the car has been run on leaded for nearly 29 years, will there be enough 'lead memory' on the valve seats to run it on unleaded?* "

AB series engines are 'high-compression'. But, by VW standards, this meant 7.5:1 rather than 7.3:1 or 6.6:1, so you don't need petrol with a higher octane rating than ordinary 'premium' unleaded. Beetle engines are also 'plodders' rather than 'revvers' and there isn't much joy to be had from revving them past 3,000 rpm anyway. So even though your engine's valve seats may be cast iron inside its alloy heads, the chances are they won't recede by much running on ordinary 'premium' unleaded. However, if you regularly rev the engine more than 3,000 rpm or cruise on motorways at 70 mph or want to be sure of protecting your valve seats, use an additive. (See the beginning of this chapter.)

A plea for better petrol

" *Mitsubishi's Gasoline Direct Injection seems to offer considerable advantages in terms of performance and economy. Why have other car manufacturers not followed suit – especially those building the more thirsty cars such as Jaguars? "*

Partly because Mitsubishi invented GDI, so have the patents. And partly because UK petrol is not of a high enough research octane number for super-efficient engines. A lot of work had to be done to get GDI engines to run properly in Europe. Even 'lean burn' engines can develop trouble with their Lambda sensors running on UK petrol. Japan has the best, highest octane petrol in the world. The UK's best petrol was recently reduced from 98Ron to 97Ron with no reduction in price, just a 2p tax cut, so it still costs 7% more than it should. At the same time Shell Germany has introduced a new 99Ron Optimax petrol which costs just a few pfennigs more than ordinary 95Ron unleaded. Low octane petrol is a principal cause of high emissions and poor economy, and the main reason why engineers are held back from giving us the advances in engine technology they could achieve on higher octane petrol.

TDI consumption

" *Using the 'brim to brim' method, over 15,000 miles I have established that my Audi A4 TDI 110 SE Avant is only delivering 43 mpg. This compares very unfavourably with the 'official' combined figure of 53.3 mpg. The Audi dealer has checked the systems with his diagnostic interrogator and reports no faults. I feel that I have either been misled or have a faulty engine. Please comment.* "

The 'official' figures are for comparative purposes with the 'official' figures for other cars and do not necessarily indicate what individual owners can expect to get. You will find the best comparative 'real life' figures for diesel cars in the data pages of *Diesel Car* magazine which averaged 45.3 mpg over its test of an A4 TDI 110 Avant. To put this into perspective, I averaged 43.84 mpg over 780 miles in one. My experience of VAG cars in general is that their odometers are more likely to under-read than over-read, so don't flatter the car's consumption figures. My VAG 1.9 litre TDI fuel consumption experience is as follows:

model	mpg	distance covered
SEAT Ibiza TDI 90	54.11	369
SEAT Toledo TDI 110	52.38	692
VW Golf Mk III TDI 90	53.66	785
SEAT Ibiza II TDI 90	50.63	479
Skoda Octavia TDI 110	46.96	278
VW Golf Mk IV TDI 110	46.49	1,001
Audi A4 TDI 110 Avant	43.84	780
Ford Galaxy TDI 90	37.39	829

For recession, check compression

" *Since running an engine designed for leaded petrol on unleaded or LRP might lead to valve-seat recession, would it not be a good idea to take compression readings every 2,000 miles or so? Of course, loss of compression may also be due to 'leak down' past the piston rings, but this would normally show up in a heavy increase in oil consumption.* "

Yes, especially with cast iron cylinder heads. But if the head is aluminium with cast iron valve seats, great care needs to be taken not to cross-thread the spark plugs when replacing them. New spark plug washers may also be needed.

For 98Ron, read 97Ron

" *Having noticed a drop in performance from my wonderful 1989 Audi 200 Turbo, I checked with Shell to find out if the company had lowered the octane of its Superunleaded. Sure enough, it had, to 97Ron, so 'Super' can be used as the base fuel for cheaper LRP. (Why is LRP cheaper?) How do I now increase the octane rating of pump petrol to a level my car prefers? Should I use an octane-enhancing additive? And should I add it to LRP or to Super?* "

Because your car has a turbo, you have to be very careful not to mix a sodium-based additive with any other. What I'd do is use lead-replacement additive-free 95Ron Premium Unleaded, and boost the octane with an octane enhancer containing no sodium. Happily, none of the FBHVC approved octane-enhancing LRP additives are sodium-based. Castrol Valvemaster Plus (from Halfords) is phosphorus-based, while Millers VSP Plus (0800 281 053) and Carplan Nitrox 4-Lead (0161 764 5981) are manganese-based. There is no reason other than profit why LRP should be cheaper than the Super on which it is based. (See 'A plea for better petrol' above.)

Zetec S or Zetec E?

" *On our Ford dealer's recommendation, we purchased a Ford Focus 1.8 Zetec rather than a 1.6. But, to date, after 2,000 miles of careful driving, we are appalled to be averaging just 30 mpg, with a best so far of 33. The car is not used for short journeys, nor is it flogged on the motorways. My Mondeo 2.5 regularly returns over 30 mpg on the same runs. We are wondering whether we bought a dog in getting the older 1.8 litre engine rather than the more up to date 1.6?* "

I got 35.53 mpg out of a Focus 1.6 Zetec on a long trip with four people and their luggage aboard (worse than from my own 2.0 litre Zetec E Mondeo). But the car is 'long geared' and was very sluggish in fifth, which is why your Ford dealer recommended the more torquey 1.8 litre engine. I'd give your Focus 1.8 another 4,000 miles or so to loosen up, then, if you don't start getting 35 mpg or more on Shell or Texaco Premium Unleaded, begin investigating why not. That said, Ford odometers can vary a lot. My own is 4% fast which means that the 40.68 mpg I recently averaged in my 2.0 Mondeo on Shell was really 39.05 mpg.

LRP = less mpg?

" *Since switching to LRP from Shell four-star, the mpg of my 1989 Renault 5 has dropped from 32 mpg to 23 mpg. Two friends have noticed the same drop, one with a similar R5 and one with a Ford. Is this to be expected?* "

We're finding out. If the Shell four-star you were previously using came from French refineries it was probably at least 98Ron, not the 97Ron Shell 'low lead' four-star which some of us had trouble with in the UK prior to the introduction of 97Ron LRP. In the UK, the oil companies have generally increased the potassium additive content in LRP from 8 mg/litre to between 10 and 12 mg/litre, but this is still a long way below the 36 mg/litre recommended by the FBHVC. The other factor could be lack of detergent additive in your petrol. This is particularly important on an island like Guernsey where cars tend to spend their entire lives plodding about at low engine revs.

Thirsty diesel

" *I have a 1992 Rover 218SLD which has covered 52,000 miles and is fitted with the PSA XUD-7TE engine. Over four years it has consistently returned about 45 mpg locally and 50+ mpg on longer journeys. Over the last few months, this has fallen to just below 40 mpg, always measured 'brim to brim'. It has been suggested that the cause is the new low-sulphur diesel fuel. Could this be possible? Should I consider seeking help from our local Citroën garage, which knows this engine well?* "

A visit to a Citroën or Peugeot franchise is a good idea. The injector timing might need to be re-set to compensate for the lower Cetane rating of the low sulphur fuel. But first, try Shell Pura diesel. Also consider adding Millers DieselPower Plus to the fuel. This additive combines a detergent with a lubricity enhancer (to help the pump) and a Cetane improver (to give a better burn). It has been reformulated with less detergent and more Cetane improver to suit low-sulphur diesel, which already contains detergent but lacks Cetane. You can get it from A1 Motor Accessory Shops or phone 0800 281053 for other stockists.

New pollutes more than old

" *An interesting story appeared in the* New Scientist *on 12 February*

2000 reporting that new cars actually cause more pollution than old cars, partly through 'specification creep'. I personally deplore the virtually universal fitting of power steering, even on small cars, which don't need it, because the system inevitably absorbs power and leads to more pollution. **"**

The National Institute of Public Health and the Environment at Utrecht University has produced figures which show that building a new car and recycling an old car creates more CO_2 than continuing to run the old car. This is compounded by the 'specification creep' of which A.K. writes: the likelihood of a new car being heavier, more powerful and much more complex than the vehicle it replaces. The Institute's figures show that reducing the average age of cars in the Netherlands by three years would actually increase CO_2 emissions by 4% overall, though the effect would be lessened if people replaced large, inefficient, old cars with small, efficient, new ones. J.T. of Standlake adds that, during a 10–12 year lifespan, the average car will never use as much energy as was taken to build it. He feels that registration tax on cars should be imposed on the basis of their projected longevity and that this would do more to combat global warming than the tax on CO_2 emissions announced in the Budget.

More than coincidental

" *My sympathy goes to D.H. of Guernsey (26 March). Since I switched from Texaco four-star to LRP the fuel consumption of my 2CV has risen from 48 mpg to 32 mpg.* **"**

There could be another reason for this. The engine might need a carburettor rebuild. (I had a 2CV once that suffered an identical malady with no change of petrol.) Other readers have found they get so much better mpg on Super rather than LRP they can justify the additional cost. Yet others have found that, without any adjustment, their 1980s cars run fine on Premium Unleaded, which suggests that some brands are more than the minimum 95Ron. (In independent tests, Shell Premium was found to average 95.6Ron against an average of 95.1Ron.)

Astranomically thirsty

" *We have purchased a Vauxhall Astra automatic for my wife and she is unhappy about the fuel consumption. The quoted figures for the model are: urban: 28.59 mpg; steady 56mph: 47.06 mpg; steady 75mph: 37.6 mpg. However, in practice, we have only been able to achieve a maximum of 30–33 mpg.* "

This must be the old model Astra because the consumption figures you quote are the old official figures which have not been used for new cars for some years. The new figures take some account of cold starts, but any car used for a succession of short runs from cold starts will use a lot of petrol because it is running on an enriched mixture for a high proportion of its mileage. A car used in this manner will drink more petrol than one cruising on the motorway at a relatively high 4,000 rpm, which generally equates to between 80 mph and 112 mph.

Giving it a boost

" *I drive a Volvo 240 which has hard valve seats and was fine on 98Ron Superunleaded (now 97Ron), but I am finding this grade of petrol increasingly difficult to obtain in the UK. As I am soon setting out to tour northern England and Scotland is there any way I can get information as to which filling stations stock 97Ron petrol?* "

LRP is 97Ron and is supplied by almost all filling stations. But you might find it better to use a good Premium Unleaded such as Shell and boost it with an octane booster such as Millers Octane+. This costs around £3 for enough to boost 40–50 litres of petrol from 95Ron to 97Ron or, for grey imported Japanese high performance cars, from 97Ron to 99Ron. For a list of Millers stockists, phone 0800 281 053.

Da doo Ron Ron

" *I recently acquired a new E46 model BMW 323iSE. I note that the handbook recommends that I use Superunleaded petrol. However, in view of the considerable price differential between Super and Premium I would be grateful to receive your view on the advisability of using the lower octane petrol.* "

Modern high-performance engines are designed to run on the best petrol, which in Europe is 98Ron and in Germany is 99Ron. Because engines have have knock sensors, they can run on lower octane petrol such as the UK's 97Ron or even 95Ron Premium Unleaded in emergencies, but on 95Ron they lose 5–10% of their power, are less economical and may develop problems. (The exception is Fords which are generally happy on 95.5Ron Shell.) Both 95Ron and 97Ron can be boosted slightly with additives such as Millers Octane+, tel: 0800 281 053 for stockists. (See 'A plea for better petrol' above.)

Unleaded railway engine

" *I have a small railway locomotive, originally built in 1909 and since fitted with a petrol engine from an Austin 8. Last year I ran it on four-star leaded. What can I run it on now?* "

It depends on the revs the engine uses. If it has to rev hard, then LRP may not contain enough potassium to prevent valve-seat recession. You can still get four-star leaded from Grizebeck Service Station, Kirby in Furness, Cumbria. Or, since the engine's standard compression ratio is only 6.8:1, you could use 95Ron Premium Unleaded plus any approved lead-replacement additive whether it boosts the octane or not (see beginning of chapter).

The 87p *gallon*!

" *In your 'De-mystified motors' on fuel tax you stated that at a pump price of 79.9p a litre, 'only' 19.8p pays for the petrol and the rest is tax. Well, in Cyprus the pump price of a litre of either petrol or diesel works out at just 16.22p (87p a gallon). Cyprus isn't an oil producer. How do you explain the difference?* "

UK property prices, UK council taxes, UK wages and the fact that petrol stations effectively work as taxing stations, collecting huge amounts in tax revenue for a tiny percentage profit on turnover. All their profit and running costs have to come out of the 19.8p they charge for the petrol – and from Kit-Kats, Cornish pasties, *Daily Telegraphs*, barbecue briquettes and anything else they can flog you.

GEARBOX AND CLUTCH

Clutchless change

" *A few months ago the* Telegraph's *'Motoring' page ran an article about a conversion of manual gearboxes to a type of automatic, avoiding the use of the clutch pedal. Similar to the Renault Twingo 'Easy' system, but possible to transfer from vehicle to vehicle. Please will you supply the name, address and telephone number?* "

You are referring to the TUV-approved Vehvac AutoClutch, which employs a button on the gear-shift knob and an electric motor to dip the clutch for you when you want to change gear. The product is AutoClutch, from Vehvac Ltd, Fircroft Way, Edenbridge TN8 6EJ, tel: 01732 868080.

CVT troubles

" *Four years ago I bought a new Nissan Micra CVT automatic. The gear change was a bit stiff, which I put down to the car being new. But last year it got much worse and I took it back to the supplying dealer for advice. I was told the car needed a new magnetic clutch, and remedial work to the gearbox which had been damaged as a result. Though the car had done less than 5,000 miles, it was out of warranty and I would have to pay the cost of approximately £1,200. I then consulted my local garage, which has looked after the car. They took it to an automatic-gearbox specialist who said the engine-management computer had a fault and would require a new 'torque converter'? We also approached Nissan who said the problem was the result of my driving with my hand on the gear lever, and revving the engine while the car was stationary. Have you ever heard of this problem with Micras? What worries me is if I pay up, the same problem may crop up again, landing me with even more expense.* "

Apart from the CVT in the Volvo 440/460 1.8 (quite rare) and the Honda Civic 1.6i (very rare), the Micra's CVT seems to be the most reliable of this type of box, and Fords and Fiats the least reliable. Like the Fiat Punto, your box has an electromagnetic clutch operated by sensors which can sometimes play up. As a general rule of thumb, if the change into gear ever feels stiff, you should seek help from your dealer immediately and not force it, or you are highly likely to damage the gearbox itself. The other essential with CVTs is to check the ATF (gearbox oil) level at least every week and if it drops below the minimum to immediately top it up with the correct ATF fluid. (Buy a bottle from the dealer.) Follow this advice and, once your gearbox is repaired, you should not have any further trouble. Nissan has shown its faith in CVTs by coming up with a new one for more powerful 2.0-litre engines, which has a torque converter instead of an electromagnetic or magnetic clutch and a sequential changer, enabling the driver to change between or hold six ratios.

More CVT trouble

" *I have a Rover 416 CVT automatic Tourer, first registered in November 1997. I bought it secondhand with 7,800 miles about six months ago and took out a two-year MBI warranty at the same time. At 9,000 miles I began to hear a rattle from the gearbox area when the engine was started from cold, which disappeared as soon as the engine and gearbox were up to running temperature. The Rover dealer says it comes from the torsion damper between the engine drive plate and the CVT box. This has a number of springs in it, which tend to be loose and rattle until they heat up and expand. The dealer says it is a design fault, but is not dangerous and will not lead to a failure. It can be eliminated by replacing the springs, but will return after around 2,000 miles. Though I can't claim on the warranty, I find this fault extremely annoying. Can I make any sort of claim against the dealer?* "

You caught me out here because, until I checked up, I was completely unaware that the Tourer model had ever been fitted with the 'K' series, 1,589 cc engine and CVT box used in the 'new' 200 automatic. These are quite reliable CVTs because they don't have the complex electromagnetic clutch fitted to Fiats and Nissans and give 'instant drive', which is great for getting out of T-junctions but does require care when manoeuvring. (Left foot braking is advised.) Had you brought the matter up earlier you might have had a case for rejecting the car under the 1994 Sale and Supply of Goods Act. But it's too late for that now. For tips on preserving the life of a CVT see 'CVT Troubles' above.

Left-leg exerciser

" *I possess a Micra 1.3 'Noddy' car with which I am reasonably happy apart from the action of the clutch. It is high-set, with a long travel and has to be floored for a baulk-free gear change. It also has a seemingly insatiable appetite for cables as, at a mere 19,000 miles, I am now on my third. In the Lakes area, the narrow, hilly, winding roads with numerous blind bends necessitate incessant gear changing, so I am wondering whether the CVT automatic version of the Micra might be more suitable?* "

Unfortunately, the previously well regarded Micra CVT is now starting to develop the same sort of problems that have plagued Ford and

Fiat CVTs, so I cannot, hand on heart, recommend it. But some time ago, D.R. of Eskdale asked me to suggest a replacement for a Peugeot 205 GTi, to be used to ferry elderly people on similar roads to those you describe. I suggested a Seat Ibiza TDI, and he and his wife are delighted with it. The car has so much low-down torque, gear changing is minimised. It romps up the hills, handles tidily, and delivers 55 mpg, which more than makes up for its slightly gruff nature.

Automatic fear-boxes

" Please could you expand on what can go wrong with Fiat Punto, Nissan Micra and Ford Fiesta CVT gearboxes? "

First, don't panic. The fact that quite a few of these gearboxes have failed does not necessarily mean that yours will. The standard precautionary measure is to change the automatic transmission fluid every year and to keep an eye on the ATF dipstick level, making a check at least every week. If the level falls, it is vital to top up the box up with the correct ATF and ask a specialist to investigate the leak. Do not drive the car with a low ATF level or the box could self-destruct. Additionally Fiat Punto and Nissan Micra CVTs have electromagnetic clutches, the sensors of which can play up. If the gear lever ever feels stiff, seek assistance from a specialist. Do not in any circumstances force the lever or you could wreck the gearbox. King Automatics of The Chalk Pit, College Lane, Epsom, Surrey, tel: 01372 728769, have come up with a modification which prevents ATF loss from CVT gearboxes – especially Fords, and are experts in all types of CVT including Rover, Honda and Volvo.

No creeping

" *I am thinking of buying a Rover 216 with the CVT automatic gearbox. I have been warned that this type of automatic does not have 'creep' and so is not as easy to use, especially when parking. Is this true and, if so, are there any other makes in this class that do offer 'creep'?* "

Fiat and Nissan CVTs have electromagnetic clutches that allow a gentle take off. With the Rover 216 CVT, take off is immediate. This is hugely advantageous when getting out of road junctions. But, unless you are adept at left-foot braking when manoeuvring in confined spaces, you could run into difficulties. If you aren't, you will be better off with a conventional small automatic, such as a VW Polo 1.6 four-speed auto or a Toyota Corolla 1.6GS four-speed auto.

Out of control

" *I wonder if anyone has had any experience of this? My friend, driving a Volvo 440 automatic, put it into reverse and it roared away and hit a bank. She then put it into 'drive' and it went completely out of control and she could not stop it.* "

What you describe is so common there is even a term for it, 'unintentional acceleration syndrome'. It kills around 20 people every year and is mainly caused by elderly drivers who drive automatics 'one footed' confusing the brake and accelerator pedals. If they could drive 'two-footed' (left foot for the brake, right foot for the accelerator) this confusion would never arise and they would always be able to stop the car, even if the engine-management system increased engine revs sufficiently to engage 'drive'. If your friend is prosecuted for the accident, she may be compelled to re-take her driving test.

Automatics are harder, not easier, to control than manuals and I am convinced that no one over the age of 60 should switch from driving manual cars to driving an automatic unless they are disabled and the car is specially adapted to offer full braking control at all times.

Automatic accidents

" My wonderful mother-in-law is both fit and well, but is fast approaching her 92nd birthday. She is considering changing her ageing Metro for another small car with power steering and automatic transmission. I read that you have reservations about the longevity of CVTs. Could you please recommend a new or 'nearly new' car that would be enjoyable for her to drive and, most of all, reliable. "

Unless an elderly driver has already been driving automatics for many years, I don't recommend this combination. Every year there are at least ten deaths caused by 'runaway automatics' driven by elderly people who are taken by surprise at their inability to control them in the same way as a manual car. So my recommendation is either a VW Lupo or a Seat Arosa SE with the 1.7SDI diesel engine. These cars are small yet tall, with an excellent range of seating and steering-wheel adjustment, power steering is standard, and the engines provide a gentle yet flexible spread of power which masks mistakes and make them both easy and pleasant to drive. They are also extremely economical, have the lowest CO_2 emissions of any car I have yet seen listed, and carry a three-year warranty. (See 'Not Automatically' in 'Horses for Courses' section.)

Automatic transition

" *I am considering buying the new BMW 320D SE automatic Touring. However, I have had seeds of doubt sown by a local garage (not a BMW dealer) which specialises in repairing BMWs and which has a very good reputation locally, telling me that the diesel engine with its powerful mid-range torque is not a good mate for an automatic gearbox. This is not the first time I have heard the opinion. Is there any reason to doubt the pairing?* "

Depends on the engine, and the transmission. Strong mid-range torque isn't as much of a problem as the lack of power and torque at the bottom end of the rev range. Even with the very best pairings, for example the Mercedes Benz 220CDI and five-speed autobox, if you lift off or brake on a steepish hill you will need to yank the box back into second gear manually to recover any kind of speed. Can't tell you how BMW's 2.0-litre diesel works in an automatic 3-Series as the only car I've driven with this engine was a manual Rover 75, in which the power output is cut from 136 bhp to 116 bhp. The BMW 530D automatic, however, is either a truly great car or the bloke in front of me didn't know how to drive his Porsche 911/996.

Sticky gears

" *My Nissan Primera 2.0SE required considerable effort from the driver to change gears. The dealer has told me it is a 'characteristic' of the model. What can be done?* "

The gearbox is a weakness of the Primera. Yours may now be damaged, in which case the only cure is a replacement box. But before you go to this expense, have the gearbox oil drained and replaced with semi-synthetic or fully synthetic gearbox oil. It's actually well worth having this done within the first 18 months of any modern car's life because it gets rid of swarf thrown off as the box beds in and works wonders for the change quality. (The reader later reported back that changing the gearbox oil had vastly improved his gearbox.)

'A' for automatic

" *I am thinking of buying a Mercedes Benz A Class. Being past 60 years of age and mindful of the ever increasing volume of traffic on the roads, I have been thinking of an automatic. I then discovered that MB do two different automatic versions of the A Class: one a full automatic, and the other a semi-automatic. What advantages does one offer over the other?* "

The first A Class I drove was an A140 semi-automatic and I can tell you it's surprisingly easy to get used to. The advantage is control over which gear the box is in. The even smaller MCC Smart car has a six-speed, semi-automatic box with a button on the side offering fully automatic changing so you can compare the two systems in the same car. It's actually vastly better in semi-automatic mode. One final advantage of semi-automatics is that in them you are far less likely to suffer from 'unintentional acceleration syndrome' because if this appears to be happening you can simply pull the box out of gear. A company by the name of Vehvac offers semi-automatic conversions for a wide range of manual vehicles, tel: 01732 868080.

Transmission transition

" *I have a 68,000-mile, 'D'-reg. BMW 520i with a four-speed, ZF automatic transmission. For the first 1,000 metres or so after starting up, gear shifts are quite smooth. But the first to second shift then de-*

generates. I should add that I live in Central London and have driven a total of less than 6,000 miles in the last five years. My mechanic tells me that 80,000 miles is the normal life expectancy of this transmission before a £600 rebuild including a new torque converter 'to be safe'. However, two Californian friends tell me that the expected life of a BMW automatic transmission over there is 250,000 miles. Since a mile is the same distance in the UK as in California, is this yet another example of 'Rip-off Britain'? **"**

No. Drive any car a huge annual distance in warm, stress-free conditions at relatively moderate speeds and you can expect to cover massive mileages before major failures. Drive the same car no more than 6,000 miles over five years in London traffic and you can expect to inflict serious damage. You now face a bill which is not far off what the car is worth (about £1,000). So it's decision time.

More automatic fear-boxes

In the same batch of mail I received letters from B.G. of Ramsey and G.R. of Verwood, both of whom own Ford Mondeo V6 24v automatics, both of whom have changed the transmission oil, and both of whom are having trouble with their CD4E boxes. B.G.'s is the lower mileage car at 28,000 and seemed to be slipping and jolting at lower speeds. Trevor King of King Automatics diagnosed possibly the road speed sensor but more likely the inhibitor switch which is a simple £26 replacement. G.R.'s 57,000-mile car has lost reverse and been analysed by a local specialist as needing a reconditioned box at £1,350 plus VAT. Trevor King confirmed that if it this was not caused by a blocked valve in the valve body, it was most likely to be a clutch problem, necessitating a reconditioned box for which he charges £1,100 plus VAT, fitted. These boxes are best changed by lifting the entire engine and gearbox up out of the car rather than dismantling the subframe and dropping the box down underneath. Trevor King at King Automatics, tel: 01372 728769; Federation of Automatic Transmission Engineers, tel: 0585 228595.

Clutchless changes

" *I have an Alfa 156, which is without doubt the best of the 38 cars I have owned in 45 years of driving. (Second best was a 1974 Renault 16TS.) I have noticed that I can make perfect, seamless up-changes without using the clutch, and if I blip the accelerator with the gear shift in neutral I can also make clutchless down-changes. Is this doing any harm? I have noticed that clutchless changes can only be made if the lever slips easily into neutral. Any stickiness and it shouldn't be tried.* "

The 156 Selaspeed has the same box with an electric clutch, so guarantees the same effect with the benefit of change buttons on the steering wheel. No, you won't be doing the box any harm, unless, of course, you muff a change.

Exploding VW gearboxes

" *The gearbox of my wife's 35,000-mile, 97P VW Golf 1.4 exploded in Derby on 11 December. The garage has estimated £600 plus for its repair. I have always maintained the car myself with specialist jobs carried out by independent garages. Do you think VW would consider a goodwill claim?* "

Possibly. It's always worth phoning VW Customer Care on 01908 601777. Another reader, B.O. of Shrewsbury, wrote to me last week about the failure of the gearbox of his wife's 32,500, 96P VW Polo CLD. In his case, the bolts holding the driveshaft worked their way out and the flailing driveshaft smashed a hole in the side of the box. VW turned down his claim because the car was out of its three-year warranty and because the repair was carried out at an independent garage, but two letters about 'P'-reg. VW gearbox failures in a week seems like too much of a coincidence.

Is a CVT for me?

" Until I read your comments I was thinking of buying either a Nissan Primera or new Almera CVT (assuming both are available with CVTs). What is it that gives CVTs, to quote your words, a 'relatively poor record of reliability'? "

Automatic-transmission fluid leaks, which lead to premature failure of the steel band through running dry, and worn or failed sensors where the clutch mechanism is electromagnetic. The Nissan 'Hypertronic' CVT M6 has a torque converter rather than an elecromagnetic or multiplate clutch, so eliminates sensor problems at the expense of tardy take-up. The new 'Steptronic' ECVT in the Rover 25, on the other hand, is by far the best automatic transmission for suburban use I have ever driven. Not only does it pull out of side roads with commendable alacrity, the electromagnetic clutch takes up drive much more smoothly than the old 200 CVT, so offers the best of both worlds. And the 200 Steptronic is the easiest automatic I know in which to shift from 'D' to 'N', then pull the handbrake on so as not to blind the driver behind with its high-level brake light. The ability to hold ratios is less of an advantage in traffic, but does offer benefits when accelerating hard, when ascending or descending hills and when driving on snow-covered roads.

No automatics

" *Have you any idea what's going on at Ford? In January, my wife ordered a Focus Ghia automatic for delivery on 2 March under the Motability scheme. She had to return her previous Motability car on 3 March yet, despite switching our order to a cancelled order so we could take delivery more quickly, there is still no sign of the car. Now we have been told that Ford has stopped all deliveries of Focus automatics due to a technical problem. What would you suggest as an alternative?* "

Ford had a lot of trouble with its CTX continuously variable transmissions in the 1990s, mainly due to ATF leaks which led the boxes to run dry and seize up. Because of this, the CTX was abandoned for the Focus and a four-speed automatic box specified instead. Unfortunately, this, too, tended to suffer from failure of the end seals, which is why production has been stopped until a solution can be found. Trevor King of King Automatics of Epsom actually developed a cure for the CTX problem and offered it to Ford years ago. I think your wife's best bet is an Astra 2.0DI automatic. Until 16 March I would also have recommended a Rover 25 1.8 Steptronic.

GIZMOS AND TOOLS

Acoustic parking

" I am trying to locate an electronic car reversing aid which warns a driver of unseen obstacles in the path of a reversing car. I am told such a product exists, but no motoring store appears to stock them. How reliable are these devices and where can they be obtained? "

Auto Express magazine tested a range of these devices in issue 535. The one they rated best was Autosonics Backminder at £175 for the kit (01259 217004). Next best, scoring four stars was Ultrapark 2000 at an expensive £346 (Laver Technology 01279 436080). Next, with three stars, the Cobra ParkMaster at £151 for the kit (01923 240525). Next, fourth equal, and also with three stars, the much cheaper £86 AlliGator (Western Brands 01242 570227). Also fourth equal with three stars, the Proximeter at £170 (020 7345 5050). Another product which uses coloured lights as well as 'beeps' was originally designed for reversing caravans. It is made by Brigade Electronics, is called the 'Backscan RI-OS', costs around £200 fitted and worked well fitted as an optional extra to a Ford Scorpio I tried. Brigade Electronics can be contacted on 020 8852 3261.

Filler finder

A small British company has been developing an electronic filler detector for use on steel-bodied cars. They sought my unpaid opinions of the prototype and the first production examples. The result is a useful 2in-long, pocketable device that can tell you if a panel has been filled or not. Proof of the 'pudding' came when I finally had some transporter damage to the roof of my Pepper Red Mondeo repaired. Sunbury Coachworks did such a brilliant job, the original damage is undetectable to the naked eye. But the Ferristor TLX-1 found exactly where the filler was and I'll now be taking my Ferristor to auction every week. The price is £14.99, including battery. The maker is Teslec Ltd, New Springs, 90A Blackburn Road, Whittle-le-Woods, Chorley PR6 8LG, tel: 01257 271105.

Torque talk

" In the 1970s I bought an Alfa Romeo and, because it had an aluminium engine, diff case, etc. a torque wrench was essential. So I went out and bought a 'Norbar SL2'. The Alfa is now long gone, the way of most Alfas, but the Norbar remained in my possession. Foolishly, I let someone borrow it and it came back broken. (I can't imagine how he broke it.) Fortunately, Norbar is still in existence, so I sent the wrench back to them for repair. Even more fortunately, instead of repairing the old one, they sent me a direct replacement. "

A company like this deserves customers. Norbar Torque Tools Ltd, Beaumont Road, Banbury, Oxon OX16 7XJ, tel: 01295 270333, email: enquiry@norbar.com

A sponger writes

" *Can you please tell me if Spontex sponges have disappeared from the market? For many years now I have found them without equal, but now I discover that neither Halfords nor B&Q stock them locally. Are they still available and, if so, where?* "

A quick grovel in my wife's under-sink cupboard turned up some Spontex 'Tough Scourers', which I can personally testify are brilliant for cleaning pans. From the pack I got a Swansea address then, with a bit of help from Directory Enquiries and Spontex Non Woven of Colchester, established that Spontex has now moved to Worcester and its number for customer enquiries is 01905 450300. It turns out that the plain Spontex 'Car Sponge' has been discontinued in name only and continues to be sold as the Spontex 'Decorator's Sponge'. You can get one from Hurst Decorating Supplies, Unit 2, 9 Havilland Road, Ferndown Industrial Estate, tel: 01202 890520. If you prefer the Spontex 'Curved Back Car Sponge', C.J. Hardware will order one for you and is situated at 125–127 Bournemouth Road, Parkstone, tel: 01202 740712. I bet you never expected an answer like this. I never expected to provide it.

GOOD GARAGE GUIDE

In Summer 1996 we ran a reader's story about the difference between big garages in Britain and small garages in France. I felt that the contrast was more likely to be between bad garages and good garages generally, so I asked for readers' recommendations. The first 100 or so came in thick and fast, and have continued to do so. The result is this updated list which now reaches into the far corners of the land.

Remember, the list is based purely on readers' recommendations (plus four from me). Inclusion is not a guarantee of quality, competence or good value, and neither The Daily Telegraph *nor me can accept any responsibility for the consequences of taking a car to any of the garages listed. Nevertheless, many of the testimonials I have received were fulsome in their praise, so if you are looking for good service, this list may be a good start.*

- ABBERLEY: Alan Hole, P. Owen & Sons Ltd Motor & Agricultural Engineers, The Abberley Garage, Abberley, Worcestershire, tel: 01299 896209.

- ABERDEEN: Harpers of Aberdeen. Main workshop, tel: 01224 697772. Rapid Fit (open 8–6 M, Tu, W, F; 8–8 Th; 8 –5 Sa; 10–4 Su), tel: 01224 663232. (Good, helpful, Ford franchise.)

- ABERGAVENNY: Abergavenny Autos, Monmouth Road, Abergavenny, Monmouthshire, tel: 01873 852712. (Reliable Renault franchise.)

- ABERYSTWYTH: Anthony Motors Ltd, Aberystwyth, tel: 01970

624444. (Good Mazda agents.)

- ALDEBURGH: Chris Copeman, Copeman & Son Engineering, Hazelwood Farm, Aldringham, nr Aldeburgh, Suffolk, tel: 01728 830640, mob: 0860 614518.

- ALTON: Neil Carpenter, Farringdon Industrial Centre, Alton, Hants, tel: 01420 587 403.

- AMERSHAM: T and F Motors, White Lion Road, Amersham, Bucks, tel: 01494 765286.

- ANDOVER: Chris Monaghan and Martin Dix, Intech GB Ltd, Unit 12B, Thruxton Industrial Estate, Thruxton Circuit, nr Andover, Hants, tel: 01264 773888. (Service and repair specialists for Japanese grey imports from Honda Beat to Lexus 'Soarer' Coupe.)

- ASHBOURNE: Hulland Ward Garage, Main Street, Hulland Ward, nr Ashbourne, Derbyshire, tel: 01335 370209.

- ASHTON-UNDER-LYNE: Quicks, tel: 0161 330 0121. (Ford agent, which has retained at least one loyal customer for 39 years.)

- AYLESBURY: Ivor Miles, Churchway Garage, Churchway, Haddenham, Aylesbury, Bucks HP17 8HA, tel: 01844 291263. Lodge Garage (Aylesbury Mazda) Ltd, Bicester Road, Kingswood, Aylesbury, Bucks HP18 0QJ, tel: 01296 770405. C.D. Bramall (Aylesbury Toyota – formerly BMG Aylesbury).

- BALLATER: J. Pringle, Victoria Garage, Ballater, Grampion AB35 5QQ, tel: 013397 55525.

- BEDALE: John Gill Ltd, Bedale, N. Yorks, tel: 01677 423124. (Daihatsu dealer and general repairs.)

- BEXHILL-ON-SEA: Peter Johnson Motor Engineer, Unit 3, de la Ware Mews, Station Road, Bexhill-on-Sea, East Sussex TN40 1RD, tel: 01424 224169.

- BEXLEYHEATH: Paul at PDQ Car Services, Bexleyheath, Kent (phone first for directions), tel: 020 8303 1618, mob: 07831 138463.

- BILLINGHURST: Geoffrey Sizzy (Automobiles), Wisborough Green, nr Billinghurst, West Sussex, tel: 01403 700661. (Independent Peugeot specialist: sales, service, very good after-sales service.)

- BIRMINGHAM: R. Newman Motor Engineers, rear of J.H. Hancox Ltd, Alcester Road, Portway, Birmingham B48 7JA, tel: 01564 824996. G. & B. Clements, Baldwins Lane Service Station, Baldwins Lane, Hall Green, Birmingham B28 0XB, tel: 0121 744 5453. Ken Hunt Auto Services, 536 Hobmoor Road, Yardley, Birmingham B25, tel: 0121 789 7273.

- BOGNOR REGIS: Middleton Garage, 169 Middleton Road, Middleton-on-Sea, Bognor Regis, tel: 01243 58276. (Very helpful Fiat franchise.)

- BOSTON: Mick Barsley, Barsley Motor Engineers, 78 High Street, Boston, Lincs, tel: 01205 355396.

- BOURNEMOUTH: Horizon Motors, tel: 01202 294341. (Honda agents.)

- BRIDGWATER: Tim Stiles Racing, Units 5 & 6 Transform Estate, Wylds Road, Bridgwater, Somerset TA6 4DH, tel: 01278 453036. (VW/Audi performance modifications at reasonable prices and labour rates.) Stogursey Motors, High Street, Stogursey (eight miles from Bridgwater near Hinkley Point power station), tel: 01278 732237. (Car, van and motorcycle repairs and MOTs.)

- BRISTOL: All Audi Used Part Stores, Units 26/26 Hanham Business Park, Memorial Road, Hanham, Bristol BS15 3JE, tel: 0117 949 4136, mobile: 0860 259567. (Good source of parts for obsolete Audis.) R.J. Auto Engineers, Whitehouse Lane, Bedminster, Bristol, tel: 01179 632029. (Saab and Alfa specialists.) Cotswold Sports cars, a38 at Thornbury, near Bristol, tel: 01454 412413. (General maintenance and repairs.)

- BROADWAY: Alan Aston Motor Engineers, Childswickham, nr Broadway, Worcs, tel: 01386 852311.

- BROMLEY: Ted and Neil Craker, The Vehicle Test Centre, 107 Southlands Road, Bromley, Kent BR2 9QT, tel: 020 8460 6666. (Very well equipped and sensibly priced servicing workshop/MOT test centre, with two 'rolling road' brake testers and full diagnostic equipment.)

- BURTON-ON-TRENT: Peter Sharp, European Car Specialists, Parker Street, Burton-on-Trent, tel: 01283 540414.

- BUSHMILLS (CO. ANTRIM): James Wylie Auto Repairs, 40A Ballyclough Road, Bushmills, Co. Antrim BT57 8UZ, tel: 012657 32096. (Citroën specialist as well as other makes.)

- CAERLEON: Autotech, Panthir Road, Caerleon, Gwent NP6 1NY, tel: 01633 423717. (One of semi-official Autotech chain of independent BMW specialists.)

- CANTERBURY: Ashford Road Service Station, Chilham, Canterbury, Kent CT4 8EE, tel: 01227 730223. Hewitt Motors Ltd, Rhodans Town, Canterbury, Kent, tel: 01227 464386.

- CARDIFF: Continental Cars (Cardiff) Ltd, tel: 029 2054 2400. (Mercedes franchise, prepared to treat elderly drivers with sympathy and compassion.)

- CARNFORTH: The Mountain family, Lune View Garage, Melling, Carnforth, Lancs LA6 2RB, tel: 015 242 21457. Mill Brow Garage, Kirkby Lonsdale, Carnforth, Lancs, tel: 015 242 71248.

- CASTLE CAREY: Moff Motors, Castle Carey, Somerset, (near Castle Carey station on Shepton Mallet Road) tel: 01963 350310. (Independent dealers with good after-sales service.)

- CASTLEFORD: Castleford VW Spares, Methley Road, Castleford, W. Yorks, tel: 01977 518254. (VW/Audi servicing and parts.)

- CATFORD: Gilbert's Motors, tel: 020 8698 7067. (Honda agent prepared to repair expensive components rather than replace them.)

- CHANDLERS FORD: Hendy Lennox, Chandlers Ford, Hants, tel: 023 8048 3100. (Good, helpful Ford agent.)

- CHELMSFORD: Mr & Mrs John Plumb and son Steve, Central Garage, Latchingdon, nr Chelmsford, Essex, tel: 01621 740284.

- CHERTSEY: Speedtest, Unit A, Gogmore Lane, Chertsey, Surrey, tel: 01932 568921. (Non rip-off servicing and MOT centre. Good with Citroëns and Renaults.)

- CHESSINGTON: Mole Valley TVR, Chessington, Surrey, tel: 020 8394 1114. (Good TVR dealer – two recommendations.)

- CHESTER: Newgate Motors, Chester, tel: 01244 374473. (Expensive but straight Mercedes agent. Charges £58.75 an hour.)

- CHESTERFIELD: Bridgegate Ltd, Chesterfield, tel: 01246 208681. (Very helpful BMW agent. Even helpful to owners of older models.)

- CHIPPENHAM: David Giddings, 14 Brook Street, Chippenham, Wilts SN14 0HN, ex-directory. (Specialist cars such including Alfas and Jensens.)

- CHISLEHURST: Paul and Tony at PDQ, 1a Albany Road, Chislehurst, Kent, tel: 020 8295 0121. (BMW and Jaguar specialists.)

- COLWYN BAY: Meredith and Kirkham, Colwyn Bay, tel: 01492 515292. (Rover agent, which has retained at least one loyal customer for 47 years.)

- CORFE MULLEN: Westover Nissan, 149/153 Wareham Road, Corfe Mullen, Dorset, tel: 01202 693681. (Former Rover dealer, now Nissan. Very highly recommended by one reader.)

- CREWKERNE: Misterton Garage, Misterton, Crewkerne,

Somerset, tel: 01460 72997. (Ford retail dealer, good for servicing and repairs, reasonable prices.)

- CROWBOROUGH: John Cottenham, Care's Garage, School Lane, St. Johns, Crowborough, Sussex TN6 1SE, tel: 01892 653519. (VW.)

- CROYDON: The Silver Wing Garage, 25 Horatius Way, Silverwing Industrial Estate, Stafford Road, Croydon, Surrey CR0 4RU, tel: 020 8680 6959. (Much praised independent garage operating a National Auto Service franchise.)

- CWMCARN: Bijou Motor Services, (rear of) 99–101 Newport Road, Cwmcarn, Gwent NP1 7LZ, tel: 01495 271033. (Citroën specialists, offering enhanced servicing for these models.)

- DARWEN: Brunswick Street Garage, Darwen, Lancs, tel: 01254 762300. (Mercedes-Benz trained independent MB specialist.)

- DAVENTRY: Dave Carvell Cars, Staverton, nr Daventry, Northants, tel: 01327 300739.

- DERBY: Citrognome, Great Northern Road, Derby, tel: 01332 345869. (Citroën specialists.)

- DORCHESTER: Loders, Dorchester, Dorset, tel: 01305 267881. (Good franchised Audi dealer service.) Old's Jeep, Dorchester. (Good franchised Chrysler dealer service.)

- DORKING: Steve Bradstock, The Coach House, Beare Green, Dorking, Surrey, tel: 01306 713424.

- DOVER: Elms Vale Garage, Elms Vale Road, Dover, tel: 01304 201077. (Good, small, independent, local garage.)

- DRUMNADROCHIT: J.E. Menzies & Son Ltd, Lewiston Garage, Drumnadrochit, Inverness, tel: 01456 450212.

- DUBLIN: Walden Motor Company, Parnell Street, Dublin, tel: 00

3531 873 0400, email cars@walden.ie. (Dublin Ford agent which has retained at least one customer for 50 years.)

- DURHAM: Volksparts, Langley Moor, nr Durham City, tel: 0191 378 0284. (German car specialists: Audi, BMW, Mercedes, VW.)

- EASTBOURNE: Visick Cars Ltd, Birch Close, Lottbridge Drove, Eastbourne BN23 6PE, tel: 01323 722244.

- EASTHAM: Mitchell Mitsubishi, New Chester Road, Eastham, Wirral CH62 8HJ, tel: 0151 328 5555 or 0151 625 4555.

- ELVANFOOT: South of Scotland Coachworks, Elvanfoot, Lanarkshire (adjacent to A74M), tel: 01864 502236. (General repairs and service.)

- EMSWORTH: Lillywhite Bros Ltd, 40 Queen Street, Emsworth, Hants PO10 7BL, tel: 01243 372336.

- ENFIELD: Stephen James, London Road, Enfield EN2 6JJ, tel: 020 8367 2626. (Friendly BMW agent with sensibly priced servicing.)

- EPSOM: King Automatics, The Chalk Pit, College Road, Epsom, Surrey KT17 4JA, tel: 01372 728769. (Automatic transmissions of all types, including CVTs.) Kwik-Fit, 166 East Street, Epsom, Surrey, tel: 01372 739955. (Replaced a reader's tyre valve free of charge.) Drift Bridge Garage Ltd, Reigate Road, Epsom, Surrey, tel: 01737 360111. (VW agent.)

- EXETER: Volkswagen Services, 11 Coombe Street, Exeter, Devon EX1 1DB, tel: 01392 493737. (VW servicing.) Carrs of Exeter, tel: 01392 823988. (Good Mercedes and Porsche service.) Reg and Paul Stephens, Snow and Stephens, King Edward Street, Exeter, tel: 01392 256552. (General car repairs.) Rockbeare Motor Services, Rockbeare, Exeter EX5 2DZ, tel: 01404 822410. (General car repairs.) Best Tyres, Verney Street, tel: 01392 411100. (Low prices, good service and excellent for suspension alignment.)

- EXMOUTH: Karl Brigham, KB Auto Services and Repairs, Victoria Way, Exmouth, Devon, tel: 01395 223330. Bentleys Garage, Chapel Hill (High Street), Exmouth, Devon, tel: 01395 272048.

- FAREHAM: Peter Cooper, Fareham, Hants, tel: 01329 288233. (Good, helpful VW franchise.)

- FERRING: John Cooper Garages, Ferring, West Sussex, tel: 01903 504455. (Very helpful Honda franchise.)

- FORRES: Pedigree Cars, Forres, Morayshire, tel: 01309 672555. (Citroën garage.)

- FRENCHAY: Frenchay Garage, Frenchay Common, Frenchay, Bristol BS16 1NB, tel: 0117 956 7303.

- FROME: Marston MOT Centre, Whitworth Road, Marston Trading Estate, Frome, Somerset BA11 4BY, tel: 01373 452352. (Proprietor Stewart Herridge. Very reasonably priced, local, independent garage.)

- GARSTANG: H. & J. Kitching, Hornby's Garage, Lydiate Lane, Claughton-on-Brock, Garstang, Lancs, tel: 01995 640229.

- GRANTHAM: TMS Garages, Spittlegate Level, Grantham, Lincs, tel: 01476 564114. (Volvo specialist.)

- GRAVENHURST: Chris Case, Town Farm Garage, Campton Road, Gravenhurst, Beds, tel: 01462 711017.

- GUILDFORD: A.H. Autos, Unit 11, Foundation Units, Westfield Road, Slyfield Green, Guildford, tel: 01483 303942. (VW/Audi specialist.)

- HARROGATE: Mr Greenwood, Western Garage, Valley Mount, Harrogate, North Yorks H62 0JG, tel: 01423 502902. Nidd Vale Motors, Harrogate. (Vauxhall agents.)

- HEMEL HEMPSTEAD: V.P. Autos, Hemel Hempstead, Herts, tel: 01442 68163.

- HENLOW: Alan Turner, Henlow Car Centre, Henlow, Beds, tel: 01462 814668.

- HERSHAM: Colin Marshall or Keith Rhoods, Wheelbase Garage, 43 Queen's Road, Hersham, Surrey, tel: 01932 252515 or 01932 252881. (VW/Audi specialists.) Sunbury Coachworks, Unit R3, Lyon Road, Hersham Industrial Estate, Hersham, Surrey, tel: 01932 254057. (Good bodyshop offering excellent Autocolor paint finish at reasonable prices.)

- HEXHAM: Fred Almond, Haugh Lane Garage, Haugh Lane, Hexham, Northumberland, tel: 01434 60 4163 or 0836 532999.

- HOLMFIRTH: M & M Engineering Services, Clarence Mills, Holmbridge, Holmfirth HD7 1NE, tel: 01484 687706. (Citroën.)

- HOLT: Eddy Lynton, Academy Garage, Castle Street, Holt, Clwyd LL13 9YL, tel: 01829 270781.

- EAST HORSLEY: Philip Stonely, The Body Workshop, Forest Road Garage, Forest Road, Effingham Junction, Surrey KT24 5HE, tel: 01483 284805.

- HOUNSLOW: Franco Motors, 29 Vine Place, Hounslow TW3 3UE, tel: 020 8570 3798.

- HULL: Jordans of Hull, 45–52 Witham, Hull, tel: 01482 222500. (Various dealerships including Mazda. Sensible service policy.)

- HYTHE: Auto Pat, 3 Hardley Industrial Estate, Hardley, nr Hythe, Hants, tel: 023 8080 4163.

- ILFORD: Whichford Rover, 404 Eastern Avenue, Gants Hill, Ilford, Essex IG2 6NW, tel: 020 8554 8888. (Rover dealer which fixes faults on recently purchased used cars at no charge and without question.)

- ILKESTON: Dave's Motors, West Street, Ilkeston, Derbyshire, tel: 0115 9441 886.

- ISLE OF WIGHT: Harwoods, Lushington Hill, IOW, tel: 01983 885500. (Very helpful Renault agent, not averse to imports.)

- JARROW: David Ellis, Jarrow Coachworks, Curlew Road, Jarrow, Tyne and Wear, tel 0191 4892715, mobile: 0860 424813.

- KIRKWALL: A.T.S., Kirkwall, Orkney. (Tyre specialists and general servicing.)

- LANGPORT: J.A. Scott, Langport Motor Co., Westover Trading Estate, Langport, Somerset, tel: 01458 251100. (Citroën specialist.)

- LEAMINGTON SPA: Brian Ricketts, tel: 01926 451545. (VW/Audi.) Midland Autocar Co., Russell Street, Leamington Spa, Warks CV32 5QB, tel: 01926 421171. (General repairs and service.) Bull Ring Garage, The Bull Ring, Harbury, Leamington Spa, Warks CN33 9HR, tel: 01926 61275. (Excellent local garage.)

- LEDBURY: R. & J. Mathews, Blacklands Garage, Canon Frome (near Ledbury), Hereford & Worcester, tel: 01531 640374.

- LEEDS: David Wood, 11 Primley Park Road, Leeds LS17 7HR, tel: 0113 268 1815; mobile: 0780 858 0859. (VW/Audi). IVC (Independent VW Audi Centre), Globe Road, off Water Lane, Leeds LS11 5QS, tel: 0113 242 0875. (VW/Audi.)

- LEEK: Andy Jackson of A&C Vehicle Services, Ball Haye Road, Leek, Staffs, tel: 01538 398227. (VW/Audi.)

- LEIGHTON BUZZARD: Tom Goodman Motors, Comptons Yard, Grovebury Road, Leighton Buzzard LU7 8TS, tel: 01525 375972.

- LEWES: Morris Road Garage, Western Road, Lewes, East Sussex, tel: 01273 472434. (Independent Bosch fuel injection specialists.)

- LICHFIELD: Central Garage (Lichfield) Ltd, Queen Street, Lichfield, Staffs, WS13 6QD, tel: 01543 262826. (BMW and Mercedes.)

- LINCOLN: Riccardo Emiliani, Lincoln, tel: 01522 531735. (Helpful Honda agent.)

- LISKEARD: Ken Rowe, Rowe's Garage Ltd, Dobwalls, Liskeard, Cornwall PL14 6JA, tel: 01579 320218. (Citroën franchise, but willingly repaired D.W.'s 1972 Humber when it broke down while touring Cornwall.)

- LITTLEBOROUGH: J. Stanton, Stantons Motor Garage, Brookfield Mill, Canal Street, Littleborough, nr Rochdale, Lancs, tel: 01706 370166.

- LIVERPOOL: Orlando Heeson, Landers Autos, 19–22a Cathedral Road, Liverpool L6 0AT, tel: 0151 263 4913. Philip Walker, Dudlow Motor Company, Menlove Gardens West, Liverpool, tel: 0151 722 2396.

- LLANGOLLEN: Kenrick's Garage, Market Street, Llangollen, North Wales, tel: 01978 861381/861382. (Friendly local garage with excellent and reasonably priced 'rescue' service.)

- LOANHEAD: Stewart McLennan Garage, 44 Lawrie Terrace, Loanhead, Midlothian EH20 9ET, tel: 0131 440 0597.

- LONDON E5: Tony, D.A.M. Car Repairs, 1–8 Broadway Mews, Clapton Common, London E5 9AF, tel: 020 8800 7121.

- LONDON N4: G. Horscraft, Supertune Motor Engineers, 2A Beatrice Road, Stroud Green, London N4 4PD, tel: 020 7272 7678. Nick Sandamas, G&N Garages Ltd, 54/58 Wightman Road, Harringay, London N4 1RU, tel: 020 8340 331. (Independent Saab specialist.)

- LONDON SE6: Gonella Brothers, 9/13 Catford Hill, Catford, London SE6, tel: 020 8690 0060. (Alfa, Fiat and Lancia specialists.)

- LONDON SW2: Hearn Bros Ltd, The Hill Garage, 94 Brixton Hill, London SW2, tel: 020 8674 2888. (Twenty-four recommendations.)

- LONDON SW17: Carpenters Garage, 69–71 Bickersteth Road, Tooting, London SW17, tel: 020 8672 4891. (Small, family-run, independent garage and MOT-testing station.)

- LONDON W8: ACE Cars of Kensington, tel: 020 7938 4333. (Specialises in older Saabs: 900, 99, 96.)

- LONDON W12: AC Automotive, 247–251 Goldhawk Road, London W12, tel: 020 8741 9993. (American car parts and servicing.)

- LOWER BASILDON: Les Allum, Allum Auto Services, Reading Road, Lower Basildon, Berks RG8 9NL, tel: 01491 671726.

- LYMINGTON: Dory's Garage Ltd, Sway Park, Station Road, Sway, Hants, tel: 01590 683432. (Citroën specialists.)

- MAIDENHEAD: Delta Motors, tel: 01628 675064. Contacts: Jerry Houdret (sales), Roger Towers (parts). (Renault agents. Shipped a new water pump to a reader in Grand Cayman to arrive within 36 hours.)

- MALVERN: Denver Davis, The Station Garage, Thorngrove Road, Malvern, Worcs, tel: 01684 574088.

- MANCHESTER: Derek Boardman, Units 12/25, Morton Street Industrial Estate, Failsworth, Manchester, tel: 0161 681 0456. (VW/Audi – further endorsed by a reader now living in Holland.) Westron, 7 Nell Lane, Manchester M21 8UE, tel: 0161 881 1061. (Citroën suspension specialists.)

- MERSTHAM, John Witty, Witmun Engineering, 67 Nutfield Road, Merstham, Surrey RH1 3ER, tel: 01737 644828. (Citroën specialists.)

- MIDDLESBROUGH: Dave Stott Motors, Charlotte Street, Middlesbrough, tel: 01642 224805. (Independent Citroën specialists.)

- MORETON-IN-MARSH: N.E. Repairs, Hospital Road, Moreton-in-Marsh, Gloucs, tel: 01608 650405.

- NEEDHAM MARKET: Richard Robinson, Robinson's Motor Engineers, Debtrac Centre, Needham Market, Suffolk, tel: 01449 722240.

- NEWTON ABBOT: K. Tapper, Decoy Motors, Unit 10 Silverhills Road, Decoy Trading Estate, Newton Abbot TQ12 5LZ, tel: 01626 68701.

- NORTH SHIELDS: John Gallagher, Collingwood Garage, North Shields, tel: 0191 296 2888.

- NORWICH: Peter Whitley Motor Services, 7 Low Road, Drayton, Norwich NR8 6AA, tel: 01603 860154.

- NOTTINGHAM: John Harrison (Lowdham) Ltd, Southwell Road, Lowdham, Nottingham, tel: 0115 966 4112. (Helpful, honest Peugeot franchise.)

- ORPINGTON: Chelsfield Motor Works, Court Lodge Farm, Warren Road Orpington, Kent BR6 6ER, tel: 01689 823200.

- OULTON BROAD: John Pope, Pope Brothers, Station Garage, Bridge End, Oulton Broad, Lowestoft, tel: 01502 573797.

- OXFORD: North Oxford Garage Ltd, 280 Banbury Road, Oxford, OX2 7EB, tel: 01865 319000. (Helpful BMW franchise.) Motor World Mitsubishi, Oxford, tel: 01865 722444. (Mitsubishi agent offering excellent after-sales service.)

- PENARTH: Bernard Cody Motor Engineers, Station Approach, Penarth, Mid Glam, tel: 029 20704293. (RMI, VBRA, AVRO and MOT testing station.)

- PENRHYNDEUDRAETH: Dafydd Williams, Garreg Lwyd, Penrhyndeudraeth, Gwynedd LL48 6AW, tel 01766 770203.

(Secondhand Twingos, servicing, advice and 'hard to get' parts.)

- PENZANCE: Autostop Service Centre, Longrock, nr Penzance, Cornwal, tel: 01736 330300. (Excellent, non-franchised service and repair garage.)

- PERIVALE: AC Delco, 19 Wadsworth Road, Unit 14, Perivale, Middx, tel: 020 8810 4595. (American car parts and servicing.)

- PETERBOROUGH: Brian Pitts, 'The Complete Automobilist', 35 -37 Main Street, Baston, Peterborough PE6 9NX, tel: 01778 560444.

- PETERHEAD: Harpers of Aberdeen, Rapid Fit (open 8–6 M, Tu, W, F; 8–8 Th; 8–5 Sa; 10–4 Su), tel: 01779 474849. (Good, helpful, Ford Rapid Fit centre.)

- PEWSEY: Stevens Cars, Nicol's Yard (rear of Post Office), Pewsey, tel: 01672 563330.

- PLYMOUTH: Simon Rouse, Peverell Garage, Weston Park Road, Peverall, Plymouth, Devon PL3 4NS, tel: 01752 266099.

- POOLE: Connellys, Ashley Road, Upper Parkstone, Poole, Dorset, tel: 01202 738700. Grand Parade Motors, Poole Road, Poole, Dorset, tel: 01202 763361. (Good Vauxhall agent.)

- PORTHCAWL: John Rogers, Station Hill Garage, Porthcawl, Mid Glam., tel: 01656 786705.

- PORTMADOC: The Glanaber Garage, Borth-y-Gest, Portmadoc, Gwynedd, tel: 01766 512364. (Rescued a reader on a Saturday.)

- PRESTON: J.C. AND M. Davis, Garstang Road Garage, Garstang Road, Pilling, Preston PR3 6AQ, tel: 01253 790322. (General repairs, but good with diesels and Citroëns.) I.J. Woodburn, Unit 4 Garage, Langley Lane, Goosnargh, nr Preston, Lancs, tel: 01772 861126. (Reliable, independent BMW specialist.)

- RIPLEY: Colbourne Garages Ltd, Portsmouth Road (old A3), Ripley, Surrey, tel: 01483 224361. (Oldest-established UK VW agent; still good.)

- SADDLEWORTH: Greenfield Service Station, Chew Valley Road, Greenfield, Saddleworth, nr Oldham, Lancs, tel: 01457 873700.

- SANDERSTEAD: Steven Pengelly, Vorne Motorsport, 145 Limpsfield Road, Sanderstead, Surrey, tel: 020 8651 5344.

- SEVENOAKS: Antwis Engineering, Vestry Industrial Estate, Otford, nr Sevenoaks, Kent, tel: 01732 450386. (Very good with BMWs.)

- SHEFFIELD: Bridgco Garage, 160 Broad Oaks, Sheffield 9, tel: 0114 2441775.

- SIDCUP: Steve King, Kings Auto Services, 313/315 Blackfen Road, Blackfen, Sidcup, Kent SA15 9NG, tel: 020 8298 9225.

- SKYE: Ewan MacRae, Portree, Isle of Skye.

- SOUTHAMPTON: E. & J. Jarvis, Motor Engineers, Onslow Road, Southampton, tel: 023 8022 9297. Hilton Motors, Bond Road Garage, Bitterne Park, Southampton SO18 1LH, tel: 023 8055 5600. (General service, repair, sales garage and automatic-transmission specialist.)

- SOUTH MOLTON: Andrew Geen, Geen's Garage, South Molton, North Devon, tel: 01769 572395.

- SOUTHSEA: John Skerratt, Owl Motor Services, Richmond Road, Southsea, Hants, tel: 023 9273 6393.

- ST. ALBANS: Godfrey Davis St. Albans, 105 Ashely Road, St. Albans, Herts AL1 5GD, tel: 01727 859155. (Good Ford servicing facility capable of correctly diagnosing problems.)

- STEBBING: Bob Rains, Drakeswell Garage, Bran End, Stebbing, Essex, tel: 01371 856391.

- STOCKPORT: Chris or Stewart, Tenby Garage, Lavenders Brow, Churchgate, Stockport, Cheshire SK1 1YW, tel: 0161 480 5075. The Dave Arnitt Citroën Repair Centre, Arthur Street, Reddish, Stockport, tel: 0161 432 0636. (Citroën specialist.) General Motors, Cooke Street, Hazel Grove, Stockport, tel: 0161 483 3883. (Independent Audi/VW specialists.)

- STOCKTON: Shearborne Engineering, Preston Farm, Stockton-on Tees, tel: 01642 677744. (Independent Jaguar specialists.)

- SUTTON: G.B. Autos, 271 Gander Green Lane, Sutton, Surrey SM1 2HD, tel: 020 8641 1999. (Independent Volvo and air-conditioning servicing specialists.)

- SUTTON COLDFIELD: G. Chamberlain & Sons, Four Oaks Garage, Lichfield Road, Four Oaks, Sutton Coldfield, West Midlands B74 2UH, tel: 0121 308 0309. Dave Buckland, D.J. Buckland (Motor Engineer), rear of 162 Birmingham Road, Wylde Green, Sutton Coldfield, tel: 0121 355 7634, out of hours tel: 0121 350 6881.

- SWINDON: Fish Bros, Elgin Drive, Swindon, Wilts SM2 6DU, tel: 01793 512685. (Several recommendations. Fiat, Alfa Romeo and Mitsubishi franchise. Good at diagnosing unsolved faults on Alfas.)

- TAUNTON: Paul Lyall, Fairwater Garage, Staplegrove Road, Taunton TA1 1DF, tel: 01823 277268.

- WADEBRIDGE: John Smith, Old Forge Garage, St. Miniver, Wadebridge, Cornwall, tel: 01208 863323.

- WALLSEND: Priory Cars, The Silverlink, Wallsend, Tyne and Wear NE28 9RD, tel: 0191 295 1295, fax: 0191 295 1123, email: priory. bmw@dial.pipex.com. (Reader-recommended BMW franchise.)

- WANTAGE: Paul Rivers, Hillcrest Garage, Reading Road, West Hendred, nr Wantage, Oxon OX12 8RH, tel: 01235 833363. T.A. Collins Motor Engineers, Denchworth Road, Wantage, Oxon, tel: 01235 768321. (Volvo specialist.)

- WARRINGTON: Horsehoe Garage, Hollow Lane, Kingsley, Frodsham, Cheshire, tel: 01928 787323. (Well equipped independent capable of servicing anything from a Mini to a BMW 7-Series, proprietor Stan Woods, labour rate just £25 an hour.) Dave Roundell Services, Milner Street, Warrington, Cheshire, tel: 01925 635958. School Lane Garage, 19 School Lane, Hollins Green, Warrington, Cheshire WA3 6LJ, tel: 0161 775 3179, ask for Chris. (Independent VW specialists.)

- WELLINGTON: Grants Repairs, Mantle Street, Wellington, Somerset, tel: 01823 662067. (Independent BMW specialist. Chief mechanic Trevor Klimpke.)

- WEOBLEY: John Simpson, Whitehill Garage, Weobley, Hereford HR4 8QZ, tel: 01544 318268.

- WEST BROMWICH: The Sun Garage Company, Sandwell Road, West Bromwich, West Midlands B70 8TG, tel: 0121 553 0296.

- WESTCLIFF-ON-SEA: J. Harold Penny of Westcliff-on-Sea. (Ford agent, which has retained at least one loyal customer for 35 years.)

- WEST KIRBY: Mitchell Mitsubishi, tel: 0151 328 5555 or 0151 625 4555.

- WEST MALLING: B. Butler, The Saab Sanctuary, Almandene, Woodgate Road, Ryarsh, West Malling, Kent ME19 5LH, tel: 01732 872722.

- WESTON-SUPER-MARE: Howards Citroën (tel: 01934 644644) and Howards Rover (tel: 01934 643434) both of Hildersheim Bridge, Weston-Super-Mare BS23 3PT. Howards Peugeot (tel: 01934 636049), Searle Crescent, Weston-Super-Mare BS23 3YX. Howards Nissan (tel: 01934 416454), Herluin Way, Weston-Super-Mare BS23 3YN. (Howards are franchised agents for Citroën, Rover, Peugeot and Nissan all, very unusually, in the same town.)

- WEYBRIDGE: S.S. Motors, 16c Hanwell Lane, Weybridge Business

Park, Weybridge, Surrey KT15 2SD, tel: 01932 821555. (Mercedes specialist run by Mercedes-trained, ex-franchise service manager.) Dagenham Motors (Weybridge), Wintersalls Road, Byfleet, Surrey, tel: 01932 332933. (Good official Ford service agent.)

- WEYMOUTH: Tyre & Exhaust World, Weymouth, tel: 0345 419937. (Friendly, honest and values its customers.)

- WIDNES: Widnes Car Centre, tel: 0151 420 2000. (Independently owned, fair and honest Nissan agent.)

- WIGAN: K. Brown & Partner Motor Engineers, 131 Upholland Road, Billinge, nr Wigan, tel: 01942 519522. (Independent garage, experienced in VWs.)

- WINDERMERE: Keith Donnelly, Oldfield Road Garage, Oldfield Road, Windermere, Cumbria LA23 2BY, tel: 015 394 46710.

- WINDSOR: New and Son, West End Service Station, Dadworth Road, Windsor, Berks, tel: 01753 862078 and 851685.

- WIRRAL: Durley Garage, Units 12–14, Badger Way, North Cheshire Trading Estate, Prenton, Wirral CH49 3HQ, tel: 0151 608 0788.

- WOKING: Colbourne Garages Ltd, 76 Maybury Road, Woking, Surrey, tel: 01483 722415. (Oldest-established UK VW agent; still good.)

- WOLVERHAMPTON: Roger Williams, Oxley Service Station, Fordhouse Road, Wolverhampton, tel: 01902 787386.

- WORTHING: Rod Denton, Denton Motors, 1–3 Park Road, Worthing, West Sussex, tel: 01903 233790.

- WRAYSBURY: George Williams, Lakeside Garage, 48 Welley Road, Wraysbury, Middx TW19 5JD, tel: 01784 482158.

- WREXHAM: Brian Jones Garage Services Ltd, Queensway, Wrexham, LL13 8UN, tel: 019878 352077. (General garage. Happy to save a customer money wherever possible.)

- YEOVIL: Eastside Garage, Lufton Trading Estate, Yeovil, Somerset, tel: 01935 31412. (Citroën specialist.) Auto Wizard, Penhill Trading Estate, Yeovil, Somerset, tel: 01935 410532. Douglas Seaton Ltd. (Ford franchise, which has retained at least one loyal customer for 45 years.)

- YORK: John Galley Motors, Pocklington Industrial Estate, Pocklington, York, tel: 01759 303716. (VW/Audi.)

- FRANCE (CHERBOURG): Garage Pichard, 124 Rue du Val de Saire, Cherbourg 51000. (Rover agent.)

- SPAIN (VALENCIA): Imperauto, Valencia, tel: 342 06 22. (Land Rover.)

HORSES FOR COURSES

Not automatically

" *I am 80 years old and feel that I now need a car with automatic transmission. What do you advise?* "

I think you may have left it too late safely to make the change. The problem with automatic transmissions is that unless the driver drives 'one footed', he or she has far less control over the car than over a manual, and that is why we read of around 20 deaths a year caused by 'out of control' automatics. What usually happens is that during the engine's warm up phase, or if the engine has been over-fuelling, the electronic control unit raises engine revs to above the point at which drive is taken up in the transmission, and the car starts to move. The driver may then panic, attempt to brake heavily but hit the accelerator instead of the brake and the car either crashes or runs someone over. (The condition even has a name: 'sudden acceleration syndrome'.) You cannot predict precisely when the car's ECU will increase revs independently, so my advice is only to buy an automatic if you can teach yourself to brake with your left foot at least while manoeuvring, which keeps the car fully under control. Skilled drivers left-foot brake automatics and even manuals all the time, but not everyone can get their heads around the technique for everyday driving, especially if they switch to and from the two types of transmission.

No licence needed

" *Recent mention in your columns of the Ligier Ambra diesel microcar being imported by Reliant (01543 459222) prompts me to ask about cars that can be driven without a licence and without road tax on the Continent. I believe that their principal use is by retired people.* "

The Ligier Ambra is one, the JDM Titane another; the Aixam, Amica and Microcar are three others (see 'Alternative Transport'). In Holland they carry motorcycle registrations on the rear only, are restricted to either 40 or 45 kph and are permitted to use bicycle tracks, which helps prevent traffic jams of cars piling up behind them. But, so far, there are no plans in the UK to allow anyone to drive any form of non-electric microcar or moped without paying VED and without passing a driving test.

A decent car

" *I am looking to purchase a new or newish car. I currently have a 1997 MGF and my wife drives a 1993 Nova. We are looking at selling both to replace with a single vehicle. It must cost less than £15,500, be five-door (but not an estate), have aircon, have legroom (we are both over 6ft), and be reliable and safe, with low running costs. Having always bought new cars tax-free whilst serving abroad with HM forces, I now find myself married and expecting the imminent arrival of a rug-rat. We have looked at a new Ford Focus Ghia, but I am concerned about their reliability, resale value and rust factor.* "

No need to worry about the Focus rusting. Like the Golf Mk IV and new Astra it is electro-galvanised and guaranteed not to rust for 12 years. For design flair and driving enjoyment, the Focus is the pick of the bunch – especially with the larger 1.8 or 2.0 litre engines. (The 1.6 Zetec S is a nice engine, but is overgeared for hauling a family and their clobber at motorway speeds.) For your money, I'd go for the air-conditioned, alloy-wheeled, 110 bhp Seat Leon TDI SE or the six-speed, 180 bhp 20VT Sport, both also galvanised with 12-year body warranties and the additional advantage of a three-year mechanical warranty.

Matiz matters

" *I am considering buying a Daewoo Matiz SE+ for my family as a school-run, supermarket, general run-around second car, but can find no technical details as to its reliability, performance, etc. as it is a relatively newly launched car. I would welcome your comments on the three-cylinder transverse engine and whether there has been any reported electrical problems due to the location of the spark plugs. Furthermore, the Daewoo Deal seems to be too good to be true. Any comments?* "

Of the Atoz, Amica, Move, Wagon R+ and Matiz, the frog-like Matiz is the only one which has been styled by Ital Design and consequently doesn't look like a telephone box on wheels. They're landed in the UK at £2,200 before VAT and in other European countries are £4,000 cars, so should be seen as such here despite the obvious attractions of the Daewoo Deal. No point in buying anything other than the base version as a runaround. The 796 cc, three-cylinder engine is a well proven design adopted from the old Suzuki Alto, and I've been in nine-year-old versions of these which are still running strong.

Haymarket Reprints on 01235 534323 can supply a copy of the road test which appeared in *Autocar* on 11 November 98 (their main reservation was stability during reverse turns at over 10 mph). No reports on reliability as yet, but *Which?* magazine will be gathering data.

£12,000 to spend

" *My son will soon have £12,000 available for a new or 'nearly new' five-door hatchback for family use, preferably 1,600 cc. It will be used daily, annual mileage about 12,000 and he will plan to keep it for at least five years. He is interested in the Ford Focus, the Astra and the Rover. Any comments on the pros and cons of these or any alternatives would be much appreciated.* "

The brilliant Ford Focus is the best car in this class and has an electro-galvanised body guaranteed not to rust through for 12 years. If you can't get at least a 1.6LX with aircon from a Ford dealer for £10,750, go to a supersite such as Motorpoint of Derby or Trade Sales of Slough. However, if he wants lively performance he'd be well advised to go for the 1.8 or 2.0.

Time to Twingo?

" *On a recent Continental holiday, I saw quite a few Renault Twingos. I understand these cannot be imported to the UK. Why is this? It would surely fit into the under 1,100-cc category which we are all supposed to be encouraged to drive these days. For a low-powered vehicle it looks remarkably presentable, without 2CV oddities, so what's the snag, I wonder?* "

We have covered the Twingo quite a lot before, in the column and in the previous *Book of Motoring Answers*. It never fitted the under 1,100-cc category because the first engines were 1,171 cc and the current engines are 1,149 cc, but it is under the 1,200-cc limit from 1 March 2001. Enthusiasts have been importing them almost since they were launched. VCA-approved, left-dipping headlights can be supplied by David Benton, Broadmeadows Garage, Padstow Road, Wadebridge, Cornwall PL27 7LS, tel: 01208 812046 at £150 a pair delivered. While Daffyd Williams (the enthusiastic Welshman) can supply a £99 module to convert the digital kph speedometer to mph (01766 770203). All that then remains is move the rear foglight over from the left to the right. It has often struck me that left-hand-drive Twingo Matics with power steering would be ideal vehicles for the disabled because they would then have a small, inexpensive, very versatile vehicle they could get out of much more safely kerb-side.

Previous attempts at a right-hand-drive conversion failed, but Alternative Vehicle Technology of Hatch Beauchamp now offer one – though it is not as yet type-approved (tel: 01823 480196; website: www/twingozone.com).

Suppliers other than those already mentioned include: South: Auto Europ, c/o 7 Clementine Close, Beltinge, Herne Bay, Kent CT6 6SN, tel 01227 769700, fax 01227 741257. Midlands: Studio Imports UK, Alscott Park, Stratford-upon-Avon, Warks CV37 8BL, tel: 01789 450480. Wales: Dafydd Williams, Garreg Lwyd, Penrhyndeudraeth, Gwynedd, LL48 6AW. tel 01766 770203, website: www.theenthusiasticwelshman.ukgateway.net.France: Diffusion Automobiles Calasiene, 58/60 avenue de Saint-Exupéry - B.P. 154 - 62103 Calais, tel: 00 33 321 19 15 58. Spain: Inaki Martin Dominguez, Twingos Aragon, Calle Sagrada Familia 3, 2- esc, 3-B, Zaragoza 50 012, mobile: 00 34 09 06 02 13, fax: 00 347 623 4917 (weekdays), 00 347 656 2366 (weekends).

Another big softie

" For reader K.W. of Westcliff-on-Sea, who needed a soft-riding car (24 April) you recommended a Mercedes Benz S320 with standard 'Airmatic' suspension, optional 'Comfort Seats' and orthopaedic backrests. Unfortunately I can't afford £50,000, so could you recommend a cheaper compromise up to £20,000? "

The Rover 75 has a softish ride quality likely to appeal to the large number of drivers who rate ride comfort as more important than sporty handling. Mind you, the handling's not bad. The Renault Safrane 2.5 Executive is a cheap but plush and cosseting car capable of surprisingly high average speeds without soaking up too much petrol.

Dissatisfaction survey

" The BBC 'Top Gear' programme sets great store by the results of its J.D. Power Customer Satisfaction Survey, but I am more than a little surprised at the results achieved by British cars. I have a Rover 600, which is the second I have owned after two Rover 200s. All four were produced during the era of the Rover/Honda partnership and were, apart from a few cosmetic touches, virtually identical to the equivalent Honda models. I have driven a Honda Accord as well as my Rover 600s and could not tell them apart from behind the wheel. True, the survey looks at franchised dealer performance as well as the cars, but I don't believe that Honda dealers are significantly different from their Rover counterparts. How, then, can one explain the Honda Accord coming out 17th from top in the 'P'-reg. survey, whereas the Rover 600 is 64th? Is the British habit of self deprecation being applied to the cars we make as well? "

In the USA, the J.D. Power Organisation has access to registration records and is thereby able to conduct a truly random customer satisfaction survey. In the UK, the Data Protection Act forbids this, so J.D. Power has to rely on data supplied as the result of appeals by Quentin Willson on BBC 'Top Gear' and in *Top Gear* magazine. It is therefore possible for dealers to 'skew' results to some extent by influencing their customers to answer favourably and thus help preserve the resale values of their cars. The other factor that upsets results in the UK is that many of the cars which do badly are company cars over which the drivers had little or no choice, and which are driven far greater distances. However, this doesn't explain why the same makes and models of cars tend to do just as well in American and German customer satisfaction surveys. So, while the UK J.D. Power surveys cannot be as statistically accurate as the J.D. Power surveys in the USA, they and the similar Consumer Association's *Which?* surveys are the best we've got and thoroughly deserve our support.

Taxi!

" *A vintage-Buick-owning friend of mine in the USA has asked me who makes the black London taxis. Can you tell me who the manufacturer is, especially of the engines?* "

London Taxis International, Holyhead Road, Coventry CV5 8JJ, tel: 024 7657 2000, website: www.london-taxis.co.uk. The engines are 2.7 litre Nissan TD27s made in Japan. They share the same capacity, but are not the same as the TD27 TDI engines made in Barcelona for the Nissan Terrano II 4x4.

Yaris 1.0 vs Polo 1.4

" *The Toyota Yaris 1,000 cc engine produces 68 bhp. The VW Polo 1.4 engine produces merely 60 bhp. Which of the two engines would you choose for day-to-day durability and why, apart from fuel economy? I only do 3,000 to 4,000 miles a year, but do occasionally need to use motorways.* "

The 1.0 litre Yaris develops 68 bhp at 6,000 rpm and 66lb ft torque at 4,100 rpm. The Polo 1.4 eight-valve puts out 60 bhp at 4,700 rpm and 86lb ft torque at 3,100 rpm, so this makes it a more restful car to drive. But the new VW 1.4 16-valve engine, as already used in the Golf Mk IV and the Lupo and now in the face-lifted Polo, offers 75 bhp at 5,000 rpm and an even stronger 92lbs ft torque at between 3,000 and 5,000 rpm. As from March 2001, annual VED for new cars first registered after that date will be based on CO_2 output per 100 km, not engine size, but older cars under 1.2 litres will retain a £55 tax advantage. For your type of use, I'd go for the Lupo 1.7 SDI diesel, which offers 60 bhp at 4,200 rpm and 84lb ft torque at 2,200 to 3,000 rpm and is the most restful to drive of the lot.

Desert stormer

" *I intend to move and work in Dubai this autumn, hopefully for a few years, and was advised that to take advantage of the off-road opportunities I should buy a 4x4 vehicle. What would you choose? I have no idea of a budget, except that fuel costs are negligible. I would also use the vehicle to commute a 20-mile round trip each day on high quality metalled roads.* "

First check that diesel fuel is available for use in private vehicles. If so, go for the brawniest and best 4x4 in the world, which is a Toyota Landcruiser 4.2 GX TD Amazon (201 bhp, 317lb ft torque, optional active suspension). But don't reckon on Dubai specification conforming to European Type Approval if you are planning on bringing it back to the UK.

Bad back

" *What is the best car of a normal size and price, for using if you have a bad back?* "

Any car with a fully adjustable driving position. By this I mean a height-adjustable seat with adjustable backrest, and a steering wheel which is adjustable for reach as well as height. The Ford Focus, VW Passat, VW Golf, VW Bora, Seat Leon, Seat Toledo, Skoda Octavia and Skoda Fabia all have all these features, as do all Mondeos with height-adjustable seats.

Camping star?

" *I am intending to buy a Mitsubishi Colt Space Star 1.3i. I am worried that it is under-powered, as I intend to use it for European camping holidays, loaded up and sometimes ascending Alpine roads. Mitsubishi claims that the 1.3i is equivalent to a 1.4 with good mid-range torque (max 86lb ft at 3,000 rpm). Is this correct? Do you think the car will be adequate for my requirements? Are there any alternatives in terms of size, comfort and cost?* "

When I tested one of these, I deliberately picked the cheapest model with the smaller 1.3i engine. It is adequate for hauling a family of four with their luggage at motorway speeds but, because the engine has to work hard, I only got 33 mpg. If you can afford it, you'd be better off with the 1.8GDI, which may even offer a VED for those buying new from March 2001 because it has very low CO_2 emissions for a petrol engine. The Space Star is a good alternative to other five-seater MPVs and is one of the few cars offering reclining rear seats. The Citroën Berlingo Multispace is a bit more basic, but more capacious, and in spring 2000 could be had with a hard-slogging but economical 1.9 litre diesel engine from just £9,000 on the road.

Sporty little number

" *Over the years I have owned over 30 cars, mostly sporting and including MGs, Alfas, BMWs, Audis, Saabs, etc.. I never keep them more than two years due to boredom, and am currently in the market for a change. My shortlist includes: Alfa 156, Audi A4, BMW 3-Series, VW Passat, Volvo V40, Mazda Xedos 6 and Honda Accord. For various reasons, I have narrowed the choice down to the Honda, but have you any other ideas? My current car is a Nissan Primera 2.0SE.* "

I'll ask you one question, that would decide the choice for me. When you open your garage door, what is more likely to stir your blood: the sight of a Honda Accord, or an Alfa 156? That said, the Honda Accord Type R is actually a better car to drive than any Alfa 156, including the 2.5 V6.

How good it IS?

" *I purchased a new Mercedes C180 Elegance 18 months ago, and experienced so many problems I have lost confidence in the car. As I intend to replace it, I would appreciate your views on the new Lexus IS 200.* "

I hope you realise how much you stand to lose by disposing of a C Class at this age (£6,000–£8,000). The IS 200 could not be more different. First, by UK standards, it's something of a bargain in terms of what you get for your £20,500–£23,000 (a 153 bhp straight six with a six-speed gearbox for starters). It has terrific 'clean sheet of paper' styling. The chronometer-like instruments are a bit odd, but work fine. The 'Sport' has one of the nicest steering wheels on any car. The steering itself offers proper road feel, unlike any other Lexus. Handling is fine, though the traction-control system of the 'Sport' tends to over-kill. But you do need to work the six-speed box because the car could do with another 50 bhp, and gear-shift quality varies from superb to sloppy, depending on the strength of the self-centering springs. The four-speed automatic is forgettable, so forget it. A supercharged 205 bhp IS 200 arrives in late 2000, while a three-litre IS 300, sadly without the six-speed box, but with a five-speed automatic is due in 2001.

Three in a row

" *My wife is expecting triplets and we will have to change our much-loved Audi A3 for something more practical. Ideally we would like a car that will accommodate three rear-facing baby seats in a row. The trouble is that all seven-seater MPVs offer no more than a lap strap for the centre rear seat and, because they are usually fitted with airbags, the front passenger seat is not an option either. Scenics, Colt Space Stars, Volvo V70s, Saab 9-5 estates, etc., all of which have three lap/diagonal rear belts are out because we will need a sixth seat for the inevitable nanny, plus space for the pram and all the other paraphernalia. This is an unusual request because only 300 sets of triplets are born each year in the UK.* "

Your answer might well be the new Fiat Multipla. This offers two rows, each of three individual seats and each with a proper lap/diagonal seat-belt. There's also plenty of space behind the back seats for prams, etc. and plenty of room to move about inside with no obstructions to prevent anyone in the front seats from getting out of either side of the vehicle. The engine of choice has to be the new 1.9 litre 105 bhp JTD diesel. The unusual body must be aerodynamically efficient because, much to my surprise, I found myself lapping the Millbrook bowl at 115 mph in a Multipla JTD. Fiat leads Europe in fresh new paint colours and promises some really good metallics for the Multipla, so a vehicle that at first seems a creature from outer space may become very fashionable.

Crisis car

" Having simultaneously reached 'that time of life' and benefited from a minor windfall, I want to spend £12,000, give or take, on a toy. It will only do about 4,000 miles a year and is likely to be a long-term affair, but I would prefer it not to cost a fortune in maintenance and not to lose value too furiously. I quite fancy a Mazda MX5 or an MGF. But would an old Elan Sprint or even an E-Type be a better bet? "

If it's sheer driving enjoyment you're after I'd go for an MX5 1.8. Make sure it's a genuine MX5 1.8, not a Eunos Roadster 'Jap scrap' import and definitely not an MX5 1.6. I wouldn't trust a £12,000-MGF to be reliable. The MX5 will depreciate while, if properly cared for, the Elan Sprint or E-Type probably wouldn't. But, unless you like tinkering with cars rather than driving them, the vastly increased maintenance cost of these classics and the constant worry of something dropping off or going wrong would soon take the shine off them.

Exciting retirement

" After 35 years of company Cortinas, Sierras and Vectras, I would like something more exciting when I retire in six months' time. The MX5 is about my price range of around £16,000. Or is there something more exciting with more street cred? "

The Mazda MX5 is the most successful sportscar ever built for one good reason: it's the best, affordable sportscar ever built. It handles very nicely. With a 1.8 litre engine, it goes well enough to be satisfying. The current model has a glass rear window. The hood goes up or down in five seconds. But be aware that the sharp handling will take a little getting used to after a Vectra. And do make sure you go for one with a 1.8 litre engine rather than a 1.6, otherwise overtaking could prove exciting for the wrong reason.

Short runs only

" *I am 77, drive a Clio diesel (for economy – very short journeys only) and have now a left-leg problem necessitating an automatic. Is there a small diesel automatic available?* "

None in the Clio class, but there is plenty of choice several sizes smaller, and all provide the ideal answer for people who only ever drive relatively short distances. These are the Ligier Ambra, Aixam and Microcar Virgo all of which have two cylinder, 500 cc, 12–20 bhp diesel engines giving up to 90 mpg (but more like 60 mpg used for short runs) and simple, reliable, open-belt CVT automatic transmissions. The MCC Smart CDI is a bit more sophisticated with an 800 cc diesel engine and a six-speed sequential or fully automatic gearbox. For your nearest supplier, speak to Reliant Cars Ltd (for Ligier Ambra), Cannock Road, Chase Terrace, Burntwood, Staffs WS7 8GB, tel: 01543 459222, fax: 01543 459444; Aixam UK Ltd, 4200 Waterside Centre, Solihull Parkway, Birmingham Business Park, Birmingham B37 7YN, tel: 0121 224 5720; Microcar UK, Park House, The Grange, Wolverton, Stratford on Avon CV37 0HD, tel: 01789 730094; MBUK (MCC Smart), tel: 0800 037 9966; KSB

Motorgroup (MCC Smart), Chiswick, tel: 020
8995 3837, website: www.ksb.co.uk.

Brand new Maestros

" *We own a property in Portugal. Getting there involves a 430-mile drive
from Bilbao, plus a 90-mile journey to and from the airport to collect my
wife who cannot stand the sea crossing. Our house is also 50 kilometres
from the nearest town which also means a lot of driving in Portugal, the
roads of which are the most dangerous in Europe. I therefore feel I need a
lhd car, and was intrigued to see an advertisement for brand new lhd
Maestros for £3,299. Can you tell me of any pitfalls in purchasing one?* "

Lifestyle Garages of Ctra de Mijas, Fuengirola,
Malaga, Spain (00 345 952 580 077) is offering
'brand new Rover Maestros' with 'full Spanish
registration' for Ptas 995,000. They are built
from knocked-down kits, originally supplied to
Bulgaria, and never previously assembled. You
can also get a newly built Maestro 1.3L, catalysed and converted to right-hand drive on a 'V'
reg. from Ian Yarsley of Parkway Service Station
of Ledbury, tel: 01531 632320, for a reasonable
£5,300. The cars you have seen are not catalysed
and, to avoid Advanced Emission System MOT
testing, must be registered as having been built
before August 1995 which is why the ad says
they will be 'N' reg. If you accept this contra-
diction in terms, and the fact that the 1.3
Maestro is a dog to drive, they seem cheap
enough. The dealer is David Hill & Associates,
2 Hadleigh House, Rectory Court, Rushden,
Northants NN10 0TA, tel: 01933 413863.

My kinda car

" *I drive a 91J VW Golf Driver, which I have owned since new and which
now has 99,000 miles on the clock. Reluctantly, but conscious of its age*

and mileage, I am looking to replace it with a newer car. Ideally I want something reliable and stylish. Does such a combination exist? And I anticipate an annual mileage of 10,000–12,000 miles. In addition to the P/X value of my car I have £5,000 to spend. As a replacement Golf is out of the question for the money I have available, I was considering a Fiat Brava but have heard mixed reports about them. What would you suggest? **"**

A Seat Ibiza TDI 90. Unfortunately you won't be able to afford the excellent new Ibiza TDI 110 which offers significant improvements in both handling and ride comfort (proving that these need not be mutually exclusive). But you have plenty for an old model Ibiza TDI 90 which will effortlessly outdrag some 'sports' cars on the motorway while delivering an even 55 miles for each gallon and proving to be a very amiable companion.

Short Shuttle

" *After close to nine years' sterling service we have decided to replace my wife's Honda Civic Shuttle and would welcome your advice as to the nearest equivalent in the range £14k–£15k.* **"**

The choice of replacements has grown enormously in recent months. Most obvious are the Colt Space Star, Mazda Demio and Mazda Premacy. If you're prepared to risk European reliability, you can add the Citroën Berlingo Multispace, Renault Megane Scenic, Fiat Multipla and Vauxhall Zafira. One reader swapped his Civic Shuttle for a Suzuki Wagon R+ 1.2 litre, while a bloke round the corner from me replaced his with a Mercedes A160.

Cheap thrills

" *Back in 1995 David Vivian wrote in the* Daily Telegraph *'Motoring' of* *a Citroën BX 16v which he had picked up for a song and which proved to be a tremendous performance bargain. On the strength of this I went out and bought one myself and it has been a delight to own. Now I am starting to think about a replacement, what other 'underrated and forgotten' delights are there that will take a load of photographic gear and deliver the same level of performance?* **"**

If you get wind of a VW Vento VR6 or old-shape VW Passat VR6 going cheap, bite the vendor's hand off.

Nurse taking care of her purse

" *I have just graduated as a nurse from Birmingham University and I am looking to spend about £5,000 to £6,000 on a small car. My choice would be a three-year-old VW Polo 1.4L. However, I am aware that I am unlikely to get this car for the amount of money I want to spend. I also like the Peugeot 106 and the Citroën Saxo. What would be your recommendation? Would I be wiser to spend the money on the Polo because they retain their value well, even though it would be more expensive to insure, tax and service? Any suggestions?* **"**

In Summer 2000, after Fiat allowed its UK dealers to buy new Puntos at a 30% discount, they were on sale at £5,999. With dual-range power steering, height-adjustable seats and steering wheels, the best planned interior of any small car, a galvanised body shell and a cheeky look you couldn't do better.

Quick petrol to quicker diesel?

" *Due to sky-rocketing fuel prices, I am thinking of replacing my BMW 528i auto with a similar engined diesel saloon. The only three models that come to mind are the Audi A6 2.5TDS V6, the BMW 530D and the new Mercedes E320 CDI. Which of these would you recommend and why, bearing in mind that all three are in the £30,000 price range? What would the annual fuel savings be?* **"**

Of the three models you mention, the A6 is the most frugal, giving between 38.1 mpg and 40.3 mpg in three tests carried out by *Diesel Car* magazine, but is a very front-heavy car. (The same 150 bhp V6 TDI engine is now available in the similar-sized, less expensive VW Passat.) With big wheels and tyres, the BMW 530D auto is so sensationally quick I found myself hanging on to the back bumper of a Porsche 996 during a test on the Millbrook 'mountain' track. *Diesel Car* got 38.1 mpg from this one. The new Mercedes E320CDI has also impressed motor noters with performance generally better than the E320 petrol version and *Diesel Car* magazine got 34.2 mpg out of the estate version. I have driven an E220 CDI auto and, if you're prepared to suspend your disbelief for a few seconds, I can tell you that this car is capable of delivering both 125 mph (briefly, at a test track) and 40.33 mpg on the same tankful of Shell Pura. What makes it work so well is the combination of an astonishing 221lb ft torque from 1,800–2,600 rpm and an excellent five-speed autobox (you only fall into a hole if forced to brake while ascending a hill). You're probably getting around 28 mpg from your 528i auto so, over 20,000 miles at current prices (£3.41/gallon petrol; £3.50/gallon diesel), you'll save £685.71 a year with an E220CDI. But if our government continues its campaign against diesel cars in the UK, this saving could rapidly disappear.

Folding ears without tears

" *To get my 1997 Rover 216Si into my garage I need to fold the door mirrors. Unfortunately, the springs are held by a comparatively weak piece of die-casting, which breaks. Because of this I have had to replace two mir-*

rors and Rover has no solution to the problem. Can you recommend a re-
placement car which does not suffer this problem?"

Yes, a Chrysler Neon. The new 2.0 litre 131 bhp
LE model lists at a very reasonable £10,995, and
comes complete with electrically folding door
mirrors. Just press a button and they automatically fold in, just like those of an S Class Mercedes.
The Neon LE also comes with standard air-conditioning, a three-year warranty and a five-speed
manual gearbox or three-speed automatic at no
extra cost. The Seat Toledo and Leon SE models
also have electrically folding door mirrors as do
all current Mercedes and some Audis.

A very Smart idea

" *What can you tell me about the 'Smart' car I snapped in a street in*

Amsterdam? Who makes them? Where? What sort of engine do they have? And can you get them in the UK? **"**

The Micro Compact Car Smart and Pure is the most basic version of the MCC Smart car, which sells for £5,350 on the road in Germany. It has a 599 cc 45 bhp engine and a six-speed gearbox with autoclutch. Next up the ladder is the Smart and Pulse, which has the same engine boosted to 55 bhp and a button on the gear lever allowing fully automatic shifting. This sells for £5,845 in Germany. Next up is the Smart and Passion, which is a Pulse with alloy wheels, rev counter and air-conditioning, at £6,515 in Germany. Top speed is artificially restricted to 83 mph, but Brabus does a de-restricted version with 70 bhp said to be capable of over 110 mph. The non-Brabus petrol models tend to average around 65 mpg. There is also a cabrio version. But the one I like best is the 83 mpg Smart CDI, which has a 799 cc 41 bhp common-rail direct-injected diesel engine which puts out 74lb ft of torque and costs £6,345 in Germany. They are built at Smartville (where else?) near Hambach in France and, though originally a joint development between Mercedes Benz and Swatch of Switzerland, the company is now wholly owned by the Daimler Chrysler Group. From October MB UK will import them to the UK (0800 037 9966). They are being purchased from Smart Centres in Europe, imported into the UK, 'legalised' with mph speedometer faces, left-dipping headlights, etc. and retailed by various enterprising dealers including KSB Motorgroup, tel: 020 8995 3837, website: www.ksb.co.uk. Prices are a bit up on Germany, starting at £5,995 and rising to £10,000 for a Brabus Smart.

Best value MPV

" *I am thinking of replacing my aged Carlton estate with a low mileage 'nearly new' diesel-powered MPV and was thinking of a Galaxy or Alhambra with a/c, etc.. What do you think are the best value MPVs for economy, performance and quality at a price up to around £14,000? Also, is this a good time to go ahead, or should I wait until winter or spring?* "

It's no oil painting but, on paper at least, the new Kia Sedona 2.9TDI S has to be on your list for the simple reason it is only £13,995 brand spanking new with a three-year warranty. The TDI engine develops 125 bhp and a monster 249lb ft torque (comparable with the Mercedes Benz V Class 220CDI). Taxi drivers are queuing up for them. The Galaxy and Alhambra may offer a better driving experience and better economy, but for £14,000 will be secondhand with nothing like the warranty.

S-Type

" *I am thinking about changing my 1994 Jaguar XJ6 3.2S auto with 25,000 miles for a new S-Type, probably the 3.0 V6 SE. From my point of view, is there an optimum time to make enquiries (year-end dealer's target, for example) and would it be prudent to try two or three dealers?* "

The S-Type Jaguar has been a terrific success. But for once with a new Jaguar, supply has met demand and it has not sold for 'overs'. You're already thinking on the right lines. The V6 manual with CATS suspension package is the best S-Type to drive and the best value. The V8 may be faster, but the one I drove was lumbered with an unpleasant Ford autobox that spoiled the car. Your problem will be getting an acceptable P/X deal on your old motor. Despite the low mileage, your XJ40 is now seen as out of date and any

P/X offer you get for it may shock you. But instead of thinking of what you can get for your XJ40, think 'cost to switch'.

Adjustable

" *We need to replace our ageing Saab 900. My wife, who is 5ft 3in tall does most of her driving clutching the steering wheel to her bosom. Are there any average family cars that offer a more relaxed style of driving to the vertically challenged?* "

When there is an airbag in the steering wheel your wife needs to sit at least ten inches from it. What follows is not a complete list, but all these cars offer a fully adjustable driving position, by which I mean that both the seat and the steering wheel are adjustable for both height and reach: Audi A3, Audi A4, Ford Focus, Ford Mondeo, Seat Leon, Seat Toledo, Skoda Fabia, Skoda Octavia, VW Golf IV and VW Bora.

55 mpg seven-seater

" *I drive a Montego turbo-diesel seven-seater estate car and average 55 mpg whether I am driving to and from work or to and from Spain for the annual holiday. I am now looking to replace it but have been unable to find anything offering 55 mpg together with seven seats, a load length of 1.7 metres, and a full-length roof rack. None of the current small or large MPVs measures up to this.* "

The only new car I can think of that might meet all your needs is a Peugeot 406 HDI 110 seven-seater family estate. You should get 50 mpg with no trouble, but you'll have to tread lightly to average 55 mpg.

Cheap family car

" *I use a motorcycle for commuting to work., but I need to buy a cheapish car for the family, for the school run, for shopping and for the odd longer weekend trip. We need an estate, and my partner wants power steering. I'm not bothered about appearance or street cred or even whether it's petrol or diesel as long as the model has a reputation for reasonable reliability and is reasonably nippy. With a budget of only £2,500 to £3,500 I've been thinking of an older VW Passat estate, Peugeot 405 estate or BMW 3-Series Touring. Do you have any views on something suitable?* "

Your budget is plenty for something quite reasonable these days. If I was you I'd go for a 'V' grille Astra Merit 1.7LPT estate. This was launched late 1994 for the 1995 model year onwards, has power steering, and a tiny bulkhead-mounted turbo which both cleans up its emissions and makes it a bit more lively than the old non-turbo Astra Merit TD estate.

Which TD?

" *I would be grateful for your advice on the proposed purchase of a used five-door hatchback, TDI diesel for economy, with power steering and a purchase cost of £6,000–£7,000. I am interested in the VW Golf and the Peugeot 306, but understand that a Seat may be the same as the Golf and a Citroën the same as the Peugeot. Please advise.* "

With Carcraft (01633 284800) just down the road you don't have far to go for a bargain. A Peugeot 306 is good looking and handles very well, but build quality isn't the best and a £7,000-example will be a TD, not an HDI, offering 40–45 mpg. Citroën ZXs and Xsaras are the same underneath, but cheaper. A VW Golf Mk III TDI 90 CL or GL is your best bet, giving 50–55 mpg as well as flexible and lusty performance. If you can find one, the comparatively rare old-shape Seat Toledo TDI will be the bargain from the VAG stable, but it is based on the Mk II Golf/Jetta platform, not the MK III Golf/Vento platform. To my mind, the latest Toledo and Leon TDI 110s are the stars of the current VAG Golf Mk IV based line-up, but, though they're sensibly priced, I'm afraid they are both well over budget.

Suspension of disbelief

" *When Ford launched the Focus, it introduced fully independent 'control blade' rear suspension which, by clever use of pressed steel components, means it is as effective as a five-link set-up. At the time it was thought that its direct competitors – Golf, Astra, etc. – would be forced to follow suit and address their rear suspensions. Have they? I continue to read that the Golf's handling is 'soggy', so I assume they have not.* "

The Focus currently out-handles everything else in its class and also maintains a compliant ride, which is quite some achievement. GM got Lotus to look at the Astra and it too handles well but, like the modified car it is, with some sacrifice in ride quality. The previous class leaders were, of course, the Peugeot 306 and Citroën ZX/Xsara, but not every driver can cope with the passive rear steering of these cars, which reduces under-steer considerably but, if the driver does something silly like brake half way round a bend, can promote more over-steer than he might expect. All Golf IV platform cars are designed to cope with the driver braking half way round bends and could be said to err slightly on the side of caution. But, while the Golf Mk IV could never be considered to be 'fun' to drive, VAG's Golf-based 180 bhp six-speed Seat Leon 20VT Sport most certainly is.

It sells for £15,000–£16,000, depending on what kind of deal you can do, and offers fun by the bucket load without any nasty dramas.

Saab to Saab

" My 70,000-mile Saab 9000CD is going as well as ever, but I am nevertheless considering trading it in for a 9-5 saloon, either a 2.0 or a 2.3. I have read a lot more about the 9-5 and spoken to some very satisfied owners, but have not driven one. And, of course, I was very interested in Matthew Carter's road test of the 9-5 Aero, which you published on 2 October. I note that new suspension bushes have been adopted across the Saab range. But please could you tell me what 'Aero' means and what are the advantages for a lot more money. Since I am not in any hurry, would it be worth waiting for UK prices to come down? "

Last things first, Saab was one of the first to cut its UK 'list prices', which went down by around 10%. Real-life deal prices might come down a bit further, but not if demand is dropping, and certainly not if sterling falls off a cliff. As Matthew pointed out, the Saab 9-5 is based on the Vectra floorpan, so what could be done to make it handle properly was always limited. Saab engineers, after consultation with Saab rallying legend, Eric Carlsson, opted for progressive under-steer with no nasty surprises. As a result, despite the new suspension bushes, Saab 9-5s are not the drivers' cars the old 9000 series used to be. The Aero is the souped-up model with 230 bhp rather than the 168 bhp of the 9-5 2.3. It rides on 17 x 225/45 tyres so is bound to tramline and to transmit shocks from contact with uneven UK road surfaces to the cabin. If you don't want, or need, its 150 mph top speed or its 6.5 second 0–60, you'd be better off with a cooking 9-5. The model comes top of its class in crash safety. And the 9-5 estate is a very well designed estate.

Luxury without the bells and whistles

" *I have long advocated 'de-contenting' of cars, but for reasons of safety rather than cost. My Renault Safrane V6 is a fine car, but its expansive array of small buttons and computer graphic displays invite one to fiddle, taking one's eyes off the road. After several frights, I now stop the car to de-mist a misted screen or set up the climate control. Comfort is essential to me, so what luxurious car can you recommend which avoids this dangerous over-loading with non user-friendly gadgets?* "

A Mercedes Benz E Class in 'Classic' spec, which includes sensible items such as air-conditioning and electric windows, but eschews the gadgets and ge-gaws you so despise. The E220 CDI five-speed automatic is astonishingly good for such a big car powered by such a small diesel engine and returns a creditable 40 mpg with ease. However, it has to be said that the ride quality is not as cosseting at that of the Safrane.

Automatic choice

" *I have a 1993 Citroën ZX Avantage diesel automatic which has given me good service for 85,000 miles. I am now looking to replace it with another diesel automatic of similar size (garage space is limited), but unfortunately neither Citroën nor Peugeot produce a ZX-sized diesel automatic hatchback any longer. Do you know of any others?* "

The Vauxhall Astra 2.0 DI automatic works very well. The VW Golf Mk IV TDI 90 is also available with an automatic box, but the engine and gearbox are a less successful match.

AD, BD or CD?

" *I am trying to choose between an Audi A4TDI, a BMW 320D and a Mercedes C Class 220CDI.* "

Not the Audi, not even the TDI 2.5V6 in this hallowed company: it's too heavy at the front and depends on its traction-control system to be drivable. A detuned 116 bhp version of the BMW 320D engine has been well proven in the very pleasant Rover 75 (it's the 75's best engine). The full 136 bhp 320D got rave reviews and Phil Llewellyn reported averaging 47.4 mpg on a 1,200 mile journey from Nice to Wales. I have averaged 40.33 mpg in the 123 bhp MB 220CDI in a heavier five-speed automatic E Class (the E Class and new C Class now have a 141 bhp version of this engine), so would reckon that most C220CDI owners will see 45 mpg. But unless you can get hold of a new C Class, the 320D would be the one I'd go for.

Punto punter

" *My wife is a confirmed Fiat Punto fan and is now on her third, an 85SX. Her Personal Contract Purchase comes up for renewal in August next year and naturally enough she is keen on test-driving the latest version, preferably a 'Sporting'. But there is now a bit more competition in the 'zippy' hatch department, not least of which is from the 'new' Fiesta 1.4 Zetec. What do you advise?* "

I ran a 'new' Fiesta 1.4 Zetec for a week and found the handling and nippiness delightful. It's easily as good as a Puma 1.4, and for a lot less money. But, compared to the Punto, which seats five adults in reasonable comfort, the Fiesta is no more than a two-plus-two. I can't sit upright in the back seat, and I'm only 5ft 9in. So if it's nippiness she's after, she should go for the Fiesta. If it's roominess, style and 'brio', the Punto wins hands-down. But there are two other contenders that should be on her list, both British-built. One is the Peugeot 206, which has the best ride quality in the class. And the other is the Rover 25 1.4Si, which is much more fun to drive than the Rover 200 was, is much better value for money and comes with a three-year warranty.

Luxury and economy, for £2,500?

" I was going to replace my 'D'-reg. Honda Accord Exi with a newer one, but things have changed and I might have to think again. I am near retirement and now work a little from home so the car has mostly short journeys and only an occasional long journey. My budget is only £2,000 to £2,500, and reliability and comfort have been main priorities. Now I must add economy, but I really need PAS and air-conditioning. My computer has come up with three suggestions: an Audi, a top-of-the-range Toyota Corolla, and a Nissan Primera. Do you have any other suggestions? "

Though you now get a lot more for £2,500 than you did over the last couple of years, you are still looking at a type of car that could be prone to very expensive failures. Features such as ABS and aircon are best avoided when paying this sort of money. A quick trawl on www.autotrader.co.uk, restricting the search to within 100 miles of your postcode, found the following numbers of cars in your price range: 33 Audi 80s; 41 Honda Civics; 23 Honda Accords; 37 Mazda 323s; 35 Mazda 626s; 7 Mitsubishi Galants; 50 Nissan Primeras; 44 Toyota Corollas. Happy hunting.

Irreplaceable Baleno

" I have A Suzuki Baleno 1.6GLX Saloon, bought new in September 1997, which has already done 49,000 fault-free and economical miles. It will reach its 60,000-mile warranty watershed in March 2000. Is this the time to change it? What is deemed in the trade to be the optimum economic time to change new cars these days? And if I have to replace it with another marque, what should I consider? "

Assuming the punters pay 'list price', most new cars depreciate by between 30% and 50% in the first year, then by 10%–20% in the second year, then by 7.5%–10% in the third year. By that time, most will start to need 'wear and tear replacements' starting with tyres, and followed by brake pads, brake discs, exhaust silencers and so on. There are, of course many exceptions. But 80,000 miles and three years is generally deemed to be the point at which bills for repairs and replacements outweigh the cost of depreciation of a newer car. A 60,000-mile, three-year-old Baleno currently trades at about £3,000 and might sell privately for £3,500–£3,750. A similar sort of car to replace it with is the Hyundai Accent. The alternative is to take a small chance and buy a dynamically superior but not necessarily as reliable nine-month-old Focus 1.8iLX for around £9,000.

J.D. Power Survey

" When Quentin Willson announced the latest 'Top Gear' J.D. Power Customer Satisfaction Survey of 'R'-registered cars, I phoned the hotline to register for a questionnaire. I never received one. Could this be because I drive a Vectra? I happen to be very satisfied with it. "

No. It's the sheer volume of Vectra drivers who had already applied for questionnaires. Once the researchers have reached a quota for each model, they stop sending out the forms. I drive an auction-bought 'R'-reg. Mondeo and also registered for the questionnaire. But I must have done so comparatively early, so did receive it and returned it in November.

Fiat Palio?

" On a recent holiday in Morocco I noted two Fiat models, the Palio hatchback and Siena saloon, which I have not seen in Europe. They bear a family resemblance to the Punto. Where do they come from? "

From plants in Brazil, Morocco and South Africa and eventually also from plants in Argentina, Chile, China, Egypt, India, Poland, Turkey and Venezuela. The Palio is Fiat's 'World Car' available as a three-or five-door hatch, a four-door saloon, an estate car, a van and a pick-up. Engines are 1.0 litre, 1.2 litre, 1.5 litre, 1.6 litre 16v, plus a 1.7 litre TD. The estate cars, vans and pick-ups are available in lhd in Europe. In Germany a 103 bhp Palio 1.6 16v Weekend estate car costs Dm 26,500. In Spain, it's Ptas 1,910,000. It may be coming to the UK, priced around £8,500.

Automatic choice

" I am considering buying a Golf/Megane/Astra-size car to drive about 8,000 miles a year. It must be automatic. Is there anything to choose from between petrol and diesel as mpg will be important? "

The Ford Focus automatic was a disaster. The Golf holds its value best, so tends to be expensive. And the only good diesel automatic that can be bought for a sensible outlay is a 15-month-old Astra 2.0DI auto, which should return between 40–45 mpg, and should retail for around £9,000.

Diesel drop-top

" Does anyone make a diesel convertible? I can't find one and it seems unfair that petrol users should have all the fun. "

VW briefly imported rhd Golf Mk III TDI cabrios to the UK. The Fiesta Mk III based Quantum kit car can be assembled using a Fiesta 1.8 diesel as the donor. More from Quantum Sports Cars, Enville Street, Stourbridge DY8 3TD, tel: 01384 834422. Westfield once offered a Ford 1.8 turbo diesel-powered version of its well proven sports car, developed by Richard Wilshire, tel: 01384 400077. There should also be an 800 cc common-rail diesel version of the MCC Smart Cabrio soon, or you could get one of the many independent suppliers to build one for you.

Ford beats Volvo

" My company car is a Mondeo 2.0GLX manual estate in Juice green with sunroof, a/c, roof bars and cycle racks. I can buy it at three years old and 60,000 miles for £5,950. I want to replace my wife's five-year-old Volvo 850GLT 20v automatic estate which may have loads of cred, but cannot safely carry half the load the Mondeo can. It may be worth twice the money, but the Mondeo is more comfortable. Is the Mondeo a good buy, and, if not, what else do you suggest? "

I agree in all but your valuation of the 850 estate. Compared to a Mondeo estate, an 850's rear load platform is no more than a shelf, and to carry a proper load the Volvo needs to be piled to the roof which dangerously restricts rear vision. But, with 60,000 miles I don't think you'll get more than £8,000 for it. While £5,950 for the Mondeo isn't quite 'trade price', the £2,000 difference gets you a better, more economical car and also pays for a good holiday. Ford now owns Volvo, by the way.

Which 4x4?

" *I am considering buying a 4x4, but the choice is absolutely bewildering. Could you give me a couple of recommendations taking into account the following: 1) no budget constraints; 2) will not be driven off road, except by accident; 3) would like it to be about one year old to offset the initial depreciation; 4) my wife and I are in our late 50s and would like to use the vehicle for towing as well as day-to-day use. Could you give a price range and mpg for your recommendations?* "

Towing is a legitimate reason for owning a 4x4 because the safe towing limits are much greater. The best 4x4 for towing is and has been for donkey's years the Toyota Landcruiser 4.2 VX diesel with manual transmission. But watch it when buying secondhand because more than a few have been towing huge chrome-plated caravans for thousands of miles, with their odometers disconnected. For a genuine UK-market 18-month-old VX 4.2 you'll pay about £30,000 and get 21–27 mpg in solo use. If you don't want something quite so big, consider the Mercedes Benz ML 270 CDI at £29,000 for the six-speed manual and likely to be capable of up to 35 mpg.

Spoilt for choice

" *I am currently considering changing my car and would appreciate your comments on the three 'nearly new' options under review. They are: Land Rover Freelander 1.8 petrol/diesel; BMW 316/318 Compact; Mercedes A160.* "

This is a real oddball selection because the three basic vehicles could not be more different. The Freelander is, of course, a part-time 4x4 and, though it's not bad on the road, its ability to go off-road compromises its on-road abilities. The similar Honda CRV is easier to live with, but anyone with a family will appreciate the five-door Freelander's high back seat which gives child passengers a good view while being held securely in place by three proper lap and diagonal seat-belts. The A160 is also a compromise in that it provides excellent interior room within a compact footprint, by sitting the driver up high over a semi-underfloor engine. This, in turn, raises its centre of gravity so it can never handle quite as well as a low-slung car. The BMW 318Ti Compact is by far the most fun to drive, but it's the oldest design with rear suspension derived from that of the 1980s E30 3-Series (note that the 140 bhp 318Ti has a lot more power than the 102 bhp 316i). So your choice really depends on what you want the car for and how much you enjoy driving.

Five seats in my saloon

" *I need to accommodate five in a saloon car: one short driver of 5ft 5in, two large passengers, and two children, both of whom are becoming larger by the day. I have been yearning for the solid clunk of a BMW, but am put off by the right-hand slant of the pedals and the not very roomy back seat and boot. Suggestions please in the region of £18k–£22k, either new or 'nearly new'.* "

New, at UK prices, a VW Passat V5 manual with optional centre rear lap and diagonal seat-belt and head restraint. You'll get bags of room, a big boot, a fully adjustable driving position, plus a beautifully matched engine and gearbox. If you hanker after an automatic, a post-June-1998-build Mercedes E240 Classic or Elegance five-speed automatic. These had a centre rear lap/diagonal belt as standard from June 1998 and your money should buy you a June–August 98R Elegance or an August 98S to March 99S Classic.

Unfortunately you will need a bit more money for the excellent E220CDi diesel automatic.

75-mile school runner

" We live on a farm, which is 450 yards up a track from the road. We also have a school run of 75 miles a day, which involves a short stretch of the A1M. Our present vehicles are a 54,000-mile 96N Discovery and a 26-year-old Land Rover Series 2, which is held together by nothing more than good luck. We need to keep the 4x4 Discovery for farm work and to replace the Land Rover with a four-door car tough enough to take a pounding from the farm track, quick enough for the motorway and economical enough for us to afford the 75-mile school run. What do you suggest for under £10,000? "

One of the last VW Golf Mk III TDI 90 estates, which are roomy, useful vehicles easily capable of 55 mpg on your school run. Alternatively, if you can find one, a Seat Ibiza TDI five-door or Seat Cordoba TDI Vario (though do remember that the Vario has a high hatchback sill). The two Seats should offer 60 mpg.

TATA for now

" Please could you comment on the TATA, which I think is a basic motor vehicle? I prefer a vehicle which does not have too many refinements to go wrong. "

You're not wrong in assuming that TATA light commercials are very basic vehicles. The Y2K range consists of an Indian-built 90 bhp turbo-charged, intercooled diesel pick-up or double cab available with two-wheel drive or four-wheel drive. The double cabs can carry over 1000 kg, so VAT is reclaimable by VAT-registered businesses, which brings the on-the-road price of a two-wheel drive double cab down to

£9,860.20. All are covered by a three-year, 60,000-mile warranty. TATA's latest model in the UK is the seven-seat, but slow, Safari which has to make do with the same 1,950 cc XUD-based diesel engine as its cheaper brethren. TATA also exhibited an attractive, modern, small hatchback named the Indica at the Barcelona Motor Show last year, so this, too, could be coming to the UK eventually. The vehicles are imported by Motor Vehicle Industries Limited based at Bridlington, tel: 01262 402200.

Which top diesel?

" *I am about to retire and wish to purchase a high quality diesel-powered saloon car with a view to keeping it for, say, 100,000 miles. A Mercedes E Class or BMW 5-Series immediately come to mind. Obviously depreciation and running costs are major factors and I would appreciate your thoughts on which you consider would be the better buy.* "

The Mercedes E320CDI and BMW 530D are both excellent cars, the performance of which compares more than favourably with their petrol counterparts. Put it this way, even I was able to stay on the tail of a Porsche 996 while driving a 530D auto on a twisty, hilly test track. *Glass's Guide Whole Life Costs*, compiled by Ron Williams, gives pence per mile figures of 42.57p for the E320CDI Elegance auto and 45.64p for the BMW 530DSE auto for four years and 120,000 miles. Ron's figures include depreciation, funding costs, fuel, service and repair, insurance, vehicle excise duty and hiring a relief vehicle during services. So the Mercedes gets the decision on costs even though the BMW offers the better drive. To subscribe to the bimonthly *Glass's Whole Life Costs* (£195 pa), tel: 01932 823823.

Removal van required

" *I own a 1989 Nissan Prairie Mk I, which is brilliant for loading tall articles up to 46in high. Because the rear bumper is part of the tailgate the height of the load deck from the ground is only 18in and there is no lip to lift things over. My problem is, I can't find anything to replace it with. Do you have any suggestions? (Yes, I have looked at the Renault Scenic.)* "

Renault Kangoo Combi.

Handling disappointment

" *For the last six years I have been driving around in a 1987 Peugeot 309 1.6XSi which, in its day, was meant to go, handle and ride pretty well. I've been thinking about a change and quite fancy a small estate, but want something with a bit of poke. The most likely contender seems to be a 1996 model Astra 2.0i 16v Sport estate, but I am a little bothered by press criticism of its ride, handling, steering, etc.. Am I likely to be disappointed with the Astra?* "

In a word, yes. Not with the performance, but compared to a 309, the steering, roadholding and handling are abysmal. Your best bet for a non-disappointing three-to-four-year-old replacement is a Peugeot 306 or Citroën ZX estate, preferably the turbodiesel which has bags of grunt once you get used to driving it and which should return more than 40 mpg. I should add that the current Astra is in a different class from the old one, just like the Focus is from the Escort.

Rustproof

" We are retiring to an apartment in a coastal region where no garaging is available. Is there a vehicle suitable for use other than farming, and appropriate for domestic and leisure use, and which would be more resistant to the weather conditions compared to the usual family saloons? "

The Audi A3, Audi A4, Citroën Xsaras and Xantias built from October 1999, Ford Focus, Seat Leon, current Seat Toledo, Skoda Fabia, Skoda Octavia, current Vauxhall Astra, VW Golf Mk IV and VW Bora are all electro-galvanised and guaranteed not to rust through for ten or 12 years. Most Fiats also have electro-galvanised panels and an eight-year no-rust-through warranty.

Downsizing

" Our 2.0 litre Mondeo Ghia X has many attractive features. We particularly like the leather trim, electric seat adjustment and computerised information display, and find the automatic gearbox to be most satisfactory. We would like to be able to change to a smaller, less powerful car while retaining all these touches of luxury. Are you able to suggest one? "

Yes. A Rover 25 1.6 or 1.8 litre 'Steptronic'. You

can specify leather seats and air-conditioning, plus plenty of other features, and even the standard car has many little 'luxuries' not found on other models of similar size. (No electric seats or computer though.) The Steptronic ECVT works really well. It's best left in fully automatic mode in town, but on the open road the ability to chose six gear ratios can be useful when accelerating, when ascending or descending hills and in slippery conditions. Handling, steering and ride comfort are much better than the preceding 200 Series.

Mitsubishi U-turn

" *In trying to find a replacement for my Montego Countryman estate I came across the Mitsubishi Lancer estate, which seems great value at £10,995, particularly in view of its three-year, unlimited mileage warranty. But, living where I do, I am a bit worried about the car's U-shaped beam rear axle, which looks as if it would collect road salt, mud, etc and possibly rust through in time.* "

This is a rare car at a bargain price and I had never seen one. So I phoned the Colt Car Company to ask and was told that the beam rear axle is indeed 'U'-shaped, but upside-down. The rest of the spec includes a 1,597 cc 16-valve engine with 83 bhp and 101lb ft torque, air-conditioning and a seats-down luggage area 59.1in long, 42.7in wide and 33.9in high. Top speed is 115 mph; 0–60 takes ten seconds, the combined fuel consumption figure is 34.9 mpg and CO_2/km 188g.

Diesel automatics

" *I have a Mazda Xedos 9 automatic and am considering changing it for a diesel automatic costing up to £20,000. What do you recommend?* "

I'll try to list all the recent diesel automatics I know of in alphabetical order: Audi 80TDI, Audi A4TDI, Audi A6TDI, New BMW 320D, BMW 325TD, BMW 325TDS, BMW 330D, BMW 525TD, BMW 525TDS, BMW 530D, Citroën ZX Avantage and Aura D to 1996, Citroën Berlingo diesel automatic (to special order), Citroën Xantia LXD and SXD to 1996, Xantia 1.9TD auto, Citroën XM 2.1TD (but not 2.5TD), Ford Granada TD, Ford Scorpio TD, Land Rover Discovery TDI, Range Rover TDI and TD 6, MCC Smart CDI, Mercedes Benz A170CDI, Mercedes 190 2.0D and 2.5D, Mercedes C Class 220D, 250D 250TD and 220CDI, Mercedes E Class 300D, new E Class 250TD 300TD, 220CDI and 320CDI, Mercedes ML270CDI, Mitsubishi Shogun 2.8TD, old Nissan Primera D (not turbo), Peugeot 605 2.1TD, Renault Megane Scenic DTi, old Renault Safrane 2.5TD Executive, Seat Alhambra TDI Tiptronic, Suzuki Vitara TD, Vauxhall new Astra DI, Vauxhall Omega TD, VW Golf Mk III Ecomatic (very rare), VW Golf Mk IV TDI 90, VW Passat TDI, VW Sharan TDI 110, VW Caravelle Multivan 2.4SD, Volvo S70TDI. Though relatively expensive, a Mercedes is likely to be the longest lasting. My personal choice under £20,000 would be a C220CDI auto.

Six appeal

" I have a Saab 900 2.5 V6 automatic which is three years old and has 34,000 miles recorded. Extras include climate control and leather upholstery. I very much enjoy driving this car, but my wife finds general visibility very poor, especially rearwards and is very nervous about reversing and parking. She much prefers her MR2, which she finds easy to park. I propose to change the car this month and much prefer six cylinders for smoothness. What can I choose which would offer better visibility for my wife and a *similar level of performance for me? Would a Saab 9-5 estate be better? Or should I break the mould and go for a Mercedes, Audi or BMW?* **"**

The Saab 9-5 estate is probably the 'safest' estate you can buy in terms of occupant protection. But it isn't easy to reverse without optional electronic sensors in the back bumper. The Audi A4 and Mercedes C Class both include excellent six-cylinder estates, but both model ranges are up for replacement in the near future. That leaves a BMW E46 3-Series estate; either a 2.5 litre 323i, or the hot new 330D diesel.

Short answer

" *We need to buy a new small car for my wife. She is five feet tall with little short legs. Even in her present old-style Micra she is almost touching the steering wheel. Having read the lead article about airbags on 18 March this is rather frightening. The car would need to be super mini sized, no larger, with good power steering particularly at parking speeds because of an arthritic right wrist. Any recommendations to fill these requirements?* **"**

The new Fiat Punto has a brilliantly designed dashboard with a very adaptable driving position. The seat of all models is height adjustable and has an adjustable lumbar support. The steering wheel is also adjustable for height, the dual-mode power steering offers two levels of electrical power assistance direct to the steering column and in 'City' mode it is featherlight. Alternatively, consider a new Skoda Fabia. The seat of this is height adjustable and the steering wheel is adjustable for both height and reach. The power steering is very light as standard, and the whole car is beautifully built from high-quality materials. But the design of the dashboard is virtually non existent and it seems merely to serve as a receptacle for VW 'parts-bin' dials, switches and vents. If the passenger airbag goes off, it destroys the entire fascia. Also try a Seat Arosa SE or a VW Lupo, a Hyundai Amica or a very small car such as a Daewoo Matiz.

Company car choice

" *I am provided with a company car by the company I work for. Until this year, I was provided with a Citroën ZX diesel followed by a Xsara diesel. But this year I will be offered a choice: Toyota Corolla 1.6GS five-door; Toyota Avensis 1.6GS five-door; Toyota Avensis 2.0TDS four-door, five-door or estate; Vauxhall Astra 1.6iCD four-door, five-door or estate; Vauxhall Astra 1.7TDI 16v LS four-door, five-door or estate; Vauxhall Vectra 1.6LS four-door or five-door; Peugeot 306 1.6GLX five-door manual or automatic; Peugeot 306 1.6GLX automatic estate; Peugeot 406 1.8L four-door. I quite fancy the Peugeot 306 1.6GLX automatic estate. I am not bothered about speed but would like economy and luxury with a decent load capability. Please bear in mind that we usually get the option to purchase our company cars after three years and 70,000 miles.* "

From March 2002 your company car benefit tax will be partially based on list price and partially on CO_2 emissions, with a penalty for diesels because although they emit less CO_2 than petrol engines, they are deemed to be less environmentally friendly. There will be no discounts for employees who drive high business mileages. That said I'd go for either the Toyota Avensis 2.0TDS estate or the Vauxhall Astra 1.7TDI 16v estate, especially if you are thinking of buying it after three years. The Peugeot 306 automatic estate may be a good-looking car, but it is not economical, the autobox isn't one of the best and the model is about to be replaced with the new 307.

Steer without fear

" *I drive a Ford Escort RS Turbo, which I have owned for some ten years. I find the performance exhilarating and the road-holding both positive and precise. I am now trying to find a new car with similar characteristics to the RS Turbo, but find that power steering is imprecise, makes me feel like I'm driving on ice and also gives me vertigo. Are there any cars with similar performance to my RS Turbo which are obtainable without power steering?* "

There's the Lotus Elise, the AC Mk IV or the Caterham Seven but that's about it. If I were you I'd check out the Seat Leon 20VT Sport at £15,995. Yes, it has PAS, but also bags of 'feel' and precision compared to the Golf its based on. And it puts out 180 bhp via a six-speed box, so definitely has the potential to exhilarate. An alternative is the 170 bhp Renault Sport Clio, which is immensely 'chuckable' and fun, but a bit more rough edged. Sharper at the front is the much more expensive Peugeot 306 GTi-6 which easily chips to 180 bhp plus, and also has a six-speed box. Be warned, though, this car has passive rear steer. Once you commit to corner in a GTi-6, don't lift off.

Bumpy ride

" *On 1 September 1999 I changed my Citroën ZX 1.6 automatic for the new Mazda 323 1.6LX automatic. Whilst I like the new car very much I find it has a comparatively hard ride and I seem to notice bumps and indentations in the road which were absorbed by the Citroën. The dealer says that the suspension is normal for the model, so I am now wondering if it is the policy of manufacturers to stiffen suspension in order to achieve better road-holding.* "

You have switched from a car with remarkable, class-leading ride comfort and bump absorption to one which is only average. I well remember selling a ZX to a chap who bought it solely for its fine combination of ride comfort and handling. If it's any comfort, your Mazda is likely to be relatively trouble-free.

More fun for my mum

" *My mother has a 1.1 litre 'J'-reg. Fiesta which is low-powered and rusting, with a dodgy four-speed gearbox, sloppy unassisted steering and very little sound proofing. She wants something quiet with five doors, five speeds, power steering and a small, injected engine for £2,000. Any thoughts?* "

The bargain basement includes an 'M'-reg. Fiat Tipo 1.4ie or a Daewoo Nexia. Alternatively, an older Toyota Corolla or Mazda 323i should still be reliable.

Soggy Saab

" *I recently bought a Saab 900SE Turbo, 'N'-reg., which is my third Saab. I previously owned an old-shape 900 and this car seemed a lot 'tighter' with regard to handling. I know that GM has now taken over Saab, but is there a lot of difference between the original 900 and the model that I now own?* "

A world of difference. The old Saab 900 was a thoroughbred left-foot braker's delight. The 1994–98 900 has a Vauxhall Cavalier floorpan and suspension, so it's not surprising that it handles like a marshmallow in a bowl of custard. The additional problem is that the 'new' 900 Turbo is far too powerful for the traction available, which exaggerates its lack of finesse. But at least it boasts excellent secondary safety. The 9-3 is much improved over the 'new' 900, but neither is the classic driver's car that the old

900 was. If you see a good old-shape 16-valve 900 convertible or 185 bhp Ruby turbo going for sensible money, my advice is to buy it.

Company-car road block

" *I am a NHS community nurse who averages 250 work miles a month and 1,700 miles a month travelling to and from my employment which is 40 miles away. For the past four and a half years I have driven a 1994M non-turbo Ford Escort diesel which has now covered 130,000 miles without difficulty and returns 52 mpg. I am now considering selling this car and taking a lease car through my employer. Similar fuel economy and reasonable comfort are more important to me than size or style. However, I had heard that Government plans to tax company-leased diesel cars more than petrol equivalents from April 2001. Is it still worth my while going diesel? And what would be a sensible choice of car?* "

A good choice would be a Seat Ibiza TDI 'Cool' which lists at £10,995 (£10,815 for tax purposes) and comes complete with climate control air-conditioning. Its CO_2 emissions are 135 g/km which will remain below the base 15% rate for company car benefit tax even when this drops to 145 g/km for the 2004–2005 tax year. The only penalty is an extra 3% because the car is a diesel. So you will pay tax on the benefit of having received extra salary to the tune of 18% x £10,815, which is £1,946.70 (22% of that plus 12% NIC amounts to £661.88, and I defy anyone to run a reliable car for 32,900 miles a year for that amount, plus the cost of their fuel). Since you will probably average 55–60 mpg, this level of economy more than compensates for the extra 4p a litre diesel currently costs over and above Premium Unleaded.

A matter of opinion

" *Motoring journalists love to sneer at MPVs. Given that most tend to be unmarried, and aged 20 to 30-something, this is not surprising. But how would you feel if a 42 year old with five children complained that your favourite sports car only seated two, and had a ridiculous top speed? This 42 year old is very happy with his Mercedes V Class – a particular butt of people like you. Grow up!* "

You obviously haven't checked the average age of *Telegraph* 'Motoring' editors and contributors (37). I would be the first to agree with you that MPVs are practical, sensible vehicles that are not and never were fashion accessories. The trouble is, you have picked one of the worst MPVs with which to make your case. My neighbour offloaded his V Class as soon as he could and still lost a fortune on it. My other (French) neighbour's Espace 2.1TD hasn't missed a beat in 110,000 miles and yes, you can fold up the rearmost seats so they take very little luggage space. The seven-seater Zafira outsells the Astra, on which it is based, something like 5-to-1 in Holland.

Bargain barge

" *Hacked off with the vast amounts of cash I was losing on the free-fall depreciation of new cars I gave them up and bought an old Volvo. I haven't looked back. It's a 1988 240 automatic estate, and I paid £2,100 for it three years ago. It looks smart, is comfortable, smooth, quiet, spacious and incredibly strong. My 5ft 1in wife has no trouble driving it. Parts are all readily available. There is even room under the loadspace for an LPG conversion which would solve its one fault of high fuel costs. There still are plenty of these cars around and Volvo dealers let part-exchanged 240s go for buttons.* "

Good point. But anyone who actually likes driving will soon discover that old Volvo 240s wallow like hippos in a mud bath.

Longbridge longevity

" At the age of 87, having owned 16 Leyland-based cars and having had no trouble of any significance with any of them, I cannot understand the deep-seated prejudice against products of the 'British' motor industry. The only car I owned that did give me trouble was a BMW 2000 which suffered engine seizure after the thermostat failed while climbing a long Welsh pass (with the sun in my eyes so I could not see the gauge). I recently took a taxi from Worthing to Gatwick. It was a Rover 820, which had done 332,000 miles, and the owner had three more in regular use, all with more than 200,000 miles under their wheels. "

The trouble is, anyone who was driving in the 1970s has bad memories of the appalling quality and chronic unreliability of many BL cars and the insufferably patronising attitude of most BL dealers. It's usually six times as expensive to acquire a new customer than to keep an old one, yet all the Japanese and Germans had to do was hook a British driver with one reliable car and the British industry lost a customer for good. It's now up to the new bosses at Rover to make the best of the Dunkirk spirit which is selling their cars by not letting customers down. Simple as that.

In clover?

" My son will be getting a company car in August and I am considering buying his 'P'-reg. Alfa 145 Cloverleaf (mileage will be around 54,000). What would be a fair price? Are there any major weaknesses or problems likely to show from this mileage on? Is it a car with good long-term prospects? "

For sheer brio and smiles per mile, this is a great little car. Like the Fiat Tipo it's derived from, the body and floorpan are mostly electro-galvanised, so it won't crumble away before your very eyes. The engine is charismatic and powerful, and the unusual shape of the front windows allows you to open them fully to enjoy the symphony of sounds without getting your hair re-styled. The steering is quick, the handling good rather than great. On the down-side, it is an Alfa; the dashboard isn't too well put together; you should look for oil leaks particularly around the cylinder head gasket; it will need a new timing belt, tensioner and camshaft end seal; and you must make sure your son has kept the infamous 'red key' or you may need to replace the combined engine-management system and immobiliser at a later stage. Expect a warm welcome from your insurance broker, and remember there's a new model about to hit these shores, so your son shouldn't be asking for more than £5,000 to £5,500 unless you regard buying his car as a tax-efficient way of transferring some assets.

Over the top

" I am considering changing my Honda Prelude for an MPV just so that I can get a better view of the countryside. Can you tell me which of the many MPVs has the highest seating position from the road please? "

The highest I remember driving is the VW Caravelle, which gives you the added advantage of a truck driver's view of the road ahead, enabling you to see hazards over the roofs of the cars in front. The Nissan Serena is quite tall, but is anything but serene to drive, so I don't recommend you go near it. The Honda Shuttle (now out of production) was a nice MPV to drive and by far the most reliable. A new, small MPV which is the best of the lot to drive and chock full of practical features is the Citroën

Picasso from which you can see over walls but not over every car in front.

Capacious cruiser

" *A nine-year-old Volvo 960 estate has proved to be ideal for transporting large loads in total comfort from our base in East Anglia to properties on the west coast of Scotland beyond Inverness and to Northern Tuscany, driving through Switzerland. We would like to continue these journeys in both summer and winter, often involving driving on single-track roads of uneven surface, using an estate car or similar specification, to include automatic gearbox, air-conditioning, cruise control and, possibly, four-wheel drive. With a budget of £20,000, we are considering a recent example of the Subaru Legacy or Outback range. Should we be looking at anything else?* "

Other possible contenders are an old-shape Volvo V70 Classic AWD or one of the Audi A6 Quattro estates, but I think that a Subaru will be your best bet. It's also likely to be the most reliable.

IMPORT/EXPORT

Internet imports

" Could you please supply me with a list of import agents who can obtain a car for me at prices which more closely reflect those in Europe? "

If you are prepared to take the risks of sterling falling against Euro currencies, rising European car prices and long delivery dates, Origin Euro (020 7381 3000) is one of the better importers, while the oldest established Euro car broker is Intercar at Brunssum in Limburg, South Holland, tel: 0031 45 525 3494, email: sales@intercar.nl. With the proviso that what follows is merely a list and that none are recommendations, other new-car and new-car-import websites include:

- www.carbusters.com (Consumers Association)
- www.oneswoop.com (£10 search fee)
- www.autobytel.co.uk (seem to be best prices)
- www.park-lane.co.uk
- www.ifm-t.com
- www.virgincars.com (or www.virgin.com/cars)
- www.showroom4cars.com
- www.paragon-euro.com
- www.jamjar.com

- www.newcarsdirect.co.uk
- www.totalise.co.uk/carsave (guarantees a sterling price)
- www.tins.co.uk
- www.eec.co.uk
- www.asl.fr
- www.wheelseci.com
- www.exclusive-eurocar.co.uk
- www.posl.com (or tel: 0870 600 0613)
- www.broadspeed.co.uk (or tel: 020 8387 9121)
- www.stenaline.co.uk
- www.interplancars.co.uk (or tel: 01603 300377)
- www.fsmotorist.co.uk
- www.eacdirect.com
- www.importcars.co.uk
- www.personalimport.co.uk
- www.realcostcarimports.net
- www.topkarz.com

This list will be regularly updated on www. honestjohn.co.uk.

Import step-by-step

" I want to import a car personally from Europe. What do I need to know? "

1 Get the relevant Government booklets and forms. First phone the DVLA on 01792 772134 and ask for the pack on personal imports. This includes a booklet, 'How to Import a Vehicle Permanently into Great Britain'; Form V100 which explains registering and licensing procedures and gives a list of Vehicle Registration Offices; and Form V55/5, which is an application form to li-

cense a vehicle in the UK for the first time. (Alternatively, phone the DETR on 0207 676 2094, write to DETR VSE1, Zone 2/01, Great Minster House, 76 Marsham Street, London SW1 4DR, or visit the DETR website at: www. roads.detr.gov.uk/vehicle/vse1/index.htm.) Then phone your local VAT-enquiry line, listed under 'Customs and Excise' in the telephone directory and ask for the 'VAT Notice 728 Pack' which includes a form appendix D 'New Means of Transport – Notification of Acquisition'. (Please don't phone C&E at either 020 7864 3000 or 01304 224372 as these lines have become overwhelmed with enquiries.)

2 Decide which makes and models you are interested in, and obtain the UK brochures for these cars. Then phone the manufacturer's UK customer helpline, say you have one of their cars and ask for a current list of Continental service dealers.

3 Choose the car and specification you want, then start phoning. When you find a receptive dealer, fax the exact specification of car you want and ask for a quote, to include temporary registration and export plates. The best countries to buy in are likely to be Holland, Belgium, Germany and France. Remember, if you buy in Europe, you will be buying a Europe-spec car with rhd as an extra. Other things, such as a radio, tinted glass, alarm/immobiliser and seven seats in an MPV, may be extras too.

4 Order your car from the dealer offering the best combination of price and delivery date.

Delivery could easily be six to eight months for a car such as a VW, Mercedes Benz or Alfa Romeo. You will be asked to pay a deposit of between 10% and 30% on receipt of order, either by credit card, Switch or by international bank credit transfer. Make sure the dealer faxes, emails or posts you a receipt for this and a confirmation of your order.

5   Decide on whether you are going to gamble on sterling rising or falling against the currency in which you will be buying the car. If you gamble on sterling rising, leave your funds in a high interest sterling account. If you gamble on sterling falling, open a foreign Currency Call Account at your bank. This is a deposit account in a foreign currency, offering interest based on the much lower base rates for the foreign currency.

6   Keep in touch with the dealer by phone, fax or email to make sure your order is being processed. Within two months of the delivery date start asking for a scheduled build-date for your car.

7   Once the dealer gives you a delivery date, ask him to arrange temporary insurance for you to drive the car back. A new EU rule now prevents you from insuring it in the UK on the VIN (Vehicle Identification Number). Then organise your flight out and ferry back and a bank draft to pay for the car.

8   When you go to collect the car, inspect it carefully to make sure it complies with the specification you have ordered. Make sure the dealer gives you a Certificate of

Conformity to European Type Approval ('C of C'); Registration Certificate naming you as the keeper; insurance document to prove the car was insured in the country of origin (often combined with temporary registration); and, of course, the dealer's invoice. Make sure you buy some petrol in the country of origin and keep the receipt. Keep any hotel and restaurant receipts. And keep the ferry ticket.

9 As soon as possible (this *must* be within seven days of arriving back in the UK with your new car), fill in the form 'New Means of Transport – Notification of Acquisition' (Appendix 'D') which came with VAT 728, and take it, together with completed form C55/5, the dealer's invoice, foreign registration document, the Certificate of Type Approval Conformity, your petrol receipts and any other foreign receipts to prove you have driven the car abroad, your ferry ticket, and your UK insurance certificate based on the VIN number to your nearest Vehicle Registration Office. On payment of a £25 first registration fee and either six months' or twelve months' VED, they will issue you with a registration number and a VED disc. The date of first registration will now be the date the car was first registered in the UK, provided this is within 14 days of the purchase date or within 30 days of the purchase date if this immediately precedes a reg. letter change. Your V5 registration document will then be sent to you from Swansea.

10 The VRO will send form 'NMT Notification of Acquisition' on to Customs and Excise,

who will then send you invoice VAT 413 for UK VAT at 17.5% of the cost of the car, which you have 30 days to settle. Once you have, you will receive a receipted VAT 413.

11 Order a set of plates. Phone the manufacturer's customer helpline number to put the car on the manufacturer's UK data bank for warranty purposes and in case of any recalls. Though C&E only insist you keep the purchase invoice and the receipted VAT for six years, as proof that VAT has been paid, it's advisable to keep all the documentation, including petrol receipts and ferry tickets, in a safe place with them to pass on to the new owner when you sell the car.

Contraband diesel

" *I have been going to France to pick up cheaper diesel in a 1,000-litre tank when I stock up with booze. I have been told that the diesel bit is not legal. If not, what should I do about it?* "

You're smuggling. The offence is no different from filling your 1,000-litre tank with brandy, because what you are doing is deliberately evading UK Customs and Excise duties in the same way as a 17th-century bootlegger. C&E will accept an emergency 'long range' tank up to 60-litres capacity, but it must be plumbed in to the vehicle's fuel system. If the vehicle is relatively new, the mod would need to conform to European Whole Vehicle Type Approval, and if it is older it would still need to conform to UK Construction and Use regulations.

Tax-free cars

" Tenerife is a tax-free island. Yet despite this, and the fact that pre-tax Spanish car prices are already far lower than in the UK, dealers in Tenerife are still offering discounts. To benefit in full from these prices, however, you would need a 'Residencia' or at least to own a property out there. "

Coincidentally, another reader also sent a list of prices culled from Canary Island newspapers. The tax-free prices worked out as follows: Alfa 146 Junior 1.6, £6,860; Fiat Seicento, from £3,400; Fiat Punto 55 (not 60), from £3,840; Fiat Bravo, from £5,776; Ford Fiesta 1.25 16v 'Tattoo', from £4,740; Ford Focus Tddi, from £8,100; Ford Mondeo 1.8i 16v CLX, £9,112; Ford Mondeo 2.0i 16v Ghia, £11,008; Hyundai Accent 82cv, £4,780; Mazda Demio, from £6,380; Nissan Primera, from £7,204; Nissan Primera estate, from £9,635; Opel Corsa 'Top' 16v, £5,152; Peugeot 106 'Max' 1.1 litre, £4,100; Renault 5 Express Combi 1.9D, £4,900; Seat Arosa, from £4,240; Seat Cordoba 'Dream', £5,180; Seat Cordoba 1.6 Vario, from £5,868; VW Polo hatchback, from £5,160; VW Polo saloon, from £5,760; VW Polo (Cordoba) estate, from £5,880.

Rhd conversion

" I will be returning to the UK later this year, bringing with me a new lhd Volvo S40 automatic. Is it possible to have the car converted to rhd? If yes, do you have any idea of the cost, and who could carry out the work in the South East? Will it be necessary to change the headlight assemblies? "

Any Volvo dealer should be able to convert the car. But this will be a major job, including left-dip headlights, probably costing between £3,000 and £4,000 using new parts. Once the work is completed, the car would then have to pass a

Single Vehicle Approval Test, costing £165, before it could be registered in the UK. The reason is that even if you can obtain a Certificate of Conformity to European Type Approval for it from Volvo, this will not cover its conversion from lhd to rhd. You will then find that the car has very little value in the UK. My advice is to consider bringing it back to the UK only if you can get an EU 'C of C' from Volvo and, if so, leave it lhd.

Four stress-free imports

" *Whilst serving in the RAF I bought three cars from Intercar at Brunssum in Holland. Intercar has been supplying cars to service personnel and civvies for 32 years and all staff speak fluent English. Last year, as a retired civilian, I ordered another car, this time a Golf Mk IV SE TDI. I was told delivery would be eight months and paid my 10% deposit in Deutschmarks. My email enquiries about progress over the following months were dealt with promptly, in February Intercar supplied me with the VIN number for insurance purposes and in March I collected the car. Intercar also supplied temporary Dutch registration and the requisite Certificate of Conformity and, had I wanted them to, would have arranged overnight accommodation. I drove back via 'Le Shuttle', paid the UK VAT and registered the car with no problems whatsoever. My total saving was just over £4,000 on the UK list price. Intercar's email address is sales@intercar.nl, tel: 0031 45 525 3494, fax: 0031 45 525 9529.* "

The Dutch Intercar is not the same company as UK based Intercar, the telephone number of which is 020 8203 3399.

Getting it covered

" *For the private motorist the incentive to buy a new car across the Channel is now irresistible. But what happens when we get our vehicles back home? Are the manufacturers' warranties pan-European, and will local distributors be obliged to offer normal service facilities?* "

Buy any car within the EU and the manufacturer warranty, which applies in the country of purchase, applies on a pan-European basis. For example, Nissan and Mazda three-year warranties apply if details of the car are registered with the UK company and a proper pre-delivery inspection has been carried out. If an extended manufacturer warranty is purchased, this also applies on a pan-European basis. But if, for example, you bought an MGF in Singapore, the warranty which applied in Singapore might not apply in the UK. And if you bought a Subaru in Japan, the UK Subaru concessionaires are under no obligation whatsoever to honour the Japanese warranty on the car. On the other hand, UK franchises for European cars rarely turn away profitable servicing business of any kind and VW even asks personal importers to register their cars with its customer care department (0800 711811) in case it needs to make a technical update to the car. Even Mitsubishi has now trained its franchises to service grey imports from Japan. But, at present exchange rates, if you buy a car in Europe and travel to Europe often, you will find it much cheaper to have the car serviced in Europe rather than in the UK.

South African import

" I own a 1.3 litre Mazda 323 bought brand new on 30 October 1996 in South Africa. It now has 60,000 km on the clock, has been regularly serviced, and is in good condition. Q1) Is it worth spending the money to bring it over here in the container with our other household effects when my husband comes home in December? Q2) Would we have to pay import duties and/or other charges? Q3) Would the vehicle have to be modified to meet UK regulations? "

Only around 100 of the '97 model year 1.3 litre three-door hatch were imported, so body parts can be a problem. It's a cute-looking car though, and definitely worth bringing back because the answer to Q2 is, in your circumstances, there would probably be no tax to pay. As long as it has a cat, it will probably conform to UK advanced emissions standards, but would need an 'mph' transfer on the speedo face and a rear fog light if it doesn't have one already. Because it is more than three years old, under the current rules it is not subject to the SVA test. A 96P with 38,000 miles is worth roughly £3,750 in the UK. You need to get yourself various booklets and documents (see import step-by-step at the beginning of this section).

Euro warranties

" *I question your reply about warranties on cars imported from other European countries. In March 1999 I purchased a new BMW 530 diesel from the main dealer in Karlesbruke, Germany. Last Friday, at 5,300 miles, the car would not start. After two hours' talking to the AA and the Nottingham BMW dealer, and making several calls to Germany, the Nottingham BMW dealer allowed the AA to tow my car to its workshops. They now say that 'because the car is an import' it is not covered by BMW England and because I bought it in Germany then exported the car, I am not registered on the computer for BMW Germany. It took seven days to obtain the necessary part and the bill was £49 plus labour.* "

The dealer you bought the car from should have stamped the warranty/service book with the date of purchase, after which a pan-European, 12-month warranty applies. If this wasn't done, the book can still be stamped by BMW (GB) Ltd on evidence of the purchase date. BMW Nottingham was not obliged to carry out warranty work without being shown a warranty book which included the purchase date and, in these circumstances, it is entirely understandable that they would charge for the work. Even if the warranty book of an import is stamped with the date of purchase, it is advisable to inform BMW (GB) Ltd of your UK ownership so that you can be reached quickly in the event of any recalls.

Another successful import

" To save money on my new Alfa Romeo 166, I personally imported it from Auto Aalbers, Holland, who advertise in your newspaper (tel: 0031 26 3397455, email: aalbers@autoaalbers.nl). They are fine people to deal with, I ended up over £5,000 in-pocket and I have now done 6,000 miles in my fabulous 3.0 V6 automatic. My problem is how now to extend the warranty to the 100,000 miles available to Alfa buyers in the UK. "

Alfa has now come up with a second- and third-year warranty for personal imports, but it isn't cheap.

EC car prices

" Where can I get hold of the official EC list which compares pre-tax car prices country to country?"

Visit the EC website by typing into your internet browser 'go' window: http://www.europa.eu.int/comm/dg04/aid/en/car.htm. Alternatively, visit http://www.europa.eu.int, go to 'Welcome', press the 'Search' button at the bottom of the page, type in 'car prices', then press the search button, go to the first item which gives the latest price list, then chose your format for display very carefully to match a programme in your computer because you don't get a second chance.

The lists are updated on 1 May and 1

November every year and are based on the exchange rate on that day, but are not released straight away (the 1 May 1999 list is dated 3 August 1999).

Safely deposited

" *I am considering using a dealer to import a Mercedes SLK. Importers advertising in your and other newspapers ask for a substantial deposit to be held over a long delivery period. Some advertise 'no risk', from which I infer there may be one. How do I protect myself against the import dealer going into liquidation, or simply disappearing with my money?* "

Either pay the deposit by credit card, in which case you are protected from default by the credit card company. Or have the deposit paid into an 'escrow' account where it is not part of the import dealer's assets until the car is delivered. I appreciate that if the import dealer asks that the deposit be paid direct to a franchised dealer in another EU country you can't do this, so you have to decide for yourself whether the potential saving you might make is worth the risk. The one advantage is you will then have a handle on the EU franchised dealer the car is coming from. Always remember, sterling could fall heavily against the buying currency. To protect yourself from this you can open a foreign currency account at your UK bank or you can use a currency dealer such as www.currencies4less.com to buy forward (tel: 020 7338 7667).

Matters of import

" *I am considering importing a BMW 323i automatic coupe either from Holland or from one of the dealers advertising in the Daily Telegraph. Why should the secondhand value of a car imported from Europe be lower than that of a car purchased in the UK, providing the import is of the same specification? I am not worried about sterling falling against the currency of the country from which the car comes because I can buy that forward at today's rates.* "

You want to buy a BMW, so I'll stick to that marque. The prices of used BMWs are determined by the careful way they are marketed by BMW dealers. When good examples appear at auction, there are always at least ten freelance buyers phoning BMW dealers on their mobiles to pre-sell the car before they start bidding, and one of the first questions the dealer will ask is, 'is it an import?'. If it is, they aren't interested, so the only way you will sell the car is via private advertising or independent dealers, in which case you will inevitably realise a lower price.

£1,600 for rhd

" *When I was in Germany recently I asked a German Audi dealer for the price of an A4 1.9TDI 110 automatic. He quoted me about £16,400, but if I wanted right-hand drive it would be an extra £1,600. I thought that putting this obstacle in the way would be against EU regulations. Is it?* "

The dealer probably did this to get rid of you because he did not want your custom. He is not obliged to sell you a car, especially if he is already close to his quota limit and knows he will ultimately make more by selling the last cars within his quota to Germans who are likely to bring them back to him for servicing and eventually for a part-exchange. However, if he told you that the manufacturer was charging him a £1,600 premium for rhd, then write to Commissioner Mario Monti, The European Commission, Rue de la Loi 200, Brussels B-1049, Belgium. A reasonable premium for rhd, usually up to £500, is allowed. Beyond that is against EU rules.

Little red lever

" *I have recently purchased an August-1991-built Nissan Fairlady 300 ZX TT automatic, imported to the UK in 1999. On the front of the gear selector is a small, red-tipped lever connected, I think, into the gearbox. My knowledge of Japanese cars is very limited, but I think that the lever must be something to do with disconnecting the box if and when the car is being towed. The local Nissan servicing expert, who claims to service a 300ZX every week, has never come across this before. Do you know what it could be?* "

The grey imported ZX service specialists are MJP Eastern Auto, Parkview, Ongar Road, Kelvedon Hatch, near Brentwood, Essex CM15 0DF, tel: 01277 374201. They hadn't seen one of these little red levers either and doubted that it was a gearbox isolator, nitrous-oxide injector, or turbo-boost control. But they have offered to take a look and see what it is connected to. Many Japanese market 300ZXs were very heavily modified. Anyone contemplating a grey Japanese import or already in possession of one should get hold of Dave Thornton's book, *The Grey Guide*, which will be the best £9.99 they ever spend. The publisher is Veloce and the ISBN: 1-901295-70-2. Also look out for *Car Import Guide* magazine at newsagents for the most up-to-date information.

Viva Espana

" *I want to purchase a left-hand-drive car to take to Spain and have found it almost impossible to get one from any UK dealer. I am looking for one of the following: a Citroën Xsara SX, a Renault Megane 1.6 or a Nissan Almera 1.6.* "

If you have purchased a property in Spain, then the obvious place to buy the car is Spain, which offers some of the lowest 'on the road' prices in Europe. Any savings you might make buying tax-free in another lhd country would be lost in the hassle of registering and taxing a 'foreign bought' car in Spain. Always remember to haggle for a deal whatever country you are buying in, especially when buying from dealer stock.

FTO blow

" *On 9 October I purchased a grey import Mitsubishi FTO with 14,014 kilometres recorded (8,800 miles). It is covered by a 24-month RAC Gold warranty. Within five weeks of ownership the clutch began to slip. The dealer told me that because this could be due to wear and tear it was not covered by the warranty. After dismantling I was told that the Ferodo disc was completely worn away. My solicitor thinks I may have a good case against the dealer under the Sale and Supply of Goods Act 1994. I am now wondering if the recorded mileage is genuine.* "

A grey market FTO is typical of the type of car which spends 90% of its mileage in Japan's notorious traffic jams and the other 10% engaged in car-park racing. Needless to say, neither activity is conducive to long clutch life. But this is one of the many risks you take when you buy a grey import with no possibility of carrying out a proper check on its history.

Which MX5?

" *I am considering the purchase of a Mazda MX5 as a second car, expect to average around 10,000 miles a year in it, and keep it for ten years. What are the pitfalls of buying a grey import? Would I be better off buying a high-spec older car or buying as new as I can afford?* "

The process and pitfalls of buying a grey import would and does fill a book: *The Grey Guide* by Dave Thornton, ISBN 1-901295-70-2, price

£9.99, publisher: Veloce. Buy as new as you can afford. Only the newer exposed-headlight models have a glass rear window. Forget the 1.6, it's too slow for a 'sports car'. Jap-market Eunos Roadsters are not rustproofed like UK-market cars and I've seen holes in the sills in eight-year-old examples.

Rover not coming over

" *I ordered a Land Rover Defender 90 TD5 pick-up with tow-pack from an independent importer in August and paid a deposit of £2,434.48. Availability was promised in 'approximately 16 weeks'. It is now 19 weeks since I placed the order and no one can tell me when my Land Rover will arrive. Land Rover UK Customer Care on 0990000 500 put me onto 'foreign imports' on 01865 746760, who gave me the Dutch number of 0031 347 366618, but I got no joy from any of these. Land Rover is quite happy to hang on to my deposit, though. Can you tell me what is happening?* "

Land Rover does not have your deposit. The Dutch supplying dealer does. What Land Rover appears to be doing is using its lack of capacity to pre-delivery inspect the vehicles in Holland as a bottleneck to delay delivery to its Dutch franchises. Unless you can prove that the delay only applies to rhd vehicles, Land Rover cannot be compelled to expand this facility and it is plainly not in the company's interests to do so. But you and anyone else whose Land Rover import has been delayed should still write and complain to Commissioner Mario Monti, The European Commission, Rue de la Loi 200, Brussels B-1049, Belgium.

Wizard deal from Oz

" *On holiday in Australia recently, I costed buying and shipping a new Ford Falcon 4.0 litre Forte automatic back to the UK. The export price worked out at less than £10,000, plus shipping at around £500 (or £250 if two cars could be fitted into the container). So what's going on in 'Rip Off Britain'?* "

To get this great-looking rhd-car on the road in the UK you would have to pay shipping insurance and stevedoring costs, plus 10% European import duty and 17.5% UK VAT, plus the cost of the enhanced Single Vehicle Approval Test to be introduced in September, which might set you back an additional £2,000. Still a lot cheaper than the £30,000 or so which the semi-official importers ask for these cars in the UK.

Non-starters

" *A friend of mine and I both bought Renault Scenic TDs in 1998 from the same Isle of Man independent importer. Both exhibit a reluctance to start when the weather is slightly frosty or colder than usual. Once started, the problem disappears. Could you shed any light on this?* "

They are probably 'warm climate' models which are missing the diesel pre-heater fitted to vehicles destined for Northern Europe. When diesel falls below zero degrees centigrade, elements of it begin to solidify and it won't pass through the fuel system properly. A pre-heater makes sure it will.

Why am I waiting?

" *I ordered a right-hand-drive BMW 318iSE through an import specialist, which ordered the car from a Belgian BMW dealer. Delivery was promised in three months but, since then, has been put back a month at a time and is now promised at nine months from order date. Neither the import specialist nor the dealer can give me a satisfactory explanation for the continuing delay. Can you throw any light on this?* "

All sorts of possibilities: BMW may be delaying delivery; the dealer's stock-allocation quota may have been used up, preventing him putting in the order; the dealer may have made a mistake on the order; your car may have reached the dealer and been sold to someone else prepared to pay more for it. These are the risks you took.

Going grey

" *I am looking to purchase an automatic car to replace my current 1996P VW Golf SE auto. The Audi A3 1.8SE auto seems to fit the bill, except for the price. I decided to check some of the personal import websites and was particularly impressed with price comparisons, offering an A3 1.6 at £11,590 compared with the Audi brochure price of £14,580, a 1.8 for 12,270 vs £16,262 and a 1.8T for £12,720 vs £18,875. The website stated that these prices include VAT and that the company will carry out all the necessary import work, including UK registration, for an additional £1,000. What am I missing here? Could the cars not be UK spec? Would they not be covered by the three-year warranty?* "

These are examples rather than actual prices. They are probably for Euro-spec, rhd cars. VAG's Euro warranty is only for 12 months, not the three years of its extended UK-dealer warranty. And you could face a long wait for the car during which sterling may plummet against the currency in which you are buying it. As soon as this starts to happen a lot of import specialists and brokers will go bust or disappear just like they did at the end of the last personal import boom. So make sure that any deposit paid to an intermediary is paid by a credit card which offers a full refund if goods ordered on it are not delivered. By far the safest way to buy a cheap car is to buy directly from stock whether it be from a specialist importer, a supersite or a franchised dealer. You don't get as much choice, but you do make sure you get the car.

Import success

" *I would like to recommend a Belgian Mazda dealer through whom I purchased a new MX5 with hardtop and 15in alloys, for a total of £13,000 on the road in the UK. He also helped me to arrange for the UK three-year warranty to be applied to it and my wait for the car was a mere five months. He is Douglas Verbancke of Hancke Mazda, which can be found at www.go.to/mazda, or fax: 00 32 58 520491.* "

Sounds good, but readers should be aware of potential problems outlined in 'Going grey' above.

Jap scrap

" *Recently a local site has opened offering what appears to be a wide range of imported high-quality Japanese cars, which seem to be three to six years old. Are there any pitfalls in buying such vehicles?* "

A giant crater sitting ready and waiting to swallow your money. The problem is muddled and messed-about rules and regulations, introduced by our current Government, which were supposed to be sorted out by 1 March 2000 but were delayed to September 2000 and have now been delayed until next year. In Japan, strict 'Shaken' testing laws mean that many cars more than three years old and most cars over five years old have no home-market value other than as scrap. But instead of being scrapped, they are auctioned off to buyers from poorer countries where they still have a value as road cars. Until things change in the UK, the strict rule is that a private buyer can privately import a car more than three years old without it having to undergo a comprehensive 'Single Vehicle

Approval' test, which costs £165, even if he imports it via an auction in another EU state, such as Ireland. But cars of three to ten years old imported to the UK for re-sale must undergo the SVA test before they can be UK registered. So, what dealers do to beat the system is import the cars under their own private names, the private names of their families and the private names of their mates, put them through a UK MOT, then put them up for sale. The car may well have no rust-proofing, unsuitable brakes, unsuitable tyres and an unsuitable engine-management system, which has not been re-programmed for lower grade UK fuel. As Quentin Willson reported in the *Daily Mirror* on 3 March 2000, 'Changing Rooms' star Anna Ryder-Richardson lost £6,500 in two years on a 1993 Mazda Eunos Roadster, plus another £3,500 in repairs and taxi fares and hire cars while her unreliable MX5 lookalike was off the road. So my advice is and always has been, only ever buy a Japanese grey import if it comes with a UK SVA Certificate or if it is being sold at a price which truly reflects its Japanese value and you are prepared to take a few risks.

On 1 August 2000 the DETR announced changes to SVA rules. As from 18 August the trade import quota limit of 50 cars per year of any one make and model was abolished. From 1 January 2001, only genuine personal imports which have been owned and driven by the importer in another country for more than six months will qualify; all other vehicles up to ten years old will be subject to the SVA test. And from June 2001 the SVA test itself will be tightened up in terms of safety, anti-theft security and emission controls.

Cutting a dash

" We have just taken delivery of a new Fiat Punto 1.2ELX 16v in Steel Grey, with power steering, five three-point safety belts, fully adjustable seat with lumbar support, side airbags, passenger airbag, ABS, fog lamps and air-conditioning. It's a little dream car: well put together, lovely interior, all sorts of gadgets and a superb, willing little engine that cruises at 80 mph turning over just 3,200 revs. The UK 'list price' would have been £11,400. But, after paying UK VAT, registration tax and VED, my total outlay was just £7,200. I bought the car from Marc and Lilian Deboo at Garage Deboo NV, Oostendsesteenweg 159, Bruges, tel: 0032 050 319598. It is a dealer for Fiat, Lancia and Saab, is 20 minutes from Ostend, and the ferry and Hoverspeed even do a special concession fare on the Dover–Ostend or Dover–Calais route for people travelling to pick up a car. The outward fare is £5, return £70, bookable 24 hours in advance. "

Nice story and likely to bring plenty of business to Garage Deboo. I'm also a fan of the latest Punto which simply bristles with design flair and has by far the best dashboard of any small car.

Meganes from France

" I found a very reliable way of importing a Renault from Europe. I imported it direct from the Renault Export Division in Paris, at a saving of £3,500. Renault provided transit plates, and registering it back in the UK was straightforward. This was back in September 1998 but, if readers want to give it a go, my contact was Bob van Duin, Renault SA, Direction de Vents Speciales Export, 186 Avenue Jean Jaures, 75019 Paris, tel: 00 33 (0)1 40 40 3232, ext 3335. My local Renault dealer in the UK has been very co-operative over servicing and warranty. "

Many thanks. Readers are advised to brush up on their French before calling, just in case they can't get straight through to English-speaking Bob van Duin. Another reader also did very well buying through InterPlan Cars of Norwich, tel:

01603 300377, website: www.interplancars.co.uk.
While yet another new website, as advertised on
BBC 'Watchdog', is www.fsmotorist.co.uk.

Import-ant news

I.W. of Sutton in Ashfield has found an easy way
to buy a new EC Type Approved car from stock
in Paphos, Cyprus and import it back to the UK
at a huge saving. His total on-the-road cost for
a rhd Honda Swindon Civic 1.5i five-door with
a/c, sunroof, twin airbags and metallic paint
was £9,035, compared to a local-dealer quote of
£13,428. He even used the Honda instead of a
hire car for his two weeks' holiday in Cyprus.
Note that the cars are transported by Grimaldi
Lines ro-ro ferries which dock at Portbury,
Avonmouth every Friday night. For more information, tel: 01623 409709.

It's a free world

" Once again I feel compelled to write to you about the prices of new cars
in the UK compared to Australia. At an exchange rate of A$2.6 to £1,
Toyota can sell a three-litre Land Cruiser TD called the Prado for £16,442
compared to a list price of £25,990 for the cheapest Colorado in the UK.
Similarly Daewoo offers the Matiz from £4,612, the Lanos from £5,381 and
the Nubira from £7,688, all on the same Daewoo Deal including the three
years' free servicing that we get in the UK. Even Subaru has introduced a
limited edition Impreza WRX Club Spec Evo IV for £16,254, which is
£4,700 less than we are asked to pay for the standard Impreza Turbo. "

There's a shipping saving of £300–£500 because
all these cars are built in the same part of the
world as Australia. But sterling is not out of pace
with the Australian or US dollar in the same way
as it has been with Euro currencies, so an inflated sterling cannot be blamed for this dis-

parity. Import specialists with the right contacts are already taking advantage and, with the relaxation of SVA quotas from next year, the flow of these cars into the UK is bound to increase to a torrent as long as they can be got through the 'Enhanced SVA' test and substantial savings can still be offered. I rather liked the second-hand Holden HZ V8 'ute' with four-speed manual box advertised on the reverse of the clipping for A$5,999 (£2,307).

INSURANCE*
AND
WARRANTIES

Free recovery omissions

" *In December 1996 I purchased a new Chrysler Neon LX, and am very happy with it. But because the 'package' included three years' Chrysler Assist breakdown cover, I let my own GEM policy lapse. Then I read the small print and found that Chrysler Assist does not cover me for recovery following an accident or vandalism (which is when one really needs to be covered). So I re-joined GEM.* "

Makes sense. GEM provides good, inexpensive cover, but first you have to join the Guild of Experienced Motorists. Even so, membership including breakdown recovery insurance is £48 a year which compares more than favourably with some of the other organisations. More from The Guild of Experienced Motorists, Station Road, Forest Row, East Sussex RH13 5EN, tel: 0645 645505, website: www.gemrecovery.co.uk

* If you have had an accident which was not your fault you need a no-fault accident solicitor. See the 'Accident Solicitors' section.

Wrong policy

" I purchased a BMW 732i, new, in 1981 and have kept it in pristine condition. Over the last 18 months I have spent over £2,000 on new tyres, radiator, exhaust system, and having the self-levelling suspension replaced by a manual system. Unfortunately I had a bad accident, and my pride and joy is a write-off. It is comprehensively insured on a standard car policy and I understand the assessors will value it from Glass's Guide and make me an offer. If the guide value is extremely low, can I appeal against it? "

Even Glass's Guide to Older Car Values does not go back to 1981, so this is not a fair way to assess the value of your car. As it stood before the accident it could have fetched around £2,000 in a classic car auction, so a fair settlement would be closer to this rather than the £195 to £955 at which Glass's values the oldest 732is it lists. Parker's Plus Guide (from newsagents) says £650 trade; £965 retail for an 'above average' 1981W or 'X'-reg. 732i automatic. The work done to your car is standard maintenance rather than improvement for insurance purposes, so is unlikely to be allowed for. You should have had a car of this age valued and insured on an agreed-value classic-car policy.

Warranty servicing

" I own an 18-month-old Hyundai Lantra which carries a three-year unlimited mileage manufacturer's warranty. According to the handbook, servicing by anyone other than a Hyundai dealer invalidates the warranty. Is this still the case, or has there been a legal ruling that states otherwise? The car will soon be due for its 30,000-mile service and the difference in cost between the dealer and an independent garage is considerable. "

There has been an EU ruling that any car sold within the EU must be covered by a manufacturer warranty of at least 12 months, and that as long as independent servicing is carried out strictly according to the manufacturer specification this will be no bar to warranty claims. But an extended warranty is different. It's a contract and, like any contract, contains terms and conditions which must be adhered to by both parties.

If it's a 'write off', should you write off?

" *Several years ago, though my car was still drivable after an accident, my insurers declared it an 'insurance damage write-off'. My broker insisted that I should not complete the transfer section of the V5 registration document, but I was not happy about this, so wrote to the DVLA giving all the details required on the form. Several weeks later I had a friendly visit from the police who wanted to know how the car had been disposed of. Apparently, someone had filled it up with petrol at a service station, then drove off without paying. I gave the police the name of the salvage company that had collected the car, and heard no more of the matter. Had I not written to the DVLA I have no doubt there would have been trouble.* "

There are some new rules about this. Formerly, where the car was repairable but the repair cost would exceed its value, the full V5 was handed over to the insurance company. It was then the insurer's responsibility to ensure it was properly completed and sent off to the DVLA on transfer to a new keeper. This rule still applies to cars with a pre-accident value of less than £2,000. But when the car's pre-accident value was more than £2,000, and estimated repair costs exceed this value, the V5 must now be destroyed by the insurer and, if it is a new-style V5, the red section (V5/3) must be sent by the insurer to notify the DVLA which salvage company, auction or trader the vehicle has been transferred to.

The red section should also be filled in and sent off when a car is sold to a trader or consigned to auction, but the rest of the V5 left blank and handed over to the trader or auction house. The car can then remain within the trade without further notification, and in a single trader's possession for three months before the trader must notify the DVLA of his keepership.

Write-off to make money

" In May, my 22-year-old daughter was involved in a traffic-light shunt which destroyed the front end of her 1990 VW Passat 1.6TD, leading the insurers, Endsleigh, to declare it an 'insurance damage write-off'. After deducting her 'excess' of £250, she received an offer of £2,000. We then offered to buy the salvage and secured it for £300 from the insurers. Using the 'Find a Part' service, within a day I was offered 90% of what was needed for the repair. Within a few days the parts were delivered, and 20 working hours later my nephew had repaired the car. Chassis alignment and radiator were tested, a new MOT was issued, and for a parts cost of £450, plus a labour cost of £400, the car was back on the road. Insurance renewal then came up and, having decided to switch from comprehensive to third party, fire and theft, we secured a quote from Hill House Hammond of £360. After all the sums are added up, my daughter is now back on the road, fully insured for a year, with an extra £490 in her bank account. "

Well done. Though a 'damage category' three or four car may be beyond economic repair to an insurer, the same is not necessarily true for a determined and resourceful owner. Unfortunately, some insurers are contracted to dispose of all their category three and four write-offs via salvage companies, so it is not always possible to buy your own wreck back.

Trade Sales warranty

" On 2 July, following your advice, I purchased a Ford Escort Ghia from

Trade Sales of Slough. The price was good, and I have no complaints about the car. But the salesman told me there were two payments beyond this: firstly a 'service charge' of £46, and secondly a one-to-four-year warranty. I did not want one, but agreed to take one as I was told I had to. When I got home I checked the paperwork and found that a warranty was not a condition of sale, so immediately phoned Trade Sales. I was advised to call back the following day and speak to the general manager. He agreed to stop the warranty and refund my £295. This has not yet happened. "

If the car is a CTX automatic, Trade Sales does insist you take out its warranty for reasons which will be well known to owners of late Ford CTX automatics throughout the country. Trade Sales' warranty is, in fact, one of the best you will find on a secondhand car. Not only does it cover the mechanicals 'bumper to bumper', it also covers the radio and consumables such as catalytic converters, batteries and clutches during the first year. However, if the car is a manual Escort, you did not need to take out the warranty. If this is the case, Trade Sales has offered to increase it to three years at their expense. As a general point, when you buy a car on 'trade terms', trade terms apply. You don't get the thick-carpet treatment. And you don't pay thousands of pounds for the thick-carpet treatment.

Insuring a 17-year-old

" *My 17-year-old son is learning to drive with an approved local instructor. At some point either I or my wife will be wanting to take him out to gain additional experience in our second car, a VW Polo 1.4. At present we pay £214.11 for a Norman insurance policy through AA Insurance Services. Norman will not consider adding our son to our existing policy. Cornhill wants £1,057 to cover him. Can you suggest anyone who might specialise in covering A-level—student learner drivers with a dozen hours of driving experience under their belts?* "

Male, 17-year-old learner drivers, along with 17-year-old 'qualified' male drivers, represent the highest underwriting risks, which is why insuring them is so expensive. I spoke to David Barratt at brokers ABM (020 8681 8986) and he recommended the following: first, forget insuring a 17-year-old learner to drive the family car. Paying for extra lessons with a qualified instructor to gain experience usually works out less expensive. Once the youngster has passed his or her test, pay the extra £100 or so for a 'Pass Plus' course which will qualify them for substantial discounts with most insurers. Then buy a small, old car in a low insurance group and insure it third party, with the youngster as a named driver. It is not usually worthwhile insuring it in their name for them to start building up their own no claims discount until they are 19. The other point David Barratt made was if the young driver is away at college for most of the year, it will be cheaper to add them to the family-car policy only when they are home on vacation. (ABM now has a website: www.abm-insurance.demon.co.uk.)

Warranting an import

" Using the information in the 1999 *Daily Telegraph Book of Motoring Answers* I recently imported a Saab 9-3S 2.0 litre convertible from Holland, saving myself an incredible £7,100 in the process. Unfortunately no UK Saab dealer will sell me a Saab warranty for the car's second and third years, and the helpful Dutch dealer, A.S.M. Utrecht, does not sell extended warranties. Is there any way I can buy one in the UK? "

Yes, from Motor Warranty Direct, tel: 0800 097 8001. If you buy an import in the UK from Trade Sales of Slough (tel: 01753 773763, website: www.trade-sales.co.uk) they offer a 'bumper to bumper' extra-cost warranty, but Nissans imported from Eire and properly PDId by a Nissan dealer there can be covered by the manufacturer's three-year warranty once the car's existance in the UK is registered with Nissan.

Green Flag – red rag?

" I subscribe to the lower level of 'recovery only' cover offered by Green Flag. In April 1999, my Citroën ZX diesel automatic refused to start while parked at the local supermarket. I called Green Flag and a commendable six minutes later a local breakdown service arrived. The mechanic diagnosed a dud battery and had a replacement on board his vehicle. He offered me a choice of being towed home or having the battery replaced on the spot. I naturally chose the latter. Then, in May 1999, I received a bill from Green Flag for £51.70 – the difference between the level of service I had paid for and the next level of service. This has now been followed up by a letter from a debt-recovery service, demanding immediate payment to 'Carrick Road Insolvency' and threatening further action if I do not pay up. What should I do? "

Pay up immediately to prevent any action being taken against you that could put you on a credit-risk register. Then take the matter up with Green Flag. If you paid the mechanic for the new battery, I don't see the problem. This is no different from the mechanic recovering your car to his premises and fitting the battery there. But if you did not pay for the battery and that is what the bill is for, then pay up and let the matter rest.

Insurance at 17

" I may have a different answer to the problem of insuring new drivers at the age of 17. Get yourself a Daewoo Matiz and insure it with Daewoo Direct. With my wife as the registered keeper, we pay £212 a year for comprehensive cover with my wife, my 18-year-old son and myself all as *named drivers. The £212 premium is after a full no-claims discount. I thought you were a little less than fair to the Matiz on 12 June when you told your readers to think of it as a £4,000-car (all it costs in some other European countries), and wrote that it was pointless to buy anything other than the basic version as a runabout. We succumbed to the £7,090 SE+ version.* ""

Daewoo came up with an even better insurance deal on the Matiz: one year's free insurance (may no longer apply by the time you read this). That makes the basic SE version at £6,440 on the road a very sensible buy for 17 year olds who might otherwise find themselves forking out £2,000 or so to get comprehensive cover. (The price includes a three-year warranty and three years' servicing.) I quite like the Matiz and gave it a generally favourable write-up in *The Daily Telegraph How to Buy and Sell Cars*. With its Giugiaro styling, it's certainly by far the best looking of the Far Eastern microcars. Just don't go reversing round any corners at top speed.

Ban kok-up

" *On 19 March 1999 I bought a new Mercedes C180 from a local independent dealer, knowing it was a grey import re-directed from a cancelled export order to Thailand. It had 66 miles on the clock and was obviously brand new. It had been imported to the UK via Jersey on 17 November 1998 and was declared 'new' by the importer. Obviously I bought at a huge discount, but nevertheless contacted MB UK regarding the warranty. I received a letter dated 11 May 1999 confirming that all MB passenger cars are covered by a 12-month unlimited mileage warranty regardless of where they are purchased, starting from 'the date of first registration of the new vehicle'. I then had a small problem with the air-conditioning system, took the car into an MB dealer, and was charged £116.33 for the work on the grounds that the car was out of warranty. So I wrote to MB UK again, only to discover that all MB 12-month worldwide warranties expire 18 months after the car leaves the factory. As my car had been built in November 1996 specifically for the Thai market, the warranty on it effectively expired in May 1998, before I bought the car. The letter went on to state 'your vehicle is clearly not new as you claimed' and that 'this decision is final'. It has been suggested that I take my case to the Small Claims Court, but I am reluctant to pay court fees of £80 plus. What do you suggest I do?* **"**

Buy an independent warranty from Motor Warranty Direct on 0800 097 8001. You cannot invoke the warranty stated in MB's letter of 11 May 1999 because you paid nothing for it and there was therefore no contract between you and MB UK. It is likely that the a/c fault was directly caused by the car sitting around unused for two years before the independent dealer bought it, and it is unreasonable to expect MB UK to honour a 12-month new-car warranty on what is effectively now a three-year-old car. Anyone buying an apparently recent BMW or Mercedes should carefully check the build date (stamped on the plastics) and should only pay what that age of car is worth, in your case a 96P/97P rather than a 99S. New UK MB cars now carry a three-year warranty.

Un-covered

" *I would like to warn your readers that some of the methods being used to sell direct insurance might leave them uninsured. I asked for a comprehensive quotation and among the disclosures I told the insurer that my annual mileage would be 10,000–15,000, the car would normally be parked on a private drive but occasionally garaged and that it would be used for personal, domestic, social and business purposes. The quotation was lower than expected, but when it arrived in writing I found it was for a maximum of 10,000 miles a year, included commuting but not business use, and was based on the car being garaged. Had I not read the quotation document very carefully, I might not have been aware that it was based on the wrong criteria, and because of this a claim might have been turned down.* **"**

Sensible advice. In our desperation to obtain an affordable quotation, many of us might end up 'under-disclosed' and find this used by the insurer to refuse a claim.

Well warranted

" *Further to your 'De-mystified Motors' about warranties, I have nothing but praise for my Car Protect MBI and for claims manager Glyn Smith. I bought a 91,000-mile 'M'-reg. Rover 414Si from The Great Trade Centre, London, in July for £2,799, and purchased a Car Protect MBI to go with it. The main condition is that the engine has an oil and filter change every 6,000 miles or every six months, whichever comes first. I forgot, and exceeded the service requirement by 1,000 miles (Auto Protect allows 500 miles). So I wrote to Auto Protect explaining the circumstances and was very pleased to receive a reply re-instating the warranty providing there were no incipient faults. So, excellent service from the GTC and from Car Protect Ltd.* "

Here's a quote from page 40 of the 1999–2000 *Daily Telegraph Book of Motoring Answers*: 'The Great Trade Centre has done more over the years to pull used car prices down to a sensible level than any other dealer in the country.'

Insurance refunds

" *In May I insured my car comprehensively for the sum of £160. Two months later, I sold the car, but because I had another on order I asked the insurer to suspend the policy until the new car arrived. I was told this was not possible. I could either cancel it completely or leave it to run. So I left it to run. Then, in October, after the dealer had continually let me down, I cancelled the policy and obtained a refund of just £60. I complained, and was refunded a further £44. But I'd be surprised if many of your readers knew that different insurers have different refund policies and that some offer no refund at all for cancellations within the first year.* "

This was covered on pages 426 and 430 of the 1998–99 *Book of Motoring Answers* and is cov-

ered on page 415 of last year's book. Some insurers give no refund at all for cancellations
during the first year (which can happen if you
re-insured with a new insurer, then bought a
new car which came with a year's 'free' insurance). Others give no refund if any claim is
made during the first year of insurance.

Over the limit

" *My wife and I are on our fifth Citroën, a Saxo East Coast, which we
bought in July, availing ourselves of a £500 cashback and the offer of two
years' 'free' insurance. Unfortunately the latter did not apply to me because the age limit is 75 and I am 79. I wrote to Citroën to complain about
not being forewarned in August and have yet to receive a reply.* "

Unfortunately due to job swaps at Citroën you
wrote to the wrong person and your letter never
got through to the right one. But there are two
pieces of good news. Citroën is anxious to make
amends in your case. And, as from 1 January
2000, the Saxo two years' free insurance offer
applies to ages 18–80, rather than the 21–75 it
was when you bought your car. As a general
rule, it's better to phone a manufacturer's customer assistance centre than it is to write.
Citroën's number is 0870 6069000. Ask for 'customer services'.

Warranty uncovered

" *At Easter 1999 I bought a used VW Sharan VR6 Carat from an independent dealer. Included in the purchase price was six months' warranty
by Olympic Warranties Ltd of Leeds. In June the a/c stopped working and
I had it re-charged, and a dye added to the refrigerant so that future leaks
could easily be located. In August the a/c failed again, so I called in the
same specialist who told me he thought the evaporator had failed, and
checked that the evaporator was specifically included within the warran-*

ty cover. I then got in touch with Olympic Warranties, and was told that they would make arrangements with another a/c specialist for an independent engineer to inspect the system prior to allowing a claim. This happened and, because a lot of dismantling was involved to get at the evaporator, a new one was installed at the same time. The a/c specialist then phoned Olympic Warranties for a claims number and was told that because the failure was in the seam seals of the evaporator and the clamped joints had lost pressure it was not a 'mechanical failure', and was not covered by the warranty. If this is the case and an evaporator is a non-mechanical part, why was it specifically included in the warranty? "

The correct name for this type of warranty is 'Mechanical Breakdown Insurance', but I take your point. Fortunately there is a proper avenue for you to follow, which is The Insurance Ombudsman Bureau, tel: 020 7928 4488. This will refer you to The Complaints and Advisory Department, Lloyds of London, 1 Lime Street, London EC13 7HA, which operates entirely independently of the Lloyds MBI policy underwriters and will make a decision binding on Olympic Warranties Ltd. (Please include your warranty number in your letter.)

Un-seamly conduct

" *My semi-invalid sister purchased a new Mini Equinox in May 1996 and drove it for around 4,000 miles, then became seriously ill. This meant long periods in hospital, including six months in intensive care. While she could not drive it, her car was only started and driven to charge the battery and distribute the engine/gearbox oil. Its next service was not due until 6,000 miles. The mileage to date is 4,800 miles. Now that the car is back in regular use, the phenomenon of 'seam bleed' has been noted under both front headlamps. The Rover agent has confirmed that the seams are rusting but has refused to do anything under warranty because the car has not been inspected on an annual basis by Rover technicians.* "

However many miles it covers, a Mini needs to

be serviced at least every 6,000 miles or every year *whichever comes first*. The service book and handbook make this very clear. Not only that, 'seam bleed' is not covered by the car's six-year 'no perforation' warranty. However, in the special circumstances, Rover will make an exception to its rules and will attend to the problem free of charge. Would readers please remember that annual service inspections are not just necessary to preserve a car. They also give a mechanic an opportunity to inspect its underside and spot dangerous defects such as half-severed brake pipes before they kill you.

Unlucky Cloverleaf

" *In August 1996 I part-exchanged my 205 GTi 1.9 for an Alfa 145 2.0 litre Twin Spark Cloverleaf. I had a few fit and finish problems (who didn't with this model?) then, at 65,000 miles and four months out of its three-year warranty, the engine failed. The prognosis was a cracked crankshaft and the estimate for a replacement engine £2,500. The garage thought Alfa GB might contribute towards this, but all I was offered was a 'goodwill' cheque for £250. Can this be correct? I haven't even finished paying off the HP on the car.* "

Round about 1960, the engine of my dad's 1956 Morris Minor 1000 packed up at 45,000 miles (the car had already needed a new gearbox). So though quality is generally much better than it was in those days and our expectations are higher, problems can still occur. I'm more interested in precisely why the crankshaft cracked. It could not be a materials fault or it would have happened earlier. So could the reason have been dirty or otherwise degraded oil? These engines love to rev, but taking one to 7,000 on dirty oil could easily have run a bearing, and generated enough heat to snap the crankshaft. When I had a 105 Series Alfa in the 1970s the oil-change regime for basically the same engine was 3,000 miles, no further.

Immobilised insurance

" I am considering buying a 1995 'M'-registered Vauxhall Corsa 1.2 E-Drive. My insurer has quoted on the basis of the car having an immobiliser as standard, but the example I have looked at does not. Should it? And am I right in assuming that a 1995-registered car is a 1995 model? "

A chip-in-key operated immobiliser system was an option on the Corsa 1.2 E Drive for the 1995 model year, on sale from November 1994 and discontinued in July 1995. If the car was registered early in 1995 it is possible it was old production built before 1995 model year.

Bike-rack racket

" Could you clarify for me the motorist's liability in the event of an accident involving a bike rack, either on the roof of the car or slung on the rear? Am I correct in thinking that ordinary car insurance will not cover for a claim if a bicycle rack or bike on the rack becomes loose and causes damage or injury? If so, there must be thousands of people driving around unaware they are uninsured in this respect. "

Large numbers of drivers are unaware that it's unwise to hang an accessory-shop bike rack on the GRP hatchbacks of cars such as the Citroën BX estate, Citroën ZX, Fiat Uno Mk II, Fiat Tipo or Renault Espace. It is illegal to obscure your number plates or rear lights with a bike rack or the bikes on it (the answer to this is a trailer board). But if the bike rack and its contents fall off and cause damage to other cars or people, your insurer is legally bound to cough up. It will not pay for the damaged bikes, though. And, though the rack itself may be covered as an 'accessory' under the driver's comprehensive policy, you would be wise to contact your insurer to make sure. Some insurers distinguish between manufacturer-approved accessories and non-approved accessories.

Braking point

" Though my home is in Scotland I travel a great deal in mainland Europe. In June 1997 I bought a year-old Audi S6 from Audi Zentrum in Munich. In February 1998, at 36,475 km, I had it serviced at S.M.V.A. S.A. in Frejus. The rear brake pads were found to be of faulty manufacture and were replaced (they had crumbled and cracked rather than worn away). I was charged Ffr 1430 for this and have since been trying to get my money back. The French garage referred me to Audi Zentrum, Audi Zentrum referred me to Ingolstadt, Ingolstadt referred me to the French Audi concessionaires, and Audi France tells me that brake pads are not covered because they are a wearing item. "

Good news. Audi UK has offered to cough up. I have emailed you details of who to contact.

Hard-boiled attitude

" While touring in the south of England in March, my Vauxhall Omega began boiling over. The cause was eventually traced to the electric fan motors, which had come adrift from their bearings. The cost of replacement was £266. Since the car was then only 31 months old, and had only covered 35,000 miles, I submitted a goodwill claim to Vauxhall for at least part of the cost but, despite furnishing a full Vauxhall service record, my claim was turned down. "

In the UK, new cars tend to be covered by either a 12-month warranty or a 36-month conditional warranty. If a car suffers a failure outside its warranty, which has not been the subject of a safety recall, then the meeting of any claim depends on how much goodwill the manufacturer wishes to maintain between itself and its customers. In your case, your continued goodwill towards Vauxhall was not judged to be worth £266 and, as a result, you probably won't buy another Vauxhall. I'm not singling out Vauxhall here. The same goes for any other rejected goodwill claim with any other manufacturer.

Unwarranted import

" *I can save £3,500 by buying a Land Rover Freelander in Holland but the warranty is for 12 months only, in contrast to 36 months if I buy it from an official UK Land Rover dealer. Is it possible to buy an extended warranty privately?* "

Yes, from Motor Warranty Direct, tel: 0800 731 7001. But, judging from the 90 files of complaint we received about Land Rover trouble following our appeal in March, I would not recommend anyone to buy a Land Rover without the full UK factory/dealer-sponsored 36-month warranty.

Cashback classic insurance

" *Your colleague Andrew English thought your readers might be interested in the features which we have added to our classic car insurance policies. All classic policies have a mileage limit, but if an owner does not reach the 8,000 limit of ours, and no claims have been made, we offer cashbacks on the following year's premium based on each 'unused' block of 1,000 miles. We also make an extra payment following a total loss to help defray the expense of finding a replacement car. For lesser damage we also grant the owner the facility to repair his or her own car, paying both the cost of parts and an allowance for the policyholder's own labour.* "

This is bound to be of interest to readers running older cars for limited annual mileages. To qualify, your car must be either more than ten years old or the model must have been in manufacturer 15 years ago but is no longer made. Lynbrook Insurance can be contacted on 01704 822661.

Not our policy

" *I renewed my car insurance last August. Following an accident in December my car was declared a 'write off', I was paid a settlement figure, and the insurance was suspended. I bought a new car in March and the deal included a year's insurance, so I wrote to my previous insurer asking for a refund. I was told there would be none. Is this usual?* "

Yes. No refunds if a car insurance policy is cancelled during its first year or after an accident.

Breakdown in communications

" *Can I advise fellow readers that when their RAC Breakdown Assistance premium becomes due they first check the cost of cover purchased via the RAC's website at www.rac.co.uk . I found that if I bought my roadside assistance and recovery cover this way it cost £65 compared to the £79 which was about to be direct debited from my account. After confirming that cover bought from the website was exactly the same as renewed cover by direct debit I naturally took the cheaper option.* "

As Quentin Willson wrote, 'ignoring the internet is like ignoring the wheel'. I am now receiving more emails than letters, and the age profile of emailers (18–80) is no different from that of letter writers.

Insurance scam

" *Have you ever heard of people making claims after car accidents in which they were not involved? I was caught up in a three-car prang in late*

1999. The three drivers all exchanged details. Then, two months later, I received a very abrupt letter from someone else claiming to have been involved and demanding my insurance details. I ignored it and six weeks later received a further letter from an unknown company purporting to act for the same spurious claimant and quoting a vehicle which was not involved in my accident. I returned this to the sender, stating that all details had been exchanged at the time of the accident. I have heard nothing since, but should I do more about this, such as report the matter to the police? "

Better to inform your own insurer who will be far more diligent in pursuing a fraudulent claimant than the police would be. This might also reveal any confusion or mistake which arose over the exchange of information at the scene of the accident.

KIT CARS

NGTA SVA

" Back in 1990 I purchased an NGTA car kit and an MOT-failed MGBGT 'donor car' to provide me with a retirement project. Under the old rules, I was able to register the new car as having an open body on the original MGBGT registration. Then, for various reasons, I was unable to retire and have only had time over the past nine years to clean and prepare the donor parts. I now expect to re-commence the project next year, but have been told that under the new rules the result will be subject to an Single Vehicle Approval test. As my TA kit and donor parts do not allow for dual-braking, collapsible steering column, windscreen design and seat-belt-mounting points on the chassis, the project would be uneconomic. But as the 'car' is already registered do I really need to submit it for an SVA test? "

According to the Vehicle Inspectorate, yes. In any case, the old DVLA points system for retaining registrations has changed for kit cars built from donor cars (though not for restorations). What happens now is the car will be issued with a 'Q' plate if less than two major components of the donor car are used, or a new age-related registration if two or more parts from the donor car are used. In the case of kits using different chassis or monocoques (such as yours) purchased before January 1998, there is a partial dispensation from sections of the SVA test relating to exterior projections and instrument panels lasting until 31 December 1999.

But dual-circuit brakes, protection from steering column intrusion and chassis-mounted seat-belt points must all be fitted. One option you do have is to buy a Heritage MGB roadster shell which counts as an 'original' monocoque bodyshell, turns the project into a restoration and exempts the finished car from an SVA test (tel: 01993 707200 or 020 8867 2000). The other is to speak to John Hoyle at NG Cars Ltd of Epsom (tel: 01372 748666) and find out the true cost of SVA legalising your NGTA kit.

LEGAL MATTERS AND CONSUMER RIGHTS

Your rights under the Act

The Sale of Goods Act (1979) was modified in January 1995 by The Sale and Supply of Goods Act (1994) which more tightly described what was meant by the requirement for the goods to be of suitable quality and 'fit for the purpose' for which they were sold. It states:

'Where the seller sells goods in the course of a business, there is an implied term that the goods supplied under the contract are of satisfactory quality ... Goods are of satisfactory quality if they meet the standard that a reasonable person would regard as satisfactory, taking account of any description of the goods, the price (if relevant) and all the other relevant circumstances.' (This differentiates a garage or even a trader operating from home from a private vendor. A trader operating from home cannot hide from the obligations as outlined above.)

'... The following are in appropriate cases aspects of the quality of goods:

(a) *Fitness for all the purposes for which goods of the kind in question are commonly supplied.* (For example, it is reasonable to expect a Rover Metro 1.1 to operate adequately on shopping trips, the school run and leisure trips. It is not reasonable to expect it to pull a large caravan or to run all day at 100 mph.)

(b) *Appearance and finish.*

(c) *Freedom from minor defects.* (For example, it is reasonable to expect a new car to be free from minor defects such as small scratches and paint chips. It is not reasonable to expect a second-hand car to be.)

(d) *Safety.* (For example, it is reasonable to expect the brakes, steering and suspension of a new or second-hand car to be safe, taking account of the nature of the deal and the price paid. It would not be reasonable to expect an old car bought as a 'non-runner', with no MOT, to be safe.)

(e) *Durability.* (For example, it is reasonable to expect a new or second-hand car to run properly without breaking down and without falling apart for a reasonable period of time, taking account of the nature of the deal and the price paid, and provided the buyer has maintained it properly and not abused it. It would not be reasonable to expect a £200 banger to immediately be capable of a long journey.)'

But these terms do not extend to 'any matter making the quality of goods unsatisfactory...

(a) *...which is specifically drawn to the buyer's attention before the contract is made.* (If defects are pointed out to you by the vendor, you cannot later reject the car for those defects.)

(b) *...where the buyer examines the goods before the contract is made and which that examination ought to reveal.* (If you are given a good chance to inspect the car and fail to notice a very obvious fault, you cannot later reject the car for that reason. However, a professional buyer is expected to know what to look for and to inspect the car much more carefully than a private buyer.)'

The Act then defines what is meant by 'acceptance'.

'*Goods are accepted where the buyer intimates to the seller he has accepted them or when the goods have been delivered to him and he does any act in relation to them which is inconsistent with the ownership of the seller.* (So, start using a car as your own, without the permission of the seller, and you are deemed to have accepted it.)

'*But where goods are delivered to the buyer and he has not previously examined them, he is not deemed to have accepted them until he has had a reasonable chance of examining them.* (So, if you order a car on the basis of a test drive or the viewing of another in the showroom, you are not deemed to have accepted the car you ordered until you have had a reasonable chance of inspecting it.)

'*The buyer is also deemed to have accepted goods when after the lapse of a reasonable time he retains the goods without intimating to the seller he has rejected them.*

'*The buyer is not…deemed to have accepted the goods merely because he asks for or agrees to their repair by or under an arrangement with the seller.* (So if you ask the seller to put right a fault and the seller does put it right you are still not deemed to have accepted the car.)'

Case law

Rejection under the Acts

There are a number of examples of case law on this section of the 1979 Act. In *Bernstein v Palmerston Motors 1987*, the engine of Mr Bernstein's new car failed after three weeks and 120 miles. Palmerston Motors fitted a new engine, but Mr Bernstein still attempted to reject the car. When it went to court, Mr Bernstein's case failed. But in *Rogers v Parrish 1987* the buyer tried to reject a Range Rover after six months and 5,500 miles for a catalogue of faults, including defective oil seals, gearbox defects and body problems. His case was upheld on appeal by the Queens Bench. Against this, in 1995 in Scotland, the case of a buyer who tried to reject a car after ten months (and two minor accidents) was rejected on appeal. And in *Carlisle v Lane 1996*, which concerned a used Range Rover alleged to be older than indicated by the date of registration, the case failed on appeal on the evidence because the buyer was adjudged to have been told the car was older than its registration date at the time of sale. In yet another, more recent case, the buyer of a VW Polo was held not to have rejected the car, because he kept possession of it rather than returning it to the dealer he sought redress against.

Termination of a purchase contract

A more recent case, *Johnson v HWM 1997* (Kingston Crown Court), set another precedent.

Mr J, an Aston Martin Virage owner, ordered a new Virage in October 1988 during the heady days of supercar speculation. He was required to put down a deposit of £20,000 of which VAT was charged as a proportion because, unlike an 'option to buy', his deposit constituted a part-payment for the car.

In 1989 Mr J decided he would like a more powerful car, and changed his order to the Vantage model. Then, over the years (there was a very long waiting list) he began to change his mind again, and, in 1993, asked to cancel the order. HWM refused to refund his part payment and instead suggested he took a new Virage which, by that time, had been uprated.

Mr J then launched a campaign against HWM alleging that, amongst other things, the Vantage was not a full four-seater and the car was not what he ordered because the automatic gearbox of Vantage models was retro-fitted. (In fact, a Vantage is merely a highly modified Virage and shares the same body shell as the Virage which Mr J already owned.)

HMW tried to settle the matter out of court, but could not reach agreement, so the case went to court.

On 15 August 1997 the judge found for HWM. Mr J not only lost his £20,000 deposit, interest on the deposit and HWM's loss of profit, he was also ordered to pay HWM's legal costs and court fees as well as his own. The precedent set here is that, in between the time of order and delivery, a manufacturer can change the specification of the car for any reason, whether it be legislation, development, changes of parts suppliers or whatever.

Misrepresentation

C.M. of Dover had a dispute with a Mercedes salesman over the paintwork of a secondhand 300TE he purchased in October 1992. No instance more perfectly confirms my advice to avoid litigation for damages over and above a reasonable settlement offered by a dealer.

C.M.'s case hinged on the salesman's description of the car as 'an original one-owner car which [his garage] had supplied new to that owner and serviced'. The car, new in 1990, had a lot of extras to justify the price of £22,950 – partly paid by a part exchange allowance of £10,995 for C.M.'s older 300TE. But the word 'original' was important to C.M. because the newer car was in a shade of solid red, the pigment of which is notoriously difficult to match.

After two years, C.M. noticed that the paint on the nearside front wing and door had 'bloomed' to a different colour from the rest of the car. It later transpired that, early in the car's life (at fourteen weeks old), the paintwork of those two panels had been damaged by a golf trolley and they had been resprayed by the selling garage at a cost of £213.47, which included replacing the grille.

In April 1995, the garage offered to 'cut back' the bloomed paint, but C.M. declined. He demanded that the garage either took the car back and refunded the original purchase price, supplied him with a better car, or paid him £5,000. This figure was based on a perceived 'trade guide' price difference between the two cars involved in the original transaction, plus £800 'damages'.

On getting no satisfaction, C.M. issued a County Court summons for £900, representing the difference in trade value between an 'original' 1990H 300TE and one with repaired damage. The case was heard by District Judge Morling in the Ashford County Court on 12 December 1996 (*Mulloy v Darren Dawkins*). The judge agreed that the car was not 'original' and should not have been described as such – particularly where the golf trolley damage had been repaired at an earlier date by the selling garage and the information was on its records. But, in finding for the plaintiff, the judge awarded a mere £500 in damages and costs on Scale 1. This left C.M. more than £5,000 out of pocket and, though he was able to recover part of this after a Taxation Hearing, his loss was still considerable.

So, though a case of 'misrepresentation' was proven against the salesman (and may set a precedent for other similar cases), C.M. has still lost out. It could be argued that, in the circumstances, C.M.'s claims were less than 'reasonable' and the system punished him for this. But as long as the costs of legal action in the UK can outweigh any benefit, even when a case is proven, private individuals are ill-advised to take a case such as this as far as C.M. did. Unless you have money to burn, it is especially ill-advised to pursue any matter through the courts on 'a matter of principle'.

Mercedes Benz UK has taken the view that the case should never have gone to court and, according to C.M., has written to the selling garage asking it to refund to C.M. the balance of his costs as a 'gesture of goodwill'. However, since C.M. has asked Mercedes Benz UK to review the franchises of both the selling agent and another MB franchise which the agent called in as an expert witness, 'goodwill' may be a little thin on the ground.

Falling out with a restorer

If you consign a car to a restorer and then fall out with him, the relevant precedent is *Peter Troy Davies v Anthony K. Divey* (Peterborough County Court).

Troy Davies claimed that in January 1994 he took out a contract with Anthony Divey who trades as Triking Cyclecars to restore his car for a price of £1,791. He then paid £2,000 in advance, and in June 1994 he paid a further £400 to Triking Cyclecars. The plaintiff relied upon the implied condition of the contract that work would be done using all reasonable care and skill and that parts supplied would be of merchantable quality. He claimed that the defendant had failed him in each case, enlisted the help of the legal department of *Which?*, and relied on an RAC report carried out five months after he had collected the car from Triking. The plaintiff had refused to have his vehicle inspected by the RAC before he removed it from Triking's premises. After collecting the car on 28 April 1995 the plaintiff had faxed and demanded a refund of £3,301.90 on 2 May 1995. The refund was to be paid by 9 May 1995, and he later increased his demand to £4,300.

He made a claim on 30 January 1996, and issued a summons on 16 February 1996. Triking filed its defence and counterclaim on 22 March 1996, but the plaintiff did not respond to this until 12 June 1996. Action commenced in the Hitchin County Court on 21 October 1996, and was later transferred to the Peterborough County Court, a transferral which the plaintiff had opposed. After various delays, the plaintiff presented his case, but was absent when District Judge Cernik heard the defendant's evidence on 12 August 1997.

The defendant's case was that there was never a written contract. He agreed he had collected the plaintiff's cyclecar in order to look it over and give the plaintiff a general idea of what could be done within the plaintiff's available budget. He then presented a fax sent to him by the plaintiff on 1 March 1994 listing a number of 'things to be done', which stated: 'Tony, if you can give me an idea of the cost of the above I will then know how much of my budget I will have left over to do the items below. As said on the phone, I am away from the end of March/April/May and possibly June, so there is no rush to get the job done. I suggest you look at it as one of those jobs to be done when things are a bit slack ... There is no rush for the job. I don't even care if you can't start on it till your six orders are complete.' The plaintiff's fax then went on to mention other jobs he would like doing, including a complete respray, a re-trim of the cockpit surround, the fitting of a removable head, some new side pipes and stainless steel silencers and two replacement rocker box covers. He paid the defendant £2,000 as an advance, but not on the basis of any quotation. After costing the work and making a number of adjustments to what the plaintiff had requested, the defendant had quoted that he could perform a number of tasks for a price of £2,450, as long as time was not of the essence.

A first attempt to respray the vehicle was unsuccessful, due to concealed accident damage which the defendant had not found on his first inspection.

The Judge declared himself satisfied that 'at no time did the defendant agree to undertake a complete restoration' and that the 'all-important fax of 1 March referring to things to be done and other jobs that he would like to do are entirely inconsistent with a complete refurbishment. ... I formed a clear impression that the plaintiff was something of a perfectionist and found it less than agreeable to have anything to do with something that was in effect a compromise. ... The notice that he gave by letter of 21 April 1995 to complete the job on 24 April 1995 was clearly unreasonable. ... The plaintiff did not challenge the defendant's case that the defendant had wanted an independent expert called there and then (before the car was removed from his premises). ... He then commissioned his report from the RAC on 8 September which was a good five months later.'

Working from a large number of photographs taken by the defendant during the restoration, the Judge decided that the vehicle inspected by the RAC was not the same vehicle presented by the plaintiff after restoration that May. Parts were missing and wear was in evidence that would not have been possible in the five months since the restoration, during which the plaintiff had anyway claimed he had been unable to use it. As a result the Judge stated, 'I frankly find it difficult to attribute any degree of reliance upon the remainder of the Plaintiff's evidence ... I believe the Plaintiff got what he paid for. What the Plaintiff did after that in the presentation of this case suggests to me an attempt to distort the true facts and mislead the Court. ... I dismiss the Defendant's counterclaim, but the Plaintiff must pay the costs thrown away by the Defendant to include the hearing on 21 April ... a total of £495.'

This seems to represent a victory for restorers working to contracts where time is not of the essence and presented with dubious claims by their clients.

Falling out over a sale 'on consignment'

Case No 96BUS188 between Richard John Leeson and Classic Automobiles of London Ltd went to trial in the Central London County Court on 13 August 1997.

In R.L.'s words, 'I had known the defendant for many years and in 1996, over a very enjoyable lunch, I agreed to allow his firm to sell a recreated Bugatti Type 40 of mine, constructed from original parts, for a net return to me of £50,000. The verbal agreement we reached also allowed me to sell the car myself at no commission to his firm on the basis of "first past the post" and I informed the defendant that some interest had already been expressed as a result of an advertisement in the Bugatti Owners' Club newsletter. Within a few days I received a call from one of the defendant's salesmen that he had an offer of £30,000 plus an Austin Healey he considered to be worth at least £20,000. I turned down this offer which was followed by a revised offer of £40,000 which I also declined. By that time, a potential purchaser I had spoken to some time previously expressed a more serious interest in the car and wanted to fly out to the UK to view it. This he did, by arrangement with the defendant's firm, and on the day he made me a firm offer of £50,000. He then expressed his satisfaction with the deal to the defendant's sales manager, and we returned to my home in Surbiton to complete the sales agreement and receipt. Two days later, I spoke to the sales manager about the sale and he told me that the car had already been sold earlier on that day to a -purchaser who took out an option on it several weeks before and had now offered the full asking price. The case went to trial and when it was heard I was totally vindicated. But, unfortunately, it was not possible to "undo" the deal between the defendant's firm and the person to whom it sold my car, so my purchaser was disappointed.'

Judgement was in favour of R.L., and Classic Automobiles of London Ltd was ordered to pay him £50,000, plus interest at £5,633.44, plus most of R.L.'s costs. What this case illustrates is the absolute necessity to put all such deals and any subsequent alterations in writing, so that any dispute can be easily resolved without the enormous cost of going to court (in this case estimated at more than £100,000).

My advice

The Retail Motor Industry runs a conciliation service for disputes between its members and used car buyers where the purchase was made less than 12 months previously. (It will not become involved in disputes over new cars.) The telephone number is 01788 538316/538317, but the RMI will only arbitrate where the dispute remains private, with no involvement of solicitors, Trading Standards officers, TV or the press. Alternatively you can discuss the matter with your local Trading Standards Office.

However, my advice is to think very carefully before you engage a solicitor and try to pursue the seller for costs over and above the amount you paid for the car. Where dealers agree to a refund, they are likely to stick their heels in over such costs. When a refund is agreed, a dealer will usually ask the recipient to sign a receipt stating that the refund is 'in full and final settlement', to preclude any further claims. This is often the best you are going to get.

If you fight the dealer for costs all the way to an Appeal Court hearing, not only may you lose the refund, you may find yourself landed with £10,000–£15,000 of court and solicitors fees – on top of a nerve-wracking delay before the Appeal hearing.

Goodwill lands Peugeot in hot water

An interesting case came before the Panel of Arbitrators appointed by the SMMT in March 1999. In essence, the claimant bought a second-hand Peugeot 605 from a Rover agent and had trouble with it. Peugeot then became involved through its agents with a measure of goodwill in mind. The first goodwill repairs did not solve the problem. A senior Peugeot employee then test-drove the car, and during this test drive it lost all of its oil. He then had a Peugeot agent carry out further repairs. Five thousand miles later, the engine suffered a big end failure. The Arbitrator ruled that though there was no contract between the claimant and Peugeot, or between the claimant and Peugeot's agents which carried out the last work on the car, a Peugeot employee and not the claimant had ordered this work. The fact that it was not done satisfactorily was Peugeot's responsibility, and Peugeot was ordered to pay the claimant £3,347.89. This payment included both the cost of rectification work on the engine and £656.36 for a hire car. As well as demonstrating the considerable intelligence of the Arbitrator, this proves that the SMMT system is fair and without bias. Many thanks to R.K. of Watford for providing full details of his case. If you wish the SMMT to consider appointing an Arbitrator to resolve a dispute with a manufacturer or a franchised agent, speak to Sean Wadmore on 020 7235 7000.

Too late, mate

" *I bought a new Renault Megane Scenic Alize in March from a Renault dealer. At the time, during and after the sale I was not made aware of changes to the specification. In this case, the vehicle was not fitted with a heat-reflecting windscreen. The dealer has since informed me that Renault has the right to change specification at any time. I have noticed numerous 'T'-reg. Scenics with blue, heat-reflecting windscreens. If I had been made aware at the time of sale that my vehicle would not be fitted with one, I would have paid extra for it to be fitted. The dealer has offered me a first free service in replacement, and informed me that as far as Renault is concerned the matter is closed. Under the Sale of Goods Act 1994, how do I legally stand in getting what I paid for?* "

A Scenic Alize had not come with a heat-reflecting screen since air-conditioning was made standard a year before you bought yours. The more expensive Scenic RXE continued to have a heat-reflecting screen as well as a/c. The supplier's right to change specifications of vehicles in between order and delivery was confirmed in *Johnson vs HWM* 1997. (Johnson had ordered an Aston Martin and sought to cancel his purchase contract on the grounds that between order and projected delivery date the specification of the car changed.) However, the Sale and Supply of Goods Act 1994 gives the purchaser the right to reject a purchase for not being of 'satisfactory quality' if he has not had the opportunity to inspect the purchase prior to payment. So, despite *Johnson vs HWM* you may have been able to reject the vehicle at the point of delivery. But case law has so far shown that if you do not do so virtually straight away, you lose the right to reject the vehicle and receive a full refund. This is reasonable because your Scenic is now 'secondhand' and could not be re-sold for anything like the price you paid for it. The solution to your problem is to wait until the screen becomes irreparably stone-chipped. Then have it replaced with a heat-reflecting screen, on your insurance. You will probably have to pay a standard £40–£50 excess for this, plus the difference in cost between a standard screen and a heat-reflecting one.

Reject it

" *I bought an August 1998 registered Nissan Almera 1.6 with 936 miles on the clock on 28 May 1999. I then drove it to the coast, but could not return until the next morning because the side lights did not work. I then returned the car to the franchised dealer I bought it from. Six weeks have now elapsed and I am still without the car. I am told that Nissan Europe is involved and a complete electrical harness is being installed. Today (8 July) I have sent the dealer a letter rejecting the car. Am I being reasonable?* "

Entirely. Send all spare keys and the V5 back to the dealer by registered post and demand the full price you paid to be returned. State that you have rejected the car as being of 'unsatisfactory quality' under the terms of the Sale and Supply of Goods Act 1994. Because the fault showed up so soon, and because you gave the dealer a reasonable chance to put it right, case law is in your favour. If the dealer kicks up, remind him that it was also a criminal offence to sell you a car that was not in roadworthy condition and, if necessary, be prepared to bring in the Trading Standards Office which covers the dealership. I will be very surprised if you don't get your money back very quickly indeed. Don't buy another car that has been sitting around doing nothing for most of its life.

Misleading advertising?

" As OAPs we were keen to get the best deal possible, and so responded to a Renault dealer's advertisement which, among other things, stated: 'We'll contribute £1,000 towards your deposit.' In the small print underneath, it stated: 'Typical Example: Clio Grande 1.2 3dr. Manufacturer's Recommended On the Road Price: £8,600. Deposit: £3,495.90. Monthly Payments: £85 x 24. Minimum Future Value: £3,064.18. Total Payable: £8,600. APR: 0%. Offers subject to status and conditions and apply to selected models. Written details and quotations on request. Finance provided by RFS Ltd, NSW House, City Road, Chester X CH99 3AN.' The sales manager told me that the £1,000 offer could not be applied to the Clio deal, blaming whoever typeset the advertisement for my confusion. Another sales executive stated that the £1,000 offer was for more expensive models. I then wrote to Renault UK and the reply stated that 'an error was made when the advertisement was placed'. Should I now go to Trading Standards? "

The small print clearly states the offer on the table for the Clio Grande, which is a standard

Personal Contract Purchase at 0% APR. (After 24 months you have the choice of paying the balance of £3,064.18 to keep the car, using any equity between £3,064.18 and the trade value of the car to part-finance the deposit on another PCP, or leaving the car with the dealer and walking away.) I find no ambiguity whatsoever in the Clio offer because nowhere does the sum include £1,000 towards your deposit. I agree that the £1,000 offer should have been qualified. But the Clio offer is cut and dried.

Thorny question

" Every autumn we suffer a serious problem in our area: thorns left in the road after mechanised hedge-clipping operations. Last week we had four punctures; two at the same time causing tremendous problems because, of course, we carry only one 'spare'. Whose responsibility is this *state of affairs? Complaints to the contractor and landowner merely elicit the response, 'prove it was a thorn from my hedge'.* "

Take these bullies at their word and prove it. Use photographs of the hedge-clipping operations and the detritus they leave behind in the road. Use photos of the thorns in your car tyres. Then take the case to a Small Claims Court. You can obtain 'How to' leaflets on the courts service website: www.courtservice.gov.uk (go to 'forms and leaflets', then go on to 'Civil Justice Reforms'). You will find a charity that might help you on: www.endispute.co.uk. You might also try www.adviceguide.org.uk and www.lawrights.co.uk. If you aren't connected, there's a book: *See You in Court! – How to Conduct Your Own Case in the Small Claims Court* by Anthony Reeves, priced £3.99 (Elliot Right Way Books). Of course, if the hedge-clipping operations are now over, you will have to wait until next year before you can start to gather your evidence. You also have to bear in mind the risk of losing your court allocation fee of £80 and an additional £20 for claims of less than £200, rising to an additional £70 for claims between £500 and £1,000. These fees are deterring claimants from pursuing the smallest claims.

A case for rejection

" *Seven weeks ago I spent £20,000 on a new Honda Accord. First and second gear are extremely difficult to use and the local Honda dealer informed me that to cure a paintwork problem all four doors must be removed to paint the door jams. Also, the rear bumper and driver's door must be totally repainted (the car is metallic silver). The car will be off the road for at least a week and they are not prepared to provide me with a loan car. What would you do and how?* "

Reject it. Return the car, all keys and the V5 registration document to the Honda dealer together with a letter stating you reject the car as 'not being of satisfactory quality' under the terms of the Sale and Supply of Goods Act 1994, specifically itemising all the faults, and asking for your money back in full. Send a copy of this letter by recorded delivery to the dealer principal at the Honda dealers, a second copy to Honda (UK) Ltd, and a further copy to the Trading Standards Office which covers the area of the garage. (In this case, rejection was accepted by the dealer with no further argument.)

Getting back more than you paid

" *When you suggest that readers reject a faulty new car and ask for their 'money back in full', what do you mean? Most people part exchange an old car for a new one, which might have been sold on by the dealer by the time they reject the new car. Can they claim back the full invoiced price?* "

Yes. They can claim back the full invoiced price, even if the dealer offers to return their old car plus what they actually paid. This has been tested in court and should make dealers very wary about over-valuing part-exchanges.

Taking it too far

" *I bought a new Silver 'Ally' Nissan Micra on 30 April. When I inspected it I noticed brown marks on the bumpers and side panels, which I was told had come from the 'tyre black'. When I got it home I found a scratch on the left side of the hatchback and the bumper. I phoned the dealer who told me to bring the car back. On 1 May, the dealer tried to remove the marks, but scuffed the paint. I ended up with a new bumper, a light respray on the left side of the hatch and a bouquet of flowers. In June, the car went in for free sill protectors to be fitted (compliments of the dealer).*

I also asked him to look at the gearbox as I was finding second gear diffi-cult to select, and complained that brown gunge was still coming off the tyres. The tyres were replaced, but the new ones have a brownish hue, which I do not think quite right on a brand new car. In August, the car was booked in again as I still found the gears very stiff. There was also a knocking noise from the rear of the car. On 26 August, the car was collect-ed from my works, a second set of new tyres were fitted and also a com-plimentary chrome tail-pipe trim. Then in the middle of September when I started the engine I heard a loud noise from it like a concrete mixer. The dealer took the car back, loaned me a courtesy car and asked if I would consider another Micra, similar to mine but with £800 of extras, as a re-placement. Though the replacement was the same age as my car it had done 5,979 miles, so I turned it down. By now it was the end of September. At the time of writing (8 October) I am still driving the loan car. What should I do? "

The dealer appears to have done all he reason-ably could to keep you happy. In the circum-stances, the offer of the replacement is reasonable and I would re-consider it. It is not reasonable to expect a brand new car on a later registration in replacement.

Mileage marathon

" *I have written to the DVLA to complain about it divulging former ownership details of cars to third parties, such as HPI Equifax, which are profit-making organisations. I have demanded written confirmation from the DVLA that this will not happen again, or I will take up the mat-ter with my MP.* "

Prepare for a complicated explanation. Under the Data Protection Act, the DVLA cannot di-vulge keepership details of vehicles to credit record organisations such as Equifax and Experian. But, under Regulation 15 of the Road Vehicles (Registration and Licensing) Regulations 1971, as amended, the DVLA can pass keepership details to organisations such as Vehicle Mileage Check and the National Mileage Register. The reason for this is that traders are required under the Trade Descriptions Act and the Theft Act to 'show due diligence' in tracing the mileage history of vehicles they offer for sale. VMC and NMR do the work that enables traders to fulfil these legal obligations. VMC and NMR also supply mileage information, but not keepership information, to HPI Equifax and AA Experian to sell on to potential purchasers as part of their vehicle history checks. For the information of puzzled readers, T.B. runs a company which imports cars from the Far East and the 'J'-registered car in question had been registered to T.B. personally from 8 June 1999 to 5 October 1999. He strongly objected to receiving a letter from NMR asking him for the mileage of the car on disposal. (HPI Equifax: 01722 422422; AA Experian: 0800 234999.)

Unbelievably cheap

" *I saw a 'V'-reg. Rover 200 with a price of just £995.00 on the windscreen. I went home, got a camera, photographed the screen price, then presented my cheque for £995 to the dealer. I asked for a receipt, but this was refused. Where do I stand legally? Has this appeared in courts?* "

You're legally legless. For a binding contract to exist between you and the dealer there must be an offer and an acceptance. A price sticker does not qualify as an offer, it is just an 'invitation to treat'. The relevant case law is contained in *Fisher vs Bell* 1961, where Lord Parker stated, 'It is clear that, according to the ordinary law of contract, the display of an article with a price on it in a shop window is merely an invitation to treat. It is in no sense an offer for sale, the acceptance of which constitutes a contract.'

Badge engineering

" *In May 1999 I took delivery of a new VW Golf. I had ordered a new Golf Mk IV GTi in February with an eye to the enhanced residual value I might expect of a GTi model. But what I actually got was a 1.8 Highline. GTi badges appear nowhere on the car and in the service record book the car is clearly described as a 'Golf 1.8 Highl 92KW'. So, though I ordered a Golf GTi, what I appear to have is a 1.8 Highline.* "

The GTi designation of the 125 bhp 1.8 litre and 115 bhp 2.0 litre Golf Mk IV, solely for the UK market, always smacked of a cynical marketing ploy. The 'GTi' badges are actually stuck on the backs of Highline models by UK dealers. Never mind that they are no more true GTis than 1.8 or 2.0 litre Highlines, if that's what the market wanted, that's what it got. You need to go to the 150 bhp GTI Turbo to get GTi performance and even that gets left for dead by cars like the 167 bhp Peugeot 306 GTi-6 and 180 bhp Seat Leon 20VT. My son's football-team manager has rearranged the letters on the back of his GTi so they now read 'GIT'.

Witness for the prosecution

" *After returning from two weeks' holiday my daughter had difficulty starting her Renault 5. Her friend's father managed to get it going for about five minutes, she drove it for about a mile, and it stopped again. The RAC was called, their man diagnosed damp ignition and got the car going again. My daughter was advised to ignore any subsequent popping or banging noises. She asked the patrolman about some 'funny ticking noises' the car was making and he told her he had no idea of the cause. When she asked if the car was safe to take on the motorway, he apparently said 'OK'. Seven miles down the motorway the car expired in a cloud of smoke.*

The RAC was called again and this time diagnosed a blown head gasket. When the engine was dismantled a piston crown was found to have melted which confirmed the effect of excess water in the combustion chamber. I have had to pay for a completely new engine at a cost of £1,100 and the RAC denies negligence, maintaining that 'the overheating occurred due to a further problem incurred during the journey on the motorway'. I think this is arrant nonsense and everyone I talk to in the trade agrees, but no one will put this in writing. Do you think I would have any chance of recovering at least part of the replacement engine cost in the Small Claims Court without a written opinion? **"**

As always with the Small Claims Court, it depends on the judge, and whether the RAC contests the case, which would lead to an expensive full hearing in a County Court. But the cause of the head-gasket failure was not the RAC man's fault. It was the failure of your daughter and anyone else in the car's past to renew the engine coolant every two to three years (or every four years if using a Trigard MPG coolant). The corrosion inhibitors in MEG coolant only last for two to three years, after which any mixed metal engine becomes a corrosion battery and the head gasket is the first part to be eaten away. RAC Roadside Assistance is there to get you going, not to perform a full service check on every aspect of a car's running gear. In any case, if a failed head gasket had caused the starting problem, white smoke would have poured out of the car's exhaust pipe once the RAC man got it going.

Pot-hole precedents

" *In October 1999 on a rain-soaked road I drove my E Class estate into a pothole, the presence of which was hidden by standing water. The result was a buckled AMG alloy wheel and a large bill. The road is the responsibility of the county council, but it blamed a poor repair by a utility company. I have asked the council for details of this utility company so I can* *press the claim against it, but the council refused to impart this information. What can I do?* "

After a similar incident, Devon County Council coughed up the cost of another reader's tyre without demure. R.P. of Whitstable, Kent has also successfully claimed for damage on two occasions. The procedure is to record the date, time of day and weather conditions, take photographs of the potholes, ask the local council for a claim form, produce receipts for the repairs and send it all back to the local council which will then forward it to the county council for payment. However, this is not what happens in Ireland. A reader who took his case to the Ombudsman's office in Dublin received an incredible reply. In Irish law, if his accident had been the result of the council's negligence in carrying out road works it would be judged as mis-feasance and the council would be liable. If however, the accident is the result of the council's failure to carry out works, it would be judged as non-feasance, and the council would not be liable.

No MOT = no insurance?

" *I don't think that you and Fenton Bresler are entirely correct in asserting that it is legal to drive an untaxed car to a pre-arranged MOT-test appointment. I recently purchased a 1947 Scott Motor Cycle. I needed to transport it across the country for an engine rebuild, so phoned my insurer to add it to my existing motorcycle policy. All went well until, at the end of the conversation, I mentioned that it did not have an MOT. 'Sorry,' I was then told. 'No MOT, no insurance.' I was then told that all insurance companies apply the same rule.* "

Not true. According to the Association of British Insurers very few policies demand an

MOT as a condition of insurance. It is the policyholder's responsibility to ensure that the vehicle is roadworthy, but an MOT is not essential for this. I think your problem came from trying to add the classic bike to an existing policy. What you should have done is insure it independently on a classic policy. If you buy a car, bike or van without an MOT at an auction you should first phone their insurer and arrange cover, then phone an MOT-testing centre near your home to pre-arrange a test. You can then legally drive to the test centre. After that, before you can drive the vehicle home, you will need to take the MOT certificate, your insurance certificate and the V5 or V62 to a main post office to register and tax the vehicle.

Neighbours from hell

" *I am in the process of trying to sell my BMW 525iSE. In preparing the car for sale I noticed several minor scratches on both the bonnet and boot lid. I was quoted £300 for remedial work and the bodyshop stated that the damage was consistent with cats walking across the panels. I have to leave my car out on my driveway at night, and both my neighbours have cats, so I strongly suspect that one of them must have caused the damage. Assuming that I would need to photograph the relevant cat on the car to prove my point, would I have any legal redress against the owners of the cats?* "

No because, unlike dogs, cats are legally defined as wild animals. And you'd better not take any measures against the cats or the RSPCA will be down on you like a ton of bricks. We should also hope that your neighbours aren't *Telegraph* readers. If the car is more than five years old my advice is to leave it scratched as recently repainted panels usually arouse suspicion.

Wrong piece of kit

" *Last December I bought an assembled secondhand kit car which came with documentation stating it had a highly tuned 4.7 litre Ford V8. It was not until I was able to drive the car on dry roads that I began to suspect the engine was not as advertised. When my garage removed the cylinder heads it was found to be a 4.2 with perhaps 60% of the power I had expected. The vendor insisted he sold me the car in the same state he had purchased it a year previously and that it had been described to him as a 4.7. It is not possible to tune the 4.2 to give the performance I expected. What remedy do I have?* "

If you bought the car from a trader, or even someone who can be proven to have sold six or more cars a year, then you bought on a false trade description and should speak to the Trading Standards Office which covers the vendor's area. But if he was clearly a private owner who may well have thought he had a 4.7, then a court would probably take the view that since it was a car built of bits and pieces you should have satisfied yourself that it was accurately described. Simply removing the air filter, for example, would show you if the engine had a two-barrel or a four-barrel carb, and given some indication of the performance potential. Sunbeam Tiger Mk Is went quite well on the 165 bhp 260ci (4,261 cc) two-barrel Ford V8, and the same engine in early Cobras was tuned to deliver 264 bhp. The 225 bhp versions of the 289ci (4,727 cc) had a four-barrel carb, but highest standard output in early Mustang 289s was 271 bhp.

LIGHTS

One fog or two?

" I recently bought a new car, and on checking the lights found that only one of the rear fog lights worked. The dealer advises me that this is to comply with EU regulations. Is this true? "

Yes. It's also to comply with common sense. Two illuminated rear fog lights look like two brake lights and could induce drivers behind into unnecessary braking, causing concertina accidents. On a right-hand-drive car, the illuminated fog light should be on the right-hand side. On a left-hand-drive car it should be on the left.

Use your dipped beams

MOT examiner Ted Craker of Bromley sent us all a reminder to use our dipped headlights at times of low light. Side lights, even those inside the headlight reflector, and 'dim dip' are not enough because, besides failing to illuminate the roadside ahead, they do not emit enough light to bounce off reflective materials worn by paper boys, school children, cyclists and workmen. Ted also warns that of the last 200 lights he examined during MOT tests, 35% were not aligned correctly and 10% of amber indicator bulbs behind clear lenses had lost their amber coating, making them illegal. The law states that we must use headlights when visibility is reduced enough to prevent us seeing further than 100 metres. But, though the Highway Code advises us to use headlights at all times at night, the RVLR 1989 does not compel us to use them on roads lit by street lamps less than 185 metres apart within the 30 mph limit.

Wet lights

" *I have a 1977 Capri, which is fitted with rectangular headlights. Last time the car was in for its MOT, the tester told me that one of the lights was full of condensation, which could corrode the reflector. I dried the light out with a hairdryer. But how do I prevent this happening again?* "

I had exactly the same problem 13 years ago with a brand new 205 GTi. I removed the light unit, dried it out with a hairdryer (as you did) then re-sealed the joint with bathroom silicone sealant, which is available from any DIY store.

Blindingly obvious

" *Regarding driving lamp/fog lamp regulations I have read in magazines that these must be wired into the main headlight beam via a relay, and there must be some form of warning light or symbol to tell the driver when they are switched on. Yet these days I keep seeing UK- and EU-registered cars with front driving lights or fog lights mounted low in the front valence which seem capable of being switched on independently of the headlights, and which the drivers sometimes substitute for the headlights. I have read that driving lamps must be a minimum of 16 inches from the ground.* "

As far as I can gather from the SVA and MOT inspection manuals, the old minimum height for fog lamps or driving lamps has been superseded by a new rule which states that the cutoff point of a dipped beam headlamp must be at least 500mm from the ground, but gives no minimum height for driving lamps or fog lamps. The operation, condition and wiring of 'optional' lamps are not included in the MOT test. That said, it is a requirement of the RVLR 1989 that drivers must switch off front fog lamps when visibility improves, to avoid dazzling other road users (Highway Code rule 94), so drivers who use fog lamps as substitute headlights could be courting prosecution. ('Using car fog lamps when road conditions did not require them led to a £40 fine for a Prudhoe man at Tynedale Magistrates' Court at Hexham last Thursday.' *Hexham Courant* 28 January 2000.) You have been warned.

Blinded by the lights

" Driving to work recently, I came face to face with an Alfa Romeo with very bright headlights, which seem to have a bluish tinge. Without any further warning I immediately began to experience double-vision, so hastily pulled over, wound down the window and looked down until normal vision returned about one and a half minutes later. I had eaten a reasonable breakfast, do not suffer from migraines, blood-pressure irregularities, diabetes or, to my knowledge, any form of eye defect. My question is, if this happened to me, how many other motorists have been dazzled by these over-bright lights? "

Under the RVLR 1989 it is an offence to use any vehicle light to dazzle or cause discomfort to other drivers, so the legality of these new lights may need to be tested in the courts. But until that happens I have three suggestions: firstly, go and have your eyes tested by the latest high-tech equipment; secondly, if you see any oncoming bright lights, look away from them; thirdly, if you are stuck behind a moron illuminating his high-level, high-intensity brake light by holding his car on the footbrake, turn down your sun-visor to blot it out.

Lighten up

" *It's not easy to replace any bulbs behind the plastic lens of my new Mondeo Zetec. The handbook instructs one to first remove the radiator grille, then remove the headlamp assembly before any bulb can be replaced. It further warns drivers who have replaced a headlamp bulb to take the car into a Ford dealer to make sure the lights are correctly aligned. Not the sort of task for a dark night, and one that could leave a lot of drivers with the choice of driving illegally or being stranded.* "

J.S.'s complaint applies to any Mondeo of 1997 model year or later. It seems to be a penalty of the facelift. Plenty of other cars share this problem, but not the brilliant new Fiat Punto on which, among the plethora of excellent design features, the backs of the high-tech front lights are all easily accessible.

Lighting up time

" *One of the greatest hazards when travelling in poor weather conditions is motorists using sidelights. These were designed for parking only, in the days when you were required to use them by law. It would be interesting to know why car manufacturers still put them on cars when they have been obsolete for many years.* "

They aren't obsolete. Under reg. 24 of the RVLR 1989 'position lamps', as they are now called, *must* be used between sunset and sunrise. Since headlights are not required until half an hour after sunset and for the half hour before sunrise, position lights do still have a legal function, even though it is much safer to use dipped beams. I receive a large volume of mail from drivers complaining of being dazzled by oncoming headlights at all times of the day and night, and there is even a campaign to ban the daytime running lights fitted as standard to some Swedish cars. 'Dim dip' daytime running lights did make sense because they never distracted anyone. But high-intensity dipped headlights can dazzle oncoming drivers when the car bounces over a dip or 'road calming measure' and also shine straight into the mirrors of a car which is being followed or overtaken by a car in an outer lane of a motorway. For this reason, a courteous driver should use the electric beam-height adjuster to turn the beams down when fully raised dipped beams are not really needed, for example in rain or fog.

MAINTENANCE

Running in

" I have just bought a new car. What is your advice about running it in and changing the oil for the first time? "

To run a car engine in, it is vital to vary engine speeds during the first 1,000–2,000 miles. If you are cruising on a motorway, vary your cruising speed by 10–20 mph every 15 minutes or so. Don't over-rev the engine, but don't under-rev it either. Never labour the engine by driving in too high a gear. Unless it is a super high performance car such as a Mitsubishi Lancer EVO VI, current thinking is to leave the factory fill of oil for the first 12 months or 10,000 miles in order to promote some wear, and enable the piston rings and bores to bed themselves in. After that, change the engine oil and filter, and consider switching from the semi-synthetic oil the car came with to fully synthetic. Also have the manual gearbox oil changed to get rid of any swarf thrown off while the box was bedding itself in before the swarf grinds itself into minute particles which get into the bearings and shorten their lives.

Minimum maintenance

" Nowadays some car manufacturers are specifying oil changes at 12,500-mile or two-year intervals and give no indication of when things

like timing belts should be changed. What is your advice? **"**

After the first year or 10,000 miles, whichever comes first, I recommend using either a good semi-synthetic oil such as Castrol Magnatec, or a fully synthetic such as Mobil 1, and changing it every 5,000 miles or every six months, whichever comes first. If you are a higher-mileage driver doing 15,000 miles a year or more, consider stretching your oil changes to 6,000 miles. If you do 25,000 miles or more and use fully synthetic oil consider stretching to 7,500 miles but no further. Always change the filter as well. Change the manual gearbox oil once after the first year to 18 months or 10,000–15,000 miles. Change the coolant every three years if it is an MEG coolant or every four years if it is an MPG coolant. Change the brake fluid every two years unless it is Dot 5 silicone brake fluid (unlikely on a mass-produced car). If the engine has a timing belt, change that every three to four years or every 40,000 miles, whichever comes first, unless the engine has no history of premature timing belt failures. (Ford Zetec E and Zetec S engine timing belts generally exceed their design life of 80,000 miles, so can be changed at 80,000 miles.) Change the timing-belt tensioner and any weeping camshaft or jack-shaft oil seals at 80,000 miles (every second timing belt change for non Ford Zetecs).

More handy handbooks

" *Recently, you suggested that readers wanting to keep running costs down should carry out routine maintenance themselves. This is something I have always done with the aid of a Haynes manual. However, there is no Haynes manual for my current car, a Fiat Bravo. What can I do?* **"**

It came out in December 1999. D.B. of Saffron Walden asked about a Haynes manual for the Audi A4 and I'm pleased to inform him that one was scheduled for publication this year. Other new and forthcoming Haynes manuals cover the Ford Ka, the Volvo S40/V40 and the Seat Ibiza/Cordoba. To check if there is a Haynes manual for your car, telephone 01963 440001, visit the website at www.haynes.com or email your order at sales@haynes-manuals.co.uk.

The pits

" *I am planning to build a new garage and would like to have a pit sunk in the floor. Are moulded fibreglass damp-proof liners available from specialist suppliers, or is it a matter of fitting a butyl liner around the brickwork? Do building regulations describe safety aspects in pit design, for example fuel spillage and escape in the event of a fire?* "

The Mech Mate Motor Pit is RAC approved, and it's made of moulded one-piece GRP by Truckman (who make Truckman Tops for pick-up trucks). The basic price works out at £775.50, including delivery and VAT. More information from Truckman Ltd, Unit C6, Baker Street, Gloucester, tel: 01242 580033, email: truckman@compuserve.com. To dig an accurate pit, R.B. of Tewkesbury suggests employing the local grave digger, who one hopes is not too busy with his day job. Another reader warns of the danger of explosions from petroleum gases which are heavier than air and tend to collect at the bottom of such pits. Pits are subject to building regulations (it costs £82.84 to submit plans) and may also be subject to planning permission. The July 1998 issue of *Practical Classics* magazine covers everything you need to know.

Motor caravan maintenance

" I have a motor caravan based on a 1995 Peugeot Boxer 2.5 litre diesel van. Can you please tell me where I can obtain a workshop manual or whether any car manuals are applicable to this engine? "

I can't find an independent manual for the van, but Haynes does a manual for the engine (ISBN 1-85010-607-X, price £14.99, order from any bookshop).

MX5, Eunos Roadster or Miata?

" I recently purchased an imported Mazda MX5 with which, to date, I have been delighted. Unfortunately there was no handbook or instruction manual. Haynes does not print one and my local Mazda dealer says he cannot help. Any suggestions? "

Imported from where? If it's imported from

Europe it might be an MX5. If it's imported direct from Japan it's a Eunos Roadster, not an MX5. And if it's imported from the USA it's a Mazda Miata. Make sure the correct model is on your insurance certificate or you may find your insurance is invalid. Haynes does do a manual for all models and engine sizes of the American Mazda Miata from 1990 to 1997 (ISBN 1-56392-289-4, price £14.99). Veloce Publishing also do 'Enthusiasts' Workshop' manuals by Rob Grainger and Pete Shoemark for the MX5/Eunos 1.6, MX5/Eunos 1.8, Miata 1.6 and Miata 1.8, all separate publications with some commonality, and each priced £20. While you're at it, you should also join the Mazda MX5 Owners' Club of 16 Williams Way, Flitwick, Beds MK45 1XD.

Simple checks

" My husband, who used to do all the regular checks on the car, is now in hospital and I visit him there daily. Is there a simple, easy-to-understand publication telling me all the regular checks I need to make on the car? My journey to the hospital is five miles each way. Am I right in thinking I am doing the car more good by using the bypass and getting in a couple of miles at 60–70 mph rather than the mere 30–40 mph possible on the other route? "

Halfords does an excellent series of clear, full-colour *Essential Guide* maintenance manuals with plasticised pages. They stop a fair way short of a Haynes manual, but their great virtue is that they are extremely easy to understand – especially for those who have never burrowed under a bonnet before. Yes, you are right to take your car via the by-pass as this will help it reach full running temperature, dispersing condensation and helping the engine and exhaust system to last longer.

Greasy screen

" *Despite using screenwash I seem to be constantly removing a greasy film from my windscreen, and wondered if you could recommend anything which may alleviate this problem?* "

Wearing rubber gloves, clean the screen with Mer windscreen cleaner, tel: 020 8401 0002 (you need gloves because you might be allergic to it). Also note this job must be done in dry conditions. Then add Holts 'Bug Shifter' to the screenwash reservoir and buy a new set of wiper blades. Methylated spirit is very useful for cleaning oily grease from windscreens and for removing stubborn adhesive left behind after removing stickers.

The route to happy motoring

" *I drive an elderly Mk 1 Ford Fiesta 1100 Bravo which, despite having covered more than 200,000 miles, has never failed to start and has always got me home. I put this down to regular, efficient servicing rather than any other factor.* "

Too right. Nothing is more likely to kill an engine off than a sump-full of degraded, contaminated oil.

Turbo trouble

" *We have a VW Sharan TDI 110 bought as an ex demonstrator at 5,000 miles and six months old. We are very happy with the car, apart from its appetite for turbochargers. When we bought it, I had the oil and filter changed, and I change them every 5,000 miles in between VW services. We get 40 mpg in the urban cycle, 50 mpg on a long run and I never rev the engine from cold. Yet, at 15,000 miles we needed our first replacement turbo, then again at 25,000, both FOC under warranty. Can you throw any light on why this should be happening?* "

The TDI 110 has a variable vane turbo, but I don't think it's this that's causing the problem. I think it's the bearings, which have been known to lose oil even on TDI 90s. As you know, turbos run red hot and the most common cause of turbo failure is coked-up oil in its bearings. If I were you I'd check what oil the VAG dealer is using at the official 10,000-mile oil changes and make sure you use that in your intermediate changes. If you stick to a very good synthetic oil, such as Mobil 1 diesel or Millers XFE Synta, this should not be broken down by the heat of the turbo.

Mobil 1 racing

" *Following your advice I am now a regular user of Mobil 1 0W/40 engine oil in my Honda Civic VTi S. My question is, what is the essential difference between the oil I use and that used in race cars?* "

In a road car, most engine damage occurs immediately after start up, so the road car's oil is formulated to provide maximum protection at low temperatures. In a race engine, particularly when turbocharged, the opposite applies and the oil has to be formulated to stay in grade at consistently high engine temperatures. Mobil has to formulate a lot of different viscosity range oils for different racing and high-performance engines.

Italian tune-up

" *I have owned a Rover 416Si from when it was first registered in June 1996 and which has now covered 22,000 miles. I mainly undertake short journeys of two to three miles and often the car runs very lumpily until warmed up. I reported this when I had my last service in June, and when the car was returned the service manager said they had increased the fuel flow to rectify the problem. Is this the correct remedy? If so, what should I now do to overcome the problem of very lumpy and uneven running when the engine is cold?* **"**

Fill the tank with Texaco or Shell petrol, both of which have adequate detergent content. Then find someone who has a reputation for driving everywhere flat out and lend the car to him, or her, for a morning. It should come back with the fuel system and combustion chambers nicely cleaned out and the engine running perfectly. After that, make sure you do at least one ten-to fifteen-mile journey at least once a week. Or part-exchange the car for something more suitable for short journeys such as a microcar (see 'Alternative Transport').

Hidden costs of a Golf Mk IV

" *Two weeks ago I had the scheduled 60,000-mile service carried out on my personal lease VW Golf Mk IV GT TDI. The work included replacing the brake discs on all four wheels and the bill was £480.00. Because time ran out, the scheduled timing-belt replacement was not carried out then, but a bit later, and was quoted at £450, though my lease service contract meant I only paid £220. Nevertheless, my total cost for the 60,000-mile service was £700, and I can expect to pay at least the same again at 120,000 miles. I think this is worth highlighting.* **"**

Timing-belt replacement on VAG TDIs has always been expensive because of the difficulty of getting both the valve timing and the injection-pump timing exactly right. The same is true of most diesels with the honourable exceptions of the GM 2.0 litre and 2.2 litre DI fitted to current Astras, Vectras and Omegas, and Mercedes Benz and BMW diesels, all of which have chain-driven camshafts; and the Toyota Landcruiser 4.2 diesel, which has a gear-driven camshaft.

Cramped, but possible

" *As a result of your recommendations I fitted a Kenlowe Hotstart to my Mondeo 12 months ago. The car is kept outside, so the benefits are most appreciated at this time of year when de-icing commences almost immediately, even in the hardest of frosts, while, of course, the engine appreciates being started hot. Fitting took a little time in the already full engine compartment, but the main work was inserting a longer internal cable to locate the socket at the rear of the car. A dedicated circuit controlled by a 3kW immersion-heater timer ensures that the engine is heated automatically every morning prior to start-up.* "

That's the way to do it and avoid the 70% of all engine wear which occurs immediately after starting a cold engine. Kenlowe, Maidenhead, SL6 6QU, tel: 01628 823303. Another, much more expensive engine pre-heater uses the vehicle's own fuel to pre-heat the block, so can be set to work when the vehicle is parked anywhere. It is made by Eberspacher, who can be contacted on 01425 482112, website: www.eberspacher.com, email: enquiries@eberspacher.com (prices from £595 plus VAT installed).

Long-life Focus

" *I am soon to collect a new Ford Focus TDI from Belgium to replace my Peugeot 405GLD, which has now done 198,000 miles. What tips can you give to help achieve a similar mileage from my Focus?* "

Follow the running-in instructions to the letter and do not change the oil earlier than recommended, or your engine may not bed in properly. After that, change the oil every 3,000–4,000 miles if using semi synthetic and every 5,000 miles if using fully synthetic. Change the gearbox oil after 10,000 miles or the first year. Use Millers DieselPower Plus additive in the Derv to keep your injectors clean and make sure the distribution pump is being properly lubricated. Use Autoglym Super Resin Polish and Extra Gloss Protection on the bodywork. Change the brake fluid and coolant every two to three years. Have the timing belt changed at the recommended times (at least every three to four years or 30,000–40,000 miles). Use the revs occasionally and never force the engine to labour in an excessively high gear for the road speed or incline.

Death Wish 4

" *I often hear of cars failing their MOTs due to scored discs and thought your readers might be interested in my tip to solve this problem. Jack the front wheel (of a front-drive car) up, and run it in third or fourth gear with an idling engine so the wheel is spinning quite fast, then run an angle grinder over the disc surface until all the scoring has gone. As long as the disc is still thick enough, the car should pass its MOT.* "

All I can say is *don't try this at home*. Most good garages have equipment to skim discs in-situ with the car safely suspended on a four-point hoist. A company that makes this skimming equipment is Vehvac Ltd, Fircroft Way, Edenbridge, Kent TN8 6EJ, tel: 01732 868080.

Golfing costs in France

" *I own a VW Golf Mk IV GT TDI, but I bought it here in France where the tax-paid price is £4,000 cheaper despite 21% VAT. The servicing costs are a lot cheaper. I paid only £138 for a timing-belt change. Replacing all four discs, ABS sensors and pads was £371. While a 30,000-mile oil-change service, including re-balancing one wheel, was a mere £50.* "

Most of the labour costs we pay for servicing in the UK goes to pay the ludicrously high costs of the building in which the work takes place. We can't have a property boom and cut-price car servicing in the same town at the same time. It's why the labour rate of £25.00 an hour at Horseshoe Garage in rural Cheshire is less than half the £58.50 charged in nearby Chester. (See 'Good Garage Guide'.) That said, Halfords Garages are now offering oil services using Mobil 1 and including a 14-point check for £50. These services are cheaper because cheaper oil is used.

Save my Sierra

" I am the proud owner of a 'J'-reg. Ford Sierra 1.8 litre TD estate, which has completed 154,000 miles. I have carefully maintained the car following your guidance with regular servicing and semi-synthetic oil changes every 3,000 miles. The car remains a pleasure to drive, still returns 50 mpg and has virtually no rust. Other than routine servicing it has needed one clutch at 100,000 miles and a cylinder head overhaul at 105,000 miles. What mileage can I expect the car to go to? Is there anything I can do to help preserve it? Is there a Sierra Owners' Club? Would additives in the gearbox and rear axle oil help preserve them? "

I have known the old 1.6 litre non-turbo Ford diesel last to 350,000 miles, but have no record of a 1.8 turbo reaching this figure. Millers DieselPower Plus will help preserve the injectors and fuel pump (from A1 Motor Accessory Shops, or freephone 0800 281053). An MPG 'Trigard' coolant will help keep corrosion at bay inside the cooling system. I can't find a Sierra Owners' Club. Additives such as STP and Molyslip definitely do help gearboxes and diffs, but it's obviously better to drain them first and replace the oils. Alternatively, switch to a fully synthetic gearbox oil, but not to fully synthetic and an additive.

Staying cool

" *Is there any way to check the operation of the electric cooling fan of my Vauxhall Astra? There have been occasions when parking after a long run that I fancied I heard a whirring noise. But when I raised the bonnet the fan was not moving.* "

The thermostatic switch is most likely to trigger the fan in a hot summer nose-to-tail traffic jam. If the fan was not working the engine would boil and the pressure would soon find the weakest point in the system. If you are 100% certain that the fan never cuts in, take the plug off the thermo-switch and cross the contacts to see if the fan works. If it does, then suspect the thermo-switch. Have an ample supply of a Trigard-based MPG coolant standing by to replace the coolant at the same time as you replace the thermo-switch.

Cut-price service?

" *I have a 1992K Volvo 440 which at the time of its last service had done only 28,677 miles and which averages significantly less than 5,000 miles a year. At each annual service, the dealer carries out a 10,000-mile service. The last one, at 70,000 miles, which included a timing-belt change, cost me £371 inclusive. This year I shall refuse the 80,000-mile service and ask only for specific work at my request, for example a change of engine oil and filter. What other service items should I ask the dealer to carry out?* "

A car registered to a London SW1 address obviously spends most of its life on short runs in traffic, many of which will be from a cold start. Just 2,500 miles of this sort of treatment is equivalent to 15,000 miles cruising on the motorway at 70 mph. So I advise a change of oil and filter every six months. Additional jobs to this at the annual service should include a thorough safety check of the underside of the car: tyres, brake pads, discs, brake pipes, power-steering rack (if fitted), suspension bushes, exhaust system, etc. In addition, if the coolant and brake fluid have not been changed within the past three years, these should also be changed.

If it ain't broke...

" *Does the old saying, 'if it ain't broke, don't fix it' apply to the average-sized car's set of spark plugs, which in my case have done over 50,000 miles and its plug leads, which have been reliable for more than 200,000 miles?* "

Yes if the car is pre-cat and you keep the leads clean of oil and dust which can trap moisture and lead to arcing. No if the car is catalysed because any misfire caused by duff plugs or leads can set off a process which destroys the matrix of the catalytic converter.

170,000-mile Vectra

" *I question your advice that oil needs to be changed more frequently than the 10,000-mile intervals advised. My Vectra DI has not had its oil changed more frequently than at its 10,000 mile services, and at 170,000 miles is well on its way to the 200,000 miles that you did not expect a 10,000-mile serviced car to see.* "

The average car in the UK does 10,000 miles a year and in my view needs its oil changed at least twice a year. You are doing around 50,000 miles a year, so are having your oil changed every two to three months. Though the oil will have degraded in the last 5,000 miles before each change, because you are doing around 1,000 miles a week, it will not have degraded to anything like the extent it would have in a car driven for an entire year with no oil changes. I'm pleased that your DI 16v engine is holding up. It was the first of a new series of GM engines with timing chains rather than belts, so in theory it should have been long lasting. You have proved it is.

600,000-mile 405

" *You were asking about high-mileage cars recently. Well how about Roy Chapman of Blackpool's Northern Ireland registered 1993 Peugeot 405 diesel taxi which has clocked up more than 600,000 miles, 560,000 of them in the last three years? According to the Blackpool Gazette, he does all his own maintenance and the car is still on its original 1.9 litre XUD engine. He drives up to 6,000 miles a week and changes the oil and filter every week. He replaces the air and fuel filters every 30,000 miles and the timing belt every 50,000 miles. He gets 52 mpg.* "

The Mobil Oil company changed the oil and filter of its E30 BMW 325i every 7,000 miles using Mobil 1 and it's still around with 1,020,000 miles on the clock. Roy obviously doesn't do 6,000 miles every week because averaging 50–60 mph would mean driving 100–120 hours a week plus pick-ups and drop-offs plus the time it takes him to service the car. If he has changed the oil and filter every week for three years and had driven 560,000 miles, he has changed it on average every 3,589 miles.

Overserviced Rover

" *The 60,000-mile service and MOT of my Rover 216i automatic was carried out at 58,121 miles on 12 November 1998 and cost £537.39. The 72,000-mile service and MOT took place at 63,040 miles on 10 November 99 and cost £769.82. At this rate it's not the ever-increasing cost of petrol I need to worry about. It's the inexorable rise in service costs.* "

Both services were carried out by a Windsor Rover agent when E.S. lived in the area. Both included replacing the wiper blades, which seemed a bit excessive 5,000 miles apart. Both included a change of brake fluid which should only have been needed every two years. Both involved engine oil flush and fuel treatment which would not have been necessary had the oil been changed every six months and the car been driven on longer runs. The high cost of the 60,000-mile service is accounted for by a scheduled timing-belt change, coolant change and brake-fluid change and an unscheduled anti-roll bar link replacement. The even higher cost of the 72,000-mile service included driveshaft gaiter suspension, bush replacements and repairs to punctures in both rear tyres. But it's still a sobering thought that this 1999 annual service cost more than the invoiced price of my first new car.

Servicing surprise

" *My wife runs my old company car, an 'L'-reg. Peugeot 405GTX estate, which is serviced every six months by the local franchise and has now done 84,000 miles. The dealer sent her a service reminder together with an offer of cheaper services, including an 84,000-mile service for £69.99. But when she went to collect the car the dealer would not stamp the book because, apparently, a proper 84,000-mile service costs an extra £100. My wife was given a list of the extra items this covered. Eventually the book was stamped 'P1' service. Why the difference?* "

The extra items on the list she was given included: check level of transmission fluid; replace fuel filter and toothed timing belt; check condition of rear brake shoes; clean handbrake drum and lining; test vehicle on the road or a rolling road. If the timing belt had been changed at the 72,000-mile service on 1 April 1999 it would not normally need to be changed again. But if it had not been changed at this service or in the past three to four years, then it is in urgent need of being changed because if it snaps the engine will self-destruct. Check your invoice for the 72,000-mile service to see what was included.

Unwarranted servicing

" The 'menu price' for a full service of a Nissan Primera at my local Nissan dealer is £230 during the three-year warranty period but £159 after the warranty expires. Is this a form of payment towards the cost of the warranty, because if the service is not carried out at the dealer the warranty becomes void? I have no complaints about the car, which is very good. "

During the warranty period there are more service checks than a customer might want to pay for afterwards, and that's why Nissan dealers offer two-tier, or even three- or four-tier servicing options. There is nothing to stop you opting for the full £230 service after the warranty ends.

Well oiled

" Prior to motorways, litres and synthetic oils, like your Blackpool taxi driver a prominent haulier decided on a weekly oil drain of his standard fleet, also replacing the gearbox and rear axle oil on a monthly basis. Envious competitors queued to purchase his vehicles at 250,000 miles and he got very good prices for them. His workshop staff shrank from eight to just one. To prove his point, a premium chassis was purchased and run to the manufacturer-recommended servicing regime. The engine lasted just 93,000 miles. His lube oil was purchased in 600-gallon lots from two independent oil blenders at six shillings and sixpence a gallon. The drainings were resold to reclaimers at four shillings a gallon, so with his oil costing

him just two shillings and sixpence he laughed all the way to the bank. Out of interest, waste oil still fetches 20p a gallon today. **"**

As part of its contribution to the environment the VAG Group prides itself on using a blend of re-refined waste oil combined with synthetic as the factory fill for its new engines.

Running in

" *I am about to purchase my first new car. Twenty years ago, during an engineering lecture, I was informed that how a car engine is treated during its first 1,000 miles will determine the engine's life. The lecturer advised no high revs and to change the oil every 100 miles up to the 1,000-mile mark. Is this advice still valid? In my youth, the rear window sticker, 'Running in. Please pass' was very common, but with modern machining methods is any of the above still necessary?* **"**

Fifteen years ago I ran in a Peugeot 205GTi 1.6 105 bhp very carefully at moderate to high speeds on the M25, changed the oil at 1,000 miles, and changed it again every 3,000 miles. The result was a 1.6 that went like stink, would clock 115 mph almost anywhere and could hit 130. Now, oils are so much better and engines are built so much tighter that one of the best ways to run in a car is to put it on a daily rental fleet and not change the oil at all for the first 10,000 miles. The worst things you can do are to drive slowly at constant engine speeds, to labour the engine in too high a gear, and to switch to a fully synthetic oil too early in the engine's life. Once the engine has done 10,000 miles (or a year's running, whichever comes first), change the oil to a good semi synthetic such as Castrol Magnatec or Ford 5W/30, or a fully synthetic, change the gearbox oil (just the once to get rid of any swarf cast off), then continue to change the oil every 5,000–7,000 miles or every six months, whichever comes first.

Used-less propaganda

" *In late 1998 I bought a fairly new Citroën Xantia 2.0i petrol model with air-conditioning and happily drove the 25 miles to and from work every day, clocking up a total of 12,000 miles a year. Now my company has restricted its parking slots and the local council has introduced residents' parking around my workplace so I am forced to take the bus. This means that the Xantia sits unused in my driveway except for the occasional weekend jaunt. Please could you advise me how best to keep my car in good running order? I don't want to sell it.* "

The only way is to drive the car regularly, which exposes the hypocrisy of government policy which encourages us to own cars but discourages us from using them efficiently. Cars under five years old are heavily depreciating assets which, including the added fixed costs of insurance and VED, cost the average owner between £2,500 and £7,500 a year. Why should anyone fork out this amount of taxed income for something they aren't allowed to make proper use of?

Independent vs franchise

" *I would be obliged if you would list the pros and cons of having one's repairs and services done by the car's authorised dealer or by a freelance local garage.* "

Good question. While the car is under warranty and for at least three years anyway I would recommend having the car serviced at an authorised dealer, particularly if the car is a new model. The reason is that while a car is in for a service, the dealer may carry out additional pre-

ventative work under a 'technical service bulletin' from the manufacturer that the car would
miss if serviced independently. Authorised-
dealer servicing also makes the car easier and
quicker to trace in the event of an official safety
recall. And as well as that there is the possibility of a 'goodwill' claim if a failure occurs outside
the warranty. Later in the car's life, whether to
stay authorised or go independent depends on
the relative quality and price of the service on
offer. If your authorised dealer is good, helpful
and reasonably priced, stay with him. If he isn't,
find a recommended independent who has to
give good service because he is not protected by
any local monopoly. Also make use of specialists, because a good automatic gearbox specialist, for example, will know a lot more about
autoboxes than any franchised dealer.

'NEARLY-NEW' CAR SPECIALISTS

Remember, most 'nearly-new' mass-market cars are ex-rental or from 'fast rotation' fleets. The supply and prices fluctuate wildly according to supply and demand, and big manufacturers such as Ford and Vauxhall have now cut back the number of cars they register through rental fleets and 'fast rotators'. You may save as much as £7,000 buying a nine-month-old 9,000-mile Mondeo or Vectra – but equally the saving may be as little as £3,000.

Beware of 'customer service returns' which can be faulty new cars rejected by customers, taken back by the manufacturers and auctioned off to the trade. And beware of Fiats lacking a 'red key' for the alarm-immobiliser system.

Finally, note that because these specialists operate on much tighter profit margins than franchised dealers, they rarely offer as much for cars taken in part-exchange – usually no more than they know they can get for the part-exchanges at auction. Nor do they offer the sort of 'after-sales service' UK car buyers have come to expect from franchised dealers.

- **LONDON:** The Great Trade Centre, Hythe Road (off Scrubs Lane), White City, London NW10, tel: 0208 964 8080 and 0208 965 5511, website: www.gtccar.co.uk (the original 'Car Supermarket'. Advertises in the *Sun*, *Exchange & Mart*, *Thames Valley Trader*).

- **SOUTH:** Trade Sales of Slough, 353–357 Bath Road, Slough, Berks SL1 6JA tel: 01753 773763, website: www.trade-sales.co.uk (advertises in *Telegraph* 'Motoring'; offers an excellent 'bumper to bumper' warranty which even includes some consumables). InterKar, Camberley, Surrey, tel: 01276 671999 (not particularly cheap).

- **MIDLANDS:** Motorpoint, Chartwell Drive, West Meadows, Derby, tel: 01332 347357, website: www.motorpoint.co.uk (advertises in *Telegraph* 'Motoring'). Motorhouse 2000, Wryly Brook Retail Park, Walkmill Lane, Cannock WS11 3XE, tel: 01543 4623000, website: www.motorhouse2000ltd.co.uk (Chris Bowen, who founded the original Motor House, sold to Car Supermarkets and then re-sold to Concept/Carland, is now back with a new Motorhouse offering similar deals to Motorpoint and Trade Sales of Slough). Rayns of Leicester, Thurcaston Road, Leicester, tel: 0116 261 2200. Ian Shipton Cars, 24 Main Street, Stretton, Burton-on-Trent, tel: 01283 542983. Motor Nation, Mackadown Lane, Garrett's Green, Birmingham, tel: 0121 786 1111. Bristol Street Motors, 156–182 Bristol Street, Birmingham B5 7AZ, tel: 0121 666 6003. Motorworld, Dudley, West Midlands, tel: 0121 520 5533.

- **WALES and WEST:** Carcraft at Empress Cars, Langland Way, Spitty Road, Newport, Gwent, tel: 01633 284800. Ron Skinner & Sons, Roundabout Garage, A469 Rhymney, Gwent, tel: 01685 842624, 01685 844370, sales hotline: 01685 844446. C P Motor company, Tonteg, tel: 01443 218600. Sanderson Motorhouse, Cheltenham, Gloucs, tel: 01242 253053.

- **NORTH WEST:** Fords of Winsford, Wharton Retail Park, Weaver Valley Road (off A5018), Winsford, Cheshire, tel: 0845 607 3208 or 01606 861234, faxback: 0891 715970, website: www.fow.co.uk. Motor Nation, Widnes, Cheshire, tel: 0151 423 3342. Reg Vardy Motor Zone, Albion Way, Salford, Lancs M5 4DG, tel: 0161 737 7333. Carcraft, Molesworth Street, Rochdale OL16 1TS, tel: 01706 752500. Reg Vardy Motor Zone, 608 Pennistone Road, Sheffield S6 2SZ, tel: 01142 834949. Discounted Cars Worldwide Ltd, Brimaur Trade Centre, 51–53 Bury Road, Radcliffe, Manchester, tel: 0161 723 0000, 070808 112233, 0385 234299 (independent importer apparently offering a wide range of new cars from stock. Not checked out, so make your own enquiries). Reg Vardy Motor Zone, Chancellor Lane, Ardwick, Manchester M12 6JZ, tel: 0161 273 2273.

- **NORTH EAST:** Reg Vardy Motor Zone, Stoddart Street,

Shieldfield, Newcastle-upon-Tyne NE2 1AN, tel: 0191 232 3838.

- **SCOTLAND:** Reg Vardy Motor Zone, 5 Seafield Way, Seafield Road (between Portobello and Leith), Edinburgh, tel: 0131 669 3000.

Ex-fleet car specialists

- **LONDON:** The Great Trade Centre, 44–45 Hythe Road (off Scrubs Lane), White City, London NW10, tel: 020 8960 3366 (turn North from Western Avenue up Wood Lane at the BBC TV Centre. The Great Trade Centre is very cheap and stocks 2,000 cars, but requires a deposit for car keys and imposes a £41 sales charge).

- **MIDLANDS:** Arriva Used Vehicle Sales, London Street, Smethwick, Birmingham B66 2SH, tel: 0121 558 5141. Motor Nation, Mackadown Lane, Garretts Green, Birmingham, tel: 0121 786 1111.

- **WALES** and **WEST:** Carcraft at Empress Cars, Langland Way, Spitty Road, Newport, Gwent, tel: 01633 284800.

NEW-CAR PROBLEMS

Out of line

" *I bought a new MGF VVC in Abingdon in April 1998 and, apart from odd bits of plastic trim dropping off, have been very happy with it. Then in March, after 9,500 miles, I had a flat tyre and was horrified to discover that all four tyres had been worn down to their wire carcasses on their inside edges. Rover said I had driven over too many pot holes and hit kerbs too often, but still refunded me 50% of the cost of the new tyres as a goodwill payment. They also re-did the wheel alignment under warranty, but the report did not look as if it had been too bad. I am now concerned that I will have to buy another new set of tyres in a few months' time.* "

The fact that yours is a Fulham car may explain the damage from high kerbs and other vicious 'traffic calming' measures. But there have been instances of misaligned subframes on MGFs which the type of alignment check you had would not necessarily pick up. Your best bet is to take the car to a body and chassis alignment specialist such as Autolign on 01604 859424, Popplewells on 01992 561571, or for a cheaper but 'state of the art' suspension alignment check, take it to Micheldever Tyres on 01962 774437.

My idol won't idle

" *I bought a VW Golf Mk IV GT TDI 110 last September. In January 1999, at approximately 2,500 miles, the engine tick-over speed dropped significantly and the engine now shudders as one coasts to a halt and engages neutral. My local VW dealer could not diagnose any problem, so the matter was referred to VW's head office, but I have heard nothing since.* "

This is a very rare occurrence, but VW acknowledges that, when 'coasting' from around 20 mph in second gear with the clutch depressed or in neutral with the clutch engaged, something can happen in the engine-emissions control system that causes revs to fall. ECUs are usually replaced free of charge under warranty, but VW has been less sympathetic to owners of personally imported cars more than 12 months old. If the problem continues after an ECU replacement it could be due to a short circuit between the flywheel sender unit and the bell housing itself.

Running in

" *Will the low viscosity running-in oil in my new Nissan Almera 1.4 provide adequate lubrication when I take the vehicle on holiday to Spain in June? I estimate it will then have about 1,500–2,000 miles on the clock. The journey will involve a shared-driving single journey from St. Malo to Northern Spain at sustained motorway speeds. The handbook recommends a first oil change at 5,000 miles.* "

This is refreshingly different advice from the usual in a driver's manual. Normally, the first oil change is at 10,000 miles in order to promote a bit of wear and loosen the engine up. But since Nissan does it differently, follow Nissan's advice. Just be sure not to 'sustain' a cruising speed on the motorway. Vary it upwards and downwards, making sure you never 'load' the engine up inclines by staying in fifth when you really need fourth. If your average speed is considerably less than the autoroute speed limit, you will need to take more breaks because the drive will be more boring and will further increase your journey time.

Pull the other one

" *I purchased a new Fiesta 1.4 Zetec in a Ford sale for the reasonable price of £9,000. For no accountable reason, delivery was not until four weeks later, then, after two weeks use, I noticed that the front discs and calipers were different from each other. One side had a ventilated disc and the other a solid disc. The Ford dealer immediately offered to put this right, but I am now suspicious about the car. What do you think?* "

Simple misbuild. One assembly line worker put a solid disc on one side of the car, while his mate, working on the other side, used a ventilated disc. Make sure you get two ventilated discs. Here are some of the VIN codes which will enable you to date exactly when your Fiesta was built: XL May '99; XE April '99; XD March '99; XK Feb '99; XC Jan '99; WG Dec '98; WA Nov '98; WR Oct '98; WB Sept '98; WP Aug '98; WM July '98; WU June '98; WJ May '98; WT April '98; WS March '98; WY Feb '98; WL Jan '98.

Service with a smile

" *Last year I bought a new three-door Freelander and am delighted with it. My pleasure was tempered slightly when a grinding noise developed from the front nearside. I reported it to Land Rover Assist and within an hour a mechanic arrived, analysed the problem and organised recovery to the nearest Land Rover dealer. Within two hours of my call, a courtesy car was delivered for my use. The next morning, the dealer rang to say my Freelander was repaired and asked where it should be delivered. Two hours later, it was back on my drive, repaired and valeted, and the courtesy car was collected. If Rover had provided this sort of service 20 years ago, sales would never have slumped and there would never have been any question of BMW having to be called in to rescue the company from extinction.* **"**

Too right. I stopped buying British Leyland back then because not only did I hate unreliable cars, I simply couldn't stand having to grovel to some patronising service manager in yet another doomed attempt to get the car to run properly. Thankfully his breed is now as dead as the Austin Allegro and no one ever has to beg a garage to take their money. H.H. reports being quoted £100 by Unipart for a cv joint. When his jaw dropped, instead of being told to like it or lump it, he was immediately offered a remanufactured cv for £35. Could be we'll soon see the new generation of Rover dealers teaching British BMW dealers a thing or two.

Left standing

" *I purchased a Ford Mondeo, reg R396 HBW, from a dealer on 22 May 1999. The odometer reading was 10,453 miles. The car was first registered on 5 May 1998 to Hertz UK who told me they had re-sold the car back to Ford in August 1998 at four months old and with 10,411 miles on the odometer. I have no problem with this as the car is as it should be, but am concerned that the car would appear to have been held by Ford for eight months doing no more than 43 miles until the dealer bought it at auction. I am concerned that either the car was 'clocked' during this period or that it may have suffered damage by being left standing doing nothing. Ford GB could offer no information as to the status of the car during its eight months in limbo. Can you shed any light on its recent history and any damage it may have suffered if it was indeed left standing for eight months?* **"**

Four to eight months in a compound is normal

for an ex-rental Mondeo while Ford decides whether to refurbish it and sell it via Ford Direct, or to auction it off to the trade. This is exactly how I acquired my Mondeo 2.0LX, which seemed to have come to no harm between August 1998 and January 1999 apart from minor transporter damage. Your car will not have been clocked during its period in storage. But it may suffer from duff battery cells and, if stored outside, from rusted brake discs and a rusted exhaust system. If air-conditioned, some of the seals may have dried out. That said, I had no trouble at all from my battery, brakes, exhaust or a/c in 18 months of use. It's the most reliable and trouble-free car I've ever run.

Stop/start BMW

" Just under a year ago my mother bought a new BMW 318iSE from a BMW dealer. The car has suffered a number of different faults, but a serious and dangerous problem is that it has now started cutting out for no apparent reason. As you can imagine, this is highly dangerous on a motorway. How should we proceed with this matter? "

A reader who has been a thorn in the side of the motor industry over real and perceived injustices suffered exactly the same problem several years ago. BMW thought he was crying 'wolf' once too often. But eventually a North London BMW dealer finally diagnosed that the car was suffering from an intermittent fault in the fuel pump relay. I'm 99% sure this is what is wrong with your mother's car.

Jeremy was right

" For the first time in three years I can be happy about my 'P'-registered Vauxhall Vectra. I have sold the wretched thing. A brief summary of my *problems with it: steering clonking from new; camshaft speed sensor failed and was replaced three times; throttle-position sensor needed modifying to prevent stalling; gearbox drained itself of oil on my driveway; radio was replaced because it would not switch off and the traffic programme did not work; door seal split and was replaced; brake master cylinder failed and was replaced. I understand from my Vauxhall dealer that I was 'one of the lucky ones' whose power-steering fluid was not also dumped on my driveway. I feel very bitter that I was forced to become an unpaid quality controller and that the car cost me a fortune in repairs and depreciation. It was my fourth new Vauxhall, but I have replaced it with a Nissan Primera and will not buy another new Vauxhall.* **"**

What did the estimable Mr Jeremy Clarkson tell us when he first presented the Vectra on BBC 'Top Gear'?

Unconnected problem

" *I recently acquired a new Lexus IS200SE which I like a lot, but which was advertised as having a 'roof-mounted aerial with built-in antenna for use with a mobile telephone'. Alas, when Vodaphone came to fit the phone, they found there was no means of connecting it to this roof aerial and an ugly extra aerial had to be fitted.* **"**

Lexus dealers now offer a connector, part number 86705-50060, price £80.93 plus VAT, enabling UK mobile phones to be connected to the car's standard roof aerial. I like the IS200, too. It has the nicest steering of any Japanese car I have driven this side of an Impreza Turbo or Skyline GTR R34 – a far cry from the usual Lexus helm which has as much feeling as General Wiranto.

Rover springs a leak

" *I bought a new Rover 216i cabrio in 1998. Ever since new there has been a leak from the roof into the boot of the car which the Rover dealer* *has failed to stop. Now I am told that the leak is not covered by the three-year extended warranty I paid for when I bought the car. Have any other owners of Rover 200 Cabriolets suffered the same problem? If so, please could they write to me?* **"**

The fault may be in the boot seal rather than the roof. Smear a thin layer of Vaseline right round the steel sealing face of the boot, close the boot, open it again and look for any breaks in the Vaseline transferred to the rubber seal. This is an old model, on sale since April 1992, so if there is a general problem (and a solution) readers will undoubtedly write to R. Kendall, 14 Lark Hall Close, Macclesfield SK10 1QW.

Assault by battery

" *The sealed battery on my two-year-old Audi A8 4.2 literally exploded. Parts of the battery and acid were deposited around the boot. Audi paid for the repairs under warranty and explained that such an occurrence was very rare. But the recovery truck driver said it was not so unusual and can occur in any make of car using sealed batteries. I am concerned this may re-occur. Is there anything I can do to prevent it happening?* **"**

VAG supplies its excellent branded batteries 'dry', in kit form. The buyer carefully fills each cell using the acid supplied in bottles. Each kit contains a breather tube for use in Audi models where the battery is tucked away. This must have become detached or blocked in your car. Check that the replacement battery has a breather tube, that it is correctly routed and that it is not blocked.

Fuelling discontent

" *I have a Vectra 2.0iGLS, which I bought in September 1998 when it was 11 months old. It has a 60-litre tank which I always brim, but the amount* *of fuel needed to fill the tank does not equate to the amount that the fuel gauge says it needs. Some Vectras built in 1996 and 1997 had a minor fuel gauge fault, but mine was checked and pronounced OK. However, I was advised on the report that the gauge is only an indicator. How accurate should a fuel gauge be?* "

A fuel gauge relies on a float in the tank, so how accurate any messages set to the gauge can be depends partly on the efficiency of the float and sender, and partly on the shape of the tank. If the tank is tall and narrow, its contents in litres can be measured reasonably accurately. But if the tank is broad and flat, as the Vauxhall mechanic wrote, its contents can only be measured approximately, even when the car is standing on a level surface.

Delayed reaction

" *In his test of the new Skoda Fabia, Andrew English was extremely critical of its throttle response, to the point of stating that it could prove dangerous in some circumstances. Apparently this was to be corrected before the car went on sale. Then, in* Autocar *three months later I read a full road test, which made the same criticism and gave the reason as compliance with EU4 petrol-engine emissions regulations which come into force for new cars in 2005. What are your views?* "

Skoda tells me that the Fabia is the first car on sale that complies with EU4, that the delayed reaction is to prevent over-fuelling in order to comply with EU4 and that 'most drivers soon get used to it'. I tried a 68 bhp 1.4 version (likely to be the most popular) and found no problem pulling out of junctions, etc.. But if I tried to make very fast gearchanges or tried to drive in too high a gear, the throttle felt heavily damped. Because the engine is very softly mounted, this can also result in 'clonks' if you drive at all clumsily.

T4 trouble

" I would be interested to hear from anyone running a Volvo S40 or V40 T4 who is experiencing the same problem as mine. This manifests itself as an intermittent and temporary lack of response from the engine under acceleration, accompanied by vibration and, sometimes, a muffled back-firing sound. I believed it to be caused by a faulty or mis-programmed engine-management unit, but the Volvo dealer replaced this to no avail. "

This reader had a useful response to his appeal. Volvo actually replaced his first T4 at no cost, but, within two months, the replacement car developed the same problem. Volvo offered to buy this car back, but he was not happy with the amount offered. Instead, on instruction from Volvo Car UK, the dealer removed the car's cylinder head, de-coked and re-seated the valves and fitted a 'one-way valve for induction'. He is waiting to find out if this has effected a permanent cure. But the real cause may have been nothing more than trying to run the engine on lower grade fuel than it was designed for. Petrol turbocharged Volvos really need 98Ron Super petrol, as stated in the owners' handbooks. Because this is expensive and not generally available, 95Ron petrol may need an additive such as Millers Octane+ (for stockists, tel: 0800 281 053). Intermittent misfiring does not seem to be confined to T4s as owners of more mundane S40s and V40s have suffered similar problems, particularly during warm-up after a cold start during which the engine appears to over-fuel. If the petrol used does not contain adequate detergent, the misfiring may be caused by sticking valves, necessitating a fuel additive such as STP Fuel Injector Cleaner.

Flat C Class

" *Within five months of buying a new Mercedes Benz C180 it refused to start due to a discharged battery. I wrote to Daimler Chrysler in Stuttgart complaining that the battery could not sustain sufficient charge to re-start the engine if the car was only used three or four times a week or if it was left in an airport car park for 14–21 days. My letter and a subsequent fax were completely ignored and, though MB UK replied to my letter, the design problem was not mentioned. Then, reading the MB Owners' magazine I find that 'All C Class buyers can now expect an adjustable steering column, a high-capacity battery and alternator, and a useful storage net in the front passenger footwell.'* "

Though the problem was not admitted to, it was addressed. You should write to MB UK pointing this out and requesting the modifications to your car. If MB UK can't sort the matter out, it will be referred to the company's European Customer Care Centre in Maastricht.

TT trauma

" *As a regular reader of German motoring magazines I'm intrigued by the lack of interest outside Germany in the stability problems of the Audi TT. So far there have been over 50 crashes, seven deaths and 350 German owners contemplating bringing a culpable manslaughter charge against Audi. A TT-owning friend here in Spain contacted the local Audi dealer who told him there was no need to worry. As rectifying this problem is going to cost Audi at least £50 million it's probably not surprising they are trying to keep it quiet. Still, I'm surprised to see favourable mention of the TT in the* Daily Telegraph. "

I have never driven a TT, but I can tell you that every expert driver I have ever asked about this feels that there is not and never was a problem with the car – rather the way it was marketed. No car I know of will stick to the road at whatever speed you try to drive it round corners, particularly if you do something stupid like lifting off or braking after entering the corner. Driving any car safely at very high speeds requires considerable skill and concentration. What I can tell you is I have driven a 180 bhp two-wheel drive Seat Leon fitted with the electronic stability system which is to be fitted to the TT. If you leave it switched on, then try to fling the car about at 120 mph, the system does stabilise the car. But, and it's a big but, if you switch the electronic stability system off, the car is vastly more enjoyable to drive. That's where UK 'expert opinion' is coming from. The main problem the TT has suffered is the nut behind the wheel.

'Ve haf vays...'

" *Since we purchased our secondhand 'R'-reg. VW Passat TDI in June 1998 we have had a problem with the glow plug warning light remaining illuminated. Our local VW agent has tried to repair it at least eight times with no success and thinks that the Clifford alarm system is causing interference. But this has been disconnected for some time and still they cannot solve the problem.* **"**

This problem plagued the first year's production of Passat TDIs and no one knew the cure. What happens is that every time you take the car in for a service, its ECU is electronically interrogated by a box of tricks known as the VAG 1552. This is an interactive interrogator, and a slip of the finger can feed the message to a manual TDI that it is an automatic. This then sets off an error code that lights the glow plug warning light. The trouble is, there is nothing in the VAG 1552 instructions to warn of this, which is why your VW dealer has been scratching his head.

I want my gal back

" I have been without my 'R'-reg. Ford Galaxy TDI since the beginning of February. It has been undergoing body repairs, but the repairer can't get hold of a pipe for the air-conditioning unit (part no. 1029758). This has been on order since the middle of February. "

The a/c units of Galaxys, Alhambras and Sharans were vulnerable to accident damage because they were within the crumple zone very near the front of the vehicles. This was acknowledged and the components were relocated from 1999 build onwards. Part no. 1029758 is still used, but is currently on 'back order' through Ford's central parts distribution depot until another run of the part is manufactured. The company checked its press garage stores but did not have one there, so suggests that you or the repairer start phoning Ford, VW and Seat dealers to see if they have the part in stock. (The VW Sharan and Seat Alhambra are virtually the same vehicle.)

PD problem?

" Am I correct in understanding that production of VAG TDI 115 PD engines has been interrupted? If so, is it because of the discovery of a significant problem? I am thinking of buying a Golf estate with this engine although I would have preferred the tried and tested 110 bhp. This is no longer available in the UK, but I believe is still available elsewhere. I would appreciate your comments. "

There have been rumours, consistently denied by VW UK both this time and in the past. Apparently 70 early production TDI 115s arrived in the UK with insufficient coating on their pistons, but these were all recalled. A close relative of mine clocked up 16,000 miles in a

Passat PD 115 between September 1999 and June 2000 with no problems whatsoever and remains delighted with the car. The Golf TDI 110 is a very good diesel, but the PD 115 (identified by a red 'D' and 'I' on the 'TDI' badge) puts it into the shade. It has a mammoth 210 lb ft torque and an excellent twin-shaft ultra-compact six-speed gearbox giving over 30 mph per 1,000 rpm in sixth. This makes it a 125 mph car which is alternatively capable of 60 mpg, and creates the main reason for a shortage of cars: demand exceeds supply.

Crack-heads

" *In January 1996 I bought a new Jeep Cherokee with a 2.5 litre diesel engine. On 4 October 1999 at only 67,023 miles, two of the four separate cylinder heads cracked. This cost me £1,581.52. Then in March 2000, just after I sealed a deal to sell the vehicle, another of the original heads cracked costing £1,304.53 to replace before I could complete the deal. I have since heard that head failures are commonplace on this engine at between 65,000 and 75,000 miles, so hoped to obtain some compensation from Chrysler Jeep, but the dealer would not even submit a goodwill claim.* "

This problem was not unknown when Range Rover TDs and Rover 825 diesels were fitted with the Italian 2,499 cc VM engine and prospective purchasers were advised to look out for white exhaust smoke (steam) or mayonnaise under the oil filler cap. But I had not heard of problems with the Cherokee TD, Voyager TD, or the new Grand Cherokee 3.1TD which has a five-cylinder version of the same engine. Chrysler is checking its records of how many individual replacement cylinder heads it has issued through its UK parts centre.

Unimpreza'd

" *I purchased a new Subaru Impreza in January 1998. At 29,000 miles it developed a loud knocking noise on start-up. I was told that this was a known phenomenon, was not serious and would be cured under warranty by the fitting of a single replacement piston. I think that all pistons should be replaced, that the bores may have become damaged and that after the work has been done I should be provided with an extended warranty on the engine. These requests have been refused. I feel that the approach of Subaru UK to this problem can only be considered as inconsiderate, sarcastic and dogmatic.* "

Subaru UK carefully explained that the knocking is caused by a change of design of piston skirts from 1997, is not detrimental to the engine, is only apparent immediately after start-up and vanishes as soon as the engine reaches normal running temperature. Replacing just one piston is all that is necessary to get rid of the start-up noise. You have all this in writing. As added reassurance, Subaru recently issued a press release showing a secondhand Forester model with basically the same engine which has covered 150,000 miles, 140,000 of them as a 'Doctor on Call' vehicle. Plenty of Impreza Turbos turn up at auction with well over 100,000 miles and still running sweetly.

Inches underneath

" *We recently purchased a new VW Golf Mk IV and were very pleased with it until the heavy rain in May. While manoeuvring at about 5 mph in a flooded supermarket car park my wife drove into a puddle that concealed a pothole. There was a thump and a jolt, but we thought no more of it until the next day when we found a puddle of oil under the car engine's cast alloy sump. The VW emergency service engineer told us this was quite common because of the low ground clearance of the sump (just 102mm, or 4in, at full compression). Repairs cost me £205, so you'd be doing a service to other owners of Mk IV Golfs if you warned them of this shortcoming.* **"**

This was worth checking with VW UK. The lowest Mk IV Golfs are the new V6 4motion, the 1.8T and, if fitted with optional sports suspension, the 1.8 or 2.0 GTi. All the others ride around three quarters of an inch higher at five and a half to six inches, sinking to four to four and three quarter inches at full compression.

ODDBALLS

A Focus for £150

" *Further to the recent letters about customer loyalty, you might be interested in the story of Dermot Condon of Dublin. He bought his first Ford, a secondhand Prefect, for £150 from the Walden Motor Company in January 1949 and has purchased Fords from them ever since. When he went to ask about the new Ford Focus, his reward for 50 years' customer loyalty was a new Focus for £150 – the same he had paid for his original Prefect.* "

That's a new record. Interestingly, Walden Motor Company of Parnell Street, Dublin is bang up to date with an email address of cars@walden.ie (tel: 00 3531 873 0400, ask for Bill Wallace). Other readers can't expect to buy a Focus for £150, but it's worth making contact to check the Irish export price of rhd Irish-spec Focuses.

New loyalty record

" *I can beat the loyalty record set by Dermot Condon of Dublin who has bought Fords from the Walden Motor Company for 50 years. I have bought Wolseleys, Morrises, Austins and Rovers from Le Lacheurs Motors (now Ruette Braye Motors Ltd) since 1934, and my father before me bought cars from them from 1910 until his death in 1956. I may have been lucky, but I have only ever had four breakdowns in all of my cars, and one of them was caused by waves breaking over the coast road.* "

But will they be as generous as the Walden Motor Co. and sell you a new Rover 200 for the same price you paid for the first car you bought from them?

Roadside wrecks

" *Over the past 18 months I have noticed an alarming increase in the number of abandoned cars at the roadside. I presume this is as a result of the crash of the Far Eastern economies, reducing their demand for scrap from the UK and significantly lowering its price. It is no longer economic to take an old car to the scrap dealer. But am I correct in recalling that the Dutch had a similar problem and to solve it demanded a deposit whenever a car was registered, refundable only when the car was officially scrapped at the end of its life?* "

The UK actually imports far more scrap cars from the Far East than it exports to other countries. Most secondhand cars more than three years old imported from Japan would have been scrapped had they remained in that country. As well as coping with a fall in the price of scrap metal, conforming to EU environmental legislation has increased car breakers costs to such an extent that they now demand £25–£50 to 'dispose of' an old car. You are correct about the Dutch interpretation of the EC 'End of Life' directive, and the same rules may be coming to the UK soon. But some of the cars you see dumped at the roadside or down a lane or track are stolen, 'joyridden' 1980s models which the thieves then burn to destroy any forensic evidence.

Guide to the converted

" *Please advise me how to convert engine power and torque from Ps (EC) into bhp and Nm (EC) and M.kg (EC) into lb ft, and also explain why manufacturers appear to use the former whereas most UK car magazines and newspapers use the latter.* "

Ps works out as close to bhp as makes very little difference. Roughly to convert kW to bhp, add a third (eg 60 kW + 20 = 80 bhp). Roughly to convert Nm to lb ft, halve the Nm, then add half of the answer (eg 40 Nm ÷ 2 = 20, + 10 = 30 lb ft). Roughly to convert M.kg into lb ft, halve the M.kg, then add half of the answer and multiply by 10 (eg 20M.kg ÷ 2 = 10, + 5 = 15, x 10 = 150 lb ft). *Auto Express* has always used Nm. Other UK newspapers and magazines use bhp and lb ft because they remain far more easily understood in the UK.

Don't get ripped off on the motorways

" *Fed up with paying inflated prices for meals, snacks, sweets and fuel at motorway service areas, I have researched a book of cheaper alternatives just off the motorway. Most motorways, plus the A1, A2, A38, A494 and A604 are covered. The book costs £4.99 from any bookshop, is entitled Duffy's Cheaper Choices by Vincent Duffy (ISBN is 0-9532284-1-X).* "

Makes sense. But readers should be aware that petrol from some of the supermarket outlets listed may be cheaper, but may not always contain the quality and quantity of detergent additive needed to keep engine fuel systems clear of tars and gums. If in doubt, look for a notice or ask for a written assurance before filling up.

Supermarket ding-dong

" *The car park of our local Tesco lies on a slope, which means that carelessly abandoned shopping trolleys naturally migrate towards the lower end until they crash into a car. Finding my new A Class Mercedes so damaged, I reported the matter to the supermarket manager who entered it in*

a thick ledger labelled, 'Accidental Trolley Damage' and made out an insurance report. Why don't supermarkets do anything about the trolley menace? If they installed passive braking as in some airport trolleys (Kuala Lumpur Sepang, but not Heathrow Terminal 3), abandoned trolleys could not damage cars of their own accord. Better still, if they worked on a coin-release system as at French and Dutch supermarkets, they would not be abandoned at all. "

Good point. But Tesco must balance the cost of its trolley-damage insurance against the additional costs of passively braked trolleys or the cost of losing customers irritated by coin-release carts.

Water, water, *not* everywhere

" *A year ago, readers of your column helped save our charity by raising enough money for us to stay in the workshops where we re-build old trucks into water transporters for areas of the world where water is scarce. Over the last year our efforts have switched almost entirely to the Kosovar refugee camps and latterly to Kosovo itself where many wells had been poisoned. Most recently we prepared three tankers in support of the earthquake victims in Turkey.* "

Heartfelt thanks to every reader whose contributions helped to save this vital lifeline. Of course, the work of Action Water is never ending and readers who would like to make further donations should write cheques to 'Action Water' at Mount Hawke, Truro, Cornwall TR4 8BZ, tel: 01209 715385, email: info@actionwater.org.uk (Registered Charity No. 292673).

Small Jaguar, rhymes with 'newt'

" *On holiday in Japan I photographed what I thought was a late 1960s Jaguar. It turned out to be a Mitsuoka Viewt. Was this model Jaguar made under licence in Japan, or is it a very good copy?* "

Pastiche would be a better word, as the Viewt is around two thirds of the size of a Mk II Jaguar. It's really yet another Nissan-Micra based 'retro' special. Roland Danes of Park Lane (01420 544300) tells me they are very expensive even in Japan and it's likely that the cost of landing one, then paying import duty and VAT could set you back £20,000 plus. The positioning of the lights may also make it impossible to get through an SVA test.

Never lend to a friend

" *J.S. of Cambridge should have learned an important lesson when the torque wrench he loaned to a friend was returned broken. Never lend your best tools to anyone. Not friends. Not family. If they need a job doing, take your tool with you and do it for them. If someone doesn't own a torque wrench then the odds are they don't know how to use it properly. No offence, but serves you right, mate.* **"**

Though K.W.'s point of view is mean-minded, having lost all sorts of things loaned to friends from a walking stick to a tent I have some sympathy with it. Certainly never volunteer to lend anything to anyone. Better simply to give it away.

Tints

" *Recently my wife and I were startled when the rear window of our ageing Cavalier suddenly shattered. When we called Autoglass we were asked if the glass was clear or tinted. I thought clear, so ordered clear. But when the fitter came he pointed out that the rest of the car's glass was, in fact, slightly tinted and apparently known as 'bronze'. It never occurred to me that the glass was tinted and might not to some of your readers.* **"**

A useful reminder. To check, from the outside, look through the side glass, then open it and look through again. You're more likely to notice the tint looking into the car than looking out from it.

Own goal

I received a sad story via a local paper from Brian Kingston who runs the Brooklands Auto Project at Weybridge. This gives underprivileged youngsters the chance to gain motor-maintenance skills and learn to drive responsibly off public roads using cars which still run but have failed their MOTs. On 5 November, vandals made a bonfire of the project's cars, completely destroying ten of them. Not long afterwards, they did it again. But they haven't been able to since because the cars have now been moved to a plot adjacent to the site security centre. If any reader from the Weybridge area has a car which still runs but has failed its MOT and would like to donate it, phone Brian Kingston on 01932 845544, ext. 5434. (Note that many breakers now want paying to accept cars for recycling.)

Not switched on

" *Six months ago we purchased a Vauxhall Corsa for my wife. She has been very pleased with it, but complained that the only way she could get the interior light to stay on was to sit with a door open. I then consulted the manual and found that pulling the exterior light knob switches on the interior lights. Neither my mother in law nor my nephew knew about this, so I wonder how many other Corsa owners have failed to find the interior light switch.* "

Could be thousands if we include other Vauxhall models such as the old shape 1991–98 Astra which has the same type of switch. Always RTFM (read the flippin' manual). That's what it's there for.

Chop-top

" *I have a 1998 Bentley Mulsanne S which I would like to convert into a four-door convertible with a power hood. Would you know of any company that can assist me in my endeavours?* "

This is not an easy, straightforward job due to the amount of floorpan-strengthening needed. But it can and has been done by Jankel International, PO Box 1, Weybridge, Surrey KT13 8XR, tel: 01932 857766, website: www.jankel.com.

Happy motoring

" *I feel very sorry for all those people who write to you about their motoring problems. I have a 1968 Cortina Mk II De-Luxe 1300 cc crossflow which was originally purchased directly from Ford by my brother in law who worked there. I acquired the car from my sister in 1976 at 46,000 miles. I replaced the engine at 99,599 miles in June 1989 and the odometer currently reads 42,409 on its second time round. Apart from a couple of clutches and some welding, the car has been trouble-free. It is looked after by a small family-owned garage, which does me proud.* "

That's nice to know. After all, it was Henry Ford who put the world on wheels with his Model T, not by increasing prices as much as the market would stand, but by cutting costs and reducing prices so that greater numbers of people could afford to buy his cars.

Vroom with a view

" *At a recent MOT I was told that the car would have failed because the tax disc encroached on the driver's field of vision. The garage moved the tax disc to the top left of the screen where it is directly in the field of view of the passenger. I thought that the law required the tax disc to be displayed at the bottom left of the screen (as it is in almost every car I see). What is the legal position, please?* "

The MOT inspection manual states that official stickers, such as vehicle licences, are only a reason for rejection if they seriously restrict the driver's view. Reg. 16 of Road Vehicle (Registration and Licensing) Regs 1971 states that the licence should be displayed 'on or adjacent to the nearside and clearly visible in daylight from the nearside of the road'. Interpretation obviously depends on the width and depth of the screen.

Metrifistupefaction

" *The letter concerning Twingo speedometers caused me to reflect that it is deeply ironic that my butcher can be up before the beak for selling me beef by the pound rather than by the kilogram, yet on his way to court he can be stopped and booked by a vigilant policeman because his speedometer reads in kilometres instead of miles.* "

Britain is riddled with ironies like this. While the rest of Europe simply ignores silly laws, we employ jobsworths to enforce them.

Breathless

" *Why is it that it is always the passenger side of the windscreen that de-mists first and the driver's side second?* "

Because if you are alone in the car your breath will condense on the nearest cold surface. It helps to open the driver's side window while attempting to de-mist.

Hot tip

" *To remove dealer window stickers without damaging the heated rear-window element use a hair dryer on a gentle setting to soften the adhesive. I refer to J.M. of Littlehampton's letter headed 'Coming unstuck' on 18 March.* "

Many thanks, but would readers please be very careful indeed if they try this. Don't get the hairdryer nozzle too close to the glass.

Sweet smell of success

" *Hanna Collip, a final year student in Professor Mark Porter's Ergonomics Unit at Loughborough University, may have come up with an aromatherapy cure for road rage. Sensors detect when a driver's stress level is rising and release a calming scent, or, when the driver is too relaxed, they release a revitalising scent. As a result, she will be receiving a grant from the Audi Foundation to develop the idea, and has been invited to the Audi plant in Ingolstadt to meet the 'nose team' who develop the way cars present themselves aurally.* "

The Audi Foundation exists to support young designers and engineers in all fields, not merely automotive, to take their ideas from concepts to working prototypes. The first grant of 31 to date was made in February 1998 and so far £130,000 has been provided. For more information, contact Michael Farmer at the Audi Foundation on 01908 601570.

Smelling a rat

" *My 'N'-registered Renault Laguna smells of fish inside the cabin. It is worse when the fan is on. Also the windscreen steams up. Any ideas?* "

The heater matrix has probably failed. Lift the carpet and if the underfelt is damp you need a new matrix and face a fat bill.

OUT-OF-WARRANTY CLAIMS

Peugeot 'goodwill'

" I am writing to ask if you can help me over an out-of-warranty claim against Peugeot. It concerns a Peugeot Boxer 2.5 litre turbo-diesel van which I purchased new from a Peugeot dealer in February 1996, and which had covered 37,036 miles when the timing belt snapped, wrecking the engine. This was by no means the first fault with the vehicle. It was constantly in and out of the dealers during the first year's ownership, after which I had it serviced by an independent garage. Peugeot has refused to consider any goodwill payment towards the cost of the £1,351 repair and £280 for the hire of a replacement van while the work was being carried out. "

I've received a spate of rejected Peugeot out-of-warranty claims, but I'm afraid I can't do anything about this one. As Peugeot's letters explained, the reason why the company would not entertain a goodwill claim was that the vehicle had not been serviced by its dealer since September 1997 at 18,000 miles. The timing belt may have failed as the result of an oil leak (usually from the camshaft end seal) and this is something the Peugeot dealer should have looked for during routine servicing and warned you about. The dealer may also have received Technical Service Bulletins to pro-actively replace certain parts free of charge during routine servicing. Though Peugeot suggests a timing belt 'life' of 72,000 miles, this assumes no other detrimental factors, such as oil leaks, failure of the tensioner or tensioner bearing, or failure of other components driven by the timing belt. On PSA engines, I have always recommended erring on the safe side with a change of timing belt, camshaft end seal and tensioner every 35,000–40,000 miles or every three to four years. As from 1 January 2000 Peugeot extended its new car warranty to three years subject to Peugeot-franchise servicing.

An amazing gesture from Mazda

" *I have an 'M'-registered Mazda 626. I began to experience problems with the handbrake, and my local garage told me the calliper needed replacing at a cost of £183. The work was done and I then wrote to Mazda expressing my shock at the cost of this failure on my low-mileage car. I did not ask for any money and wasn't expecting any, but Mazda wrote back asking me for the car's service record and a copy of the bill. Within a very short period of time they refunded the entire amount. I will, of course, be buying another Mazda 626.* "

Rear handbrake callipers on disc-braked cars tend to fail more due to age, lack of use and being left applied for long periods than they do due to mileage. If your garage floor is level, it's usually better to leave the car in first or reverse gear with the handbrake off than to leave it pulled up hard. This also helps prevent localised rusting of the disc underneath the pads when you park up on a wet day. But all credit to

Mazda for looking after its customer – and keeping him. This seems to be Mazda policy as several other readers have informed me of similar cases.

Rusty E Class

" *In May 1996 I collected a new Mercedes Benz 200E from the factory having paid a UK MB dealer £35,000 for the privilege. At the 54,000-mile service, I was told the car needed a new water pump and a goodwill claim would be made to MB UK for reimbursement. I have also discovered rust around the boot lock and the MB dealer has quoted £334.04 for the necessary repairs. Even though new Mercedes Benz cars carry a three-year warranty, MB UK refused goodwill payments for either problem. Do you think I am reasonable in expecting MB UK to help me over failures which were totally unexpected on a £35,000 car?* "

Unless the engine has been overloaded, the water pump should not have failed so soon on any car, never mind one of this quality, and I am surprised that the MB 'goodwill' system let you down. As for the rust, yours is the second case readers have alerted me to, and I have noticed exactly the same problem around the protective outer shields of the boot locks on E Class Mercs seen parked. If this is the result of key damage, then MB can't reasonably be held liable. But if there is a fundamental problem, then a solution should be found, even if it merely consists of treating the affected area and installing a larger-diameter protective plastic shield.

I would have if I could have

" *In December 1997 I bought an ex-demonstrator June 1997 Rover 214 from my local Rover dealer. I dutifully had it serviced there in 1998 and 1999. Then, in November 1999, at 16,000 miles, the gearbox failed. I wrote to Rover seeking a goodwill payment towards the cost of this (£744), but was told that since the Rover dealer had recently lost its franchise its servicing did not count for 'goodwill' purposes. But where else was I supposed to get it serviced if the local franchise had been withdrawn?* **"**

Happily, after just one phone call, Rover saw the unfairness and offered 75% of the parts cost. If there's a lesson to be learned here, it's to phone Rover Customer Services on 0800 620 820 rather than to write. We now live in a world of immediate responses, and though I will sometimes plough through a reader's 50-page file, it's too much to ask of a customer services person who could have responded to 20 phone calls in the same amount of time.

Water over the bridge

" *I have owned a Renault Megane 1.9 turbo-diesel since I purchased it new from Arriva Derby three years and 27,500 miles ago. It has always been serviced, as scheduled by Arriva, Lowmoor Road, Kirkby in Ashfield and no one else had touched it up to the point at 26,000 miles when the water pump failed, seven miles from home and I was obliged to have it replaced locally. At the time, I was told the pump bearings had failed because the drive belt was over-tight. I complained to Arriva and was told that had they replaced the water pump they would have submitted a goodwill claim to Renault on my behalf and that it would very probably have been paid. I was also told that the belt tension had never been checked or altered as part of any service they had carried out. That means that the belt must have been over-tight since the car was new and, so I feel that Renault is to blame and should pay up. What can I do?* **"**

Phone Renault Customer Relations and point all this out. The manufacturer will have a policy of only meeting goodwill claims if the remedial work is carried out at one of its franchises. But if you explain the full circumstances it should at least meet part of your claim.

PARTS AND ACCESSORIES

Milosovich motors

" One thing NATO planners neglected to take account of was the effect of a prolonged war on Yugo drivers. The spare parts situation is a nightmare. Any idea where I can get hold of some? "

NATO has even bombed the Yugo factory. But three years ago, J.R. of East Barnet, kindly supplied the name and address of a Yugo parts specialist, which is GGB Engineering Ltd, 98 White Hart Lane, London N22 5SG or on a mail-order basis (tel: 020 8888 2354). GGB also carries parts for Alfa Romeo, Fiat, Lancia and Lada cars. Some Fiat parts will fit or can be adapted to. Other Yugo parts people include: Yugo Cars, tel: 01202 822154/896290, fax: 01202 813250, website: www.yugo.co.uk; Nottingham Road Car Sales, 271–275 Nottingham Road, Derby DE21 6AP, tel: 01332 343011; and John Childs (Garages) Ltd, Brabourne, Ashford, Kent TN25 6QQ, tel: 01303 813118, email: ChildsCars@aol.com.

Anyone got a light?

" Normally I carry a selection of spare bulbs and fuses in the car. But, having given my spare side-lamp bulb to a neighbour, I noticed one of my

own had failed while I was filling up with City Diesel at Sainsburys in Banbury. No problem, I thought. I'll get one in the service station shop. Some hope. Not only did Sainsburys not stock replacement bulbs, neither did the next three service stations on my journey to Kidlington. I could have had hot pies, sandwiches, a cup of coffee, even tulip bulbs, but none had any side-lamp bulbs. I eventually found one in an Asian grocery store in Kidlington. They also had fan belts, fuses, oils, filters – and some very tasty samosas. Surely filling stations should get back to catering for the motorist instead of merely catering? **"**

With limited shelf space, these places try to stock products which offer a high turnover at a reasonable margin. But I've never had any problem picking up spare bulbs, fuel injector cleaner, the *Daily Telegraph* or anything else I needed at Shell Select shops.

Exhaust blow

" *I drive a 95N VW Corrado VR6, which now has 41,000 miles on the clock. At the 40,000-mile service I was told that I needed a new rear silencer box and clamp which would cost around £500 including labour and VAT. Do you feel that this repair seems excessive at such a low mileage? The part I need is 'dealer supply' only as I have tried a couple of VW specialists in an effort to get a cheaper one.* **"**

Hilton Holloway of *Car* magazine mentioned exactly the same point to me. The Corrado seems to be the only VW model for which there is no cheap aftermarket supply of parts. A blown rear box after four years and 40,000 miles is run of the mill for a catalysed car partly because it's the last section of the exhaust system to heat up and evaporate acidic condensation which rots the box from the inside out. If you get together with other owners, you might be able to secure 'bulk buys' of parts direct from Germany and the best way of doing that is to join the VW Corrado Club of Great Britain, c/o Chris Rochford, 20 Melford Drive, Macclesfield, Cheshire SK10 2TW, tel: 01625 511783.

Mirror images

No manufacturer bothered to respond to my offer to publish low prices for door mirror part replacements. However, A.B. of Shelsley Beauchamp tells us that Peugeot supplies door mirror shells for 405s for a mere £10. While C.R. of Rutland was quoted £8.83 plus VAT for a door mirror shell for a Ford Focus Ghia, plus £45.53 plus VAT for the heated, electrically adjustable mirror itself. When T.H. of Melksham was quoted £320 to replace the entire electric folding mirror of his Chrysler Neon, he followed my suggestion and went to American car service specialists AC Automotive of London W12 (020 8741 9993). They had a new glass made and fitted for £25 plus VAT.

Rubber dub dub

" My Australian mate Bruce is an old car enthusiast who owns, amongst others, a Model T Ford and a Humber Vogue. The Vogue is a 1964/65 Series III, which was based on the Hillman Super Minx and was sold in the UK as the 'Singer Vogue'. He and I are both having terrible trouble trying to get hold of sealing rubber strips for the front quarter-lights. I have tried the Hillman Owners' Club (which failed to reply to my letter) and several specialists all of whom say that the parts are unobtainable. Can you help? "

Clubs sometimes buy up manufacturers' spares stocks for obsolete models. Are you sure you wrote to the correct club address? The latest I have for the Hillman Owners' Club is c/o C. Gore, 6 Askham Grove, Upton, Pontefract WF9 1LT. Also try the Association of Singer Car Owners, c/o Anne Page, 39 Oakfield, Rickmansworth, Herts WD3 2LR, tel: 01923 778575, email: http://www.uk-classic-cars.com/singer.ht. I tried East Kent Trim Supplies (01304 611681) who are very good and do windscreen rubbers for the model but told me that demand for quarterlight rubbers was insufficient to justify the tooling costs required to produce reproductions. This is often the case with trim parts for older saloon cars.

The £714 spark-plug lead

" *I own a 1992 Audi V8 4.2 litre and need to replace the ignition leads. Audi wants a staggering £714 for the parts. Yet I was quoted £238 for the same parts from a Canadian Audi dealer. This unfair UK pricing must end, I would appreciate your comments.* "

Though VAG reckons to make two to three times as much profit on the sale of parts throughout a car's life as it makes on the original car, the company will look at parts price anomalies like this and I brought it to VAG's attention.

Quieter Cinquecento

" *I would like to add soundproofing to my Fiat Cinquecento, but cannot find a supplier.* "

B.J. Acoustics, 289 Featherstall Road North, Oldham, Lancs OL1 2NH, tel: 0161 627 0873.

Heavy bill for light

" *The glass lens of one of the foglights of my Nissan Primera was recently stone damaged. The light still functions perfectly and the lens is removable. However, the Nissan dealer does not sell lenses separately and will only quote me for a complete foglight at £70. This is a total rip-off and extortionate. Parts costs of this nature would put me off buying this model again as a matter of principle.* "

This situation is not unusual, but there is a way round it. Nissan will not have made the foglight, so what you need to do is find out who did, then order a new lens through your local motor factor. Your motor factor may even be able to help you find the part as they have a commonality cross-referencing system.

Three-in-one

" *1) Can you recommend a high-quality car battery? 2) Can you recommend a high-quality exhaust system? 3) Are pattern-type oil filters worth buying and, if so, which?* "

1) AC Delco Freedom battery from AC Delco, 19 Wadsworth Road, Unit 14, Perivale, Middx, tel: 020 8810 4595, or from Vauxhall dealers. 2) If the car is a Japanese or a VW, the original equipment exhausts are best. Alternatively, talk to the London Stainless Steel Exhaust Centre, 251 Queenstown Road, London SW8 3NP, tel: 020 7622 2120. 3) Don't touch pattern oil filters because they may not contain the correct internal valving and you can't tell by looking at them. There's no point in saving £2, then doing in your engine. Only buy OE filters or those made by the parts manufacturer who supplies the car manufacturer.

Dry batteries for cars

" *If the breather of a wet battery becomes blocked, it will result in an expensive mess as sulphuric acid is highly corrosive. A much safer option is the Optima 'dry' battery, developed and manufactured in the USA and now available in the UK (01243 514214). These offer exceptionally high*

starting power, longer than normal operating life and will even continue to work for several months having sustained damage such as a 6in nail through them. "

Thank you for this. Other readers have asked about similar batteries in the past and I was unable to help them.

On deflection

" *On a recent holiday in Madeira I was very impressed with the plastic rain/wind deflectors that seemed to be fitted to most cars there. These allow you to drive with a window partially open for ventilation but prevent any rain being blown into the vehicle. I cannot find them in the UK. Do you know of a supplier?* "

ClimAir of Sidcup offers a range which are German TUV approved, are available to fit 95%

of current vehicles. They cost £49.95 a pair for the front windows and £35.95 a pair for the rears. ClimAir also offers sunroof deflectors for £49.95 (tel: 01208 309 7744, fax: 0208 309 5177, or write to ClimAir UK, 1 Station Parade, Sidcup, Kent DA15 7DB). E.R. of Keighley tells us that another firm still makes deflectors for certain older vehicles. This is: Exhaust & Injector Co. Ltd, 11 Wadehouse Road, Shelf, Halifax HX3 7PF, tel: 01274 679524.

Not-so-lucky mascot

" *I have an old and coveted car mascot, which has been proudly displayed on my cars over the years. I now have a new car and wish to fix the mascot to it, but I am not sure about the present legal requirements.* "

I quote from *Hughes Guide to Traffic Law for the Enforcement Officer*, which is updated every six months (to subscribe, tel: 01908 639233/234): Reg. 53 Road Vehicles (Construction and Use) Regulations 1986: 'No mascot, emblem or other ornamental object shall be carried by a motor vehicle in any position where it is likely to strike any person with whom the vehicle may collide unless the mascot is not liable to cause injury to such a person by reason of any projection thereon.' This seems to mean folding MB stars and RR Spirits of Ecstasy are allowed, but not bonnet mascots which could penetrate a person's skull.

Bugged by flies

" *Motoring in the autumn when there are a lot of insects I seem to collect a great number on the windscreens of both my Honda CRV and my wife's A-Class. They prove resistant to normal windscreen washer chemicals. Is there a stronger washer fluid?* "

When I remember I use Holts BUG Shifter, which seems to do the job. *Autocar* magazine recommends Comma Xstream as best value for winter use, but STP Windscreen washer as the most powerful.

Deflecting down

" *Months ago I wrote to you seeking information about exhaust pipe deflectors so I could avoid sooty marks on my garage door, trouser cuffs and caravan. You gave a couple of names, both too far away, but I never gave up and finally located a source of supply. This is Big Wheels, 14 Flexi Units, Budlake Road, Marsh Barton Industrial Estate, Exeter, tel: (enquiries) 01392 215661, (sales) 01823 259184; Cardiff branch, tel: 029 2036 1030. The cost was a mere £11.13 for a deflector to fit the 65-mm pipe of my Nissan Terrano II.* "

Many thanks for this information. But it should be noted that some cars, notably late model Escorts and Mondeos, already have exhaust pipe outlets pointing at the ground.

Double-edged wipers

" *I have yet to find really effective windscreen wipers but I do recall, some years ago, that a manufacturer started producing double-edged blades, which were far more efficient. Do you know if these are still available?* "

Bosch make 'twin-rubber' wiper blades that combine a soft synthetic spine with a hard rubber edge. You can get them from any branch of Halfords at sensible prices, as I did just before Christmas. They take a few days to 'wear in', but after that are very good. The only downside is that the 'universal fitting' does not look as good as that of the standard items.

Bully bars

" What do you think of 'bull bars'? What do you think of magazine or paper editors who advertise them? What do you think of journalists who are prepared to test and write about vehicles fitted with them? "

I think that bull bars perform a useful function in protecting the bodywork of vehicles driven across open moorland, through jungle terrain, and on roads through wilderness areas where animals such as kangaroos are a hazard. In towns or suburbs, the functions they serve are to intimidate other drivers and to kill pedestrians, especially children. Strange that you see so many fitted to large 4x4 vehicles used by housewives for the suburban 'school run'. Steel bull bars have already been outlawed for road use in the States of Jersey. The EC should issue a directive to outlaw them throughout the EU. But until this happens manufacturers and some motoring journalists will continue to pander to the aggression of the public.

Perfectly exhausted

" I am writing to recommend Longlife Stainless Steel Exhausts of Cardiff. They recently fitted a stainless steel exhaust system to my BMW and went to exceptional lengths to ensure I was perfectly happy with the system. The exhausts are tailor made to suit the car and I am now benefiting from an improvement of 3.7 miles per gallon as well as a much more pleasing exhaust note and the satisfaction of knowing the system will probably outlast the car. "

Directory Enquiries tells me that Longlife Stainless Steel Exhausts of Cardiff can be contacted on 01222 489657. The address is 1 Shakespear Street, Cardiff CF24 3ES.

Fun in the sun

" I am desperate. Please help if you can. I own a Mercedes 280S five-speed manual and wish to install a new 380 engine with auto gearbox, at the same time changing the front springs, drive-shaft, rear differential, etc.. My local Mercedes agent can't help and various attempts to obtain what I require from suppliers in Germany, Holland and Belgium have not produced any results. Can you provide me with the names and addresses of possible suppliers, please? "

I have to say, I find this a very strange request because a new 380 V8 engine and gearbox will cost many times what a 1981–91 W126 S Class Merc is worth. You'd be far better off buying a complete car. That said, your best source for parts is a German magazine entitled, appropriately enough, *CRASH*, which is published by the same people as the famous *DAZ* (required reading for anyone thinking of importing a second-hand lhd from Germany). The publisher is Crash-Mobiles, DAZ Verlag (GMBH & Co.), Mediateam KG., Postfach 1854, 22908 Ahrensburg, tel: 00 49 41 02 47 87-0, email: Anzeigenannahme@t-online.de. In the six-month-old issue I have, complete W126 380SEs with 136k to 196k km were going for Dm 4,000–Dm 4,800.

Musical chairs

" We have just bought a 20-month-old Galaxy and would like to install two integrated child seats. But out local agent tells us that these cost £300 each. Is there anywhere you could recommend I go to in order to get some cheaper, or even secondhand. Do any breakers specialise in this sort of kit? "

The best parts-finding services are Find a Part One Call on 0891 662706 and National Parts

Locator on 0800 525 030. Others include Premier Spares on 0800 092 6700 and 1st Choice Spares on 0906 910 8400. But, having had a request for a clip-in portaloo only last week, it strikes me that there might be a lease market for seats and accessories, such as Eskies, shower reservoirs and internal bike racks which clip into the seat mountings.

The part is over

" *I bought a new Nissan Primera in August 1996. On 16 May this year the throttle cable broke. When I contacted my local Nissan dealer I was told that the part could not be delivered before 23 May. Nissan Motor (GB) Ltd confirmed that this was the case and that the part would have to come from its European parts centre in Amsterdam. I expressed my shock and horror at this, but was told that such parts for four-year-old cars were not kept in stock and would have to be specially made. Fortunately my local Nissan dealer was much more helpful and agreed to remove one from a similar used car in its stock. Nevertheless I will not be purchasing another Nissan.* "

This problem is by no means confined to Nissans. Earlier this year, to name but a few, it was impossible to get rear wings for Rover 600s and air-conditioning parts for Ford Galaxys. The reason is that parts for obsolete models either have to be individually made (Nissan's 'just in time' policy) or batch-made then held in stock (less efficient because it interrupts current production and ties up capital). The way to be reasonably sure of instant or overnight parts availability is to run a very popular current model car, or to run a long-lasting older car such as a VW Golf Mk II, parts for which are still readily available from VW dealers and aftermarket suppliers.

RECALLS
1998–2000*

1998 recalls

- Audi A3: 2,822 cars recalled due to possibility of rear seat-belt fixing brackets cracking.

- Audi A4, A6, A8 with 2.8 litre V6 30-valve engine: 4,574 cars built between August 1997 and February 1998 recalled due to possibility of jammed throttle.

- BMW E30 3-Series (1983–90): 170,000 UK-market cars recalled because valve in radiator cap may seize up, over-pressurise cooling system and cause hot coolant to leak into cabin.

- Chrysler Voyager and Grand Voyager (old model not marketed in UK): recall in USA after fatalities due to faulty rear-door latches. Voluntary recall in Europe.

- Citroën Xsara: 14,000 owners of cars built September 1997 – February 1998 notified that may be a delay in airbag inflating in the event of an accident. Also possibility of faulty seat-belt pre-tensioner.

- Ferrari F355: possible fault with steering-column bolt.

* SMMT Recall Hotline: 0171 235 7000 – ask for Consumer Affairs Department. Or Department of Transport Vehicle Safety Branch: 0117 954 3300. Please note, these lists include known 'in-service modifictations' as well as official safety recalls.

- Fiat Punto (March '97 – Nov '97 build): faulty seat-belt pre-tensioner.

- Fiat Tempra 1.8, 2.0 and 1.9TDS (1993–96): front coil springs could fracture.

- Fiat Bravo/Brava 1.4 and 1.6 with ABS built before Oct '97: check for chafing of brake hoses.

- Fiat Marea 1.6 16v, non-ABS: check for chafing of brake hoses.

- Ford Ka with ABS (Mar '98 – Sep '98): brake master cylinder may fail.

- Ford Fiesta, Courier, Courier Combi (July 1995 – June 1996: 67,000 cars): possibility of brake failure due to front brake pipe chafing on bracket. Modified pipe and bracket to be fitted to both front brakes. (Announced on radio 12 February 1998.)

- Ford Fiesta with ABS (Mar '98 – Sep '98): brake master cylinder may fail.

- Ford Fiesta (with passenger airbag built August '96 – Feb '98): passenger airbag may go off while car is stationary.

- Ford Puma with ABS (Mar '98 – Sep '98): brake master cylinder may fail.

- Ford Escort (with passenger airbag built August '96 – Feb '98): passenger airbag may go off while car is stationary.

- Ford Mondeo (with passenger airbag built August '96 – Feb '98): passenger airbag may go off while car is stationary.

- Ford Mondeo V6 with ABS (Dec '97 – Jan '98): ABS system may fail.

- Ford Scorpio (with passenger airbag built August '96 – Feb '98): passenger airbag may go off while car is stationary.

- Ford Explorer (1996–98): oil pump recall notice issued January 1998.

Explorer TSBs (Technical Service Bulletins) include curing transmission shudder. Accelerator may be jammed open by the driver's floormat.

- Hyundai Accent built 1994–97: possibility of road-salt corrosion to front coil spring, causing spring to damage tyre.

- Jaguar XK8 and XJ8 (July – October 1997: 11,221 cars): may suffer sudden deceleration due to weak retention bracket on accelerator cable. Extra clip 'costing pennies' solves the problem. (Announced on radio 7 February 1998.)

- Land Rover Freelander: clutch system for part-time 4x4 system found to be failing. Replaced 'in service' by Land Rover agents. (Not an official recall.) Worldwide recall of all Freelanders built June '97 – June '98 (22,300) due to possibility of rear suspension collapse owing to faulty welding on suspension arms.

- Land Rover Discovery (Jan '94 – Mar '97): airbag may go off involuntarily.

- Land Rover Range Rover Classic (Jan '94 – Mar '97): airbag may go off involuntarily.

- Land Rover Range Rover V8 (all current shape models): official recall to check and replace underbonnet cooling-system hoses.

- Lexus LS400 (built April '95 – June '96): risk of underbonnet fire due to faulty wiring.

- Lotus Esprit: 200 V8 models recalled for new timing belt, idler pulley bearings, new clutch and fifth gear locknut, cost to Lotus at least £1,500 per car. Also check rear alloy wheels for hairline cracks.

- Mazda 121 (Fiesta shape, built Dec '95 – June '96): possibility of brake failure due to front-brake pipe chafing on bracket. Modified pipe and bracket to be fitted to both front brakes.

- Mazda 626 (Nov '96 – May '97): possibility of timing-belt failure leading to total loss of engine power and power assistance to steering and brakes.

- Mazda 626 diesel (to May '98 build): faulty fuel injector may stall engine.

- Mercedes Benz V Class and Vito van (1996–98): tread may separate from tyres.

- MGF (Aug '95 – Jul '98): faulty driver's seat-belt.

- Nissan Almera (Dec '97 – May '98): inertia reel sea-belts may not lock on impact.

- Peugeot 106 (Jan '98 – Mar '98): engine wiring harness may chafe.

- Peugeot 306 (Sep '97 – Oct '97): steering-wheel hub may crack.

- Peugeot 306 (Nov '97 – Apr '98): front suspension may collapse.

- Porsche 911 Carrera (1998 model: 540 UK cars): wrong size pulley fitted driving ancillaries drive belt which may slip affecting PAS, brakes, water pump and alternator.

- Proton Persona and Compact with 13in wheels (Aug '97 – Aug '98): front tyres may lose pressure.

- Renault Clio (June '97 – Nov '97): possibility of 'inadvertent deployment of airbags'.

- Renault Megane Scenic (June '97 – Sep '97): roof bars may fail under load. Replacements redesigned and sourced from a different manufacturer.

- Renault Laguna: 'plip' key transmitters can go out of sequence due to static or fiddling with them in the pocket. Improved 'plip' key transmitters now available free of charge to Laguna owners. (Per BBC

'Watchdog' 12 February 1998.)

- Renault Laguna diesel: cambelt tensioner may lead to premature failure of cambelt – to be checked as a TSB item at services.

- Renault Laguna (June '97 – Dec '97): 17,000 cars recalled due to possibility of 'inadvertent deployment of airbags'.

- Renault Laguna: not an official recall but large numbers of Laguna heater matrixes replaced free of charge when they began to emit coolant into the interiors of the cars.

- Skoda Felicia (with airbag): wiring for airbag may chafe.

- Suzuki Vitara two-door (Oct '91 – Oct '93): front seat-belt stalk may fracture.

- Vauxhall Corsa diesel ('K' to 'N' reg.: 26,000 cars): live cable may rub against bonnet hinge, lose insulation and cause a fire. (3 June 1998: helplines 01189 458500, 0800 455466.)

- Vauxhall Corsa 1.0 12v ('P' to 'R' reg.: 8,000 cars): cable may touch engine inlet manifold. (3 June 1998: helplines 01189 458500, 0800 455466.)

- Vauxhall Vectra (all 200,000 built 1995–98): handbrake cable subject to premature wear. Modified cable free replacement service.

- Vauxhall Vectra automatics: in-service modification to autobox ECU mapping.

- Vauxhall Sintra: catches for removing the seats may sever fingers. Covers to be fitted to seat-release lever mechanism.

- All 16-valve and 24-valve Vauxhalls from 'L' reg to 'P' reg.; also Vectras and Omegas 'P' to 'R': general warning issued to refer vehicle to a Vauxhall agent to have timing belt and timing-belt idler wheel replaced before car reaches 40,000 miles or four years old, whichever comes first. Otherwise idler wheel may disintegrate and timing belt snap, wrecking engine.

- VW Passat (Dec '95 – Mar '98): may be airbag-activator fault.

- VW Passat Synchro (Dec '97 – Apr '98): throttle and brake hose problems.

- VW Passat: 11,450 Passats built between May and November 1997 recalled due to potential fault affecting front seat-belts. Involves replacing complete belt units.

- VW Sharan (Aug '96 – Feb '98): loss of power due to wiring loom failure.

1999 recalls

- Alfa 156, June, 1999: safety recall No. 4054 to modify rear hinge mounting on all four side doors to prevent hinges splitting from doors.

- Audi A4: recall of 'S'-registered cars for brake modification.

- Audi A4: recall of 2.5 V6 TDIs for major engine modifications.

- Audi TT: German recall of Audi TTs to alter suspension anti-roll bars and fit a rear spoiler to overcome tendency to oversteer on high-speed corners.

- Bentley Arnage: possibility of short-circuit in heated seats.

- New BMW E46 3-Series from April 1998: safety recall over failure of brake-pedal clip which can allow the pedal to become disconnected and over sensitive side airbag trigger switches. (*Daily Telegraph*, 28 May 1999.)

- Fiat Barchetta: problem of sticking control valve for engine variable valve timing – makes engine sound like a diesel. Announced on BBC 'Watchdog' 21 January 1999.

- Fiat Cinquecento: recall of 50,000 cars to replace rusted fuel tanks (actual date of recall not known).

- Ford Focus: 61,000 card built September '98 – March '99 recalled for better waterproofing of alternators to prevent short-circuits. Announced *Daily Telegraph* 16 July 1999. Cars built September – November 1998 recalled in October 1999 to cure possible failure of door latches.

- Ford Mondeo: cars built September – November 1998 recalled in October 1999 to cure possible failure of door latches.

- Ford Cougar: cars built September – November 1998 recalled in October 1999 to cure possible failure of door latches.

- Ford Galaxy, Seat Alhambra, VW Sharan: 80,000 vehicles recalled to check for contamination of brake fluid through vent. Announced *Daily Telegraph*, 15 December 1999.

- Land Rover new Discovery: October 1999 recall of all 9,296 new Discoverys built to date to cure problem with ABS brakes. Ten minutes' work required.

- Lexus GS300: all GS300s built July '95 – July '97 recalled to replace potentially faulty suspension links. Announced June 1999.

- Renault Laguna: leaking heater matrixes continued to be replaced free of charge.

- Rolls Royce Silver Seraph: possibility of short circuit in heated seats.

- Rover Mini: 5,000 Minis built from August 1996 recalled for rectification of a braking system fault. Announced on BBC radio news 14 May 1999.

- Saab 9000 range 1993 and 1994 (5,300 cars): possibility of moisture corrupting computer chips which control passenger-airbag trigger mechanism.

- Seat Arosa: cold weather fault with the 1.4 automatic, manifesting itself in a loud noise when changing up from first to second gear. Replacement parts are fitted free. Announced *Auto Express*, 24 February 1999.

- Seat Alhambra, Ford Galaxy, VW Sharan: 80,000 vehicles recalled to check for contamination of brake fluid though vent. Announced *Daily Telegraph*, 15 December 1999.

- Vauxhall Corsa 1.4 and 1.6 16v (Sept '93 – Sept '96): timing belt and GF50 plastic idler pulley must be replaced before 40,000 miles or four years old, whichever comes first, or pulley may disintegrate and belt snap leading to engine failure and loss of power assistance to steering and brakes. (Helpline 01582 427200.)

- Vauxhall Astra: noisy power-steering pump on some 1998/1999 model year Astras. Will be replaced FOC. Announced Auto Express, 24 February 1999.

- Vauxhall Astra 1.4, 1.6, 1.8, 2.0 16v (Sept '93 – Sept '96): timing belt and GF50 plastic idler pulley must be replaced before 40,000 miles or four years old (see Corsa).

- Vauxhall Cavalier 2.0 16v and 2.5 24v (Sept '93 – Sept '96): timing belt and GF50 plastic idler pulley must be replaced before 40,000 miles or four years old (see Corsa).

- Vauxhall Vectra 1.6, 1.8, 2.0 16v and 2.5 24v (Sept '93 – Sept '98): timing belt and GF50 plastic idler pulley must be replaced before 40,000 miles or four years old (see Corsa).

- Vauxhall Calibra 2.0 16v and 2.5 24v (Sept '93 – Sept '96): timing belt and GF50 plastic idler pulley must be replaced before 40,000 miles or four years old (see Corsa).

- Vauxhall Omega 2.0 16v, 2.5 24v and 3.0 24v (April '94 – Sept '98): timing belt and GF50 plastic idler pulley must be replaced before 40,000 miles or four years old (see Corsa).

- Vauxhall Frontera 2.2 16v petrol (April '95 – Sept '98): timing belt and GF50 plastic idler pulley must be replaced before 40,000 miles or four years old (see Corsa). All 'new' Fronteras built from June 1998 to September 1999 (6,557 vehicles) officially recalled for 'a check on steering components'.

- VW Sharan, Seat Alhambra, Ford Galaxy: 80,000 vehicles recalled to check for contamination of brake fluid through master cylinder vent. Announced *Daily Telegraph*, 15 December 1999.

2000 recalls

- Audi TT: all 2,430 official UK imports recalled to Germany for extensive modifications to be made, including the fitting of ESP stability and traction control. Work will take several weeks. Owners will be supplied with an A4 courtesy car. Source *Auto Express*, 16 February 2000.

- Audi A6: 'In Service Action' to replace brake pads affected by salt from roads.

- Chrysler Prowler: 500 cars recalled in January 2000 because an alloy front-suspension component may not have been properly heat-treated and could crack. Affected cars to be completely recalled and replaced with a new 255 bhp Prowler.

- Chrysler Voyager: 15,000 UK vehicles recalled because cable routing of parking brake leads cable to stretch making brake very difficult to apply. Announced Radio 5 news, 3 May 2000.

- Daewoo Nexia: all cars built between 1995 and 1997 recalled for seat belt buckles to be checked. Announced 3 July 2000.

- Daewoo Espero: all cars built between 1995 and 1997 recalled for seat belt buckles to be checked. Announced 3 July 2000.

- Ford Explorer: Firestone to replace ATX, ATXII and Wilderness tyres free of charge, regardless of age or wear.

- Ford Focus: rear light bulb holders may rust around the bulbs. New rear light fittings are installed under a Technical Service Bulletin if a rear bulb fails. (Discovered 28 February 2000.) 101,000 Focuses recalled: 1.8 litre and 2.0 litre Zetec E engined Focuses recalled because oil filler cap can come adrift and oil be blown out over engine. Wiring harnesses also to be checked for correct routing. ECU's of 1.6 litre Zetec Ss to be re-programmed if engines suffer from intermittent loss of power. (Announced *Daily Telegraph*, 18 March 2000.)

- Ford Mondeo: 1997–1999 cars with rear drum brakes – Technical Service Bulletin to replace rear brake compensator; issued to dealers July 2000.

- Land Rover Discovery: June 2000, 11,000 vehicles recalled. Flywheel could fail on TD5 engines with manual transmission; a plastic engine pulley could fail on V8s.

- Mazda 626: July 2000 recall of 5,341 petrol-engined 626s built May–November 1997 to inspect the spring of the timing belt tensioner (inspection/replacement takes 1.6 hours). Helpline: 0800 387942.

- MCC Smart: June 2000, official recall by Daimler Chrysler via DVLA records on all MCC Smarts built before July 1999 to uprate part of the stability control system software and to check the front axle and throttle pedal module. Any replacements free of charge wherever the car was purchased.

- Mercedes Benz E Class: 1997-build cars recalled in January 2000 to have both sills re-treated with cavity preservation.

- Porsche 911/996 Carrera 4: 1,179 rhd Carrera 4s built between October 1998 and April 2000 recalled to correct software fault which affects fuel gauge reading. (*Auto Express* issue 598.)

- Renault Twingo 2: 14,000 second generation Twingos recalled to correct airbags which could trigger prematurely.

- Rover 75: cars built between February 1999 and October 1999 recalled for correction of 'engine fault'. Announced Radio 4 news, 10 March 2000.

- Vauxhall Astra: 600,000 old-shape Astras built 1992–98 recalled to check for water contamination of brake fluid. (*Daily Mirror*, 31 March 2000.)

- Vauxhall Zafira DI: 262 vehicles recalled for check on fuel line in engine compartment which could rupture in a front end crash. (Press release received 22 April 2000.)

- Vauxhall Vectra/Calibra/Omega V6: June 2000 recall of 17,000 cars due to problem related to the crankshaft.

RESTORATIONS

Elan rebuild

" I have a 1972 Lotus Elan Sprint with the big-valve 126 bhp engine. It is currently laid up on blocks in North Wales, but I plan to restore the car to a roadworthy condition in the near future. Can you please advise what engine modifications will be required in order to run on the fuels available in the UK after 1 January 2000? Also can you recommend a company that specialises in Lotus engines who could carry out the modifications, if required? "

Mick Miller has been building and rebuilding Elans since 1963. He tells me that all the twin-cam heads are fitted with steel valve seats which are hard enough even for unleaded, but if he was rebuilding a head he would fit chrome steel exhaust valve seats. The ignition can be retarded to run on 97Ron petrol. But if the car has been standing for a long time, there are two obvious problem areas. One is internal corrosion and sludging up of the water galleries which will lead to overheating (especially on unleaded) if the engine is run without a very thorough flushing out. The other is corrosion of the chassis, which will probably need to be replaced. Mick Miller Classic Lotus Restoration, Carlton Cross, Kelsale, Saxmundham, Suffolk IP17 2NL, tel: 01728 603307.

'B' coincidence

" I have a lhd 1966 Californian import MGB roadster for sale, which I re-imported in 1996. Having been in a warm, salt-free climate it is in much better condition than 'B's which have lived in the UK and not been fully restored. It also has a cylinder head converted to take unleaded. I have advertised the car and am not getting any response. What do you suggest? "

Two weeks ago A.B. of Mold wrote asking where he could find a lhd 'B' roadster for a friend who lives in Seville. I have put you two together and hope you can do a deal at around the £4,000 mark. 'B' owners might like to know that Ron Hopkinson has now come up with a computer-designed telescopic shock-absorber kit for MGBs that transforms the handling from far worse than an MGA to as good as a 1990s hot hatch. Price £445. Tel: 01332 756056.

SAFETY

Piggy in the middle

" *I have three children aged 13, 12 and 8 and do not like to use a lap belt as the only means of securing the youngest in the rear centre seat. Currently I augment the lap belt with a harness which is secured in the boot of my Fiat Tipo. I am now looking to replace the Tipo with a Skoda Octavia, and my only reservation is the lack of a three-point central belt. I have a 60-mile commute each day to work (30 miles each way) with no available public transport. Consequently I need an economical car and am looking in the £10,000–£15,000 region, providing good finance is available. What would you suggest?* "

You'll find all your answers in the Seat Toledo TDI 110 'S' at £15,895, which I think is the best value, most sensible package in the entire VAG 'A' floorpan range. The old strap-hanger harness bar for hatchbacks and estate cars has not been manufactured for about five years because there is now a new EU standard and no one has been able to make a harness bar that complies with it. The In-Car Safety Centre (01908 220909) offers a device known as the 'Vario' which fits over the centre child's stomach, protecting it and also usually bringing the buckle to the front where it is more comfortable rather than to the side. This can be used by children up to six to seven years old and up to 25 kilos, but is obviously not as good as a proper three-point harness.

All the cars I am about to list come with proper lap and diagonal centre rear seat-belts either as standard or as an option. They are: Alfa 156 (£97.53 option), new BMW 5-Series, Citroën Berlingo Multispace Forte 5-door, Citroën Xantia Estate, Citroën Picasso, Fiat Punto from 2000 MY (standard in HLX and above; £75 option in base models), Fiat Multipla, Ford Mondeo from 1997 MY, Honda Accord from 1999 MY, Hyundai Santa Fe, Land Rover Freelander five-door, Land Rover Discovery from 1999 MY, Mazda 626 from July 1997, MB C Class estate, MB E Class estate from May 1996, MB E Class from June 1998, Mitsubishi Galant from 1998 MY, Mitsubishi Space Star, Nissan Almera four-door, Nissan Almera Tino, new Nissan Primera SLX, Peugeot 306 Sedan, Peugeot 406, Renault new Clio from May 1998 (not base models), Renault Kangoo Combi RXE model, Renault Megane and Scenic, Renault Laguna from 95M, Renault Espace from 1997 MY, new Rover 200, Rover 25, Rover 45, Rover 600 from 1997 MY, Rover 75, Rover 800 four-door from 94M, Saab 900 from 94L, Saab 9-3, Saab 9-5 (saloon and estate), New Seat Toledo (from 1999 MY), Toyota Corolla from July 1997, Toyota Avensis, Toyota Camry from 1997 MY, Vauxhall Astra from April 1998 (not Zafira), Vauxhall Vectra from 1997 MY, Vauxhall Omega, 1998 VW Golf IV and Bora (£100 optional extra, but standard on Golf V5 Estate), new VW Passat (£100 optional extra), Volvo S40, Volvo V40, Volvo S70, Volvo V70, Volvo 850, Volvo S80, Volvo 940, Volvo 960, Volvo S90, Volvo V90.

Over the shoulder number

" *Regarding 'Piggy in the Middle', we can fit almost all cars with a prop-*

er lap/diagonal belt for the centre rear passenger. If the car is a saloon, we can fit an inertia reel under the rear parcel shelf, giving the impression of 'original equipment' from £115 plus VAT supplied and fitted. If the car is a hatchback or estate, our solution is a dual-function adjustable belt arrangement, which firstly restrains the seat-back and secondly restrains the passenger in the seat. To give proper restraint, this takes up a bit of luggage space, but can be quickly detached if more luggage space is required or the rear seat needs to be folded. The cost of our static lap/diagonal rear belt is from £75 plus VAT, but for some cars, for example Saab 9000s, the cost can rise to around £120 plus VAT. A static centre rear belt can usually restrain a child seat more securely than an inertia reel belt. We can also supply longer belts where required. **"**

This is the company I mentioned several years ago following a recommendation from Britax. They offer a useful service not provided by car manufacturers. But I have to add that whenever the standard safety equipment of a car is altered, it no longer conforms to Type Approval for the car. The Quickfit Safety Centre has its equipment tested to EU standards by the TNO in Holland (the Dutch equivalent of BSI) or by the TRL, Crowthorne, so its products are properly tested. But if an accident occurred where questions of liability of the car manufacturers arose, they could not be held liable for any injuries arising out of failure of the aftermarket belts. Quickfit Safety Belt Service, Inertia House, Lowther Road, Stanmore, Middx HA7 1EP, tel: 020 8206 0101. Citroën now fits all Xsara and Xantia models with a keyswitch to disarm the passenger airbag, allowing a rear-facing baby seat to be carried in the front. Alfa 156s also have this feature.

Bully bars

" *A recent statement by the Minister of Transport said that the*

Government was planning to 'push' for an increase in safety margins for pedestrians when they are struck by motor vehicles. This was widely publicised on TV and the rest of the media. The Government statement made the officials seem so concerned I was surprised that no mention was made then or since regarding 'bull bars' being fitted on vehicles on the public highway and the increased risk that these accessories can bring of injuring humans and causing damage to other vehicles. With such accessories seemingly negating the vehicle designers' attempts to improve safety in this area I was surprised that the Government statement was not quickly followed by a total ban of 'bull bars' on the public highway. "

A ban could be effected relatively simply, without causing significant hardship. Unfortunately, road accident statistics are insufficiently detailed to ascribe causes of deaths and injuries to these bars, which is why they were not banned after the campaign several years ago. The States of Jersey did have the good sense to impose a ban several years ago.

Airbag anguish

" *I am writing to enquire if it is possible to switch off airbags. In a recent article in the Daily Telegraph this was mentioned. What is the action needed to achieve this please? The car in question is a Suzuki Wagon R+. I am retired, 5ft 2in tall and am concerned how near to the wheel I have to sit to drive.* "

A few cars, such as the Alfa 156, have passenger airbags which can be disabled by a keyswitch. But most manufacturers will refuse to disarm the driver's airbag for fear of US-style liability suits should any death or injury occur as a result. The standard advice is that you should not sit closer than 10in to a front airbag. If the steering column of the car is not adjustable for reach, and the only way you can operate the foot pedals is to sit within 10in of the steering wheel airbag, then one answer is universal vehicle pedal extensions. These are now being actively marketed by Eze Drive Ltd of 169 London Road, Leicester, LE2 1EG, tel: 07970 571407, email: EzeDrive@aol.com.

Full circle

" Instead of messing up the appearance of the interior with black velour-faced Fablon, there is a better way to eliminate windscreen dashboard reflections. It is to buy a pair of polarising sunglasses. "

Funnily enough that is exactly the suggestion I made back in 1996 which was followed by D.S. of Ottery St Mary's alternative of the black Fablon. Spectacle wearers can also buy polarising 'clip ons' for their glasses. Other readers came up with all sorts of non-reflecting materials, some of which I put to the test and found that they did reflect. Richard Ould, 01242 222350, email: rould@freek.com, has offered to make custom-shaped non-slip black velour mats for owners of Audi A3s or other makes with the same problem.

Safety scare

" In August 1997 I purchased a Mitsubishi Space Wagon, solely for use as a spacious four-seater estate car. I am now alarmed by the recently published accident tests which gave this vehicle only three stars for safety. I would be very grateful to learn whether this scare will affect the second-hand value of MPVs. "

It can't affect the value of yours because NCAP did not test yours. They tested the new model. And, though the Space Wagon performed relatively badly in the frontal impact test, it did a lot better than the now defunct Vauxhall Sintra

and the very popular Chrysler Voyager. Used values of the top performing Renault Espace and Toyota Picnic might rise slightly as a result of these tests and Sintra and Voyager values may fall. But the middle-runners in the tests will probably remain in pretty much the same place in the market.

You can't take your test in that!

" My eldest daughter is learning to drive. Sometimes she drives the driving-school car, and sometimes our family Volvo 340DL. We are now informed that she cannot take her test in the Volvo unless a separate rear-view mirror is provided for the examiner, the front 'L' plate is taped to the front of the car rather than displayed in the screen, and the front passenger seat is fitted with a head restraint. All this came as a surprise to me and I wonder if any more surprises are in store before the test. "

Driving examiners are entitled to do all they can to ensure their own safety. Times have changed since I passed a no-reverse gear, three-wheeler test in an Isetta 300 bubble car at the age of 16. With no seat-belts and virtually no protection at all, the then-obligatory emergency stop was particularly exciting for the examiner and it's possible he passed me to avoid repeating the experience. Nine months later I passed a full test in a driving school Simca 1000 and I have always thought that a pre-test instruction session followed by a test in the same car was the most sensible way to go.

Could this be a lifesaver?

" We have developed a brake-light activation system which we believe could avoid huge numbers of deaths and injuries each year. One part is an LED brake light which lights up in one millisecond compared to 250 milliseconds for a conventional brake light. At 90 kph, or 25 metres per second, a vehicle travels more than seven metres in this time. The other part is a sensor which detects the driver's foot moving from the accelerator to the brake pedal. When the movement is relatively slow because the driver is uncertain whether he will have to brake or not, this can light the brake lights two seconds before he presses the pedal during which, at 90 kph, the car will have travelled more than 50 metres. This is important because, for example, the driver may have seen a child or animal invisible to the driver of the following car and has no other way of forewarning that driver of the possibility he may have to brake hard. In some countries, lifting off the accelerator at speed automatically switches on the car's hazard warning lights. This could also be incorporated into the system circuitry. We have called the combined device the Shuntgun and believe it could be made original equipment in new cars for as little as £10. "

I would obviously support any new technology which I believed would save lives. But I am not 100% convinced because of the increased brake-light pollution Shuntguns would inevitably create in heavy traffic, especially on motorways, and the problems they could cause to the driver of the car two cars behind the one with the Shuntgun. But anyone who believes it could be a lifesaver and would like to learn more can do so by writing to John Birtles, Spinal Injuries Association, Liberty Garden Workshops, Williamstrip Park, Cirencester, Gloucester GL7 5AS, or fax: 01285 750 227.

MPV centre-rear safety

" Why is it that all people carriers only provide a lap belt for the centre rear passenger in the middle row of seats? "

Because the seats are removable, and the top mounting point would therefore have to be the centre of the roof which is not strong enough without special reinforcement. A reinforced roof mounting is provided in the Brotherwood conversion of the VW Sharan in order to safely secure the occupant of a wheelchair in the centre of the vehicle between the two other rear seats (tel: 01935 872603). Most five- or six-seater MPVs, such as the Citroën Picasso, Renault Scenic, Fiat Multipla and Colt Space Star do have a three-point centre-rear seat-belt secured to the rear roll hoop or 'D' pillar.

Beware of exploding seats

" Most buyers of new cars never bother to read the driver's manual thoroughly. A new danger this can create became apparent when, after failing to read my new Citroën's manual, I fitted covers to the seats. Thankfully my Citroën dealer was sufficiently alert to warn me that seat covers should not be fitted to any car with side airbags installed in the seats. "

Well, yes. I get at least two letters a week from

readers who never bothered to RTFM (read the flippin' manual).

No place for slackers

" *Occasionally I notice that the bottom part of the driver's seat-belt of my car has become lodged under the boot release lever or the seat adjuster. This creates a foot or so of slack, which could mean the difference between life and death in an accident.* "

Good point. Particularly to owners of older cars in which the seat-belt retraction spring has become a bit weak. It is always a wise precaution to check that your seat-belt is correctly routed.

Child casualties

" *Depending on which figures you take, deaths of child pedestrians in the UK amount to either 150 a year or 208 a year. While this is desperately sad, I do feel that the statement 'around 5,000 children are killed or seriously injured on Britain's roads every year' is misleading and that there is no correlation at all between speeding on motorways and child pedestrian deaths. Surely what we should be doing to combat this is to improve children's education on road safety. I firmly believe that teaching of the Highway Code should be made part of the National Curriculum.* "

I could not agree more and this now seems to be enshrined in government policy. In the meantime, drivers should never assume that a child on the pavement might not suddenly jump into the road. Watch them instead of your speedometer and, after passing them, you may find that you have automatically slowed to 20 mph or less.

Belt and braces approach

" *I own a 1980 Corvette which has tan-coloured seat-belts, the webbing* *of which is wearing out. I can get replacements in black for $50 a seat from the USA, but they want $600 for the same thing in the original beige/tan colour. Is there anywhere in the UK that could make up a set for me using the original buckles and shackles?* **"**

Yes, the Quickfit Safety Centre, Inertia House, Lowther Road, Queensbury, Stanmore HA7 1EP, tel: 020 8206 0101. The centre has webbing in most colours including tan and red, and is open on Saturday mornings for drive-in quotations. Or try FDTS in Byfleet, tel: 01932 342073.

SECURITY

Failed to raise the alarm

" I am a new owner of a Toyota Land Cruiser Amazon. Soon after this momentous purchase I went out to find the rear window smashed, hazard lights flashing, but not a peep from the alarm. My insurers asked, 'didn't your alarm go off?'. I checked with Toyota to make sure I had set it correctly and sure enough I had. Soon after the vehicle's return with new rear window glass, exactly the same thing happened again. I checked with Toyota again, and got a lot of waffle: the alarm was 'Thatcham Approved', the movement sensors only detect movement in the footwells, and in any case a determined thief would take whatever he or she wanted from my car undeterred by the noise of an alarm. "

BBC 'Watchdog' discovered the same problem with another make of large 4x4 last year. (In running the story, 'Watchdog' may have unintentionally tipped off the nation's vandals.) The front-mounted volumetric sensors inside the vehicle are not sensitive enough to pick up glass breakage or movement in the rear luggage compartment. To do so, they would have to be so sensitive that the alarm would go off at the merest gust of outside air through the ventilation system. Your remedy is to retrofit an additional pair of volumetric sensors in the rear luggage compartment.

Locked out

" Away from home, I left both my dog and my keys in my car for a moment. The dog jumped up against the door and pressed the central locking button. Fortunately I had left a window open, but this should serve as a warning to others never to leave their keys and an animal in a car. "

> Or children. Particularly children.

Alarming

" I own a 1998 Toyota Avensis CDX estate. The roof light failed, so I removed the bulb and tested it. The terminals were a bit loose, but it worked so I replaced it. I then heard a series of low beeps, the security system stopped working, the central locking stopped working, the clock reverted to 12.00 and the digital trip meter self zeroed. The Toyota dealer told me I had blown a fuse by inserting the bulb incorrectly. When I replaced the fuse, everything worked again. But please can you tell me why the security system is protected by the same fuse as the interior light and central locking? "

> Because they are all part of the security system. The little plunger switches that turn the interior light on when you open the door also send a signal to the alarm.

Passive lock-out

" I recently bought a new battery for my ten-year-old BMW 520i. When I disconnected the old battery, the doors locked, locking my keys inside. Fortunately I was at home and was able to use a spare set of keys, but I feel your readers should be warned. "

> The way to avoid this, and to avoid decoding a radio which contains a long-forgotten code, is to use a set of jump leads to keep the car's battery leads connected to the new battery while you disconnect and remove the old one.

Stolen Saab

" My much loved Saab 900 V6 SE should have been impossible to steal. As usual, I checked it at 11.15 at night. The alarm LED on the dashboard was flashing and the transmission was locked in reverse. Yet at 7.15 the next morning the car had gone. How? There were no visible signs of a forced entry. "

The alarm remote signal may have been cloned, by-passed or reprogrammed using a special remote device and a notebook computer. Or, more likely, your key and the chip in it may have been copied while the car was in a garage for work, such as servicing, tyres, exhaust or body repairs.

Staying in trim

" How can I make it more difficult for thieves to steal my car's plastic wheel trims? I'm sure such a device would be of interest to many car owners. "

Pull-through plastic ties, available from DIY stores and garden centres. Daily rental companies use these, and Micheldever Tyres fit a set as part of the service when they sort out your car's suspension alignment. Alternatively, Streetwise Accessories do a range of reasonable-looking aftermarket trims which are claimed to have a unique anti-theft and anti-loss fixing system. Tel: 01204 572200 or email sales@streetwise.co.uk to order a set.

STARTING AND RUNNING PROBLEMS

Intermittent faults

Some common reasons for intermittent faults are as follows:

● **Carburettor icing** The air entering a carburettor needs to be heated because at speed, condensation in the air can freeze in the air intake, restricting the orifice and cutting off the air. Once the car has stopped for a short time, the residual heat of the engine melts the ice and the car can be re-started. If the inlet is water-heated, check water pipes; if electrically heated, check electrics. If the air filter trunk has a 'summer' and 'winter' setting, switch it to the winter setting so it picks up hot air from the exhaust manifold.

● **Faulty carburettor** The Pierburg carburettors of older VWs can suffer loosening of the brass needle valve seat when the engine is hot. This leads to flooding of the carburettor, leading to an over-rich mixture, which makes the engine difficult to start. Stripping the carb, pushing the needle valve seat firmly home, and peining the surrounding aluminium, to keep it in place will solve the problem for a while.

● **Faulty fuel pump or fuel pump relay** An electrical contact in the relay to the fuel pump or the fuel pump itself could break or 'dry out' causing intermittent mis-fires in a fuel-injected car. After correction, the condition of the catalytic converter (if fitted) should also be checked.

● **Air leaks** in the injection system or the diaphragm pressure switch.

● **Blocked exhaust system** In pre-cat days, rust caused by condensation inside one of the silencer boxes could eventually block passages inside the exhaust, preventing the car from 'exhaling', and stopping the engine. The same can happen if the ceramic core of a catalytic converter breaks up and blocks the rest of the exhaust system.

● **Badly routed cable** An electrical engine-management cable routed over a part of the engine subject to movement could rub the insulation from the cable leading to a short.

● **Faulty contact** A damaged contact plug may let in moisture leading to corrosion of contacts and possible short circuits.

● **Moisture inside ECU** Most car ECUs are situated in a safe, warm, dry place. But if they are ever affected by water or moisture ingress, such as from a burst heater matrix, internal damage may result and the circuits inside are so complex that replacement is usually the only cure.

● **Automatic cold-running control** Many automatics have automatic choke controls which are supposed to prevent suddenly increased engine revs which can alarm drivers, but which often malfunction and cut off fuel supply.

● **Internally broken cable** Any cable suffering internal breaks can lead to intermittent breakdowns, for example, 'The earth contacts at the Plenum Chamber to rocker cover were producing a short circuit caused by two unsecured bolts on the rear rocker which had become stripped.' (Alfa 164 Cloverleaf).

● **Dried-out contacts in coil or ignition system** The remedy is to check all contacts and clean where necessary.

● **Coil failure** Either the coil contacts may be faulty or the coil itself has burned out. Easily checked with a multimeter.

● **Spark plug or spark-plug cable failure** The insulation of the cables from the distributor to the spark plugs can eventually break down, but first try cleaning any accumulated dirt from the outside of the cables as this can harbour moisture which diverts the high-tension current.

● **Dirt in fuel** Swarf or rust in a steel fuel tank can block the fuel pipe or fuel filter (though this is less common now that many cars have plastic fuel tanks) causing an excess of back pressure.

● **Fuel-line air lock** Often due to a sticking gravity valve, this can stop a carburetted car where the fuel is sucked by an engine-driven pump rather than pumped from the tank by an electric pump.

● **Blocked fuel-tank breather (pipe or filler cap)** By preventing air being drawn into the fuel tank to replace the fuel sucked out, this can stop a car.

● **Faulty inlet air-temperature sensor** Part of the 'choke mechanism' on a fuel-injected car which sends messages from which the ECU decides to enrich or lean off the fuel/air mixture.

● **Faulty fuel-flow meter or air-flow meter** This can cause intermittent or total failure in a fuel-injected car.

● **Interference with ignition lock** Heavy house keys on the same ring as the ignition key, and the motion of these can cause the key to move slightly in the ignition switch, separating the contact.

● **Interference with immobiliser circuit** Any electronic device carried on the same ring as the car keys may interfere with the car's immobiliser circuit.

Thanks to Colin Marshall and Keith Rhoods at Wheelbase garage, Hersham (01932 252515) and to BBR, which now offers a motor fault-finding helpline. The number is 0897 161123, is open 9.00–5.30 and calls cost a maximum of £1.47 a minute.

Something's burning

" We have a 1986 Renault 5 which is reliable, safe, comfortable and in super condition. Recently, the wiring loom partially burned out when the radiator-fan motor failed. Apparently, this is a common problem, which can be prevented by fitting an in-line fuse into the positive cable from the loom to the motor. Since the cost of repairing or replacing the loom can be more than the car is worth, this tip may save some perfectly serviceable Renault 5s from the scrap heap. "

Thank you on behalf of Renault SuperCinq owners.

Failing the hill start

" The engine of my son's Mercedes Benz 190 recently stalled, apparently due to fuel starvation while the front of the car was up on ramps. Since then it has happened several times when parked facing up-hill. The tank

has been around half full on all occasions. What could be the cause? It has been suggested that it might be the automatic fuel cut-off which is designed to cut off the fuel supply in the event of an accident. "

It could be an over-active fuel cut-off. But I think it's more likely to be dirt or globules of emulsified fuel in the tank blocking the pipe. If I'm right, the tank needs cleaning out and the fuel system needs flushing through.

Non-starter

" *I have a 97P VW Vento. At just 2,200 miles, the starter motor failed. The Bosch dealer had never seen such a mangled unit and retained the bits for reference. Its reconditioned replacement lasted four days before turning into a chewed-up mess. A brand new starter motor was then fitted and after four starts it too shattered. All concerned are thoroughly baffled by the cause. The fourth replacement has a special cut-out which isolates it after ignition and so far has not failed. What caused the failure of its predecessors?* "

At first I thought a chewed-up starter ring on the flywheel. But starter-motor alignment is also critical. According to VW independents Wheelbase of Hersham (01932 8252515) the bush at the gearbox end of the starter motor also needs to be replaced. Bosch motors come complete with this bush and a sticker stating that it must be replaced. If it isn't, starter-motor life will be very short.

Connector con?

" *I have a 92K Fiesta Flight 1.4CVH. Recently it began to cut out, then refused to start at all. The RAC man immediately diagnosed a poor connection between the cable and the flywheel ignition sensor, which apparently is a common fault. He wiggled the connector and got the car going again. I now know how to solve the problem but would like to eliminate it. So I was shocked to discover that Ford does not offer the connector as a separate part. It is only available already fixed to a complete cable harness, which costs hundreds of pounds and is a major job to fit. Ford Customer Assistance Centre confirmed this. The best advice I have received is to cut a connector from the wiring on a scrap Fiesta and fit it to the cable myself.* **"**

Flywheel sensor connectors have become quite a common problem area. One briefly immobilised a Renault Megane I was testing several years ago. One possibility is to dry out the joint thoroughly then use Frost 'Liquid Electrical Tape' to seal the joint against moisture (£7.50, tel: 01706 658619). Alternatively, I'd check Yellow Pages for a local car electrical specialist and see what he can come up with. Even if you source a replacement connector yourself from a breaker, he should be able to fit it correctly and waterproof it properly. J.K. of Crawley tells us that Ford itself used to sell a £15 'fix kit' consisting of one foot of cable with a gold male connector at one end and a gold female connector at the other. Running this between the flywheel sensor and the loom solved the problem, apparently caused by heat tarnishing the base metal of the original plug.

Rattling Mercedes

" *I recently bought a 1988 Mercedes 300CE with a 'genuine' 90,000 miles. There do not seem to be any serious mechanical problems, but on cold starting I hear a diesel-type rattle for about ten minutes which becomes inaudible once the engine is hot. The noise is especially noticeable when the engine is under load and 'piston slap' has been suggested after no wear was found in the timing chain or camshaft lobes. What do you think is causing this noise?* **"**

If a cheap oil filter has been fitted without a

non-return valve, the top of the engine will be starved of oil for a short period after start-up. If the oil has not been changed religiously every 3,000 miles, this engine can suffer wear in the camshaft bearings. If the oil is not perfectly clean, bits of dirt may prevent one or more of the hydraulic tappets from pumping up. Dirty oil can also lead to problems with the timing-chain tensioner. Another possibility is pinking from trying to run the engine on a lower grade of petrol than it is set to expect.

Millennium Pug

" Do you know whether the engine control unit in the Peugeot 406 is susceptible to failure? According to our local retailer it is not a common occurrence. I enclose all correspondence I have had with Peugeot who are more or less saying, 'that's your hard luck'. With the cost of replacement being £500, it seems a pity that Peugeot is not offering some compensation. My car had done less than 22,000 miles in just over three years. "

Peugeot had a lot of problems with the ECUs of 2.0 litre 406s during the first six months after the car's launch, but cured them by re-chipping the ECUs. This may still be possible at a much more modest cost than the £500 quoted and if Peugeot can't do it, speak to BBR of Brackley (tel: 01280 702389). In Peugeot's favour, all new official UK-market Peugeots are now covered by a three-year warranty.

T5 trouble

" I have a 1995M Volvo T5 manual estate, with 40,000 miles on the clock. When accelerating moderately the car seems to have a very noticeable flat spot at around 3,000 rpm. My Volvo agent says there is nothing wrong, but replaced the fuel pump relay 'just in case'. I don't use supermarket petrol. What can I do to achieve a smoother ride? "

RTFM (read the flippin' manual). This tells you that the engine is designed to run on 98Ron Super petrol (no longer available in the UK) but can be run on lower grade fuel in emergencies. What is happening is you are hitting the point in the engine's mapping where the ECU runs the car leaner to achieve reasonable 120 kph fuel-consumption figures for 'official' EU tests; and additionally, trying to run on a lower grade of petrol adversely exaggerates the effect on the power output. Using 97Ron Superunleaded should give closer to the performance provided by 98Ron Super. Pity we can't get the 99Ron Shell Optimax available in Germany.

All revved up

" *I have a 1997 Fiat Punto 75, which had done 20,000 miles without trouble. Recently though, in urban driving the engine has intermittently started to idle at 2,000–2,500 rpm instead of the normal 900 rpm. This does not happen in motorway driving. A local tuning company could not detect any fault. What could be the cause?* "

One possibility is that the Lambda sensor in the car's exhaust system is not functioning properly because it is dirty. Try switching to a high-detergent petrol such as Texaco or Shell. If this does not cure the problem, then the Lambda sensor may need cleaning or replacing. Alternatively, the engine may be over-fuelling when idling in traffic. If so, a properly working Lambda sensor will detect an over-rich mixture and, to protect the catalytic converter from contamination, will send a signal to the ECU which then increases engine revs to ensure that the fuel is more completely burned.

Pop goes the Quattro

" *I drive a 1988 Audi Quattro Turbo coupe, which has done just over 100,000 miles. When slowing down with the engine on overrun it makes an unpleasant sound. The local Audi agent tells me it is caused by crankcase vacuum sucking air past the rear crankcase bearing oil-seal. He has cleared the breather tubes, but the problem persists. Any ideas?* "

This was one for Colin Marshall of Wheelbase (01932 252515) who has spent most of his life working on VWs and Audis. He told me it's most likely to be a split in the 3in hose from the intercooler to the manifold which causes a fluttering noise on overrun. The waste gates of some turbocharged cars 'pop' on overrun, but this is unlikely on an Audi unless the ECU had been chipped to deliver considerably more turbo boost than normal.

Non-starter

" *We have run a 1992J Peugeot 405GR for the past five years. Last summer it began to refuse to re-start after running for 20 minutes or so in warm weather. If we left it for 15 minutes or so, there was no problem. What's wrong?* "

Assuming this is a GR and not a GRi, it could be due to fuel vaporisation in the Solex carburettor – a fault which plagued 309s and 405s. Peugeot dealers used to have a mod for this that sometimes worked and sometimes didn't but, assuming the problem is the carb, the best cure is to replace it with a Weber (Webcon, tel: 01932 788630, website: www.webcon.co.uk). If it's starter related, it could be a damaged starter ring on the flywheel. Replacing the motor without replacing the starter ring won't solve this.

Make sensor this

" *Recently you published a letter from a reader whose car engine ran at varying speeds. I experienced a similar intermittent problem with my 'G'-reg. 2.0 litre Montego and cured it relatively cheaply. My garage recommended a new ECU at a cost of at least £250. However I noticed that whenever it occurred, the car temperature gauge read 'cold' however hot the engine really was. From this I deduced that the fault must lie with the thermistor in the temperature circuit sending the wrong message to the ECU. I had this replaced at a cost of £25 and my problem was solved.* "

Good thinking. First check your temperature gauge for false messages from the engine block coolant-temperature sensor. But a catalysed car may also have air-flow, air-temperature and air-pressure sensors as well as a fuel-flow sensor, an oxygen sensor in the exhaust, a knock sensor, a throttle-position sensor and an oil-temperature sensor (instead of a coolant-temperature sensor). A fault may occur in any of these, or their connectors, or the ECU connector, or the fuel-pump relay. In any case, the ECU will always attempt to protect the catalytic converter from over-fuelling, especially during the engine's programmed warm-up cycle, and this explains why engine response may sometimes feel at variance with the input from your right foot.

Sprung back to life

" *Recently I wrote to you about problems with the carburettor of my Peugeot 309. You suggested that I probably needed a new carburettor from Webcon (tel: 01932 788805) at a cost of around £200. But while awaiting your reply I cast my inexpert eye over the problem and realised that there was obviously wear in the ends of the choke butterfly shaft allowing it to stick. So I got hold of another external spring, added it to the original and this was enough to overcome the sticking. So until the wear becomes so severe that it sticks again, I've cracked the problem and put off the day when Webcon gets my £200.* "

This is a good tip for a temporary bodge. But the extra spring could actually increase the rate of wear at the ends of the butterfly shaft. Fingers crossed.

Fuel for thought

" My 92K Vauxhall Cavalier SRi suffers from fuel fumes entering the passenger compartment intermittently. No one has been able to explain the cause. It can happen when starting from cold and on short journeys when held up in traffic queues especially on particularly cold or wet days. "

This has come up before on Cavaliers. You should suspect the plastic filler elbow between the car body and the tank itself. If it is not seated properly or is fractured, petrol fumes can enter the car.

Cavalier with attitude

" I have a 115,000-mile 90G Cavalier 1.6 which has developed a starting problem. This only occurs from cold first thing in the morning. After that it's okay. The dealer had made four attempts to repair it and now suggests fitting a new choke unit at a cost of £98 plus VAT. What do you suggest? "

It could be the right answer. The choke system of carburettors on pre-1992 Cavaliers can start to give trouble and a new carb costs around £800. Because of this, Vauxhall came up with a £98 repair kit, which is what you are being offered. But another reader suggested that, before you go to this expense, you check that the water-heated section of the inlet manifold or the hoses leading to it are not blocked with corrosion sludge, preventing it from heating up quickly after a cold start.

Chronic Motronic

" *I have a BMW 525E which I have owned since new in 1984 and which has now covered 104,000 miles. Mechanics have been trying for months now to cure a cold-start fault. The engine always fires, but when put into gear the revs fall dramatically and on a really cold day the engine will stall. The only remedy is to keep the throttle pressed until the engine has warmed up. At present, the tick-over revs have been increased which largely overcomes the problem but this leads to excessive 'creep' and difficulty in stopping smoothly. Any ideas, please. BMW itself has not been able to help.* "

Only a couple of days ago I came across a friend who owns a slightly newer, manual 520i and has exactly the same problem. Both models are fitted with Bosch Motronic fuel injection on which the idle speed cannot be adjusted except by altering the idle mixture or the position of the throttle stop, which the mechanics must have done in your case and which, because your car is automatic, is dangerous. Your engine has 'mapped ignition and fuel injection, metered air intake with fuel cut off on over-run'. But D.B. of Leicester came up with the cure. The cause of the poor cold running is usually dirty or corroded electrical terminals on the bulkhead-mounted auxiliary air device. If the contacts are dirty, the valve sticks.

STORING AND RE-COMMISSIONING

Seven-week lay-off

" *In early January I shall be going on holiday for seven weeks, leaving my 1998 Alfa GTV in the garage. What precautions should I take to avoid any long-term damage and to be assured of it starting when I return?* "

Change the oil if it's more than three months old, clean and polish the car, take it for a ten-mile drive in the dry to evaporate any moisture in the exhaust system and put it away dry. Then hook it up to an Airflow battery conditioner which will keep the battery fully charged but never over-charged (Airflow UK, tel: 01635 569569, website: www.airflow.uk.com), and cover it with a cotton sheet. That's what I did to my 76,000-mile Jetta 16v this summer and after three months it started perfectly first time.

Recommissioning

" *Several years ago I purchased my old company car, a Honda Accord 2.0i, for my wife, and it has now done 115,000 miles. For various reasons she had not been able to drive it since last July when its VED and insurance lapsed. We now want to get it back on the road again and I have three questions: 1) What can I do to minimise engine damage from its eight-month incarceration? 2) Will I be breaking the law by driving an in-*

sured but untaxed car to the MOT testing station? 3) By not taxing the car since July, have I lost the right to the cherished registration on the car? **"**

1) Have the car transported to a garage to be re-commissioned. This will probably involve a new battery, and draining and replacing the brake fluid, coolant, engine oil and, possibly, the petrol which may have gone 'stale'. Much depends on the state of the fluids when the car was put away. You may also need new tyres if the existing tyres have flat-spotted and can't be over-pressured to get them round again, and new brake discs if condensation in the garage has caused them to became pitted with rust. 2) No. 3) Presumably the car is on a SORN (Statutory Off Road Notification) that came with its last VED reminder. If not, you are breaking the law. But because the registration is on a car rather than a Certificate of Entitlement you should not have lost your right to keep it.

Tucking it away

" *Some of my relatives are going abroad for one year. Their car will be in my garage. What should be done to keep it in good order so that it is ready for use on their return?* **"**

Overpressure all the tyres to at least 40 psi to help prevent them from flat-spotting (or put the car on blocks). Before it is put away, have it fully serviced with fresh engine oil and filter, fresh brake fluid and fresh coolant to help prevent contaminants in the old fluids from causing internal corrosion. Tell the garage generally to prepare the car for storage by greasing hinges, runners, battery terminals, etc.. Leave only a minimal amount of petrol in the tank (petrol goes 'stale' from emulsified condensation and the globules block fuel ways). For longer storage if the tank is steel rather than plastic consider draining the fuel system and refilling partially with paraffin. Make sure the car is put away perfectly dry by taking it for a fast run of at least 20 miles on a dry day to make sure all engine-generated condensation moisture is dried out of the exhaust system. Hook the battery up to a mains-powered Airflow Automatic Battery Management System (£40, tel: 01635 569569). Leave the sunroof and windows open just a crack to allow interior ventilation without rodents or birds being able to get inside. Cover it with a cotton or decorator's sheet to keep dust off. Send a Statutory Off Road Notification (SORN Form V890 from the Post Office) to the DVLA. Remember, unless you take the car to be MOT tested when it becomes due, the car will need to be filled with petrol and be freshly tested before it can be re-registered. Before re-starting the engine, turn it over a few times with a wrench or by using the underbonnet starter-motor button with the ignition off to try and circulate some oil.

TAX*

Oil company exploitation

" Am I the only person who suspects we are being taken for a ride by the petrol companies? Before the 1999 Budget, all the filling stations were selling unleaded for 59.9p per litre. In the Budget, unleaded went up by about 4p, but the pump price went up by 8p, and I do mean everywhere. By June 1999 it has gone up a further 2p to 69.9p, without exception. I thought cartels were illegal. "

Before the 1999 Budget, my receipts for Premium Unleaded show I was paying an average 65p a litre. So there must have been a price war in your area which pulled prices down. The Association of British Drivers worked out some figures based on the immediate post-1999 Budget figure of 67.9p a litre: 47.21p of this was 'fuel duty', 10.11p was VAT, and only 10.58p paid for the petrol itself. This works out at a total rate of tax of 542% on that 10.58p of petrol and hardly indicated that it was the oil companies who were exploiting the motoring public. But by June 2000 the price of a litre of Premium Unleaded had gone up to an average of 86p a litre. Of this, 48.82p was 'fuel duty', 12.81p was VAT and 24.37p paid for the petrol itself. So by spring 2000 the total rate of tax on the fuel itself had fallen from 542% to 253% – less than

---

* See also 'De-mystified Motors' 25 and 31.

half the rate it had been the previous year, but it still represented 72% of the pump price.

Discrimination against diesel

" Why, if diesel-engined cars emit less CO_2 are they discriminated against in both the new VED and new car benefit tax regimes? Surely it is hypocritical to introduce a new tax based on CO_2 emissions, then artificially discriminate against the vehicles which emit the least CO_2 "

Fuel tax on diesel, the new VED scales and the new company car benefit tax regime discourage the use of diesel in the UK because the oil companies cannot produce enough of it to supply total European demand. A barrel of crude oil can be refined into a split of LPG, petrol, kerosene and diesel or heating oil, but it can't all be refined into any one of these. I think that a deal has been done between the oil companies and the UK Government to put a cap on the demand for diesel for these reasons. It's nothing to do with protecting the environment because the buses we are encouraged to take from 'park and ride' car parks into 'no car' towns virtually all run on diesel.

'Historic', or not?

" I own a Triumph 1500TC, which I purchased new and which was first registered on 17 September 1974. The qualification for exemption from VED applies to 'historic vehicles' manufactured before 1 January 1973. As the registration document does not state the date of manufacture, is there any way I can find if my car was built early enough to qualify? "

Many 1970s cars did sit around in fields and on airport runways for as much as two years before they were registered, but yours can't be one of them. The front-wheel-drive Triumph 1500 which had a longitudinal engine with the gearbox underneath (like the Triumph 1300), ran from August 1970 until November 1973. It started to be replaced by the Triumph 1500TC in October 1973. This has live axle rear-wheel drive (like the Triumph Toledo), which means your car cannot have been built before Summer 1973 and cannot therefore be VED exempt. In fact the first Triumph 1500 chassis number of 1973 was 61754, so even a Triumph 1500 would need an earlier chassis number than that to qualify. (Source *Glass's Guide Car Check Book 1970–1979*.)

VAT's all this?

" How much VAT does a dealer actually pay to Customs and Excise if I negotiate a discount on a new car? Is it 17.5% of the published list price, or 17.5% of the price I actually pay? "

If the car is listed at £11,750 (before registration tax and VED, but including VAT), and you pay £10,000, to calculate the VAT the dealer divides £10,000 by 1.175, then multiplies the result by 17.5%. The VAT proportion of £10,000 is therefore £1,489, or 14.89% of the price you actually pay. In the evil old days of purchase tax and special car tax, these taxes were fixed percentages levied on the car's ex-works, pre-tax, 'list' price, so still applied whatever discount you negotiated.

Picking up some VAT back

" I have been told that VAT is now reclaimable on double-cab pick-ups as they carry over a tonne. Is this true? "

As from 1 December 1999, double-cab pick-ups

that can carry one tonne or more have been treated the same as vans for VAT purposes. This means that a VAT-registered business can reclaim the input VAT after purchase, but must then charge VAT on the re-sale price of the pick-up when they sell it. The same does not apply to 'Kombi'-type vans which have seats behind the driver, and side windows for the rear-seat passengers but are vans from there to the back. VAT remains reclaimable on all vehicles, cars included, which are purchased to be leased or hired out or to be used for business purposes only and returned to the business premises (which must not be a private residence) every night.

More time to pay

" I am becoming increasingly irritated by the DVLA's policy of sending out VED renewal notices only about ten days or so before they become due. This takes no account of work commitments, holidays and the lack of main post offices in rural areas. Surely it should be possible to go to a main post office at any time armed merely with V5, insurance certificate and MOT certificate to buy a licence. "

A reasonable point. I suggested to the DVLA that it should be possible to send out renewal notices a calendar month before they are due and allow renewal up to a month early, but it hasn't happened. In the future, it should be possible to scan V5s, old VED discs and insurance certificates and apply for a new VED disc by email. Very soon, the DVLA will have MOT information supplied on-line by MOT stations anyway.

Historic Marina?

" I gather from 'De-mystified Motors' that cars first built before 1

January 1973 are eligible to be VED exempt, even if they were not first registered until 1973. My Morris Marina 1.3 was first registered on 4 May 1973, but I have no idea when it was built. The VIN is MA4S9S-254897M. Can you tell me if there is any source from which I could get a build date for the car? **"**

I have an old *Glass's Guide* checkbook which lists some (not all) Vehicle Identification Numbers against build dates. But I'm afraid that MA4S9S-254897M is shown as having a 1973 build date.

Scrappage tax

" *Surely the best way to prevent people dumping old cars at the roadside would be to impose a disposal deposit either when a car is first registered or the first time it changes hands after a given date. Half the deposit would cover the cost of disposing of the car at the end of its life and the other half would go to the owner as an incentive to either take it to a breakers or to pay a breaker to come and take it away. Obviously, only an owner registered on the V5 could avail himself of the refund.* **"**

There is already a scheme along these lines in some European countries, but we would need to reform the way V5s are issued before we adopted the idea. The European Parliament has now decided to make manufacturers and importers responsible for the eventual disposal of cars at the end of their life as from 2006. There is some doubt as to whether this rule can be made retrospective so that it covers all existing vehicles either on the road or dumped somewhere. Of course, it's the EC which got us into this mess in the first place. If it had not imposed expensive environmental measures on breakers yards, breakers could still afford to take old cars away free of charge.

Car-tax confusion

" *I am about to take delivery of a new Toyota Yaris automatic, 1,299 cc, which has an emissions rating of 157g CO_2 per kilometre. As from 1 March 2001, this would put it into a VED band of £120 a year, but only for cars first registered on 1 March 2001 or later. It appears that my car will be taxed at £160. I wrote to the DVLA questioning this, as it is taken directly from their two leaflets 'INF83' and 'INF96'.* "

Not much point in writing to the DVLA as all it does is administer VED. Far better to write to the man who imposed the tax, Gordon Brown.

TIMING BELTS AND CHAINS

Timing trouble

" Watching BBC 'Watchdog' I was concerned to learn that on some Vauxhall models including Cavaliers a problem has arisen causing loss of power and considerable engine damage. Apparently, this is caused by the failure of an idler wheel, part number GF50, and can affect models registered between September 1993 and September 1996. I own a Cavalier 2.0i automatic registered December 1993, which has done just 24,000 miles (I am retired and now 80 years of age). The RAC is said to be concerned about the safety aspect of such a failure at speed and would like there to be a safety recall. What advice can you give on this matter, please? "

Phone your nearest Vauxhall franchise and book the car in for a timing-belt replacement, specifying that you also want the tensioner and any idler wheels replaced. Your car is well overdue for a timing-belt replacement anyway and when cars are in for this job at Vauxhall dealers, the suspect idler wheels are routinely replaced as an 'in service modification'. The problem is mainly with GF50 plastic idler wheels on Vauxhall 16- and 24-valve engines fitted to Corsas, Astras, Tigras, Cavaliers, Vectras, Omegas and Fronteras between September 1993 and September 1996 ('L' to 'P' reg.) and, announced on 'Watchdog' on 21 May, all 16-

and 24-valve petrol-engined 'P' and 'R' reg. Vectras, Omegas and Fronteras. The Vauxhall Customer Service Helpline is 01582 427200. Anyone worried about imminent failure and in possession of a few tools should remove the engine timing-belt cover and inspect the plastic idler pulleys for signs of cracks. If you find any, don't start the engine.

Expensive precaution

" *I have a 1996 Audi A6 TDI five-cylinder. At the 50,000-mile service, the Audi dealer told me that the manufacturer now recommends a timing-belt change every 40,000 miles and that the cost is a prohibitive £422. I feel that this is a major additional servicing cost and a real hidden extra.* "

Your Audi dealer probably has a high labour rate. And I'm afraid this is a complicated, labour-intensive job because the injector distribution-pump timing as well as the valve timing also need to be re-set absolutely spot-on. The dealer probably also includes a replacement tensioner and replacement of any camshaft or jack-shaft oil seals which may be weeping oil. As you know, the consequence of timing-belt failure is a very much bigger bill. The job is likely to be even more expensive on a Volvo 850, S70, V70 or S80 fitted with the same engine transversely because access is more difficult.

More teeth to their belts

" *I recently part-exchanged a 1994 Astra LX estate for a 1998 Astra LX estate. Reading the service booklet, I noticed two significant differences. Previously, Vauxhall insisted on a timing-belt change at 36,000 miles. Now they refer to a 'toothed belt' with an 80,000-mile change. Is this due to a more robust construction? The second difference is 'spark plugs to be changed at 40,000 miles'. Are these special plugs? How can they last so much longer than previous plugs?* **"**

The need for timing-belt changes on most Vauxhall engines at 35,000–40,000 miles or four years, whichever comes first, is well documented, especially in view of the possibility of GF50 plastic idler wheels failing before the belt itself does. But I would not bank on a timing belt lasting beyond four years or 40,000 miles unless that type of belt on that type of engine has a history of lasting much longer. Ford gives a life of 80,000 miles, or five years, for timing belts on post-March 1994 Zetec E engines and so far this seems to be a safe bet as long as idler wheels and tensioners are replaced at the same time. For the newer Zetec S engines, timing-belt life is given as 100,000 miles or ten years, so improvements can and have been made.

Shattered

" *The plastic timing-belt tensioner of my girlfriend's Fiat Bravo recently shattered, throwing out the timing and resulting in £600 of engine damage. The car was just over three years old and had done 36,000 miles at the time. The handbook gives a timing belt life of 72,000 miles. Is this a common fault with Bravos? Is it worth approaching Fiat?* **"**

This is the same problem as recently reported to occur with GF50 timing-belt pulleys on Vauxhall 16-valve engines if belts and tensioners are not changed regularly. What seems to happen is that the steel bearing in the centre of the plastic tensioner wears out and as a result overheats. This, in turn, cracks and eventually shatters the plastic pulley. Owners of cars such as VWs with steel timing-belt tensioners get plenty of warning because you can hear the bearing shrieking long before it seizes up and throws the belt off. Vauxhall's standard service procedure for many years has been to change the timing belt and tensioner every 40,000 miles or every four years, whichever comes first, and this has also always been my standard advice unless a belt, tensioner and associated pulleys and seals are well proven to have a longer life. Yes, it's worth approaching Fiat Customer Care.

Chain reaction

" *I am faced with a £2,800 bill because the timing chain of my 'K'-reg. BMW 320i snapped at just 57,000 miles despite having been properly maintained. BMW and the dealer between them have contributed most of the cost of the replacement engine, but I still feel I have been unjustly treated.* "

This is entirely understandable because BMW switched over to timing chains rather than belts to avoid the disaster you find yourself faced with. Timing-chain failure on the M50 engine is extremely rare. It could be due to contaminated oil (unlikely if the car has been properly maintained throughout its life), to something breaking or to a foreign body somehow getting into the chain case. But BMW has paid out most of the cost of the new engine and, as the company points out, the car was six and a half years old at the time of the failure.

Snap, crackle and pop 1

" *Recently the timing belt of my four-year-old 2.0 litre Vauxhall Omega snapped at 33,500 miles. Within 15 minutes, the AA arrived and towed it to the Vauxhall dealers with whom I have been dealing for years. On finding that the car had a full Vauxhall service history, the dealer agreed to replace the engine FOC and the job was done in a couple of days. Next day*

I received the AA proposal to sell off to Centrica, which will net me £240. This morning I received a prize from ERNIE. I propose to enter the lottery this Saturday. **"**

The belt was right on the limit for scheduled replacement, so your luck certainly changed.

Rollover jackpot

" *I have a 1994 Vauxhall Cavalier 2.0 litre, 16-valve model. In line with the service recommendations I have had the timing belt changed twice and each time the plastic belt rollers were also replaced. When I found out that these were replaced due to cracking rather than fair wear and tear I appealed to Vauxhall and was reimbursed with the cost of £63.33. It is possible that other Vauxhall owners whose timing-belt rollers were replaced at the same time as their timing belts may be able successfully to make a similar claim.* **"**

I think you have done rather well to get reimbursement for two because in my experience the all-steel timing-belt tensioner on VAG engines only lasts 75,000–80,000 miles. The problem in both cases arises from wear and tear in the tensioner/roller/pulley bearing. When it starts to fail on a Vauxhall engine the heat generated cracks the plastic outer pulley. When it starts to fail on a VAG engine, there is no plastic outer pulley to crack, but the shriek of the failing bearing should be enough to alert any driver that a failure is imminent and obviously if the bearing seizes up completely, the belt will snap.

Brace yourself for a belting

" *Apropos recent letters about timing belts, I enquired of my local Ford servicing dealer about replacement of the belt on my six-year-old 'K'-reg. Mondeo 1.8LX and was told that eight years or 80,000 miles, whichever* *comes first, was the recommended interval. As I have done 42,000 miles in six years, would you accept this verdict?* "

No. Ford's 'New Service Schedules' booklet published May 1998 for vehicles built from September 1989 to August 1998 states: 'Camshaft drive belt: Renew Zetec 3/94 (every *five* years or 80,000 miles whichever occurs first)'. Though timing belts aren't a Zetec E engine problem area, I'd have the belt changed straightaway whatever the service schedule may have said for your older, 1993 Mondeo.

More drastic plastic

" *The plastic-rimmed timing-belt tensioner in the engine of our Ford Fiesta shattered at 60,000 miles causing £1,000 worth of damage to the engine. The timing belt was changed when recommended, actually at 52,000 miles, but no advice was given about the tensioner. The fact that Ford has now replaced the plastic tensioner with a metal one gives an indication of a faulty component.* "

Which engine was this? Was it a 1.25 Zetec S, a 1.6 or 1.8 Zetec E, or a diesel? Plastic timing-belt tensioner wheels have been failing in Vauxhall engines and in Fiat Bravo/Brava engines. When the metal bearing in the centre heats up, heat is not dissipated as it would be into a metal pulley, and the plastic pulley shatters.

Snap, crackle and pop 2

" *The timing belt of my three-and-a-half-year-old 113,000-mile VW Polo 1.4 recently snapped, resulting in a bill of £861.17, despite the car having been regularly serviced. I later discovered that VW makes no recommendation for the age and mileage at which timing belts and associated tensioners should be changed.* "

For the past five years I have been recommending readers to change their timing belts every three to four years or every 35,000–40,000 miles, whichever comes first. Some belts, notably the thick ones on Ford Zetec engines, genuinely do seem to last at least 80,000 miles. VW's don't, so our 115,000-mile VW is on its fourth. You say your car has been regularly serviced, but the records you supplied show that between 99,319 miles and the 113,000 miles when the belt snapped the car had not been serviced at all. (In support of the campaign against clocking I feel duty bound to inform readers that the registration of this high-mileage Polo is N562 GUD.)

Tigra trouble

" I bought an 'M'-registered Vauxhall Tigra privately in 1996. Soon after I bought it I became aware of a recall over timing-belt pulleys and phoned the recall line. I was told my car was not one of those affected. Then, in December, at moderate speed on the M1, the engine failed. The car was towed to an independent garage and the cause was diagnosed as timing-belt failure. The mechanic told me that the rollers had shredded, throwing off the timing belt and that eight valves, the pistons and the cylinder head were damaged. I then phoned the recall line again, to be told that the toothed-belt rollers had been checked by a Vauxhall dealer in Kent in 1997. This was not true. The dealer had not seen the car since 1996. Though I have always had the car independently serviced I am concerned that I have been given incorrect information by the recall helpline, and the false impression that my car was okay. I now face a big bill. "

The problem with any plastic timing-belt roller is heat related. If the bearings of a steel timing-belt roller begin to wear, the heat this creates is dissipated throughout the roller. You usually get plenty of warning from a shrieking noise, like that of a loose fanbelt or a worn alternator bearing, before the bearings seize. But if the bearings of a plastic timing-belt roller begin to wear, there is nowhere for the heat to dissipate and the plastic simply cracks, then shatters. The 'inspection' was to make sure that the plastic had not started to crack. But your problem is that your car was overdue for a timing-belt change anyway. See page 12 of the service guide which states that the timing belt should be replaced at the fourth annual service or at 40,000 miles, whichever comes first. At this change, at a Vauxhall dealer, the GF50 plastic timing-belt rollers would have been routinely replaced and would probably have then lasted for another four years.

Good timing

" I have just experienced my worst nightmare. The timing belt of my 96P Vectra 2.0i 16v decided to snap while it was pouring with rain on a busy road and I had my wife with me in the car. I called the service manager at Burton Brothers of Ramsey, Cambs, which has always looked after the car, and within an hour it had been collected. The happy outcome was that because the belt failed within the four-year or 40,000-mile life laid down by Vauxhall, the engine was rebuilt at no cost to me and I was loaned another car until it was ready. Naturally enough, this restored my faith in Vauxhall and its dealers. "

The belt is most likely to have failed because the bearing in its GF50 plastic tensioner pulley overheated, shattering the plastic pulley and throwing off the belt. But I'm pleased that the company and the dealer willingly put up their hands and, as you say, 'restored your faith' in them.

Snap!

" The timing belt of my Audi A4 snapped at 85,000 miles, 5,000 miles after its 80,000-mile service. The engine was badly damaged. The service *schedule shows that engine codes AAD, AAE, ABK, ABT, ACE, ADA and ADW need a timing-belt change as part of the 80,000 mile service, but there is no recommended change point for my engine, which has an ADR code. Only the ancillary drive belts are scheduled for a change at the 80,000-mile service. I was offered a 50% discount on remedial work which brought the estimate down to £1,539 plus VAT, and, after losing the car to the dealer's workshop for three weeks, I eventually paid £835 under protest. What chance do I have of getting this and my hire car costs back via the Small Claims Court?* **"**

For five years I have been warning readers to change their timing belts every three to four years or every 35,000–40,000 miles, whichever comes first. The only exceptions are Isuzu diesels in Vauxhalls which have a virtually zero failure rate at less than 70,000 miles or four years, and Ford Zetec engines which have a virtually zero failure rate at less than 80,000 miles or five years. It looks to me that the dealer has already made a goodwill compromise. And before you could take him to a Small Claims Court he has to agree to allow the judge to arbitrate and to abide by the judge's decision, otherwise the case could go to full County Court and cost you a fortune.

TOWING*

Keeping your cool with a caravan

" I have a Mercedes E200 estate which I use for caravan towing and which has a four-speed automatic gearbox. I now want to change it for an ex-demonstration E300TD automatic estate, which has a five-speed automatic gearbox, but have run into two problems. One is the astronomically expensive price of the official MB tow bar. The other is that I have been told that if I want to use the car for towing I must have the cooling system upgraded. I will be fitting a Witter or equivalent instead of the MB tow bar, but what should I do about the cooling system? "

The problem arises when an automatic car is fitted with a 'tall' top gear for economy. Depending on the weight of the caravan, the overall gearing and the incline being ascended, the autobox torque converter will either slip and get very hot, or the box will 'hunt' between the two highest gears. It would obviously help the box to shift it manually from fifth to fourth on inclines when towing, and sometimes even to third. But an additional gearbox ATF oil cooler is the solution proposed by MB. I think the dealer may also have quoted you for a socially responsible removable tow bar, such as those made by Brink, to prevent parking ball damage when not actually towing. But, so far, these are

* See also the 'Campers and Caravans' section, and note that *Practical Caravaning* magazine runs a service matching cars and caravans to each other.

only required by law as long as leaving the tow bar in place when not towing does not obscure the towing-car's number plate. New Witter equipment conforms to the way Directive 94/20/EC has been interpreted by the VI in the UK. Having avoided a dangerously snaking caravan on the M18 recently, I don't recommend anyone to tow a caravan without fitting a stabiliser bar. Also, make sure the nose weight of the caravan is correct and never tow a caravan on tyres more than six years old because, though they may look fine externally, the inside of the carcass could have badly deteriorated and the tyres may blow out at speed.

Towing the line

" *I own a Citroën BX19GTi which I use to tow a small dinghy around. The car has 110,000 on the clock, of which I've done 80,000 in the last five years, and it has been remarkably reliable except for an ECU and three replacement clutches. I now want to upgrade to a larger boat, which is likely to result in a trailed weight of a ton to 24cwt, and I suspect that the BXGTi will not be up to it, bearing in mind that a lot of the launching ramps I am forced to use are rather steep. Could you recommend an alternative in the £3–£5k bracket? I'd be very happy if your answer was a Xantia. And does diesel represent any advantages over petrol when towing? I could even convert to LPG because there is an LPG centre in my area. Finally, is it worth considering automatic transmission to avoid clutch failure?* "

Forget autoboxes for heavy towing because you will probably experience constant slippage, resulting in overheating of the ATF and the premature demise of your transmission. 20–24 cwt translates to 1016–1219kg and, ideally, you should not be towing more than 85% of the weight of the tow-car if it is a normal road car rather than a 4x4. Your car therefore needs to

weigh 1196–1435kg. A BX19GTi weighs 1025kg. Diesels develop high torque at low revs which is good for towing, but a Xantia 1.9LXTD weighs 1210kg, which means it's only just within the limit for even the lightest of the boats. If I were you I would go for a Subaru Legacy 2.2GX estate car which weighs 1375kg, has the right gearing for towing and has permanent four-wheel drive which will be a great help on those 'slip' ways. An LPG conversion could be an option for one of these, using a tank which sits in the spare wheel well. Talk to the LP Gas Association on 01425 461612.

Tugboat required

" *After many close shaves while towing my boat out of the water I should now like to consider a four-wheel drive version of a Mondeo-sized car (not an 'off roader') as my next company car. My lease allowance should translate to roughly £16,500 and I am prepared to consider any make, petrol or diesel, saloon or estate, as long as it has air-conditioning, automatic transmission and day-long comfort. Are there any disadvantages to such cars?* **"**

Yes. There aren't many with automatic transmission. The best all round is a Subaru Legacy Classic LX estate, which has standard a/c and comes in at £15,325 for tax purposes, plus £1,000 for the autobox (the manual is far better). The Subaru Forester is smaller and dearer. The Honda CRV auto with a/c has a better autobox and with a bit of bargaining will meet your budget.

Comfortable towers

" *My wife and I are hoping to purchase a Bailey caravan – either a Ranger 450/2 which has an unladen weight of 844kg, or a Pageant Magenta which has an unladen weight of 907kg. We wish to know the best car to tow with. At present we tow with a Citroën BX 17TD which my wife likes because she has a neck problem and it offers a comfortable ride. Can you direct us to a car with good suspension capable of towing the caravan mentioned?* **"**

The most obvious choice is a Citroën Xantia HDI 110. But the conventionally sprung Xsara HDI 90 has an excellent ride and is a good tower. (Xantias and Xsaras now have galvanized bodies with 12-year warranties.) Or you could look at something from the VAG group. The Seat Toledo S TDI 110 is comfortable, a good tower and sensibly priced. But the new VW Golf TDI 115 Pumpe Duse models with their phenomenal torque output of 210 lb ft and a six-speed gearbox to make the best of it should be brilliant towers. All the cars listed are heavy enough to tow the 907kg caravan, and all but the Toledo are available as estates, enabling you to transport more of your camping kit inside the car.

That's blown it

" *Your advice to a caravanner to trade in his Citroën BX17TD for a Xsara HDI 90 was very sound. My wife and I made this change last July, and in October towed our Sprite Europa 390/2 to Locarno, a round trip of some 2,700 miles. We found the Xsara to be an even better tower than the BX with full torque available from 8 mph in first gear. But I must remark on how clever it was of Mark Hales to experience 'the mid-range kick of the turbo' when testing the Xsara Picasso HDI. This engine is atmospherically aspirated and if he doesn't know the difference between a non-turbo and a turbo, what credence can we place in the rest of his report? In fairness to him, he is not the only journalist making the same mistake. The press, even the specialist press, seem not yet to understand the principle of the common rail engine.* "

Thank you for the endorsement, but I'm afraid you are going to wish you had taken a look at your engine's exhaust and inlet manifolds before you sent this letter. Like the HDI 110, the HDI 90 is a turbo-diesel, the main difference being that it has no intercooler and the turbo wastegate is not electronically controlled. The principle of common rail direct injection is that, instead of using a distribution pump, the fuel is pumped at much higher pressure into a 'common rail'. It is then metered very precisely by electronically controlled individual injectors directly into the combustion chambers where, in the Xsara's case, it mixes with air compressed by the turbocharger fed in through the inlet manifold.

A weight on his mind

" *Last September I bought a 'nearly new' Rover 420TD to replace my older Rover 218TD which had proved to be an excellent car for towing a caravan. The salesman extolled the 420's virtues as a tow car and it was not until I read the technical data in the handbook that I found it had been set a towing limit of just 1,000kg. Similar-sized cars by other manufacturers can legally tow up to 1250kg, so I cannot understand why Rover cut off such a potentially important part of its market for the 200/25 and 400/45 diesel models.* "

The generally recommended towing limit is 85% of the tow-car's weight, though 4x4s usually have much higher limits and, for various reasons, manufacturers often set lower limits. A quick trawl through the towing limits in the tables of *Diesel Car* magazine shows that Rover's 1000kg is far from the lowest, and there are plenty of surprises. According to *Diesel Car*, Citroën sets 655kg for the Berlingo Multispace, Ford sets 700kg for the Courier Kombi, Mercedes Benz sets 800kg for the A170 CDI, Nissan sets 800kg for all Primera diesels apart from the estate, Skoda sets 750kg for the Fabia and Felicia, Vauxhall sets 900kg for the Corsa 1.7D and VW sets 850kg for the Golf Mk IV SDI estate. Others set at 1000kg include the Citroën Xsara 1.9D, the Fiat Punto D, the Ford Focus TDI, the Peugeot 306LD, the Renault Megane TDI, the Seat Ibiza TDI, the Toyota Corolla TD, the Vauxhall Vectra 2.0DI and the VW Polo 1.9 SDIs and TDIs. France imposes additional autoroute lane and speed restrictions where the towed weight exceeds the weight of the towing vehicle.

TYRES

Fit to burst

I received a letter from a worried R.L. of Bedford concerning pre-puncture and post-puncture liquid tyre sealants. Post-puncture sealants are only intended to effect a temporary repair after which, under BS AU 159, the tyre must be removed from the rim, the carcass thoroughly inspected and a proper vulcanised repair made. Sealants sold as preventing punctures can not only leave the driver unaware of tyre damage, but can make such a serious mess of the inside of the carcass that it cannot be properly repaired. Despite this, it appears that a lot of motorists are treating liquid tyre sealants as a permanent cure. This is particularly dangerous among caravan owners to whom 'puncture preventing' sealants have been actively marketed. There can't be many of us who have not witnessed the result of an unstabilised caravan tyre blowout. Now that summer is here and readers are planning long car or car and caravan journeys which subject tyres to extreme conditions, we should all remember to have any aerosol liquid sealed tyre properly repaired. We should, in any case, inspect all our tyres thoroughly for tread depth, cuts, nails and sidewall deterioration (caravan tyres particularly) and ensure that they are inflated to the correct pressures for the weight carried and the speeds we will be driving.

Tyreless royal Daimler

" *I own two vintage Daimler limousines of 1925 and 1927. These huge six-litre vehicles, as formerly used by the royal family, run on 700/750 x 23 tyres. In spite of all my searches, including Vintage Tyre Supplies, I am unable to get brand new tyres. The best I have been able to obtain are old secondhand tyres, the youngest dating from 1946 when the moulds were destroyed. Is there anywhere in the world where I could get a small production run of 50 or so done specially? As far as I know there are only likely to be a dozen or so Daimlers still running on these size tyres.* "

I tried a different supplier, North Hants Tyres, and the closest they could find suitable for 23in rims were 600 x 23 in the United States. It might be worth buying a pair to check suitability and if they are simply too narrow it may be possible for the maker to space out the mould to produce 700s or 750s. Speak to Paul at North Hants Tyres on 01252 613261.

Tyred out

" *I have always averaged 40,000 to 50,000 miles on a set of tyres. I then purchased a new Land Rover Freelander 1.8XEi five-door in May 1998. In June 1999 I received a standard notice from Land Rover to Freelander owners suggesting that, for normal use in lightly laden driving conditions, reducing tyre pressures to 1.8 bar (26lb sq in) would enhance tyre life and improve ride comfort. Then, on 23 July 1999 I was appalled to find that, at a mileage of 16,950, the centre tread on both front tyres was worn to below the legal limit. The Land Rover dealer offered a 25% discount on two new front tyres, which I declined. Land Rover itself offered a 25% discount, which I also declined. After taking matters to a higher level I was offered a 50% discount, and two new front tyres have now been fitted at a cost to me of £76.81. I still find this unacceptable. I paid £22,500 for the vehicle and do not feel I should have to pay £76.81 for parts which have worn out prematurely due to a mistake in the owners' handbook. "*

While it is true that some careful car drivers manage 50,000 miles or more from a set of tyres (usually Michelin Energy), this is by no means the average. A Freelander is a front-wheel-drive vehicle with part-time four-wheel drive. In normal use, I would expect road-pattern front tyres to last 20,000–25,000 miles, which was the basis of the 25% offer. Even with careful driving, I would not expect them to last beyond 30,000 miles, which was the basis of the 50% offer. I can't understand why you would expect a wearing component that has already given a life of 16,950 miles to be replaced free of charge.

Unsuitable tyres

" I run an 'R'-reg. Peugeot 306 turbo-diesel which I purchased second-hand and on which, with the encouragement of the dealer, I replaced the standard 14in wheels with 5in alloys. These are fitted with 195/50 x 15 low-profile tyres. Due to the poor state of the roads in Herefordshire and Gloucestershire I have now needed seven replacement tyres and two replacement alloy wheels. I have tried to recover some of the costs from the county councils with no success. Now I am wondering whether the wheels and tyres were not 'fit for the purpose' for which they were sold? "

Obviously not. But the appalling way in which the roads have deteriorated over the past year, despite the government extracting £4.2 million in 'Road Fund Licences' over the same period, is not the dealer's fault. Since the government has no intention of improving the condition of our roads, anyone buying a car would be well advised to avoid those fitted with tyres of an aspect ratio below 60%. Wide, low-profile tyres do improve ultimate grip, but at the cost of reduced ride comfort, higher wear rates, increased fuel consumption and a greater likelihood of damage to tyres and rims.

Tip worth a trip

" Just a note to thank you for putting me in touch with Micheldever Tyres of Micheldever Station, near Andover. I needed to buy five Pirelli P6000s. Their charge came to £330, whereas the quote from my BMW dealer was £488, so I saved £158. "

Micheldever Tyres is consistently good. If you live within 50 miles of Micheldever Station, Hants, phone first for a quote on 01962 774437, check your local fitted tyre prices and work out for yourself if a visit will be worthwhile.

Snow grip

" Can you settle a friendly argument we are having in our local pub? Which tyre gives the best grip in snow: a broad one or a narrow one? "

On ice or hard-packed snow, a relatively narrow tyre with spikes or studs is best. But on soft snow a light 4x4 with relatively wide tyres such as a Mitsubishi Pinin or Daihatsu Terios might ride on the top of the snow rather than sinking in. My late uncle had a mutant farm cat years ago which had two paws on each leg. While all the other cats sunk up to their bellies in the snow, 'Big Foot' could prance around on the surface.

Under pressure

" Some time ago you recommended a tyre pressure gauge that was easy to use. Could you please give me the name and stockist? "

The 'Accu-Gage S60XA', priced £15.00 from the

International Tool Co. which has once again moved, this time to: 82 Tentor Road, Moulton Park, Northants NN3 6AX, tel: 01604 646433, website: www.international-tool.co.uk, email: sales@international-tool-co.uk. It has a clear, circular dial face and is about the most accurate gauge you can buy below the super expensive devices used to check the pressures of racing tyres. I've used them for four years.

Front-drive tyre wear

" I have a 1995M Rover 623i. I replaced the original Michelin 195/60 VR 15s back and front at 27,000 miles and will have to repeat the exercise fairly soon at 50,000 miles. I find this very disappointing as my previous Rover 216 and several 2.0 litre Sierras averaged 40,000 miles a set. Can you advise me of alternatives to the Michelins which might offer better tyre life? "

The reason why Rover 623is handle and grip much better than 618s and 620s is that they run on wider, lower-profile tyres and the suspension is set up to take advantage of this. Usually, a decent-handling front-drive car eats its front tyres in 15,000–25,000 miles, but its rears can go on for 40,000. I don't think you'll find a longer-lasting tyre than Michelin Energy, but for maximum life (at the expense of grip) you may have to go for a different wheel and rim size. The other factor is tracking. Proper front and rear tracking and alignment will cost you £30 on the latest rig at a specialist such as Micheldever Tyres (01962 774437).

Tyre gamble

" My employer insists that low-cost tyres are fitted as replacements to company cars. How do these tyres compare with those fitted by the car *manufacturers as original equipment, and are there any safety issues?* **"**

This is typical of fleet operators. Saving a few quid is far more important than the safety of the car drivers, especially towards the end of the car's fleet life. Hard compound cheap replacement tyres may offer reasonable tyre life, but grip can be severely compromised, particularly under braking in the wet. Original equipment tyres are a bit of a lottery, but if you happen to get a bread-and-butter car fitted with Continental Eco Contacts or Pirelli P6000s you can consider yourself lucky.

'Spare' wheel warning

A helpful reminder came my way from the 'We Can Work it Out' TV consumer programme team. If your car is fitted with alloy wheels, but has a steel 'spare', make sure you can find the special set of bolts for fitting the emergency wheel. If you try to use the bolts for the alloy wheel they may be too long and damage the car's braking system.

Driven spare

" *I bought a 97R Nissan Primera with 14,000 miles from a Nissan dealer in February 1999. When it reached 30,000 miles I decided to fit new front tyres and hoped to economise by buying one new tyre and utilising the 'spare'. Unfortunately, this turned out to be on a 15in wheel while the road wheels of the car are 14in and I can't take it back to the dealer because it has gone into liquidation. So please remind your readers when buying a car to make sure that the 'spare' is the same size as the road wheels.* **"**

Some 'spare' tyres are space-savers. Some are on steel wheels when the rest are alloys. Some are a slightly different size, though the rim should be the same diameter. Unless the front tyres were new when you bought the car you got very good mileage for a front-wheel-drive car. Generally it is much better and much safer to replace both front tyres together as this ensures that both will be of the same tread compound.

USED-CAR PROBLEMS

Corsa cracks

" In your book *The Daily Telegraph How to Buy and Sell Cars*, under Vauxhall Corsa 'What to Watch Out For' you mention, 'Cracking around door hinges on 'A' pillars of two-door models (also look for cracks in the paint on 'B' pillars)'. My wife has owned a 1993 Corsa 1.4SRi virtually from new and we recently noticed a small crack in the paintwork of the 'B' pillar on the shoulder, level with the base of the window. We did not think much more about it until the car failed its MOT and we were quoted £400 to put the fault right. The dealer sought financial assistance from Vauxhall, but the company was only prepared to pay for the work on two series of Corsas build in 1995. How general is the problem with Corsa 'B' pillars? "

The 'A' pillar problem is general knowledge (and is not just confined to Corsas). But the new metallic green Corsa 1.2 litre I hired in Majorca in Summer 1997 had a crack in the paint on the shoulder of the 'B' pillar so, unless that car was late registered by two years, the problem is not confined to 1995 Corsas.

Blowing a fuse

" I have a splendid 1992 Nissan Sunny 1.6 which has now done 13,000 miles since new and performed faultlessly until I tried to start it in an air-

port car park after a holiday. Though the battery indicator showed fully charged, nothing happened when I turned the key, so I called out the AA. Their knowledgeable mechanic immediately diagnosed that the fusible link between the positive terminal and the loom had melted. He told me it was quite common, replaced the link with a piece of wire and got me on my way, recommending that I replaced the fusible link as soon as possible. I did, but you might like to warn your readers that carrying a spare could save them becoming stranded. "

The fuse is there to prevent other parts of the wiring from overheating if, for example, a starter-motor failure occurs. You were lucky that your fuse gave up the ghost through age rather than through doing its job.

Rattling Rover

" *We recently bought a 1991J Rover 216SLi automatic with 51,000 miles from a small, local garage with an excellent reputation. There is quite a diesel-like clatter when starting from cold (not tappets) which disappears after a mile or two. The dealer says this model of Rover has a Honda 16-valve engine and gearbox and because it is an all-alloy motor there is a clatter in these models until they warm up. If so, what is the cause and is it harmful to the engine?* "

I think you will find that the noise is from the tappets. It could be that the engine has been fitted with a cheap aftermarket oil filter which does not contain a non-return valve and allows the oil to drain from the top of the engine. But most Honda engines of this period did not have hydraulic tappets and tappet clearances are a maintenance item needing occasional adjustment. Honda dealers tend to know more about this than Rover dealers.

Mercedes myths

" *Five years ago I bought a 39,000-mile three-year-old Mercedes 230TE. I paid £20,500. Four months later, the exhaust dropped off and I was quoted £1,000, by the MB dealer, to replace it. I went elsewhere. Also not covered under the £500 MBI I purchased with the car was failure of a tailgate gas strut. However, despite sometimes having to pay £800 plus, I stuck to genuine MB servicing because I was told this was essential to maintain the car's resale value. The dealer mis-diagnosed the cause of coolant loss as a failed pump, charging me £250 for an unnecessary replacement. An independent Mercedes specialist correctly diagnosed the cause as a failed head gasket. After five and a half years, with 80,000 miles on the clock and with full MB service history, the best trade-in offer I could get was £5,500. (I didn't get a peep advertising the car privately in Auto Trader.) Now I drive a one-year-old 3.0-litre Omega Estate, which cost me £18,500 minus the £5,500 trade-in. It is modern, has all the bells and whistles, and goes like the wind.* "

You should have been able to get £6,500 or so for your 230TE auto at the time of the trade-in (trade 'book' was £7,525). Only the wrong specification such as a manual box would have killed it stone dead in the market. Merc 230E autos always were a bit short of puff compared to a 3-litre Vauxhall (136 bhp pulling 1,400 kg compared to 204 bhp pulling 1,435 kg in the Senator 24v and 208 bhp pulling 1,724 kg in the Omega 3.0i Estate). And my experience is that they are more troublesome than 300TEs, which can remain good, solid cars even at 13 years old. Long-term, big engines are usually best.

Blistering row

" *I have a silver 1995 'M'-reg. Lexus LS400, which I bought in November 1996 from a Lexus dealer. Having previously hand-washed it, I switched to a brushless car wash 15 months ago. Last week, when drying it off, I noticed patches of small blisters on the offside front and rear doors, just below the windows. There are also less noticeable patches on the rear quarter panel and boot lid. I thought that the blistering indicated poor preparation prior to painting. The Lexus dealer suggested that it could be due to the car wash water being too hot, but I checked this and the car wash provides only cold water in the cycle I have used. Can you suggest the probable cause and any form of treatment I can use? Can you also venture an opinion as to whether or not Toyota will meet any of the costs?* "

It might be that, in the words of the trade, the car has 'had paint'. In layman's terms, it might have suffered a minor accident or scratching and been re-painted before you bought it. This can be tested for with a magnetic paint-thickness indicator, which most garages specialising in luxurious cars will have in order to check cars offered in part-exchange. If your Lexus turns out to have 'had paint', then your remedy is against the dealer who sold it to you. However, to help preserve the reputation of the Lexus marque, Toyota itself may be prepared to put matters right.

Oil burner

" *After 137,000 miles my 1989G Citroën BX 16 TRS still runs like a bird, but needs a litre of oil every 200 miles unless I add 'Stop Leak' and STP Oil Treatment in recommended amounts – in which case a litre of oil lasts 1,000 miles. How long can I go on doing this safely before getting a new or re-conditioned engine?* "

Until you get stopped and fined for excess emissions and a 'prohibition of use' order slapped on your car. First get a compression test (or 'leak down') test done. If it's okay in all four cylinders, then the reason for the oil consumption is worn out valve stem oil seals – a £100–£120 job to put right. If compression isn't okay, the engine is worn out. You then have to make up your

mind whether to soldier on and risk a pull for excess emissions, to replace the engine with a rec-con, or to scrap the car.

Square wheeler

" I recently acquired a two-year-old, 18,000-mile 'R'-registered Mazda 626 automatic. I have established that my car had been virtually unused for a year and sat in the same compound for at least six months. So I was concerned to read your comments about cars sitting on airfields. When delivered, my car had a very bumpy ride, which was more or less rectified by the dealer. What should I do to protect my position? I have a 12-month Mazda UK warranty unexpired which can be extended (at a cost) for a further two years. "

The bumpy ride was due to the tyres having flat-spotted while the car sat on them in the same position for a long period. The dealer probably over-pressured the tyres and drove it around like that to try and restore the tyres' shape. Check your current warranty and the warranty you are being offered to establish whether or not they include 'consumables' such as batteries, brake pads, brake discs and exhaust systems. Probably not.

Gone to its head

" I have a Rover 416, first registered in August 1997 and purchased secondhand via Rover Direct. At its last service, at 36,000 miles, it was noted that a new cylinder head gasket and manifold gasket were required due to leaks. Rover covered the cost of this, for which I was grateful and the dealer, Haslemere Rover, could not have been more helpful. But is this a known problem area with the Rover 'K' Series engines? "

Yes. The 'K' Series are modular engines with ten particularly long stretch bolts from the top of the head, through the block, to the crankcase. Sometimes these can give a little more than they are designed to. The other problem is cracks developing in the head itself. However, though all sizes of 'K' Series engines can be affected, happily the failure rate is comparatively low and tens of thousands of these engines have covered well over 100,000 miles. P.G. of Rover dealer Lockwood & Greenwood of Audenshaw, Manchester advises that head-gasket failure with the 'K' Series engines fitted to this model is usually the result of coolant loss, not the cause of it. So be sure to renew the coolant and keep a close eye on its level.

Surging surgery

" I bought my Honda Accord 2.0i 'nearly new' and have had it for just over two years. For the whole time I have had it the car has suffered from

power surges during acceleration and at steady state high speeds. Honda dealers and Honda UK have been involved, replacing the ECU and re-setting the valve clearances but nothing has made the slightest difference. I have been unable to find another Honda Accord owner with the same problem. What do you suggest? **"**

A lot of engines don't respond as crisply to the accelerator as engines used to because the ECU often takes over to reduce emissions and protect the catalytic converter. If you have been using supermarket petrol, switch to a brand such as Texaco or Shell. If that doesn't solve the problem, get an independent performance specialist to take a look at it and, if necessary, re-chip the ECU. The one I know best is BBR of Brackley, Northants, tel: 01280 702389, though you may be able to find one closer to you in Yellow Pages (see 'De-mystified Motors' no. 16). You must inform your insurer if any changes are made from the car's standard specification.

Waterpump under the bridge

" *I purchased a secondhand 1996N Mercedes Benz C180 from an MB dealer under the 'Signature' programme. During the course of its 36,000-mile service I was told it needed a new water pump. I wrote to MBUK asking that a 'goodwill' payment be considered, but this was turned down. All I received in reply was what looked like a standard pro-forma letter with the relevant details inserted. Should I have expected such a failure so soon with a Mercedes Benz?* **"**

The German reputation for rock solid build quality is taking a bit of a hammering generally. While there is no doubt that German cars are among the longest lasting in the world, the cost of repairs and replacements during their long lives can add up. In your case, the cost of the exchange water pump was a comparatively low

£100.51, plus labour at £70.20 plus VAT (total: £200.58). The coolant needed changing anyway to prevent internal engine corrosion. I'm pleased to see that the 37,500-mile 'B' service itself included a change of automatic transmission fluid, something which is all too often neglected.

Burning question

" *I own a Volvo 940 2.0 litre turbo estate with a recorded mileage of 83,000 miles. I am concerned with what I think is excessive oil consumption of one litre every 2,000 miles. I recently read of a Volvo 740 with more than 300,000 miles under its wheels, which does not require a top-up in between oil changes. Is this a symptom of an impending engine problem?* "

The two most likely reasons for this engine to start using oil are turbo oil seals or valve stem oil seals starting to give way. Get a friend to follow you and see if there are any puffs of black exhaust smoke when you accelerate. If so, blame the turbo oil seals. If not, blame the valve stem oil seals. But if you are changing your oil every 3,000–5,000 miles, you don't have to have the valve stem oil seals replaced until the oil consumption becomes worse and starts to affect the engine's emissions. On the other hand, if you have been leaving oil changes until 10,000 miles or so, the intense heat generated by the turbo will have badly degraded the oil, possibly leading to engine bore wear and this could be causing the oil consumption.

T5 trouble

" *In June 1995 I bought a new Volvo T5 automatic estate with a five-year warranty. Since then I have had more than 30 failures. These included the gearbox, turbo, valves and seats, brake callipers, front wheel bearings, central locking, cruise control, heater fan motor and sunroof motor. After some argument, in most cases the warranty underwriters paid up. My dilemma is that the warranty runs out this June, by which time the car will have covered 85,000 miles. Should I sell it, or stick to my original plan of keeping it for ten years and 150,000 miles? I am now in my sixties and my mileage is falling.* **"**

The police sell their T5 auto estates at up to 155,000 miles. But, of course, police T5s have a comparatively easy life plodding along the nearside lane of the motorway at 50–60 mph most of the time. And they don't have extras like electric sunroofs. That said, in my experience, replaced components on cars tend to last longer than the originals. And what you can get for your car in today's volatile market will also have a strong bearing on the option you take up. In December an ex-police 95M T5 estate with 114k sold at auction for just £5,500. Yet at BCA Blackbushe on 4 February I saw a high-spec 96N T5 estate with 68k make a high £9,050. So if you can get £9,000 for your 95M, sell it and buy something more suited to your current lifestyle, such as a brand new Mitsubishi Space Star for £9,995 on the road with a three-year warranty.

Shafted by cam

" *I have a six-cylinder single overhead cam BMW 730iSE automatic. When it was six years old and had done 37,000 miles the camshaft needed to be replaced due to excessive wear on some of the cams. Now, at 11 years old and at 74,000 miles it has needed to be replaced again. Is this a common fault with the model? It may be relevant to mention that the bulk of the mileage is short runs with only the occasional long journey.* **"**

This is an engine that needs a good supply of

clean oil to the camshaft, especially on start-up. If the wrong oil filter is fitted, the oil will drain back into the sump so there will be little lubrication of the cam on start up and this will lead to increased wear. If the oil is dirty and emulsified (having not been changed at least every six months) this could lead to partial blockages of the oilways.

Teapot with drinking problem

" For all but one of its seven years of life and most of its 63,000 miles I have happily owned an unsung and rare rival to the Golf GTi in the shape of a 115 bhp 8-valve Fiat Tipo 2.0ie. I never bothered to check the fuel consumption but, moved by the onset of old age, poverty and Gordon Brown, I did and was horrified to find it drinks at the rate of a gallon for every 23 miles. Everything has been checked. There are no leaks. The injectors and the rest of the fuel system have been cleaned. The engine has been punctiliously maintained. The only probable cause is a slight intermittent misfire. Yet she regularly sails through the MOT. What can be done? "

I used to buy and sell a fair few 'Teapots' because I could make £400 and still give the buyer excellent value for money. But I noticed the same intermittent misfire on one of mine, and eventually traced it back to a single duff spark plug. So that's a good place to start. Also make sure there's no sparking across the leads which you can see happening in the dark (it may need a new set). Another possibility is that the valve stem oil seals are starting to go, but that would use a noticeable amount of oil. This isn't an economy model, so 23 mpg may be all you will get on a diet of short runs. But you should manage 30 mpg on longer journeys. I used to get 39–40 mpg out of Tip 1.4ie models.

Cruise bruise

" A week ago I had a scare from the cruise control on my 1990 Mercedes 300TE when it was not set. As I was slowing down to turn right, the car accelerated as if keeping to a pre-set speed, but fortunately the cruise control disengaged when I applied the brake. The problem was traced to a faulty switch, which has now been replaced. But I think this was a very dangerous fault which should never occur on a car, whatever its age or mileage. I had intended keeping the car for some time yet, but this incident has made me wonder if I can expect an increasing incidence of failures? "

Of course you can. The W124 300TE was an excellent car, but yours is ten years old and is of the age when you can expect failures to start to occur. Keep it maintained properly, though, and despite a few more minor failures, it should see you through at least another five years before the failures start to get seriously expensive. Also see if you can learn to 'left-foot brake'. This gives a driver much better control over the sometimes wayward behaviour of an ageing automatic when out on the road and especially when manoeuvring.

Taking a leak

" My son has an 'H'-reg. Ford Escort hatchback with a sunroof. It has a leak which he has not been able to locate. The door seals have been replaced and the windscreen surround re-sealed and there is no coolant loss from the radiator. The carpets are now saturated and giving off a dank smell. Needless to say he is now desperate. "

Early production of the rounded-shape Escort introduced in October 1990 on the 'H' registration had a double bulkhead which was prone to rusting. This could be where the water is coming from. Had it been the earlier model I'd have blamed the sunroof surround drainage pipes.

Big bills

" We have owned a 93L Peugeot 405 diesel estate since new and it has now covered 100,000 miles. It has always been dealer serviced and in April 2000 we had a new timing belt fitted. But there are a number of oil and coolant leaks for which the dealer has quoted more than £1,000 to put right. The car is lightly used most of the year, but two to three times a year takes the family on a 2,000-mile round trip to the Alps. My dilemma is whether the £1,000 expense can be justified by a further 50,000–80,000 miles use of the car. "

Lots of older cars can chug around the suburbs on runs of up to 20 miles or so almost indefinitely. But as soon as they are subjected to the relatively harsh treatment of a 2,000-mile round trip all sorts of failures are likely to occur. Paying £1,000 to have its present leaks stemmed won't prevent this from happening. If I were you I would find a local garage prepared to do the work for half as much, then sell the car and buy something newer which is likely to be more reliable on long journeys.

Torn itself apart

" My 1994M Vauxhall Cavalier V6 has split its bulkhead at the base of the steering column. I am told this is caused by forces exerted from turning the steering wheel while stationary. Have you heard of such a thing before? "

I've heard of 'creaking' power steering on Cavaliers so this may well be the cause. I've now included it in my 'Car by Car Breakdown' data bank at www.honestjohn.co.uk.

Stretching a point

" Did you know that the cylinder head stretch bolts on four-cylinder Mercedes Benz engines have been stretching a bit further, leading to

cylinder head oil leaks? MB dealers will replace them on cars not covered by the current three-year warranty on a 'goodwill' basis, but for my four-and-a-half-year-old, 38,000-mile C Class, MBUK would only contribute 50% of the cost. I'd also like to point out that the addition of climate control to the air-conditioning of a C Class is £1,007 in the UK, but just £333 in Germany at the current exchange rate. Using the argument that this anticipates a fall in the value of Sterling against Euro currencies doesn't wash because Sterling would need to fall to 1dm to £1 for the price to be the same. "

After reading this letter, six more readers complained of leaking Mercedes Benz cylinder head gaskets due to the stretch bolts stretching. The problem seems to be confined to C and E Class 1.8 litre, 2.0 litre and 2.2 litre four-cylinder engines built between 1993 and 1996. R.D. of Leighton Buzzard's 58,000-mile 96N C180 is now on its third cylinder head gasket and, despite bills of £504.30, 'goodwill' from MB UK has amounted to £31.50. Others did rather better: F.M. of Edinburgh received a goodwill payment of £282.81 when the head gasket of his 96N C200 failed at 44,566 miles; DB's 94L C200 was repaired FOC in August 1996 at 24,125 miles; and H.B. of Aylesbury received £250 (half the cost of the repair) when the head gasket of his 96N E200 failed at 63,000 miles. But R.N. of Ringwood had to fork out £642 when the head gasket of his 'L'-reg. E Class failed at 22,000 miles in May 1999; and G.B. of Swansea faces having to pay £700 to repair his 90,000-mile 'L'-reg. E220 if a leak cured by re-tightening the stretch bolts re-occurs. Since this amounts to only seven cases in total out of thousands of these cars owned by *Telegraph* readers, the cause cannot be a design fault.

Micra reminder

" *I bought a secondhand 'N'-registered Nissan Micra 1.3 in May 1997. It had a Nissan B Service on 6 May 1997, a Nissan A Service on 16 February 1998, and a Nissan B Service and MOT on 29 October 1998. Being out of warranty it was not serviced again until 1 September 1999, this time by my local garage which is not a Nissan franchise. It then began to lack power, so I tried to book it into a Nissan franchise for diagnostic testing, but none could supply a courtesy car until the end of October. The car broke down on 11 October at 44,000 miles and the cause was diagnosed as a broken timing chain. The total cost of the subsequent repair was £1,244.78. Nissan's attitude is that the car carried a three-year 60,000-mile warranty and that had a Nissan agent undertaken the service prior to the chain snapping, it would have diagnosed that this was about to happen. I am a widow on a limited income and feel very disillusioned with Nissan.* "

A snapped timing chain due to failure of the tensioner is a known problem with the 16-valve twin-cam Micra. The best preventative maintenance is to ensure the engine is running on clean oil, which means an oil change every six months. After having had your car serviced regularly up to October 1998, you then left it for 11 months and entrusted the job to your local garage which would not necessarily have realised that a failure was imminent.

INDEX

596   Index

Megane 14, 19, 210, 340, 354, 363, 386, 425, 493, 508, 519, 537, 567
Safrane 331, 350, 363
Scenic 14, 51, 189, 191, 340, 360, 363, 389, 425–426, 508, 519, 525
Twingo 291, 329–330, 488, 515
Riley 45, 110, 138–139, 264
Elf 272
Rolls Royce 65, 70, 89, 139, 511
Rover 10–11, 14, 17, 49–50, 53, 58, 60–63, 65–66, 86–89, 93, 97, 140, 242, 248, 263, 271–273, 286, 292–295, 297, 301–302, 311, 315, 323, 325, 329, 331, 339, 342–343, 351–352, 356, 358, 361, 363, 370, 388, 405, 407–408, 411, 416, 418, 424, 432, 449, 456–457, 465, 467–468, 470–471, 477, 481, 492–493, 504, 507, 511, 514–515, 519, 567, 569, 572, 576, 580
RoSPA 242

Saab 27, 41–42, 161, 259, 309, 317, 323, 336, 346, 349, 363–364, 367, 393, 401, 512, 519–520, 530
Salmson 141
salvage 398–399
seat belt 357, 513–514, 519
Seat 15, 83–84, 86, 90, 160, 188, 191, 196, 271, 278, 294, 296, 328, 334, 340, 343, 346–348, 358, 361, 363, 365–366, 368, 379, 433, 445, 475–476, 511–513, 518–519, 565, 567
Arosa 86, 188–189, 191, 296, 365, 379, 512
Cordoba 15, 358, 379, 445
Ibiza 283, 294, 340, 358, 368, 445, 567
servicing 48, 51, 61, 201, 210, 310–313, 316, 318, 320–323, 381, 385–386, 393–394, 397–398, 403, 448, 452–453, 458, 461, 491, 493, 530, 554, 557, 577
shock absorbers 60
short circuit 510–511, 533
side-screens 184

Single Vehicle Approval (SVA) 29–30, 56, 164, 167, 380, 382, 389, 392, 395, 414–415, 439, 484
Skoda 15, 30, 84, 161, 271, 283, 334, 346, 361, 364, 472, 509, 518, 567
Favorit 115
Felicia 15, 509, 567
Octavia 15, 30, 84, 161, 283, 334, 346, 361, 518
snow 240, 571
SORN 545–546
spark plug 284, 584
SPECS, see speed cameras 181
speed cameras 181, 229, 237, 239, 260
Gatso 219–220, 225, 232, 238
SPECS 181
speedometer 29, 263, 330, 344, 488, 526
speed record 115, 137
Malcolm Campbell 137
Pendine Sands 126, 137
starter motor 536
Subaru 29, 53, 372, 381, 394, 478, 564–565
Impreza 29–30, 394, 470, 478
subframe 300
Sunbeam 145, 437
sunroof 36, 107, 355, 394, 500, 546, 583, 585
supercharger 123
Suzuki 11, 15, 192, 202, 328, 340, 352, 363, 509, 521
Alto 247, 328
Vitara 363, 509
Wagon R+ 15, 192, 328, 340, 521

Talbot 110, 145
targa top 187
tax 34, 55, 79, 101, 111, 158, 167–168, 177–178, 182–183, 221, 224, 240, 273–274, 279, 282, 287, 290, 327, 333, 341, 365, 368, 382, 393, 436, 487, 547–549, 551–552, 565
taxi 186, 205, 274, 370, 392, 456, 458
Thatcham security devices 37, 67, 148, 528